Marybeth Nelson

MINE EYES HAVE SEEN THE GLORY

A Medical Missionary's African Challenges

By

Lowell A. Gess, B.D., M.D.

RLE Press
2002

First Edition
First Printing, 2002

ISBN 0-9672527-1-7
Library of Congress Control Number 2001132077

Graphic/layout design and prepress production:
RLE Press and P. Kai Mitchell,, East Lansing, MI, 48823
Printer: Spectrum Printing, Alexandria, MN

Books ($19.95 plus $3.55 S/H) may be ordered from:

Central Global Vision
111 15th Ave. East
Alexandria, MN 56308

Telephone: 320-762-1888
email: gessla@rea-alp.com
www.africanmedicalchallenges.org

...For we preach not ourselves,

but Christ Jesus the Lord;

and ourselves your servants for Jesus' sake.

II Corinthians 4:5

Dedication

To God, my Creator
To Jesus Christ, my Savior
To the Holy Spirit, my Comforter and Guide

To my wife, Ruth, my helpmate and
mother of our six gifted children

To all who prayed and sacrificed
for the fulfillment of my calling
to medical missions.

Without this HELP,
the journey would never have begun,
let alone continued for nearly fifty years.

Foreword

Missionaries once meant people who left home and friends to follow a "call" for extended terms of service in far away, inaccessible areas of the world. The parents of Lowell and Ruth Gess wondered in 1952 if they would ever see them and their grandchildren again. That was the year when a life-long commitment of serving others began.

I first heard about Dr. and Mrs. Gess when I was in Sierra Leone in 1985 on the initial Advance Team to start Operation Classroom. We visited the Kissy UMC Eye Hospital in Freetown and were surprised to see a fully functional, up-to-date eye facility in West Africa that had been built in 1983. It was a place where the blind were made to see by the grace of God and the skilled hands of Dr. Gess and the other volunteer ophthalmologists representing modern day Albert Schweitzers.

Ultimately I was to meet the Gesses in 1998 at the Minnesota Annual Conference of the United Methodist Church. They seemed to be quite ordinary people. I have since learned that God has done many extraordinary miracles through their medical mission work.

The background of the Kissy UMC Eye Hospital and other challenging aspects of their missionary career are encompassed in *Mine Eyes Have Seen the Glory*, which I have found intensely interesting. This is a book about healing people, missionary medicine, modern miracles, and Christian faith.

From Dr. Gess' first surgery to repair an ugly spear wound, I was captivated by the drama of practicing medicine in difficult places. This book will inspire you to look beyond the common experiences in life and see the hand of God at work. In reading these stories, I felt the joy of that "Amazing Grace" that sings, "I once was blind, but now I see."

You will feel the joy of God's work written on these pages.

Bishop John L. Hopkins
Minnesota Area
United Methodist Church

Acknowledgements

Mine Eyes Have Seen the Glory was written with the blessing and support of my wife, Ruth, who spent hours and days searching through letters, diaries, and albums for anecdotal material which might prove interesting and worthy of presentation.

I have great appreciation for typists Lucy Radatz, Renae Nepper, and Britta Gess and my computer coaching staff of sons John, Paul, and Andrew Gess, along with my son-in-law, Steve Boehlke, who established the web site www.africanmedicalchallenges.org and shared organizational methods. Esther Megill rallied to help in the search for the names of missionaries (and their dates of service) who served the United Methodist Church's programs in Nigeria and Sierra Leone.

It was a pleasure to have Enid Young consent to produce a color map of Africa for the book's cover. Her murals grace some of the walls of the Kissy United Methodist Church Eye Hospital in Freetown, Sierra Leone.

Special thanks are given to Lorraine and Howard Pierce whose offer to handle the vicissitudes of publishing a book, encouraged me to make the attempt as Kenneth Krueger had done for Lorraine.". The expert help of their friend, Kai Mitchell, made the production efficient and enjoyable.

In her book, *Marching Through Immanuel's Ground*, Lorraine Pierce quotes the Reverend Albert H. Utzinger in his *History of the Minnesota Conference 1856-1922*, when he stated:

> *Some of the dates and other facts may be incorrect, but we endeavored to get as near to them as possible. If any of our readers discover mistakes, think the information correctly, and read on, remembering that we are human, and did the best we could under the circumstances.*

I would plead for a similar understanding, all the while taking full responsibility for the content and presentation of these stories of my life's challenges. It is my fervent prayer that because of the publication of *Mine Eyes Have Seen the Glory*, people in need in the far flung mission fields of the world will be blessed by interested, compassionate, and skilled "hands and hearts" reaching out to them.

Lowell A. Gess

Table of Contents

Chapter Two: Sierra Leone – Rotifunk 57

Chapter Three: Taiama 125

Preface

That *Mine Eyes Have Seen the Glory* might ever materialize as a book seemed unthinkable to me for many years, even though many people asked if I planned to write about Ruth's and my experiences as medical missionaries in Africa. This viewpoint changed, and the decision was made to write a book after I received a birthday letter from our youngest son, Andrew. He wrote:

> *There are so many stories that you tell that need to be written down, stories of incidents which have and do motivate you - like the man in Nigeria from whom you withdrew extra blood to save his wife's life. After all, there may come a time when you can no longer go overseas. Your stories, however, could inspire others to go, which would be an answer to your prayers.*

It is true we have seen "the glory of the coming of the Lord" in the lives and hearts of people who have been ill or blind. With renewed health they have gained insight into the love of God as revealed in the Lord Jesus Christ. The people Jesus healed wanted to follow him. It was my heart's desire to be in a position to bring health and healing to needy people that they might want to follow Him. My calling as a medical missionary involved the physical and spiritual aspects of healing. The medicine and surgery had to be the best if we were to expect our patients to accept the Gospel. I wanted to be Christ's hands and feet, the preacher of His message of love, forgiveness, and the healing of mind, body, and soul. I wanted to say like Ambrose Pere, "I bandage the wounds, God heals."

It is striking to me that while events played an important role, it was personalities that gave life and interest - going all the way back to my parents. This is evident in the anecdotes that comprise *Mine Eyes Have Seen the Glory.* Some thoughts and practices of others have so intermingled with mine that it is difficult to say where one begins and the other ends. I am profoundly grateful to all who have influenced and molded me – as noted in the closing portions of this book.

Many pictures are included because pictures tell stories. To gain prayerful support photographs were needed to show what we were doing and whom we were serving. Captured on film was the incident that dealt with our very first surgical patient in Africa. With the inclusion of pictures less wording is necessary. A particular picture that looks interesting prompts a closer look at the script.

The first three years of our missionary service excluded the plight of the blind; general surgery held center stage. Following a period of general surgical residency, the presence of blind people could no longer be ignored. The reader will see that after the early chapters, the book describes the transition to, and emphasis on, the compassionate care of the blind.

Ruth and I have enjoyed researching old diaries, letters, and pictures which allowed us to relive our adventures and challenges. What resulted was a compendium rather than a novel, a documentation and reporting, rather than an attempt to administer advice. We wanted to tell it as it is (and was) without intentionally trying to "preach." I was guided by the words of D. Elton Trueblood who said:

> *The most important thing a man has to say is not some speculation about what may be true, but rather a direct and unself-conscious reporting of what has occurred in firsthand experience. The only testimony which has any value is that which necessitates the first person. It is not possible to find anything more basic than the report of the one who says, simply and humbly, "Whereas I was blind, now I see."*

It is my sincere hope and prayer that these recorded anecdotes may inform and encourage others to lend a helping hand, "For inasmuch as you have done it unto one of the least of these, my brethren, you have done it unto me." (Matthew 25:40). We serve God by serving others.

The plea of *Mine Eyes Have Seen the Glory* is that it may be used by the Holy Spirit to make the claims of Christ real and practical – that it may cause people to be receptive to His call to serve others in His name – that it may encourage the launching out of others into the vast uncharted seas of the future, taking Jesus as Pilot – so that whatever happens, there may be confidence in His power to prevail while experiencing the peace of His presence. Many of the waters into which Ruth, the family, and I sailed were unknown. With the enouragement of Paul (Mark 13:11) we believed that it would be given us in that hour what we were to say and do. We were simply to be "workmen ... rightly dividing the word of truth." (II Timothy 2:15). We tried to make every effort to prepare for all exigencies, but ultimately had to rest in the confidence that God would overcome.

Lowell A. Gess

Chapter One

Nigeria

Guinter Memorial Hospital, Bambur, Nigeria, Africa, 1953.

The First Surgery – The First Challenge

I was deep in the abdominal cavity of a young man. It was Monday, January 12, 1953. The scene was Guinter Memorial Hospital, Bambur, Adamawa Province, Nigeria, Africa. My wife Ruth and I, along with four of our children, had just arrived two days earlier. Yesterday, Sunday, we attended church where Dr. Harold Elliot preached in Hausa. He did very well with his newly learned language. I remember other Sundays when teacher and evangelist Kura Tella had the rapt attention of the congregation.

Today was my first day of work at the hospital. The patient I was attending had been brought to the hospital on a litter managed by four men from an inaccessible area behind a range of hills. At a wedding feast there had been an altercation which turned ugly, and a spear had been thrust into his abdomen. Jean Baldwin was administering the anesthetic. Ruth was circulating. One of the five Nigerian attendants was assisting me. We had only met that morning and were not aware of each other's abilities or capabilities.

Figure 1.1. Kura Tella preaching and supported by staff of Guinter Memorial Hospital.

Preparation as an Intern

The small one and a half inch spear wound was extended to over five inches to allow for adequate exposure. It was evident from the extensive contamination that the bowel had been perforated. Miraculously the spear had impaled on the vertebral column between the vena cava and the abdominal aorta without damaging either of them. After examining nearly twenty feet of small and six feet of large bowel, I found the segment of intestine that had been lacerated and prepared to repair it. I had been shown how to do this by Dr. Anderson, a surgical resident, at Ancker General Hospital in St. Paul, Minnesota where I interned. He had warned me that some day I would be required to repair intestine if they became gangrenous following prolonged hernial incarceration – not knowing that my very first patient would involve such a repair.

Dr. Anderson had taken me to the orthopedic supply room. With appropriate instruments and stockinette which was to serve as the make-believe intestine, we did reconstructive surgery. Continuous inverting Connell sutures were placed to attach the severed ends. Musculo-serous stitches were used to approximate the posterior and anterior surfaces before the original inverting sutures were withdrawn. That was it.

Now, six months later, I could not remember if it were, "intima to

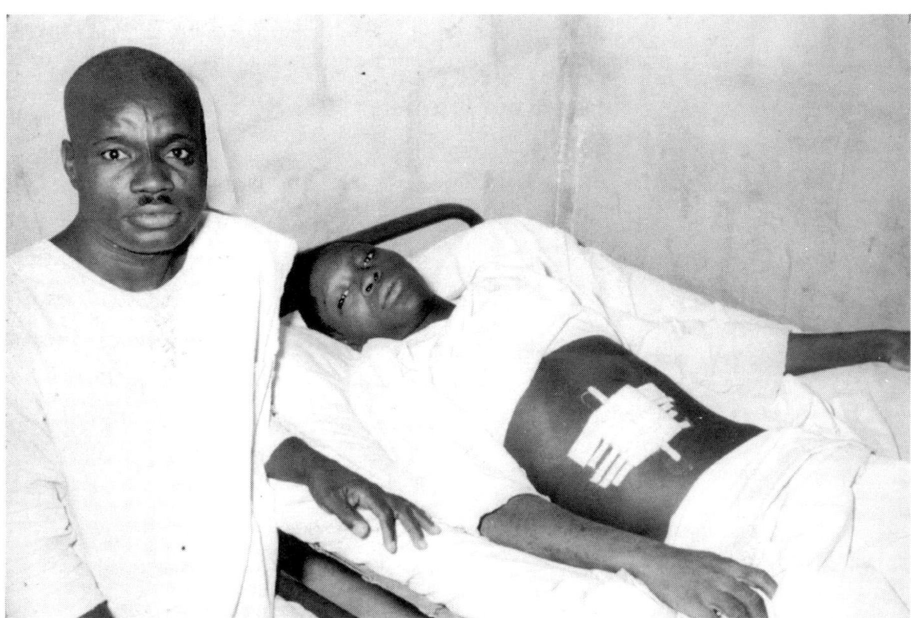

Figure 1.2. Yusufu postop.

intima, or serosa to serosa." Unless done correctly, overwhelming peritonitis would prove fatal. One might have said, "Flip a coin and at least do one of them. That would give a fifty percent chance of success."

Help, Lord!

I started to panic. This was tragic – pathetic! I was holding the life of a 21 year old young man in my hands, and I couldn't remember how to proceed. How could a Minnesota farm boy be put in such a situation as this? Surely the Lord would come to my assistance. There was no one else available to help. Any helping hands would have to be mine. "O Lord – HELP!"

While all of this turmoil was going on in my head, nothing was being done at the table. The silence was awkward and embarrassing. After about a minute, Ruth asked, "Are you alright, dear?" In what seemed appropriate to me, I responded by saying, "Let us pray. Lord bless this young man with your love and your healing. Show me how to do my part."

At that moment I clearly remembered Dr. Anderson's warning. "Be sure to carefully place the inverting serosal sutures." He didn't even mention the intima. It became clear – serosa to serosa. I even remembered that in the case of intestinal laceration, with which we were dealing, his counsel was to close in a transverse diameter so as to not narrow the passage.

I was not content with a single layer closure. I fashioned a double inverting repair, and then quickly ran the gut to rule out any additional lacerations. Four units of saline were used to irrigate the soiled abdominal cavity. A newly developed antibiotic, chloramphenicol, was used. Mildred Rebstock, a classmate of mine at North Central College, Naperville, Illinois, had synthesized it at the Parke Davis Laboratories. Later she was to be presented to President Harry S. Truman for her achievement. Her brother, John Rebstock, a lifelong friend, provided a supply of this wonder medicine just prior to our departure for Africa.

It would take some tact to explain the extensive five inch incision when the original spear wound had caused only an inch and a half opening on the skin surface. Furthermore a rubber drain would be sticking through the incision.

It was only after the surgery had been completed, that I stopped to realize how all of this must have sounded to the nurses and to the staff. This was my first surgery. They had no idea if I were even a real doctor. Here I was, literally coming in on a wing and a prayer. Did they, or did they not, have a doctor?

A Fellowship is Born

In his condition Yusufu was willing to believe and trust in me. His belief and trust went beyond the care of his body. We were to realize this two years later after his brush with death. An evangelist learned of a Christian gathering in his remote area. Yusufu had listened to the hymns, prayers, and the testimonies of the staff during his time of recuperation. He came to trust God with his life and yielded to the Lordship of Jesus Christ. His spared life made an impact for good on his family and friends. A church fellowship was born.

With the strength of his youth, Yusufu pulled through a most serious life threatening experience. The almost certain massive infection never happened. Within days he was up and about, easily handling a slight spike of temperature. It was not only God's grace that led to his recovery. Help came from the supporting staff of nurses and people like

Dr. Anderson and the Rebstocks. It was my privilege to be on hand to participate in the saving of this young man's life.

I often wondered how long it would have taken for my acceptance by staff and community if the first patient I touched had died.

Four decades later I still have a fond and remarkably clear memory of Yusufu and answered prayer in a time of need. My only regret is that I never had the opportunity to visit with him again as a fellow believer.

The fact that Yusufu was alive, well, and active in living out his new found faith reminded me of my widowed great-great-grandmother, Mrs. Paul Wolf, who on the Minnesota prairie opened her home for worship services when circuit riders came to the Nerstrand, Minnesota area in the 1860s. She never would have believed that some day, a great-great-grandson of hers would be preaching and healing in deepest Africa.

Love, A Beautiful Story

A young mother who had just given birth was brought to us with the complication of a retained placenta. She was bleeding and in shock. No longer was she conscious. One of the bearers was her husband. I explained to him that his wife needed to have blood or else her life would slip away. I proceeded to take a small sample of blood from each of the four men who had carried her on a makeshift litter of branches. They didn't understand why I was checking them when it was the patient who needed help. It was found that three of them were incompatible for transfusion. The one that was compatible was her husband. We took him along with the patient to surgery. We placed him in a little room off to the side while the nurses prepared the woman for surgery. I explained to him that I needed to take a little more blood. My wife Ruth, had been giving him glass after glass of orange juice and sweetened water. He didn't understand all this attention. We had him lie down and put a needle into his vein. Underneath the bed I hid the flask which was to receive the blood. He looked young and strong. Instead of taking just one unit of blood, I took two. We hurried it into surgery and began the administration to his wife.

In the moments that followed, her life hovered between life and death. After a half hour, her pulse began to strengthen. We immediate-

Figure 1.3. "She Has My Blood!" A beautiful love story.

ly did the surgery that was required, and her condition continued to improve. The entire staff was elated and was beginning to rejoice when suddenly I turned and found that I was looking into the face of her husband. He had tired of being on the bed in the other room and he wandered into the surgery without cap or gown to see what was going on. His gaze was transfixed on the bottle of blood. He knew that it was his blood, and in Africa you don't give blood because it is known that with the loss of blood, people die, whether it's from the result of being mauled by an animal, wounded by a spear, or any other trauma. His face was set with a firm and hard countenance. I cringed because I feared what was in his mind. We had deceived him. We had taken a large amount of blood and now he was observing that blood being given to his wife. No one spoke. Thankfully at that moment his wife stirred, and she murmured something that was audible only to her husband and to me. It was unbelievable. She spoke the name of her husband. His face melted and changed from being stern and aloof to one that showed a genuine love and compassion. He was looking at his wife. His heart went out to her. She was much dearer than simply being property.

In the days that followed, as she gained strength, he would go about saying, "See my wife, she has my blood." He was proud to say that his blood was coursing in his wife's veins. The staff understood his language and said, "That's not unusual. You were redeemed not with corruptible things such as silver or gold, but with the precious blood of Jesus." (I Peter 1:19). That scripture struck home and took root in his life. During the time of recuperation many wonderful things happened. The day came when she was alert and strong enough to move. As I came to her bed, she did something that women never do in this part of Africa. She reached out her hand and took mine in hers and said, "Na gode Allah." By translation it meant, "I thank God." Her husband, who was standing on the other side of the bed, smiled at her unusual gesture of reaching out to touch another man, but seemed to intuitively realize that this was a laying on of hands for health and healing.

This lovely couple came to know and experience the grace of God during the time of recuperation. They became firm believers in the Lord Jesus Christ. They were so glad to be alive that they took all their possessions, and going from bed to bed, they shared them with other patients prior to their departure from the hospital. Then they set off, she following her husband respectfully two steps behind in acceptance of his protection, each swinging their arms completely carefree. To this very day my eyes still well up with tears as I see them disappearing down the road unencumbered by any possessions, simply happy to be alive. Skeptics say: "That healing wasn't special, it was just good nursing care, good doctors." I say, "Not so."

They shall lay hands on the sick and they shall recover.
Mark 16:18

Meningitis Epidemic

A young African mother was receiving an intravenous injection in a grass hut during the January, 1955 outbreak of cerebrospinal meningitis. The numbers were so great that the wards could not accommodate the patients being brought in for treatment. The magnitude of the meningitis outbreak was greater than the elders at Bambur, Nigeria, could remember.

We kept building huts a short distance from the hospital compound

Figure 1.4. Meningitis Village.

as everyone was afraid of becoming infected. Without treatment the mortality rate ran 80 to 90 percent. With the overwhelming numbers, we were faced with dwindling supplies of penicillin and chloramphenical. Patients who were strong enough to take oral medications responded to triple sulphas.

The Guinter Memorial Hospital was located about 300 miles by road travel from the nearest pharmacy at Jos. The roads had only recently become passable following the rainy season, which isolated the hospital from the outside world for a four to five month period. Not trusting only in the four-wheel drive Land Rover to get through, arrangements were made to send runners as well. Seven to ten days would be required for such a direct trip over a hostile landscape. This route had been taken by Dr. Ira E. McBride on his 1000 mile motorcycle trip up from Lagos in the beginning of the rains in June during the latter 1930s. On the last lap of his journey he had set out from Vom and had to deal with streams and the Pai River. Runners would manage these barriers more easily than his six-horse motorcycle. The distance would be reduced to just over 200 miles.

The fateful day came when the antibiotics were exhausted. The seriously ill patients who were unable to swallow the triple sulpha were dying. While kneeling in prayer over a seriously ill patient with only a slight response left, the Holy Spirit-led thought came, the only plausible course was to inject the sulpha tablets. Granted, we only had one or two stomach tubes to feed the patients the sulphas. It was a matter of handling dozens of patients, of getting the tube into the stomach rather than the lungs, which, if it happened, would drown the patient.

A mortar and pestle were sterilized and placed on a sterile towel. With cap, mask and sterile gloves, the tablets were ground up. Measured saline was added for proper concentration. Then the dispensers, armed with large syringes and very large needles, began the rounds of injections. We anticipated sterile abscesses because of the tablet material that carried the sulpha, but were delighted to find that few developed. Those that did were considered a badge of honor because the patient was alive to have the abscesses drained. It was an exciting time to realize that family members were not carrying away expired loved ones.

The Land Rover did not return before the runners. They had made the return trip in just over a week's time. We enthusiastically received the penicillin and thanked God for the subsequent healing of the patients. The two runners enjoyed a notoriety of which they had never dreamed. They were the true "helping hands" in the handling of the epidemic.

After another two weeks, as suddenly as the outbreak had occurred, it vanished.

Leprosy

The man preaching at our newly established leprosy village near Bambur, Nigeria, in 1952 had difficulty keeping the pages of his Bible from turning in the wind. His fingers were missing. He was suffering from a prolonged infection of leprosy, one of the most feared diseases in the world. AIDS had not appeared on the scene at that time. His form of leprosy was tuberculoid, a type with skin lesions and nerve damage with loss of sensitivity resulting in damage from trauma or burns so that eventually the fingers and toes became ulcerated and on occasion would be resorbed by the body.

The before and after picture of the twelve year old girl with lepromatous leprosy attests to a six month effective treatment with dapsone, (diaminodiphenylsulfone – referred to as DDS). It took another year for her features to normalize. In the 1950s medication had progressed

Figure 1.5. Leprosy patient before start of treatment.

beyond the use of chaulmoogra oil which was administered by injection. The dapsone was given in tablet form which required a careful check to be assured that the capsules were actually swallowed. These good results, however, were clouded by the subsequent development of resistance to the use of dapsone alone. By 1991 the World Health Organization had launched a leprosy elimination program which reduced the prevalence of leprosy to 1 in 10,000 people in 90 of the 122 countries that had reported leprosy infections. They did this by instituting a multi-drug therapy program consisting of dapsone, rifampin, and clofazimine which prevented the development of resistance. The all too common erythema nodosum leprosum was effectively treated with the notorious drug thalidomide which in the early 1960s caused severe birth defects in many babies born of women who had received it to alleviate morning sickness. In 1998 the FDA approved thalidomide for the treatment of erythema nodosum leprosum.

The leprosy village at Bambur is no longer in existence. The multi-drug therapy program has effectively cured over eight million leprosy patients worldwide in the last ten years. Patients are no longer being isolated as they were down through the centuries from the time of Christ. Reconstructive surgery pioneered by Dr. Paul Brand, is helping patients

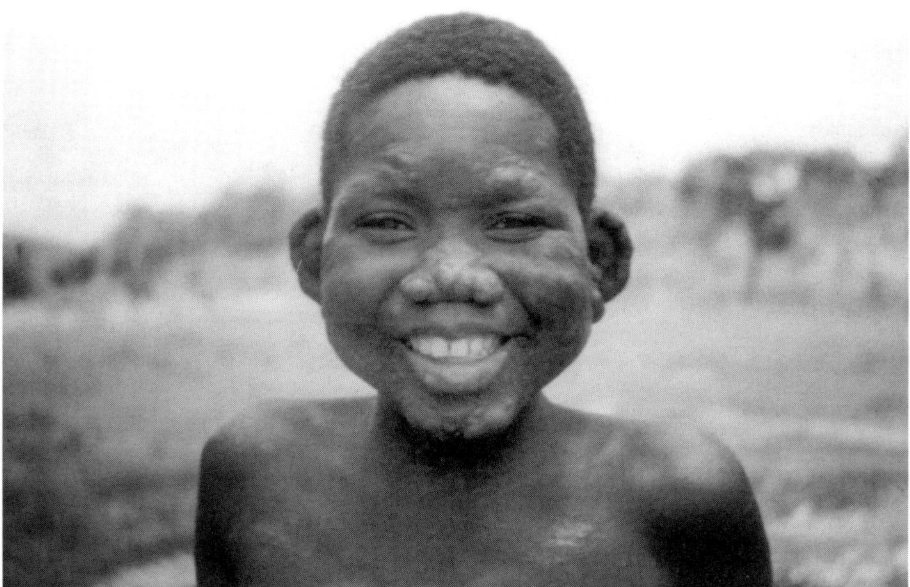

Figure 1.6. Leprosy patient six months after treatment.

who have not been treated early enough to prevent the crippling aspect of the disease.

It is the hope and prayer that leprosy may go the way of smallpox and eventually be eradicated. Governments, voluntary groups, and churches are engaged in a wide range of medical, surgical, educational and rehabilitation programs to provide holistic care to meet the physical, psychological, and spiritual needs of leprosy sufferers and their communities. Christ's ministry to those with leprosy continues to be the motivation force for today.

Figure 1.7. Leprosy patient holding the Bible minus some of his fingers.

Figure 1.8. Nurse Crystal Springborn with leprosy patient under treatment. The ravages of the disease did not become manifest.

Sharing Life's Blood

January 10, 1955, was full of many surprises. The inguinal hernia repair turned out to be a "sliding" hernia with part of the urinary bladder drawn into the large herniation. An extra hour of surgical time was needed and it was already far into the afternoon.

The long line of patients was eventually seen. One young Fulani girl was a special concern. Postpartum bleeding had left her in shock. Plasma expanders were immediately set up. What was needed was a blood transfusion.

Dr. and Mrs. Ira McBride were scheduled for their routine physicals later in the afternoon. At the close of the examination when it was revealed that they were in great shape, Dr. McBride made the comment, "What I really need is a hair cut."

Within moments the hospital guard was dispatched to our residence on the hill, and he returned with barbering equipment.

While doing his hair, he asked about the young Fulani girl. Earlier in the day he had been hunting in the Lau swamp to secure some venison. After a successful hunt he started home and would pass the hospital on the way.

Suddenly he came upon a small group of excited women. One raised her arm for him to stop. He did stop, and learned that a young mother had lost her new born child and now was near death as a result of post partum bleeding. He agreed to transport her to the Guinter Memorial Hospital. Men, according to custom, are not allowed to touch women in the delivery period. They stood by in a removed circle. Two ladies climbed into the back of Dr. McBride's truck. Other women lifted the patient to them. They cradled the patient for nearly ten miles over rough and bumpy roads.

On arrival at the hospital this was the patient who was immediately treated with the plasma expanders.

Continuing my conversation with Dr. McBride, I mentioned the need for blood for this Fulani girl. Relatives and friends were unwilling to donate blood. Childbirth deaths were not considered unusual.

There was a period of thoughtful silence. "If my blood is compatible, I would like to finish my Samaritan act of compassion," replied Dr. McBride. His blood was compatible, and a unit was transfused. Within an hour the patient was able to converse. The following day she walked, though a bit unsteadily.

For this is My blood of the new covenant,
which is shed for many for the remission of sins.

Matthew 26:28 NKJ

Nutrition and the Lau Swamp

The people in the Bambur area were meat hungry like most African tribes. Beef, pork, goat, and chicken were available on prescribed days in the local market. To many people these meats were not affordable. Children deprived of protein developed kwashiorkor which was characterized by anemia, edema, pot belly, depigmentation of the skin, and loss or change of hair color which assumed a reddish hue.

Whenever we suggested an outing for the staff, the selection was always the same – "Let's go hunting." That would mean going to the Lau Swamp between Bambur and Lau where our nearest post office was located. The swamp stretched along the Benue River for 100 miles, and was approximately ten miles deep. Kob (Mariya) antelope roamed in

Figure 1.9. Warding Off Evil Spirits. The Closing Months, 1967.

herds. Leopards, hyenas, and bush cow buffalo were present but not always seen.

Whenever we planned a hunt, we would rarely be disappointed. If by chance no animal was captured, guinea fowl, ducks or geese could be secured.

During the dry season our four-wheel drive Land Rover could manage the swamp area. On one occasion a group of antelope was spotted. In response to a dare as to how close our approach could be made with the Land Rover, we suddenly realized that we were less than thirty yards from a magnificent buck. He refused to give way to the mechanized vehicle. He was brought down with an easy shot. We ran to the quarry. To my hunting companion I asked in Hausa, "Ina wuka?" which meant "where is the knife." A voice answered "Yana non," which by translation means, "it is here." Dr. McBride, whose voice it was, emerged from some tall grass. He had been tracking and stalking this same antelope for an extended time, only to have me drive up and steal "his" animal at the last moment.

One never could be sure how many animals were being dealt with in the thick and tall grasses, and what the game was for sure. Gerald Faust came upon what looked like three large wild pigs. When the shooting

Figure 1.10. Gerald Faust with his father, Dr. A.J. Faust, bringing home three buffalo.

had ended, three buffalo were downed. Hearing the shots, men came running from a nearby village to help with the butchering and loading of the meat into the back of the jeep. The beef was shared with these men, eighty-seven people living at the Bible Training School compound, and fifteen missionaries and many of the local people. Gerald enjoyed the status of an honorary member of the Wurkum tribe. This story can be found in its complete form in *From Pero Station* by Dr. Arthur and Aletha Faust.

Protein, carbohydrate, and fat were not the only shortfalls in the people of the Adamawa and Taraba States. Iodine was suboptimal in the dietary intake allowing for colloid goiters. The American public is assured of iodine in the commonly used iodized salt, but in West Africa there was no such source. Provision of iodine in the present age has become a major emphasis in the Kiwanis world outreach projects.

It is only fair to note that some of the most delicious food in all the world can be found in West Africa. Ruth and I along with our children are thrilled with luscious mango and guava sauces, groundnut (peanut) and palm oil stews, and above all, jollaf rice, especially if it were prepared by Betty Carew, Theresa Renner, or Malcolm Albert's grandmother. Just thinking about it creates a strong longing.

Figure 1.11. Ant hill.

Early on we learned to carefully observe our food servings. The bits of stone gathered during the grinding of Guinea corn, which we used as a breakfast cereal in Nigeria, had to be experienced by chewing rather than being envisioned. Errant cockroaches were often a problem. The ubiquitous ant was less of a shock. First term missionaries often were unable to eat the soup when an ant was spotted. Second term missionaries would remove the ant and consume the soup. Third term missionaries would ask, "Where is the ant?"

Some ants could be either helpful or dangerous. An immobilized animal could be destroyed by some types of ants. Driver ants, sometimes called "soldier ants," could be dangerous. They moved in columns flanked by the larger soldiers. Accidentally stepping on their column could lead to being swarmed over and being punished with many bites. Ruth nearly stepped on such a column which had included our house in their marching orders. Their numbers seemed endless giving doubt to the effectiveness of the small quantity of insecticide that we had. We protected our food in covered receptacles and prepared to observe their advance. Methodically they proceeded from room to room leaving only the parts of cockroaches that were not edible. Lizards (geckos) and mice made hasty retreats. For a period of time, we had a "clean" house.

Figure 1.12. Rickets.

Less casual was the invasion of rats. They announced their presence by leaving large holes in unprotected bananas. Their scampering about on our ceiling was not appreciated. We felt some protection at night from our tucked-in mosquito nets. It seems that the African rat has an unusually high I.Q. They tripped traps without getting caught, enjoying the bait without much adieu. The recent availability of glue which is spread out around a piece of banana or cheese confirms their vulnerability. We found this to be the only effective way of dealing with rat intruders.

One of our patients from whom we removed a forty pound scrotum enlarged by filariasis, explained that the ulceration on the bottom was not only from injuring the floor level appendage but also the work of rats in his grass hut while he slept.

Other potential invaders included the bat, and of course, the snake which was after mice and rats. On occasion the snakes injudiciously select such hiding places as clothes drawers. Philip Galow had this surprise in Bo. Thankfully there was no biting or spitting during this encounter.

During a prayer meeting one worshipper was looking up with opened eyes rather than down with closed eyes. A viper was spotted on the rafter two rows ahead of me. The leader announced that he would usher out this critter of a different faith and poked him with a long stick. Instead of slithering out, the snake dropped to the aisle just in front of me and began his exit. As he passed me, I encouraged his progress with a hymn book. The impact was so great that "the Lord took him."

Malaria

It was past noon. It had been a busy five hour morning's work in the clinic of the Guinter Memorial Hospital in Bambur, Nigeria. I had had a headache and was unusually tired and thirsty. In the midday heat I could not tell if a fever were present. On my way out the door, a dispenser asked me to see one more patient, a teenaged girl on a makeshift stretcher. It had taken the party of concerned family members all morning to make the trip to the hospital. The patient's eyes were closed. I saw no respirations. The stethoscope recorded no heartbeat. Her forehead was still very warm. A history of severe headache, drowsiness, confusion, and delirium revealed a typical cerebral malarial infection which is often fatal. I consoled the parents, expressing disappointment that I had not been given the opportunity to administer treatment. Placing my hand on her head I prayed, "The Lord bless you and keep you; the Lord make His face shine upon you and be gracious unto you; the Lord lift up His countenance upon you and give you peace." (Num. 6: 24-26).

Some days I drove the four-wheel drive Land Rover from our house on the hill down to the hospital complex below. Today was not one of those days. Several times on the way up the hill, I paused. It seemed that "I was running out of petrol."

At the dining room table when the food was served, I sat staring at it. Before touching it, I began to violently chill. Ruth helped me to the bedroom. Before allowing me to lie down, she brought four tablets of chloroquine and a glass of water. In bed, I kept asking for more blankets. Ultimately she resorted to placing some throw rugs on top of my shivering body.

I would need another dose of medication in a matter of four to six hours. If vomiting were to be a problem or if my sensorium were affected, Ruth wrote down the doses of intramuscular medication that would be needed.

Only when the shaking chills began to subside, did the picture come before my eyes of the teenaged girl that I had just attended before leaving the hospital for lunch. She was a native Nigerian and most assuredly had a gradual immunity to malarial infections. I was an expatriate, ripe for the overwhelming paroxysms that accompany falciparum malaria. I didn't even consider the other three types that might be involved. Would my fever and chills ultimately develop into cerebral malaria?

The World Health Organization continuously grapples with the problem of malaria. More than 400 million people suffer from the disease each year and at least one million die from the infection. Even though most of the fatalities are with children, I wondered about the rest of that million who make up the group. I was not concerned about how malaria affected the economic growth of highly malarious countries or that Africa's gross domestic products would have been $100 billion greater in the year 2000 if malaria had been eliminated according to research by Harvard University, the London School of Hygiene and Tropical Medicine, and the WHO.

I was not willingly going to allow sleep to take me from consciously dealing with this crisis. However, I knew that with confusion and delirium Ruth would have to assume the treatment and care. I still was alert by the time the next two tablets of chloroquine needed to be taken. However, it was time that I needed to be willing to let Ruth and the Lord assume complete control.

I dropped off to sleep.

The following day I was a bit pale, and moved a little slower, but I was back at my post.

Figure 1.13. Snake. Perhaps the most deadly viper (carpet viper, echis carinatus).

Snakes

Is Any Help Possible?

Snakes were an ever-present life-threatening danger. The area around Bambur, Nigeria, has been known for many generations as one of the most dangerous places in Africa for poisonous vipers. Sometimes it is referred to as "the most lethal snake pit in Africa." While serving at the Guinter Memorial Hospital, two pastors were bitten by vipers while on the way to their churches. The vipers crawled out on the paths which were warmed by the sun during the day and retained the heat well into the evening hours. Tragically both pastors died following their bites.

We had brought with us snake antivenin. We felt that with this in our treatment bag we would be able to help people who were bitten by these snakes. And yet each time we were presented with a snake bite victim, the patient died in spite of all the care we gave. In addition to the antivenin we also used some new treatments such as wrapping the extremity in ice in order to slow the absorption of the poison. We were able to do this at the hospital compound because there were a number of missionaries who had kerosene refrigerators that made ice cubes.

One evening about 8 p.m., a ten year old girl was brought to the hospital after having been bitten by a viper (kububuwa). Already she had begun to hemorrhage from her gums and later on she vomited blood. We treated her with all our known armamentarium but eighteen hours later she was dead.

It was obvious that we were dealing with a problem that was not being reached by our antivenin serum. Not only was the venom of this type of snake hematoxic, it was neurotoxic as well.

Shortly thereafter a 16 year old young man who had been sweeping the school compound that afternoon was brought to the hospital. He was a recent convert to Christianity despite protests from his Muslim family. His family believed that calamity or destruction would befall him because he betrayed his Muslim faith. He was brought to the hospital soon after he had been bitten. His friends were wild eyed with terror. Everyone was aware that our treatment with other patients had been totally ineffective. In addition to the overwhelming neuroshock, blood loss was probably responsible for the demise of our previous patients. Patients lost blood even at the sites where the antivenin was administered by injection as well as at the injections sites where antibiotics were used. We could not let this boy die. We asked for blood donors and ten students volunteered. Three of them were compatible. As he was receiving the third transfusion the following day he died.

The Christian community was devastated. We prayed for spiritual guidance and even came upon the scripture in Mark 16:18 (Good News Bible) where Jesus says that signs such as this will be coming where "one can take up the serpent and not be harmed." It was apparent that what we were doing was not adequate.

Research into the type of snake with which we were dealing revealed it to be a saw scaled viper (carpet viper). We were able to find no antivenin that was specific for this type of snake. It is classified as an Echis carinatus of the family Viperidea, found in deserts and other arid regions from northern Africa to Ceylon. Though probably the most venomous of vipers, with an oft-fatal bite, it rarely exceeded more than two feet in length. It is a ground snake, active mostly at night. It is generally pale sandy in color with reddish mottling and wavy, whitish bars, usually bordered with black, in an irregular pattern. It is one of the few snakes that can be called aggressive.

Since we were unable to find specific antivenin, we would have to make our own.

Handling Vipers

Following some spirit-filled prayer meetings it was finally decided that we would pursue the production of a specific antivenin for the Echis carinatus snake with which we were dealing. It was not unusual to hear the expression, "Oh, help, Lord."

Dr. Dean Olewiler and I visited paramount and district chiefs in the area. We expressed to them our desire to be of help in saving the lives of people bitten by poisonous snakes. They were quite willing to help as all we asked of them was to immediately inform us if anyone saw or was aware of one of these snakes. We would come for the capture.

We placed the snakes that we caught in secure pens and fed them mice from time to time. It was our intention to milk them of their venom and then send this venom to a place where it could be injected into horses and the antivenin produced. The milking chores were shared by Dr. Dean Olewiler and myself.

On one occasion while preparing to milk a snake, I was suddenly surprised by the snake's turning its head in the loop in which it had been secured. Normally I would pick up the snake with a stick that had a looped cord at the end. While secured in this cord, I would grasp the snake's head behind its jaws and bring it to the rim of a small vial. Instinctively the snake would open its mouth as the vial touched it and the snake would squirt venom into the vial through a pair of fangs. On this occasion as I was preparing to grasp the snake, it somehow was able to turn and it sank its fangs into the stick by the looped cord. The fangs remained stuck in the stick, the venom dripping down. I put the snake back in the pen assuming that without fangs, it would not be able to capture the mice that we fed it.

The next week I included this snake with the others that were being milked. It performed normally. We learned that it had about five extra pair of fangs on the roof of its mouth, so that if one pair were damaged during a bite, another pair would move down into its place. That experience was not without its effect. For many years afterwards I had occasional nightmares of snakes about to turn and bite me.

The penned viper received mice from time to time. We would pay small boys to catch the mice. On one occasion, I found the snake dead, having been completely gutted. Scampering around in the pen was what turned out to be a shrew, a very small mouse-like mammal, to which scientists ascribe the greatest ferocity and courage of all animals in a pound for pound comparison.

Following the harvesting of a number of snake venom ejections, we learned that only South Africa had the facilities for the production of antivenin. South Africa was isolated from other African countries because of apartheid. The venom, therefore, had to be carried to New York by missionaries, and then sent to South Africa from the United States. The return was by the same route.

Soon after the return of the antivenin the son of Mai Doki, our cook, was bitten by an Echis viper. His was the first life to be spared with the use of this antivenin. There was great praise in the church and in the community.

During the time that we were milking vipers a dramatic incident happened. The hospital yard man, while cutting grass, was bitten on the back of his hand. I was at lunch. A hospital messenger breathlessly appeared at the door. In the excitement, his Hausa, the native dialect, was too rapid and complex for me to understand. Our seven year old son, Tim, standing at my side, tugged at my leg. He translated that I was to hurry to the hospital as our yard man had been bitten by a snake. Because everyone had rushed away for the lunch break, the instruments had been left out on the table and were no longer sterile. Following a quick local injection of anesthetic, the tissues on the back of his hand were removed with the unsterile instruments, leaving only the tendons. Miraculously he suffered no infection. Later we were able to graft his hand and rejoice with him in being alive with a functional hand. He was our first successful treatment of an Echis bite!

As parents of small children we wondered if ever that day might come when a finger or some other part of the body might have to be sacrificed to preserve life. We were afraid for our children.

Forty-five Years Later

Since these events of forty-five years ago, much has been learned about snakes and how their bites may be handled. There generally is an arbitrary division of snake venoms such as neurotoxins, hematoxins, and cytotoxins. We have come to know that the bite of an Echis snake is one of the most deadly. We were well aware of the effects of these bites years ago, but now they are classified. There are marked cardiac and vascular changes to be sure. We also now know that there are defects in coagulation and changes in vascular resistance. This causes massive bleeding into the area where needle injections are done for the administration of the antivenin as well as antibiotics. We were aware that bleeding occurred from the orifices of the body, from the gums, from the stomach, in the lungs, peritoneum, kidneys, and the heart. Cadaver studies carried out in succeeding years substantiate what we unhappily experienced more than four decades earlier. Neurologically the patient's nervous system was involved to the point where they could not control their muscles and their minds became confused. Thankfully they may not have been conscious and aware in the latter stages prior to their death.

We also became aware that dealing with cobras was somewhat different. Cobras have short fixed fangs that cannot be retracted and lie against the roof of the mouth as in vipers and rattlesnakes. In order to secure a successful injection of their venom, they would hold on to their prey longer and deliver multiple bites to insure penetration. They were also accurate up to ten feet in their spitting at the eyes of their victims or intruders.

Figure 1.14. Snake bite victim treatment today (forty-five years after antivenin developed).

Miss Vivian Olson, a saintly missionary, was much closer during the middle of one night when she awakened with the sensation of movement in her bed. To clear her senses she got up and took a shower. Finally, fully awake, she returned to her bed and gingerly lifted one corner of the sheet. Her breath left her – she was observing part of the black body of a cobra. She screamed for the night watchman who came running with a long stick. He dispatched the four and a half foot spitting cobra which never was given the chance to spit. Miss Olson's experience of the feel of the snake was an electrifying one, especially when one does not have control of the situation.

I had been laid up for over two weeks with a type A viral hepatitis. I had already gone through the anorexia, malaise, nausea, and vomiting. The fever was supposed to end with the dark urine and the jaundice. I was expected to feel better despite my yellow eyes and skin. However, this was not the case. An abnormally high temperature developed. There was a fear of delirium. When Ruth heard my call from my bedroom to bring a shovel, she assumed that I was "out of my head." Dutifully she came running with the shovel in hand.

She found me, standing on the bed, wild-eyed, pointing to a green four foot snake slithering out the doorway. With the help of the visiting mission superintendent, the Rev. Clyde Galow, the snake was never allowed to rejoin his family.

Reconstruction of the incident was as follows: In a half sleep, I had suddenly become aware of something moving over my feet. On opening my eyes, I saw the snake going from point A to point B. He never made it because every muscle in my body contracted at the same moment. The snake was sent flying into the air and the call was made for the shovel.

Ruth and I were concerned about the persistence and progression of the fever. Our medical backgrounds made us aware that a favorable prognosis or outcome could not always be guaranteed with a mortality capable of reaching ten to fifteen percent. It was sobering to think of the persons who constituted those figures.

Thankfully, following the snake incident, I began my recovery under the care of Dr. Sama Banya, who in later years was to politically guide the destiny of the country of Sierra Leone. Eventually I was able to return to work. The privilege of work had never been more sweet.

While all these incidents have a happy ending, such was not the happy experience for our family's favorite black cat who courageously tried to stand up to a cobra. The cobra spit into the eyes of Blackie and she became frenzied with pain, literally clawing at her eyes. It was apparent that the cat would be without sight; and so in the tradition of the rider who places a gun to the head of his horse with a broken leg, we mercifully sacrificed our cat.

The picture at the beginning of this anecdote is one of a young man seen in 1999 who had been bitten by an Echis viper. He was in the hospital of the United Methodist Mission Outreach at Zing, Nigeria. It shows him with his right arm swollen and with a breakdown of tissue. Wonder of wonders, however, he is alert and alive. He was one of the fortunate people living in this age when specific antivenin was available. We continue to thank God for the help of all involved in producing this life saving antivenin and for those who are ministering in these far away mission stations.

Beyond the Help of Human Hands

While serving at the Guinter Memorial Hospital, Bambur, Nigeria, our fifth child Paul was born May 29, 1954, a bonny boy! Several weeks later he became ill. The infection did not respond to antibiotics. Convulsions developed and continued throughout the following day and night. There was no letup of the spasms the next day in spite of heroic measures.

Dr. Dean Olewiler and the attending nurses were wonderful in their care. Everything possible was done. There was a general consensus that our little boy was beyond the help of human hands.

During that second day, we continued to give antibiotic injections as well as medications intended to control the convulsions. Going over in our minds repeatedly were the statements that were being made, such as, "there are some things that we have to accept," and "sometimes diseases get beyond human control, and we have to accept them as the permissive will of God." We realized that medicine is not the answer in some impossible situations, but we continued to pray for Paul's renewal.

With the coming of evening we were beginning to be drawn to accept the inevitable. We had helplessly seen so many patients die with meningitis, who in their situations also were beyond the reaches of medical help. We wanted to know if Paul's general infection invaded the central nervous system. We had to know. This meant doing a spinal tap on this very small infant – our son. Would Ruth agree? With a look of trust, and possibly resignation, she positioned him on the dining room table, and the procedure was done without difficulty.

During the polio epidemic in 1952 at Ancker General Hospital in St.

Paul, Minnesota, I was required as an intern on duty in the emergency room to perform countless spinal taps. I could tell without doubt when the needle entered the spinal canal. At this moment in faraway Bambur, Nigeria, while dealing with my own son, I knew that the needle was in the proper place. There was no spinal fluid. That was the moment of greatest anguish. Had he gone beyond the point of no return? Ruth gathered him in her arms and we huddled together on the front room couch.

After a period of prolonged silence, Ruth spoke "We haven't even baptized him." I went to the kitchen and got a cup of water. We opened the Bible to Matthew 19:14, where Jesus says, "Suffer the little children to come unto Me, forbid them not, for of such is the Kingdom of Heaven." We baptized him with the name of Paul. We both prayed, and then emotionally exhausted, we were silent. We truly felt the presence of the Holy Spirit and were relieved that we had finally come to the place where we were willing to let our son go that he might return to God, his Creator.

About a half-hour later Ruth said, "Lowell, he's not convulsing. Oh, he's gone." Instinctively I took out my stethoscope and placed it over his heart. It was beating normally and strongly. His breathing was regular. And then that wonderful moment when he moved his arms, and shortly began to nurse.

The recovery was rapid.

It was now close to midnight. The other children were in bed. Following the nursing, we too went to bed. We placed Paul between us. One of us tried to sleep while the other watched. We were not going to let anything happen now!

In the years that followed, Paul developed into a beautiful boy. He was a joy to his parents. He knew the Lord as his Savior. Although we wondered about the effects from such a serious illness, it was exciting to see him develop and become strong. On the football field in Bismarck, North Dakota, he starred as an all-state tailback for his championship football team. He was committed in his loyalty to the Lord Jesus Christ. He was willing to get on the loud speakers and address his fellow high school students about coming prayer meetings and Bible studies that were being arranged. Being a big jock, the students listened to him.

Paul went on to Seattle Pacific University and played championship soccer. At Fuller Theological Seminary he completed a master's degree to qualify him for individual, family, and marital therapy. He continues to be called upon to perform as a mental health counselor with special leadership as a domestic violence treatment provider.

The Lord had much in store for Paul following that midnight baptism.

Bambur, Nigeria in Review

Bambur, 1952

It was 1952. We were ready to go to Africa. Our calling as medical missionaries was about to be realized after a preparation that included grade school, high school, college, seminary, medical school, and internship. Residencies in general surgery and ophthalmology would come later, bringing the total number of years of preparation to thirty.

We sold our home and repaid Dick and Sylvia Rassmunson the $5,000 they had loaned us at no interest to originally purchase the house in which we lived during the internship at Ancker General Hospital. Legal transactions were handled at no cost by Bob and Betty Elliot. Our car was so old we gave it away. We had no assets in the U.S.A. We were Africa bound.

Scores of friends and relatives helped pay last minute expenses. We would be assured of an annual salary of $2,800 for our family of six. While in Africa it was raised in August, 1953 to $3,400.

We packed barrels with medicines, equipment, four cartons of SMA milk for infants, supplies, sheets, dishes, toys, and clothing for the children. Approximation of sizes had to be made for the children's growth. Some of the medical and surgical textbooks would be my constant companions for the next three years. Crates of staple food items from Leggetts in New York awaited our sailing. A Servel kerosene refrigerator provided largely by the Nerstrand Evangelical Church congregation with a gift of $253.85 would ultimately arrive in Bambur in working condition, unlike Hank and Jean Baldwin's which was dropped when being off-landed in Lagos, Nigeria.

Prior to leaving for Africa we served at the Red Bird Mission in Beverly, Kentucky, during the July and August holiday of Dr. and Mrs.

Everett Schaefer. It was great being a real doctor rather than an intern under supervision. It was an exciting time taking care of emergencies. Not so happy was son Tim's being attacked by a swarm of yellow jacket bees. A ne'er do well and supposedly shiftless mountaineer came to Tim's assistance with a daring rescue.

On August the 7th, less than twelve hours after the Schaefer's return, Dr. Schaefer assisted our son John into the world shortly after midnight. Later during the night I was called to attend another patient. Ruth was sleeping following her exhaustive delivery. Going to the nursery to admire our newborn, I was horrified to see John cyanotic, laboring to breathe because of obstructing mucous. The only rubber aspirating syringe available was not sterile, having been used for a meningitis patient. Frantically I removed the mucous orally, hoisted him up by his feet, and slapped the back of his chest. He coughed and then was able to cry – oh that beautiful cry. For a time he was assisted by an incubator which Ruth insisted be positioned at her bedside.

In the fall while packing and preparing for the trip, our physician, Dr. Gillespie, who had arranged for all our injections of typhoid, paratyphoid, tetanus, smallpox, yellow fever, and DPT shots, introduced me to Drs. George and John Earl, and arranged for me to observe and participate in surgery at the Midway Hospital in St. Paul, Minnesota. Only the future would tell how important this exposure was, as from day one on the field, I would be faced with every kind of surgical condition and emergency.

A trip was taken in September and October to Humboldt Square Evangelical Church in Buffalo, New York, pastored by Rev. Schooping, along with faithful missionary supporters Helene and Cornelia Metz. The next stop was in Cory, Pennsylvania, where Rev. Harris was the pastor. Then it was Junior, West Virginia, with the Rev. Bill Hamilton, and finally to Kendallville, Indiana, where Erv Petznick was serving with his wife Beverly, sister to Ruth. While I did a great deal of speaking, the high moment came on September 30, 1952, when I was able to hear in person Dr. E. Stanley Jones speak on "One church, one book, one Christ." Another delightful occasion took place several weeks later when I was able to hear the Rev. Ralph Esterly give his famous sermon, "The Knock on the Door."

In the closing months of 1952 we had the privilege of visiting with many of our friends before leaving for Africa. Friends such as Rudy and Eleanor Strand, Ray and Agnes Paetznik, Verna Lofstrom, and Earl and Marion Koester who brought along a beautiful Hallicrafter short wave radio for our use during our isolation in Africa.

November 1st opened very dramatically. Our car was stolen. I went fishing. It wasn't quite as dramatic as it sounded. I had agreed to speak several times at the Brainerd Evangelical Church, and while up there, my father and I had decided we would do some fishing. I spoke and we did go fishing. On our return to St. Paul the car had been recovered by the police. In spite of it's being a rickety old car it had a tankful of gas. When it was recovered it was parked on the side of the street because the tank was empty.

November the 9th was our commissioning at the Calvary Evangelical United Brethren Church. The service was led by Bishop E. W. Praetorius. The Rev. Frank Spong, and the Rev. Floyd Bosshardt also participated.

December 1st was the day that we boarded the train in St. Paul, Minnesota for our trip to Africa. Arriving in New York we were introduced to fellow missionaries leaving for Africa. Present were Eugene (Hank) and Jean Baldwin, June Hartranft, Ethel Brooks, and Ruth Elmer. Les Bradford was on his way to Sierra Leone for his wedding with Dr. Winifred Smith. Our first glimpse of him was his coming down the steps walking on his hands.

On December 5th we boarded the ship *America* for our trans-Atlantic crossing. It was rough, causing our entire family to become violently seasick. Especially surprising was the fact that our four month old John also suffered seasickness.

By December the 11th we viewed beautifully green Ireland and sailed past Guernsey Isle. The following day we docked at LeHavre, France, at 3:30 a.m. By 5:30 p.m. we docked in Southhampton, England. We traveled by train to Waterloo station, London. Duane Dennis and Mr. Edwards assisted us. Our St. Margaret's Hotel was cold during this time of the winter. We could not feed enough pennies into the coin operated burner to keep the room warm. A transfer was then made to the Bedford Hotel with central heating.

During these days hurried trips were being made to get proper visa clearance. We found out that we could board the vessel going to Lagos without a visa; so on December 18th we were on board and headed

Figure 1.15. Children playing deck games.

south to Nigeria, Africa.

The children enjoyed the trip with deck games, swimming, and other organized activity. The only serious event took place when in the swimming pool, Tim went down for the second time before being rescued by an Englishman relaxing at poolside. Tim's memory of the incident includes the fact that the man still had a wet cigarette in his mouth as he assisted him out of the pool.

Visits were made in Las Palmos, Bible study was conducted on board ship, daughter Mary's long braids were clipped before reaching tropical waters, and a visit was made to the headquarters of the Evangelical United Brethren Church in Freetown, Sierra Leone.

Four days later we docked at Lagos, Nigeria. Still without a visa, we were the last ones allowed off the ship. A sympathetic British Counsel ultimately allowed us to disembark. We were met at the S.I.M. quarters by telegrams from Betty and Bob Elliot and Dr. and Mrs. Arthur Faust. This act of kindness illustrated why the Nigerian people felt so warmly about the Fausts.

It was New Year's Eve. We were happy to share on this last day of 1952 the tropical warmth of Nigeria.

Bambur, 1953

Following our arrival in Lagos December 31, 1952, it took until January 10, 1953 to arrive in Bambur. The two day rail trip from Lagos to Jos was an experience never to be forgotten. Three of our four children developed boils during the trip requiring treatment by Dr. Roger Troup in Jos. Our welcome in Jos was by Dr. Ira McBride, Walt Erbele, and Mrs. Richmond who arranged for our housing. The overland trip from Jos to Bambur took from 5 a.m. until 8 p.m. on January 10, 1953. We were put up in the maternity ward until the end of February as Dr. Elliot and his family were still occupying our future home.

The next day, Sunday, found us in church listening to Dr. Harold Elliot preaching in Hausa. Monday morning we were introduced to the hospital staff. Within hours I was doing emergency surgery for a serious abdominal stab wound on a young man by the name of Yusufu. This incident is described in the opening pages of this book.

Several days later, Walter Erbele, the driver who brought us to Bambur, suffered a broken arm when the station wagon steering gear went out. Occupants J. Arthur Rank, and Richard Tholin were unharmed.

On January 22nd, Dr. Elliot safely brought Emmy Tschannon, Ruth

Figure 1.16. Guinter Memorial Hospital Dedication.

Figure 1.17. Guinter Memorial Hospital staff with nurses Amy Skartred and Virginia Draeger.

Wittmer, and Florence Walter in spite of an accident with that vehicle. The third car driven by Dr. Ira McBride escaped any incident while chauffeuring Bishop Warner and Dr. Ziegler. Bishop Warner became especially interested in the patient, Yusufu, the first surgical repair I did in Nigeria, and interviewed and recorded him on tape. Little did he know that years later Yusufu would be leading a Christian fellowship in his far away village unvisited by evangelists or local pastors. The arrival of Martin and Ruth Stettler completed the ferrying of passengers. All this activity at this time of the year was dictated by the weather. The heavy rains during the months of June into December made the roads impassable.

While still in the month of January, I was introduced to what was to be our greatest frustration – snake bites. In spite of antivenin treatment and heroic measures, patients died. We set about typing and cross-matching the missionaries and staff at Guinter Memorial Hospital for help in dire emergencies. Even with transfusions, snake bite victims still died.

By the month of February, 1953, in less than two months, I had already performed surgery on an obstructed inguinal hernia as well as having to manually remove retained placentas. How could I face such daunting challenges with only a rotating internship training? There was no one else to help. I was God's man, inadequate as I felt. And yet the

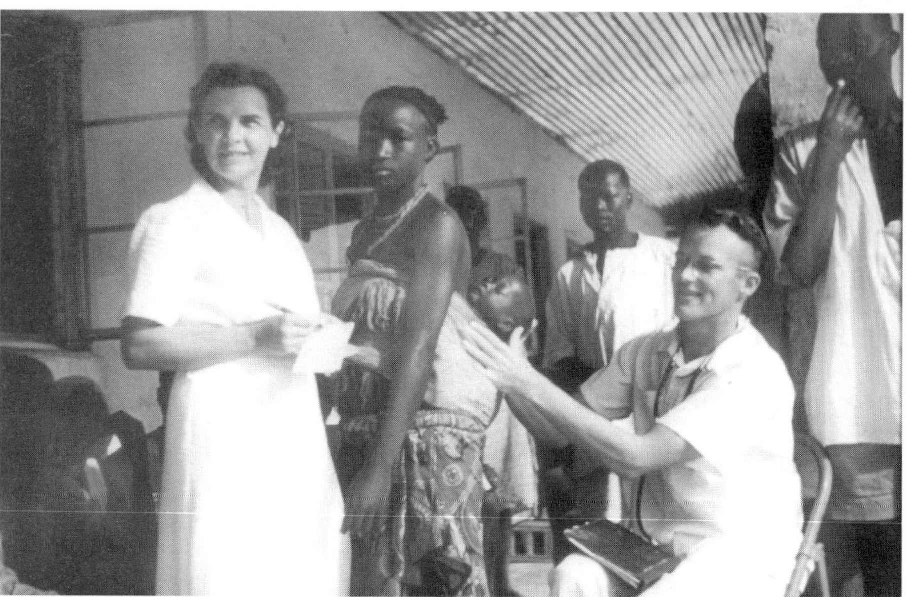

Figure 1.18. Ruth and I seeing patients on the overflow veranda.

Figure 1.19. Welcoming Doctor and Mrs. Benfer.

Figure 1.20. Women carrying water to our home.

successes were amazing. Members of the staff and our own cook, Mai Doki, decided to have their herniae repaired when they saw the successes of other patients.

In later years I reminisced about the hosts of people whom I had been privileged to serve in Jesus' name for healing. It was important to provide the best medicine and surgery possible if others were to believe that we were sharing the best Gospel.

We were delighted to welcome Dr. and Mrs. Kenneth Benfer February 11, 1953. He was a seasoned general practitioner with a bent for doing excellent surgery as Dr. Dean Olewiler did when he arrived at the end of the year. It was a bit difficult for him one day when he faced fifteen patients with disfiguring yaws. He was unbelieving that some of the other patients who appeared healed, formerly had been stricken with this disease.

Patients with fractures presented unusual challenges. The carpenters were willing to go along with some strange setups to handle the various bone breaks. It took some time for the staff to gain enough confidence in me to accept a hanging cast for a fractured humerus. Several successful results finally brought all on board.

Anesthesia occasionally went beyond a spinal, soliciting in order the help of vocal, local, pentathol, and ether. Amputation of filarial scro-

Figure 1.21. Ground breaking for Leprosy Village by Dr. Ira McBride.

tums sometimes made the patient as much as forty pounds or more lighter. Successful vesico-vaginal fistulae repairs brought many young mothers to the hospital inquiring about repairs for them. A routine appendectomy might uncover an unbelievable amount of abdominal adhesions, the result of previous tropical infections.

In the mid-twentieth century leprosy patients were isolated. We established a leprosy village for 150 patients. Evangelists could not always turn the pages of the Bible while they preached as their fingers had been absorbed. DDS (diamino diphenol sulfone) came upon the scene as a godsend.

In spite of the isolation during the rainy part of the year when we were confined to our home and our work at Gwatin compound where the hospital was located, there were lurking dangers. Son John developed an illness that included convulsions, which eventually was proven by blood smear to be malaria, the imitator of so many different kinds of illnesses. Doing a spinal tap on one's own small son needed to be reinforced by prayer.

A poisonous Echis viper was killed as it was attempting to gain entrance to our house. A leopard came out from behind our garage. He stopped, and then I stopped, frozen with fright. The leopard ambled away; I resumed breathing. Other dangerous occasions occurred with faulty brakes on the ancient Land Rover that was available for our use at the hospital. On a return trip from a clinic visit to Zing, the brakes gave out. While careening down a long incline, we were horrified to see that the bridge was missing. Shifting down the gears for some slowing, we were able to bounce through the dry stream bed without overturning.

Another incident occurred when the brakes did not hold while parked at our house. Suddenly I saw the car starting to move down the hill. Without thinking I ran and jumped into the car and applied the foot brake just as it was about to go over the terrace ledge in the direction of John who was playing on the road. We thank God that through all these experiences we were kept from harm.

One day Tim was playing on our phonograph "Softly and Tenderly Jesus is Calling." This led our five year old Mary to witness to Sambo, one of our house helpers. She spoke in Hausa, "Jesus is my Savior. Is he yours?" He replied, "Not yet." The children invited him to come to church and learn.

It was unbelievable how our children took up Hausa phrases while playing with other children. They were far better than their parents. On occasion, I elicited the help of Tim to translate for me.

The year ended with the anticipated arrival of Dr. Dean and Jane Olewiler with their children, Deborah and David. 1954 would be a better year with their help in the demanding program.

Bambur, 1954

January 2, 1954, began as a busy year. Dr. Dean Olewiler, who had just arrived with his family, did his first of many tooth extractions. Minutes later he was scrubbing with me on a vaginal hysterectomy. Dr. Merlin Brubaker was visiting us for a short time during these activities.

From February 10 to 18, both Dean and I were privileged to participate in a leprosy workshop organized by the Sudan Interior Mission in Kano, Nigeria. Specialist Dr. Robert K. Cochran was the resource leader. While in Kano, we were entertained by Dr. John Dreisback and his family. The following night, Dean, Ross Bell, John Erb, and I attended a Youth for Christ gathering.

Our introduction to the tremendously high peanut (ground nut)

Figure 1.22. Pyramids of peanuts awaiting shipment, Kano, Nigeria.

pyramids of Kano was unbelieving. Storage was done in this manner during the dry season while transportation to the coast (usually Lagos) was being arranged.

I was allowed to visit the ECWA Eye Hospital and was enthralled by the eye surgery of Dr. Douglas Hursch and Dr. Ben Kietzman. I had never given much thought to the importance of eye surgery before. A new appreciation was "seeded" that day and was enhanced while a table guest the next day with Dr. and Mrs. Hurst and their children, Patty and Bobby.

Dr. Ross came to Bambur following the Kano meeting and helped us with our workups and diagnoses of leprosy patients. While returning him to Pero, we had a dramatic confrontation with a baboon.

At the Guinter Memorial Hospital we were doing great numbers of surgeries. We had taken to doing intubations with the use of our Heidbrink anesthetic machine. On a visit to the hospital in 1999, the Heidbrink was still there 47 years later. It seemed that none of the hernial repairs were ever uncomplicated. Often in the hernial sack we had to deal with structures other than small bowel, such as bladder and even the appendix. Many herniae were obstructed which prompted their coming to us in the first place. Some were at the point of incarceration which required segmental resections. There were also the unusual happenings of having to deal with placenta accretia, intussuception of bowel, and urinary retention demanding a suprapubic prostatectomy.

Within a few days of each other the Woodrow Mackes had the good news of Wilma's delivery of a baby girl, (which Woody regretfully missed while making a trip to Jos), followed by the bad news when little John Macke swallowed a dozen ferrous sulfate pills. Ruth Wittmer and I ceased to be his friend after we lavaged him with a large stomach tube. Several weeks later our son John drank DIMP and experienced the same treatment. Also Wilma had a sacral strain which incapacitated her for several weeks requiring special nursing care by Crystal Springborn and Jean Baldwin in Jos. Later she had a baffling skin reaction. Dean and I were relieved to have the respected Dr. Barndon's help with her treatment.

Vipers continued to plague us. Dean captured one in their kitchen. Another one was found on our front steps as well as one in the tree beside out bedroom window. We had our first successful treatment of an Echis bite with the removal of the outer surface of the back of the involved hand. Our penned vipers were ready for milking. Dean caught the snake with a small rod and I grabbed it behind its head and brought it to the lip of a flask which the viper promptly attempted to bite, depositing its venom inside the glass container. Antivenin produced in South Africa brought the first ever protection for this deadly bite. We were quite relaxed in our snake activities until the day we discovered a viper had escaped his bounds. Everyone was afraid to open a drawer in the lab until it was found, cornered, and recaptured.

The isolation of the West Africans in this region produced an inordinate number of maternity complications. Not all of the uterine ruptures proved fatal. Dean was on hand when one occurred. With a flurry of activity, he was able to save both mother and child. Along with other cases, we were asked to submit to the West African Medical Journal a paper on "Uterine Rupture" which Ruth dutifully typed.

In the midst of all these life and death scenarios, time was made available for hunting. Guinea fowl and bush fowl were as tasty as any Thanksgiving turkey. To capture seven ducks with one shot may seem impossible but a dense flock on a small lake near the hospital made it possible. To be able to share venison or pork with fellow missionaries and hospital staff was an exciting event.

Fun times might mean the Baldwins and Olewilers coming up for a game of monopoly with the women in their best dresses and the men with ties. At other times the missionaries fellowshipped with hilarious performances of costume shows. Usually the climax would be a spirited hymn sing with, for example, beautiful quartet music by Dorothy McBride, Virginia Draeger, Florence Walter, and Ruth Wittmer, and then a deadly serious Bible study or prayer meeting.

It was July 22, 1954, during prayers at the hospital, I was asked to pray. Ruth Erbele, Dorothy McBride, and Art and Leth Faust had been schooling us in Hausa for over a year. That day I launched out with a prayer in Hausa. From that moment on I had to be prepared frequently to pray in "their" language – whether in the Bambur or Zing churches.

> *Ubanmu wanda ke chikin sama, A tsarkake sunanka. Mulkjinka shi zo. Abinda ka ke so, a yi shi, chikin duniya, kamar yadda a ke yinsa chikin sama. Ka ba mu yau abinshin yini. Ka gafarta man basussuwanmu, kamar yadda mu kuma mun garfart ma mabartanmu. Kada ka kai mu chikin jaraba, amma ka cheche mu daga Mugun.*
>
> **Matthew 6:9-13.**

> *Our Father who art in heaven, hallowed be thy name. Thy kingdom come. Thy will be done on earth, as it is in heaven. Give us this day our daily bread. And forgive us our debts, as we forgive our debtors. And lead us not into temptation, but deliver us from evil, For thine is the kingdom, and the power, and the glory, for ever. Amen.*

Bambur, 1955

Infectious hepatitis, that constant plague of missionary personnel, settled upon Wilma Macke, January 8, Woody Macke, February 3, and little John Macke, February 4. Also on February 4, Martin Stettler brought icteric Duane Dennis to Bambur where we made a comfortable cubicle for him in the maternity ward. It was only until March 7, before Duane's wife, Heidi, came down with the same hepatitis. On April 14, Eugene Wesley completed the hepatitis epidemic in early 1955.

Unusual for the dry season was the difficulty in getting through the Lau swamp. Dean Olewiler got stuck while taking Wakeman and his family to Djen. On January 3, Walt and Ruth Erbele, Duane and Heidi

Figure 1.23. Visit of Dr. Carl Heinmiller, 1955.

Dennis, Virginia Draeger, Dorothy McBride, and Florence Walter left Bambur to go to Zing. They were unable to cross the Benue River and had to return to Bambur. On January 6, I took Mai Doki's peanuts to Usmanu and needed fourteen men to pull me out after getting stuck in the swamp. I was very solicitous of the Land Rover even though on occasion I needed to drive through water so deep that the headlights just barely showed. On one occasion the starter refused to turn over the motor. I set about removing the starter, cleaning it, and then replacing it. My "delicate" surgery worked!!!

Of special significance was the arrival of Dr. Carl Heinmiller. He visited every station and was part of a conducted tour through the Guinter Memorial Hospital. He happened in at the surgical wing while I was doing a vesico-vaginal fistula repair. He took to heart my comment, "I need further training to handle these surgical challenges." At the mission council meeting he confirmed that I was to receive surgical training which eventually took place at the Akron General Hospital, Akron, Ohio.

On Dr. Heinmiller's return to the USA, he cabled suggesting that on our way home for furlough, a stop should be made at Freetown, Sierra Leone. He had arranged for Dr. Mabel Silver to meet with us along with Mrs. James, and Vivian Olson. Later I was to learn that the Board of Missions was planning to transfer us to the Hatfield-Archer Hospital in Rotifunk, Sierra Leone, which had no surgeon at the time. Guinter

Figure 1.24. Dr. Mabel Silver, Vivian Olson, Ms. Caulker.

Memorial Hospital in Bambur, Nigeria, was to continue to have the services of Dr. Dean Olewiler. That was a great blow not to be able to continue working with Dean, but within a short time at Rotifunk, we welcomed Dr. and Mrs. George Harris and family. He was especially gifted in surgery as well as being a general practitioner. The heavy surgical load at Rotifunk, usually found both of us doing surgery at the same time at two different tables. However, that did not prevent the enjoyment of our repartee. He had many interesting and comical experiences to share as well as some dangerous ones related to his WW II service as a pilot.

The final months at Bambur went by very quickly. Two fearful challenges occurred on April 19, 1955. Dr. Faust and our other Hausa teachers had prepared an examination that lasted from 8 a.m. until 1 p.m. They were anxious to know if all their many hours of hard work had paid off. Ruth did especially well.

The second challenge later in the day was facing up to a black cobra. Perhaps I did better at this than I did with the Hausa examination.

By the end of May, our barrels had been packed and were ready for shipment. At the last moment we were able to sell our Land Rover for a reasonable and fair price to the Bisicti Mines Company Ltd. near Jos. We were relieved to know that Kathleen McBride's episodes of illness were finally dealt with when Dr. Roger Troup and I did a cholecystectomy in Jos just prior to our leaving.

Except for Tim and me, the family had the thrill and convenience of being flown to Lagos from Jos. It was uneventful except when John dropped his little metal car on the floor of the plane. It startled the pilot who wondered if something serious had happened to the plane. Tim and I spent two days on the train accompanying our freight.

Ruth and I shall never forget May 19, 1955. As we were leaving Bambur, we stopped at the hospital where the staff had assembled for our send off. Their kind and encouraging words prompted a tear or two. After they sang, "God Be With You Til We Meet Again," they asked if I would pray in Hausa. Included in the prayer was Numbers 6:24-26 which they had heard me include many times before as I prayed with the sick and the dying. "Ubangiji shi albarkache ka, shi tsare ka; Ubangiji shi sa fuskassa ta haskaka wajenka, she nuna maka nasiha; Ubangiji shi saka maka fuskatasa, shi ba ka salama."

> *The Lord bless thee, and keep thee: The Lord make his face shine upon thee, and be gracious unto thee; The Lord lift up his countenance upon thee, and give thee peace.*

Nigeria, The Land of Our Calling

In 1952, when we set foot in Nigeria, West Africa, it was already the most populous country on the continent of Africa, numbering about 80 million people. In the year 2000, it was estimated to be 114 million. In geographic size it measures slightly more than twice the size of California (which has somewhat over 32 million people). Lagos, the capitol in those days, was a teeming metropolis with steaming heat. We were dead tired after the trying events of the day. We had arrived without a visa. British authorities took it as an affront that we would continue our journey from the USA and then from the UK without official documentation in our passports.

There is a story behind this. Up until the last moment before boarding the *S.S. America* in New York, we had been scurrying around for word about our visa. We were all ticketed, and it was decided to get on board for our trip to England. Surely the visa to Nigeria would catch up with us by then. During the five-day layover in London, I kept contacting the mission board in New York while visiting the American and Nigerian embassies in London to see if the visa papers had been sent to

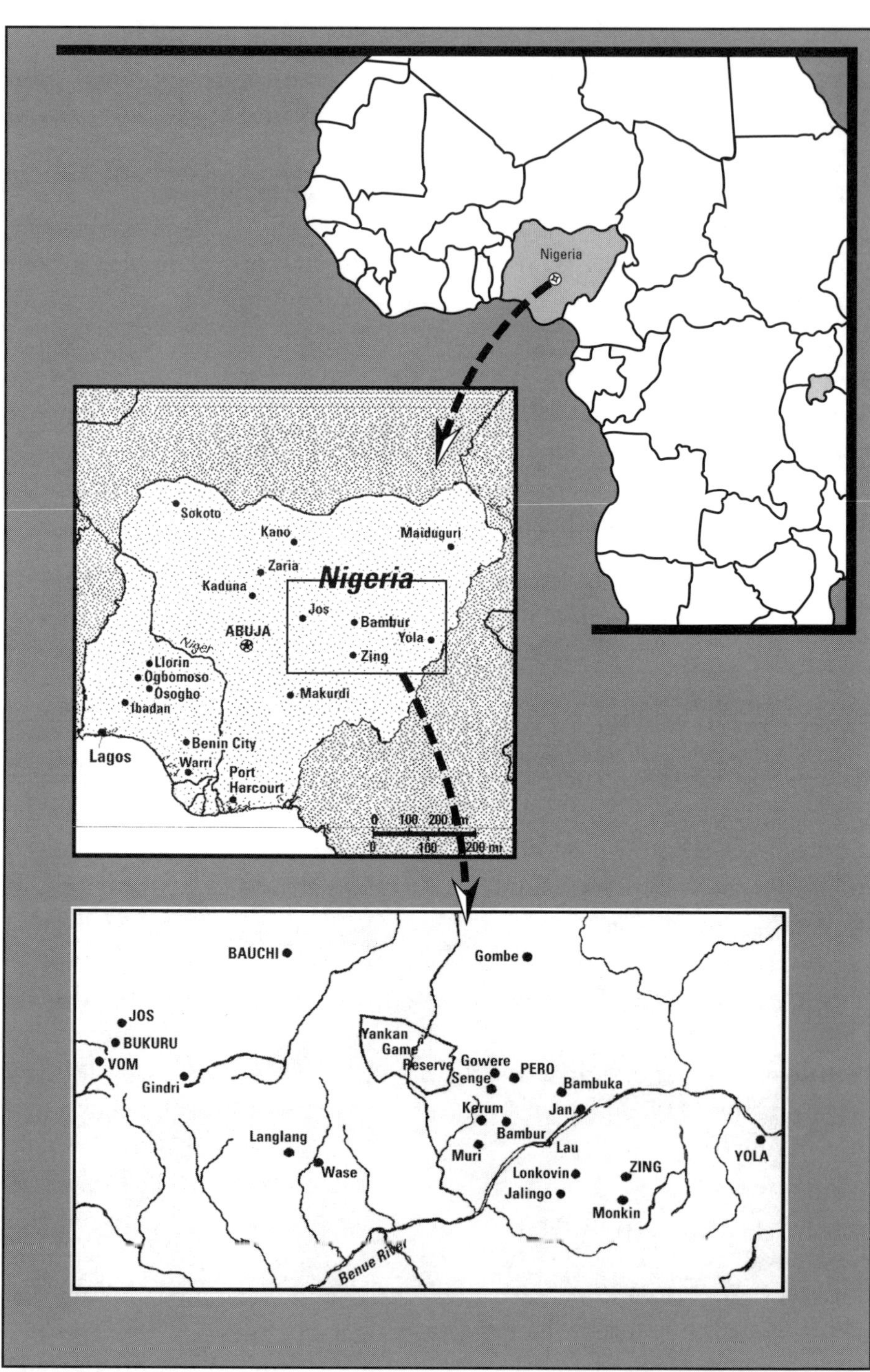

Figure 1.25. Map of Nigeria.

them. When no word arrived, we needed to make a desperate decision. Elder Dempster's steamship, *Accra,* was departing from Liverpool the next day. Our freight had been put on board automatically from our first ship of passage. It would be serious not to accompany our baggage and have to remain in London for an extended time waiting for another ship to Nigeria. We had learned at the last minute that it was possible to board the ship without a visa. We were politely ushered to our staterooms.

It was quite another story at the other end. The British officials called me into the captain's office and explained that for us to be allowed off the ship would be a breach of policy and law. How could we have been so presumptuous? I explained the intense activity all along the trip to try to right the situation, but I had no success. My statement that we felt called by God to minister in Nigeria, caused an extended silence. Apparently the official did not feel that he could subvert the will of God and relented. We were the last to leave the ship.

It was New Year's Eve. We were happy to arrive at the comfortable missionary guest house in Lagos. Thankfully the children were able to drop off to sleep. Such was not the case for Ruth and me as the seemingly greatest of all New Year celebrations was taking place just outside our window. Without air conditioning the window could not be closed. We ushered in the early hours of 1953 very much awake.

The next stage of our journey was by train. It took two days to reach Jos, which is on a plateau rising to over 4000 feet above sea level. Understandably, the engine of the train required much more time on its ascent than it did on its return trip to Lagos.

After leaving Lagos, we passed through jungle foliage with myriads of birds and animal life. The savanna territory gave us an extended view of the countryside with the many villages and their grass roofed huts.

Jos was delightfully cool. The missionaries at the Sudan United Mission guest house assumed complete care of our family. The children were bathed and fed early in the evening. After 8 p.m. the adults sat down to English cuisine, which occasionally included brussel sprouts. The matron insisted that we be as independent as possible. Instructions were given as to how we were to communicate with the Nigerian employees. "Kawo mani ruwan sha" meant "Please bring some drinking water." "Kawo mani ruwan wonka" indicated that we needed water for bathing.

The final segment of the trip to the Guinter Memorial Hospital,

Figure 1.26. Our home at Gwatin.

Bambur, was a long, dusty, and hot day's journey. Leaving the elevated plateau and returning to the savanna countryside brought stifling heat. Senge pass had to be manipulated just outside of Pero. Riverbeds needed to be crossed. Those which still had not dried up necessitated maneuvering a four-wheel drive vehicle through water that occasionally came up as high as the headlights.

Arrival at Bambur

It was a genuine Christian welcome when we finally drew up to what was to be our home for the next three years. It rested on a hilltop overlooking the hospital complex. Those years were to be some of our most delightful, and yet dangerous, times of our lives. The actual occupation of the house was delayed nearly four weeks while Dr. Harold Elliot and his family were packing for their return to the United States. We were made comfortable in the new maternity ward of the hospital.

After three weeks of traveling the high seas and crossing jungles, savanna, and plateau lands, we were finally "home." As was our practice throughout our life with the many homes that we occupied, we gathered as a family and thanked God for His presence and preservation "thus far" and for the assurance of "future care."

During the 1952-1955 years, we did not face the challenges and dan-

Figure 1.27. The view from our Gwatin home.

gers experienced by early missionaries. The Rev. C.W. Guinter arrived in Nigeria in 1906. He served under the Sudan United Mission which had been formed two years earlier. In 1909, after a furlough, he returned to Wukari with his new bride, the first white woman to see that section of Nigeria. Many times during the first weeks on the compound the matting on the fence was deftly parted to permit curious dark eyes to peep through at the new arrival. The Women's Missionary Society of the Evangelical Church assumed the support of the Guinters and his station in 1918. By the time of the merger in 1922 of the two Evangelical churches, Dr. Paul H. Eller reports in the *History of Evangelical Missions,* the W.M.S. had in hand $12,744.06 for the founding of an African mission. The Rev. and Mrs. I. E. McBride accompanied the Guinters back to Africa after they had received an appointment by the Board of Missions.

The Church officially declared its support of the Wurkum District as their denominational mission field, and later granted additional appointments to the Rev. and Mrs. J.J. Arnold and the Rev. and Mrs. V. E. Walter.

In the 1930s the work and literature of Christian missionaries threatened that of the Black Muslims who emphasized religious devotion to Allah. Consequently, anti-missionary writings appeared. The founding

Figure 1.28. Dodo.

of the University College of Ibadan in 1948 opened up the Western tradition of writing dealing with universal themes such as labor, corruption, and justice, in addition to religion. Following the October 1, 1960 independence from the United Kingdom, regionalism became a powerful force resulting in the Biafran war during the 1966-1969 period. While attending Hillcrest school in Jos, Nigeria, our daughter, Beth, had the perilous experience of seeing dead bodies along the road on the way to school. Ibo patients in the hospital were killed in their beds. Hausas were killed in the Eastern region.

Nigeria has remained intact as a republic, transitioning from military to civilian rule in 1998 based on a legal system incorporating English common law, tribal law, and Islamic law. In some areas since 1999, some Muslim states have declared that the Islamic Shari'a law is the official system. In 1991 the capitol was moved from Lagos to Abuja.

Culture and Traditions

Have the traditions of Nigeria changed during our lifetime? In the early 1950s Fulani initiation rites for young men were rigorous. I was allowed to view and photograph their stoic endurance of pain during ceremonial flogging. Barechested, they held up a mirror and peered intensely into it, never knowing at what moment they would be struck from behind. The whip that was used was a four foot green bough of index finger size. When struck flat upon the back, it curled around to the front of the chest. The drumlike sound was vibrant in that it involved the hollow chest cavity. Stoically the facial features recorded neither surprise nor grimacing of pain. Several chances were given each young man. Those whom I witnessed, along with their families, and especially the teenage girls, successfully passed their puberty rites and proved their virility for marriage.

Primitive animism was still present during our tour of service at Bambur in the 1950s. Some people lived in mortal fear of "Dodo," a power spirit, and the masquerade that surrounded it. At times weird processions to sacred sites were carried on by the men, the elders being in leadership. This deception was used by men to maintain power over women. Women were shut up in their houses during the time of the parade and if caught outside were required to bury their faces in the

Figure 1.29. Women carry the loads.

ground. A woman looking on the procession might die, become barren, lose her first born, or become a leper.

Returning in our car to Bambur on one occasion, we were aware that not a single woman could be seen on the road or in the passing villages. We were flagged down, and men excitedly ordered that Ruth go to a hut or be covered over in our car. Ruth is not easily cowed. She insisted that we drive on, rigidly sitting in the front seat looking straight ahead.

Women in Nigeria assumed a different role from European and Western cultures. In precolonial days according to researcher Alyssa Qualls, women retained certain economic opportunities within the social system. They traditionally played a more significant role in society than did Western women. Tribal society in Nigeria expected women to be significant wage earners of the family. They worked with pottery, cloth-making, and craftwork, as well as being involved in herding, farming, and fishing, alongside of the Nigerian men. Traditionally, they had the right to profit from their work, although it was a foregone conclusion that they contribute to the general family income. This economic freedom was practiced at a time when Western society women had to fight for the right to work. Women in Nigeria were world pioneers except for the pagan rites which kept women "in their place."

Figure 1.30. A devil dancer.

The freedom of the Nigerian women was not appreciated by their husbands. They consistently took their wives for granted. Nigerian women lacked basic legal rights in the accepted practice of polygamy. The men could abandon their wives and children and expect the women to carry the financial burden of the family. Women could expect little from men in terms of companionship, personal care, and fidelity. Their relationships often existed without the emotional elements.

The traditional and Islamic system of polygamy was accepted by the African women. In fact it was important in many womens' lives to depend on the other wives, especially the younger co-wives to take on many of the household and financial responsibilities. As they got older they had the comfort of knowing that the burden of their marriage did not fall solely on their shoulders, and they had the status that goes with being the "first" wife.

The really difficult problem was that a woman's position was that once she married, she became the possession of her husband, with few rights in her husband's family. The husband's mother, and even sisters, had more influence over him than did his own wife. Understandably, control and respect in their marriage was a great burden for women during the time that we lived and ministered in Nigeria. The woman was

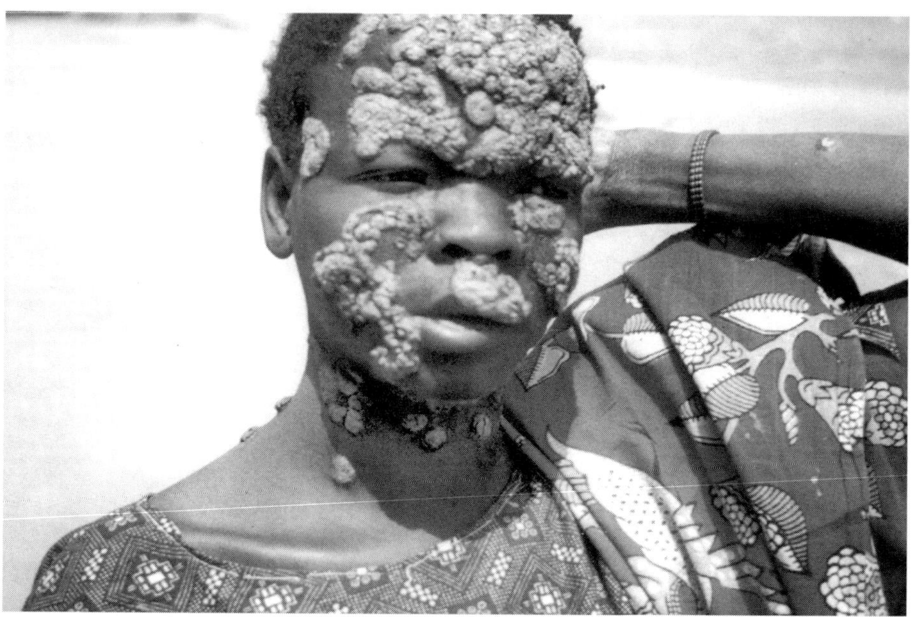

Figure 1.31. One injection of penecillin completely clears Yaws.

expected to bear children and was condemned or shunned if there were none.

In recent years, education, urbanization, and capitalism are changing Nigerian society. Educational opportunities have expanded since independence in 1961. Men have begun to see the value of higher education for their wives and daughters. Today, the rite of circumcision is not universally being done. Tremendous strides have been made for women through popular organizations as the "Zummata Mata" which held massive women's meetings. These were organized by Christian missionaries such as Mrs. Aletha Faust and Mrs. Ruth Erbele in the Pero, Bambur, and Mumuye areas. The Gospel was taken directly to women in their villages. Mrs. Faust concluded an article in the *World Evangel* with the statement: "If we would not have witnessed, we would have failed Jesus."

Mission Medicine for Nigeria

It is appropriate that the early missionary medical outreach be mentioned. Missionaries with their understanding of "cleanliness is next to godliness," were in a position to minister to the many debilitating ulcers as well as the problems created by contaminated water and food. They

Figure 1.32. Nursing staff – Guinter Memorial Hospital, Bambur.

were unable to deal with serious diseases, either among the Nigerians or among their own number in spite of the fact that in 1937 the British government had made it mandatory that all missionaries have six months of instruction in tropical diseases. The evangelistic staff did as much medical work as they were capable of doing, while continuing to make urgent requests for the appointment of a doctor. Death stalked the mission as Ruth Lowell McBride was taken on October 10, 1933, and Elizabeth Conboy McBride on March 25, 1941. Dr. McBride narrowly escaped death while experiencing "black water fever."

In my teens, I remember Bishop E. W. Praetorius at the Koronis Assembly Grounds, Paynesville, Minnesota, announcing on a number of occasions the need for a doctor for Wurkumland, Nigeria. I felt that he was speaking directly to me, but I resolved rather to answer the call to the Christian ministry, not as a doctor in some far off deep jungle in Africa. Ultimately a doctor was found in the person of Dr. Harold Elliott. Instead of a mud-walled dispensary, a concrete block hospital with wards was built in 1950-52 under the supervision of Mr. Chester Reinhardt and the Rev. Walter Erbele. Mr. Woodrow Macke completed the unfinished wards. It was dedicated as the Guinter Memorial Hospital. A succession of doctors followed: Lowell Gess, Dean Oleweiler, Kenneth Benfer, David Hilton, Charles Arnett, Ronald Willey, Marvin Piburn, Jerrel Mathison, Clifford Lumbert, and Rudolph

Hoffman. Chuck and Pearl Arnett returned to Zing, Nigeria, in 2000 for a three and a half year tour of surgical service, teaching and administration. A new hospital complex is envisioned at Zing.

The nursing staff with whom we worked included Swiss Deaconess Emmy Tschannon and Americans Amy Skartved, Virginia Draeger, Crystal Springborn Mercer, Jean Baldwin (wife of Eugene "Hank" Baldwin), Florence Walter, and Ruth Wittmer, who eventually married Mr. Alfred Bolliger and settled with her husband in Switzerland. Nurse Lucy Rowe was assigned to use her gifts in the translation of Scriptures. Crystal was especially adept in Hausa. In palavers at the hospital or on the compound, we always wanted her to mediate.

Evangelists and educators included Dr. and Mrs. Arthur Faust, Rev. Karl and Thekla Kuglin, Rev. Armin "Tex" and Margaret Hoesch, Rev. Walter and Ruth Erbele, Rev. Martin and Ruth Stettler, and Rev. Eugene and Helen Westley, and Ms. Ardis Janke. The year after we left Nigeria, Dr. Dean and Lois Gilliland arrived. We closely followed their important ministries, marveling at their command of Hausa which had eluded us. Dr. Gilliland assumed a number of roles as evangelist, director of the Muri Christian Training School at Banyam, field representative, and principal of the Theological College of Northern Nigeria. Later, among others, the Rev. Alfred and Marianne Bohr continued to share the good news of Christ to save.

Guinter Memorial Hospital at Gwatin was eventually taken over administratively by the Nigerian government. Presently the Principal Medical Officer is Dr. Anuye Rimamskeb Jeremiah. Working through the General Board of Global Ministries, the German branch of the UMC has underwritten an eye clinic at Wuram in Bambur which is close to the hospital. Across the Benue River at Zing, they have conducted an active medical facility with nurses, midwives, and Dr. Dashe. It was my pleasure to know and be entertained by Michael and Doris Vitzthum, Sabine Hanke, and Ina Schoenfeld-Dabale, and see their wonderful ministry.

The Church in Wurkumland and Beyond

During our last year (1955) of service in Nigeria, the formal articles of the constitution of the fellowship known as the Tarrayan Ekklisiyoyin

Kristi a Sudan (TEKAS) were signed at Randa. By 1967, at the time of Dr. Ira McBride's retirement, he reported to Dr. Dean Gilliland that the Evangelical United Brethren Church numbered 950 baptized members. By 1985 it numbered 59,000 and by 1999, 295,000, as was noted in the recently published *The History of the United Methodist Church in Nigeria* authored by the Rev. Peter Dong and others. On my volunteer eye surgery trips to Zing in 1996 and 1999, I was thrilled to see the growth that had taken place in less than 50 years. Karim Lamido, on the edge of the swamp, had only a mosque in the 1950s. In 1999 I passed three Protestant churches on my drive through the town.

The Bible school which opened in Kerum in 1944 was moved to Banyam in 1947 and was known as the Muri Christian Training School. In 1989 a four-year diploma course in theology commenced and was called the Banyam Theological Seminary (BTS). Especially impressive is its library. It was a privilege to fellowship with Wolfgang and Gerlinde Bay and stay overnight in their cleverly solar equipped house. Wolfgang was able to minister to fellow Pastor Para recently during a time of great stress. Fellowship was also had with former hospital staff members. It was an honor to be able to congratulate Bambur Chief Baba on his important role of leadership. Mr. Mai Doki, our cook during our stay at Bambur, stood as tall and regal as ever.

On my two volunteer eye surgery visits to Zing, Bishop Done Peter Dabale was cordial and encouraging, providing transport and housing. He is very much in touch with world events as well as with his own constituents. He is concerned about the 22 million Africans who are infected with HIV (as compared to 1.5 million Americans), especially the 13.5 million African children orphaned by AIDS deaths. With his spiritual leadership even greater and enlarged ministries of the United Methodist Church will come to pass.

General Olusegun Obasanjo's democratic election to lead Nigeria to civilian rule in early 1999, gives great hope for the future of Nigeria. Its impact as the leading regional power in West Africa has been felt even in Sierra Leone, where it has taken on leadership through ECWAS in stabilizing that war torn country. With its manpower and oil reserves, Nigeria will continue to be a major influence on the continent of Africa.

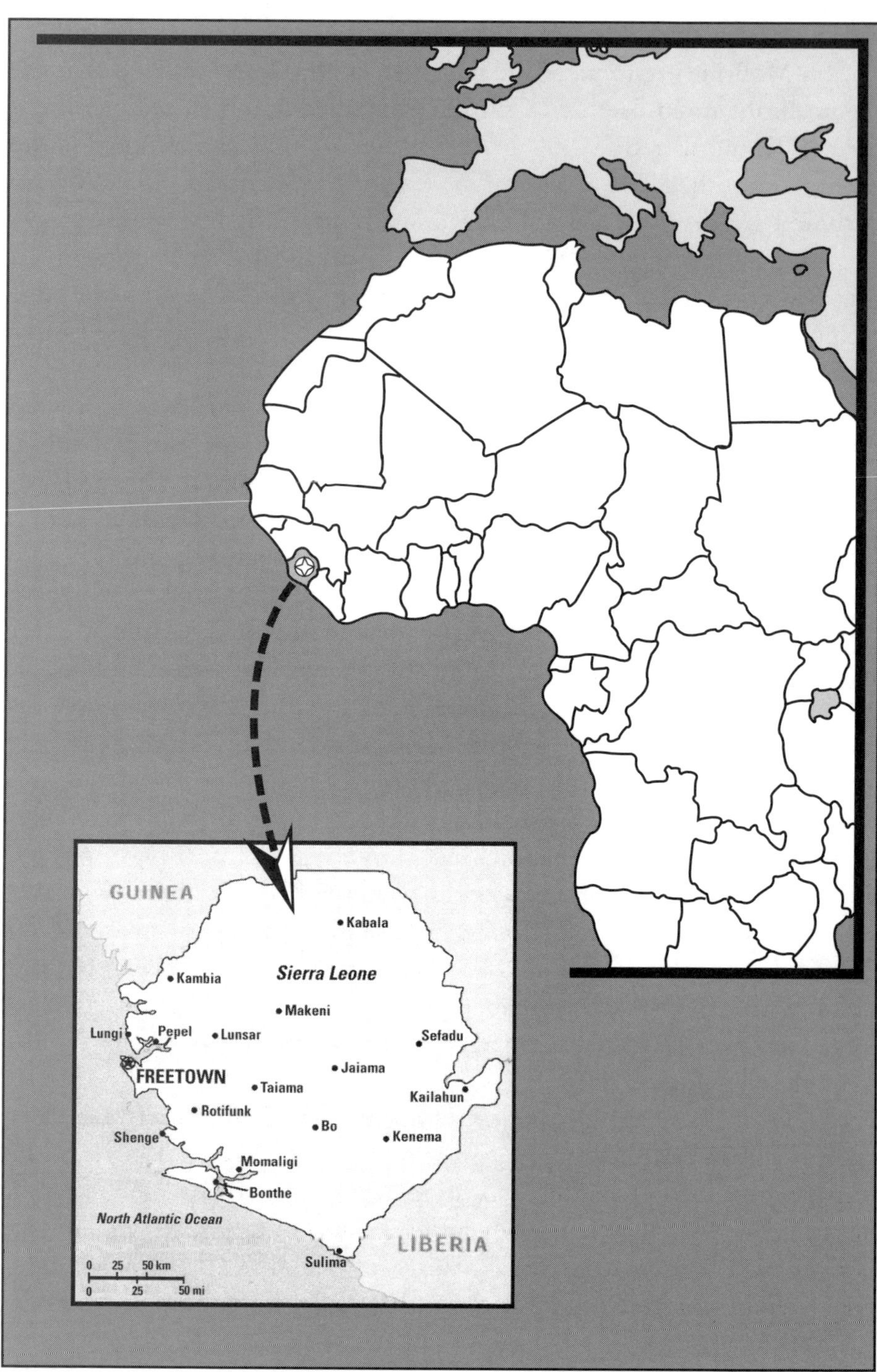

Figure 1.33. Map of Sierra Leone.

Chapter Two

Sierra Leone – Rotifunk

Train Wreck.

Train Wreck

It was Christmas Eve, 1959. I was repairing a rocking chair. Ruth enjoyed singing "Love Lifted Me" as she cradled our three month old son Andrew. Our home on the Rotifunk Hospital compound overlooked the Sierra Leone railroad tracks to the southwest. The express from Bo to Freetown was due any time.

Suddenly we heard it – the train's whistle and screeching brakes, as the engine pulled into the station several hundred yards to the south. Within moments there was the figure of a train employee running up the incline. At our gate, he frantically called for the doctor. I grabbed my doctor's bag and went down to meet him. His report was brief. Earlier on a curve, five cars had left the track and rolled over. Only the engine and coal car remained on the tracks. These were dispatched to Rotifunk eight miles down the roadway where they knew there was a hospital and surgical staff.

I was bundled into the engine cab along with Tim, our twelve-year old son, and we took off for the site of the accident. The story began to unfold. The crew and passengers were all eager to get to Freetown on

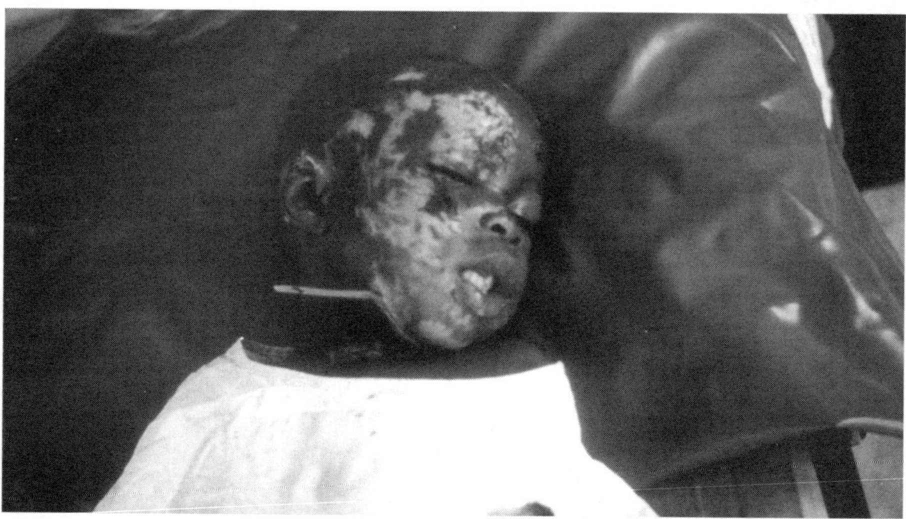

Figure 2.1. Unconscious little girl following surgery. No anesthetic had been used.

this special late afternoon of the year. The speed of the train was too great to negotiate one of the curves. Tragedy struck.

Seven or eight miles to the east of the wreck was Bauya, a train terminal. An engine with some empty passenger cars had been dispatched to the scene from that location. There was such an entanglement of cars at the site of the wreck, that the train could not proceed to Freetown. It could only go back to Moyamba, a district headquarters, where a government hospital was located. The injured were to be put on this train and taken to the Moyamba Hospital.

On dropping down from the cab, I was hardly prepared for the scene – bodies lying in the ditch with some being pinned under the overturned passenger cars. Blood was splattered around. The moaning of the injured was drowned out by the crying and shrieking of relatives and friends. Thirteen already were dead.

Realizing the urgency of the situation, I gave my supplies and bandages to others and hurriedly did a triage – going from body to body to determine if care could be given. The wounded were put on the Bauya train for transport to Moyamba Government Hospital. I was to accompany this train. I spent Christmas eve until 1 a.m. Christmas morning doing emergency surgery.

Ultimately the situation came under control sufficiently so that I could leave the doctor and staff at Moyamba to complete the care of the

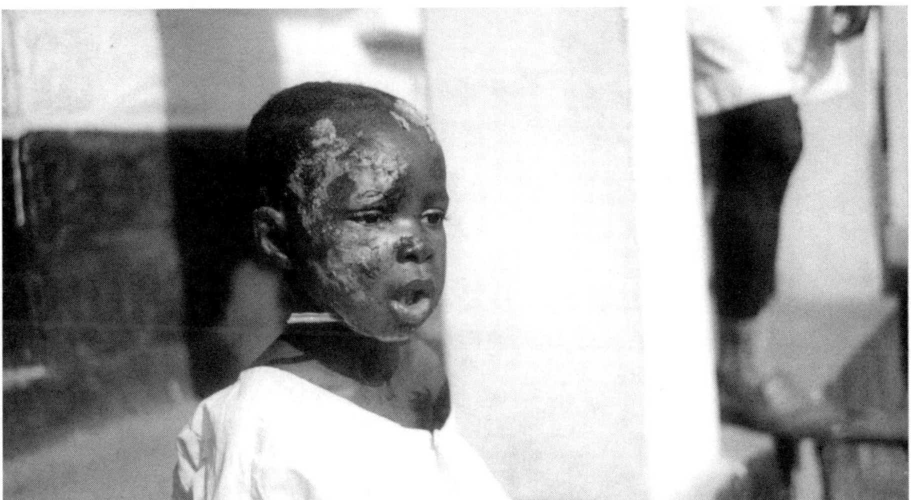

Figure 2.2. Awake the following day.

injured. A four-wheel drive Land Rover had been dispatched from Rotifunk to take me back home. The driver was Ruth, accompanied by our children and Metra Heisler, a nurse from Rotifunk.

Arriving at Rotifunk in the wee hours of the morning, dead tired, I was informed that there was an injured child lying in her mother's arms at the door of our Rotifunk Hospital. Approaching the mother and three-year old daughter, I couldn't believe my eyes. I had seen this child at the wreck. When we had moved this unconscious child to examine her, the head toppled to her back. Her neck had been cut from side to side completely severing the muscles that hold the head forward and erect. I had spent no time on this hopeless condition and had moved on to the next patient.

The mother had stuffed leaves and grass into the gaping wound in an attempt to control the bleeding. She then carried the child eight miles down the track to Rotifunk where I met them nearly eight hours later. The child was still unconscious but alive!!!

We immediately took her to surgery where we found that the major arterial vessels were still intact. Only the venous vessels had been severed along with the sternocleidomastoid muscles. A surgical repair was quickly done but only then was it discovered that there was a depressed skull fracture. No anesthesia had been used since the patient was unconscious. Towel hooks grasped the depressed fracture and the pressure on the brain

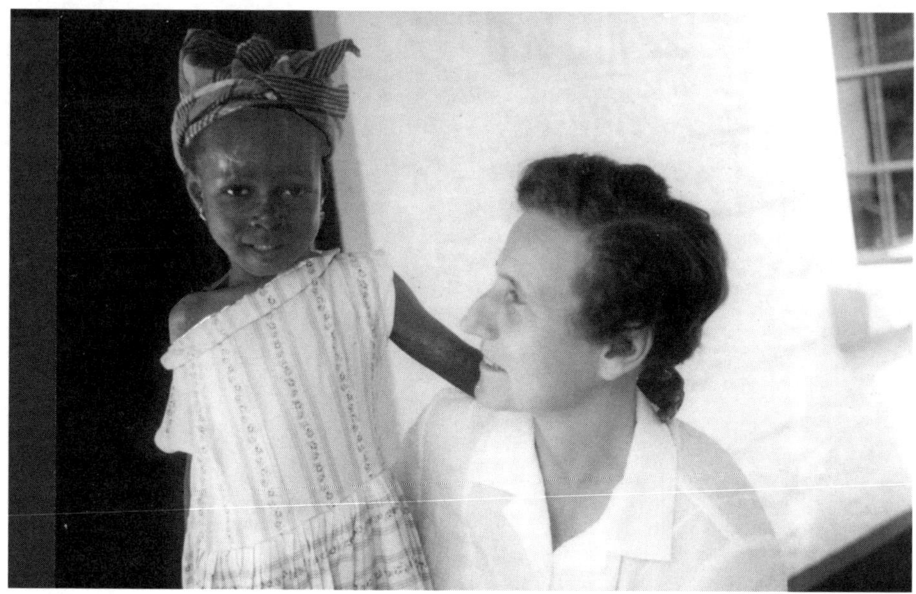

Figure 2.3. Ten days after the train wreck (with Betty Beveridge our charge nurse).

relieved. At the completion of surgery, multiple drains were left sticking out from the head and the neck because of the gross contamination. Supportive care was instituted and we all dropped into our beds.

In the morning the child, Marie Jones, was still alive. She received excellent nursing care with nurses hovering over her hour by hour. That afternoon a nurse came running to report that Marie was responding and crying for her mother.

In the days that followed, Marie became a pet with the nurses. Frequently they would tie her to their backs in typical African style. Children loved to be close to their mother, or in this case, their nurse.

Ultimately the day came when Marie left the hospital. The mother asserted that she had been thoroughly spoiled by all the attentive care of the staff but there was such joy as they left – this time Marie was tied to her mother's back. The Lord is kind. This little flower was allowed to bloom.

Seven years were to come and go, when one day at Taiama, where we were now conducting an eye program, a mother and her daughter came to the door. They were all smiles – as though we were supposed to know them. Both were beautiful. Suddenly I noticed some slightly perceptible scars on the neck of the daughter running all the way across. And there it was, the scar on her right forehead where the depressed skull fracture had been elevated. She was not only a normally developing young person but a bright student in one of our Christian schools. We were never to see her again, but there was a deep feeling in my heart that confirmed the call to enter a medical missionary career realized so many years before on the shores of Lake Koronis and Lake Geneva.

Fast Descent ➻ A Broken Back

The ascent of an African tree climber is a thing of wonder. Utilizing a sling of vines wrapped around the tree and his body, the climber climbs up the palm tree trunk. He leans his body back and his bare feet assure a secure hold.

Some tree climbers are after coconuts and other fruit. Others capture the sap of the palm tree and arrange for it to age. When a cut is made into the palm tree, the sap coming out is very sweet and not intoxicating. It is dropped into calabashes and is left to ferment. Its strength grows day by day and its sweetness diminishes, until it has turned into "real" palm wine, strong and without sweetness, being alcohol and vinegar.

Palm wine differs from grape wine in that it contains sucrose instead of the glucose and fructose of the grape wine. The fermentation is started by the complex and varied flora of bacteria provided by the insects attracted to the sap. The palms are tapped in the morning and in the evening. The evening harvest is said to be a better quality, as it has been submitted to higher temperatures and ferments better.

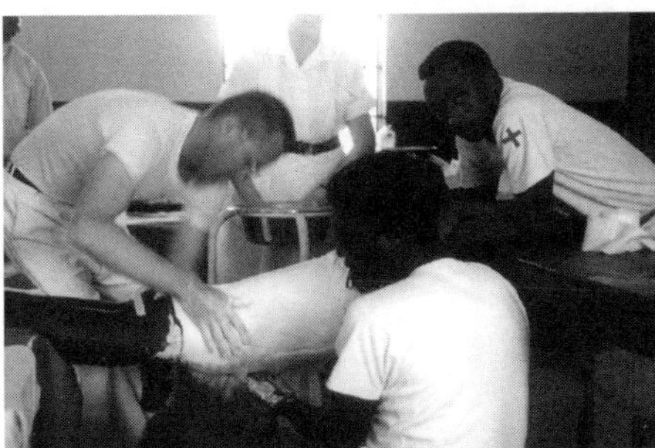

Figure 2.4.a. Fast descent (broken back). Body cast being applied.

Figure 2.4.b. Fast descent (broken back). Patient was able to walk one day after the body cast was applied.

The African declares that man is like palm wine, youth is sweet but without the wisdom of old age, and old age lacks the sweetness of youth.

On January 23rd, 1960, Sallu climbed to check his "palm wine." Apparently he tested and tasted his brew. In any event he tarried up in the tree. Ultimately the alcoholic content of his brew had its effect. Fumbling with the climbing harness, he suddenly was going through the air in a free fall. He crashed to the ground. He did not lose consciousness, and he was sober enough to realize that he could not get up. His back pained unmercifully. Friends fashioned a stretcher from tree boughs and branches and brought him to our Rotifunk Hospital.

Examination revealed movement of his toes and feet. However, the fracture of the spine just above the lumbar area could be seen grossly after it had been identified by "feel." With slight hyperextension, proper alignment of the back could be realized.

Sallu was placed face downward between two tables which supported his upper chest and lower thighs. Stockinette was curled around his body and then rolls of plaster of paris applied. Courageously he maintained this position until the body cast had dried sufficiently for him to be moved. Along with Sallu, we were relieved to find that on the following day he was able to partially support the weight of his body and the applied body cast. In fact he took several steps. There was rejoicing in that it was apparent that the fracture had not severed any portion of the spinal cord. In several days he was walking.

To wear a plaster of paris body cast in the heat of the tropics was a great trial. Even before the end of the second week, Sallu was requesting that the cast be removed. We kept putting him off with the warning of great danger if his back had not healed sufficiently.

Ultimately his requesting became begging. When he realized that the intense itching that he was experiencing was partially from the invasion of body lice under the cast, he could stand it no longer. Sometime during the fourth week Sallu, on his own, chipped away and removed the cast. Thankfully healing had been sufficient. No ill effects were suffered. Thanks be to God.

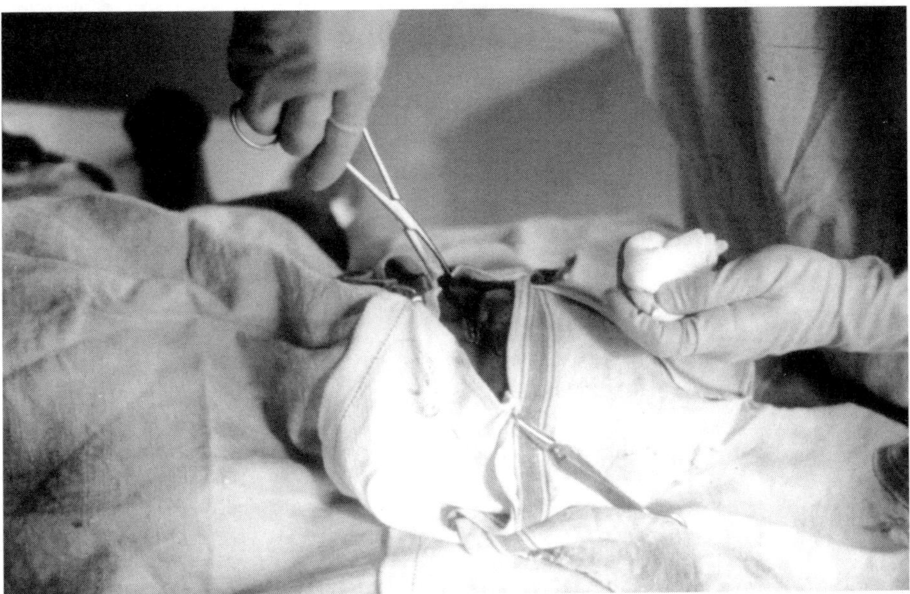

Figure 2.5. A bolt in the head.

A Bolt in the Head

In the bush African hunters often build their own guns. Too large a powder supply caused one to explode, driving a two inch bolt into a hunter's skull through the medial aspect of the right eye socket.

In preparation for surgery the instruments that were sterilized included large Craftsman pliers. Preparations also were made to deal with the escape of cerebrospinal fluid, or even worse, of brain tissue.

At the moment of removal of the bolt, only fresh red blood emerged. Rather than use a drain because of the contaminated missile, the wound was left unclosed for drainage. The flow of blood was controlled by pressure dressings.

The patient was up and about the following day. We learned that he continued to hunt, but with a "store bought" gun.

Color Print 1.1. Bishop Hopkins and Dr. Gess. (see page v)

Color Print 1.2. Enid and Loman Young with her painting for Kissy UMC Eye Hospital. (see page vi)

Color Print 1.3. Lorraine and Howard Pierce whose skills brought this book into being. (see page vi)

Color Print 1.4. Yusufu postop. (see page 4)

Color Print 1.5. Land Rover and swollen stream. (see page 8)

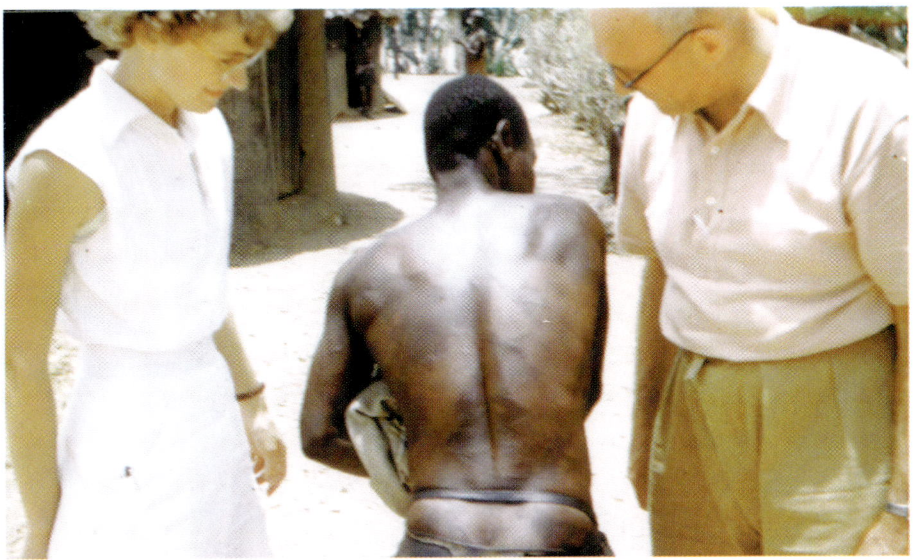

Color Print 1.6. Tuberculoid leprosy patient attended by nurse Florence Walter and specialist Dr. Ross. (see page 9)

Color Print 1.7. Ruth receiving flowers from leprosy patient she befriended. (see page 9)

Color Print 1.8. Sharing life's blood. (see page 13)

Color Print 1.9. Hunting: A 170 pound Kob (mariya) antelope nine miles from the hospital in the Lau Swamp, 1954. (see page 13)

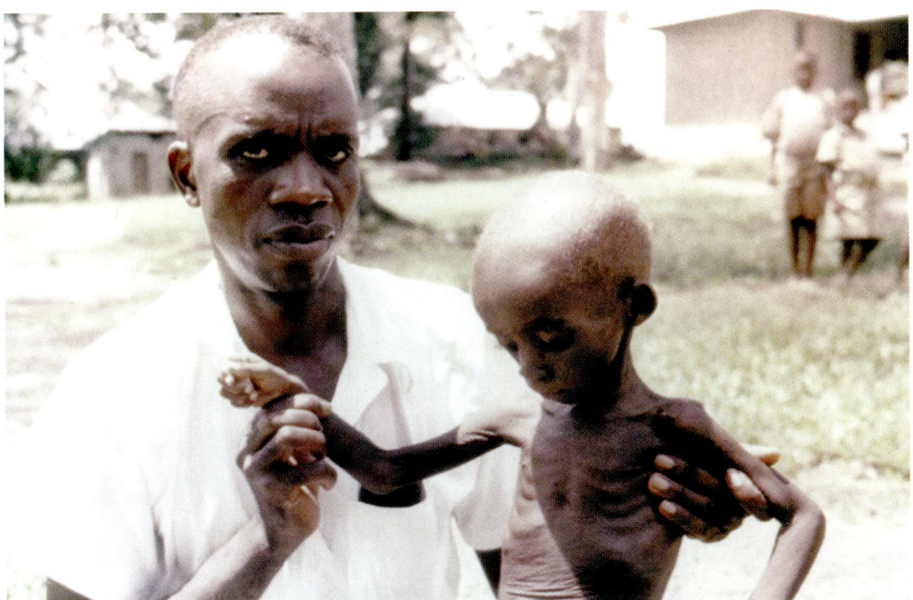

Color Print 1.10. Taiama senior dispenser, Abraham Lavaly, with kwashiorkor patient. (see page 13)

Color Print 1.11. On the way to market. (see page 13)

Color Print 1.12. A Gess family trip on the Benue River. (see page 13)

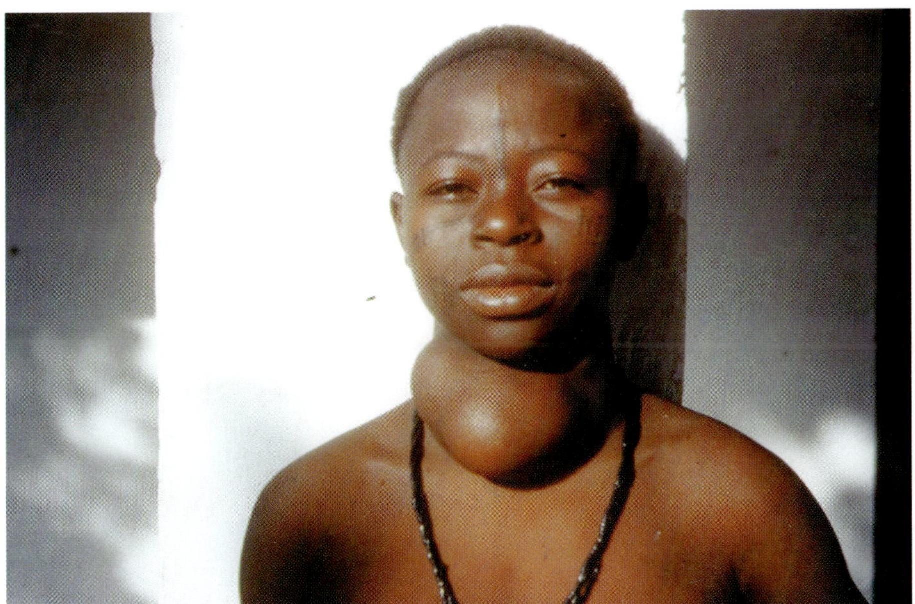

Color Print 1.13. Iodine deficient diet. (see page 15)

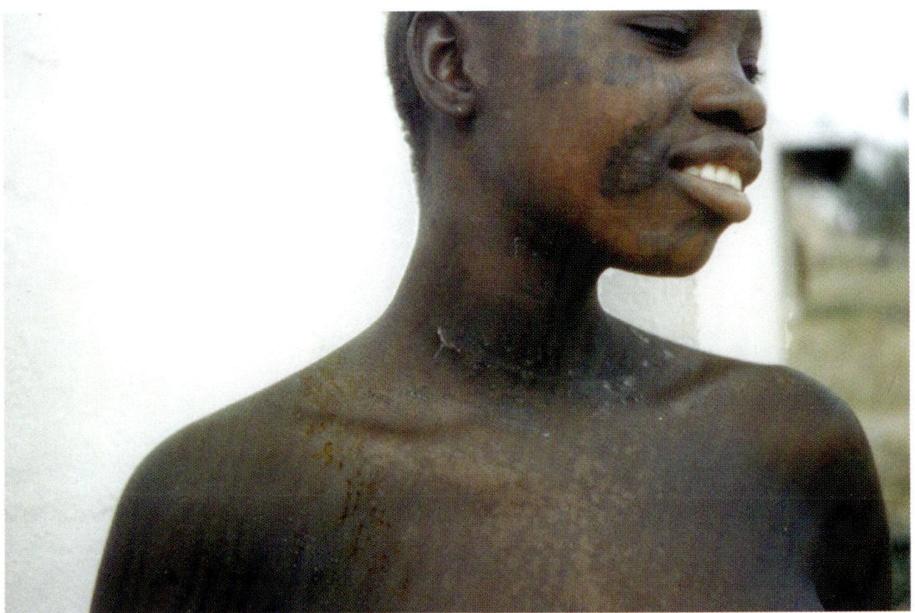

Color Print 1.14. Iodine deficient diet. Postop thyroidectomy. (see page 15)

Color Print 1.15. Gecko, the ubiquitous insect eater, being harmless, is tolerated in our homes, until they decide to hide under our sleeping pillow. (see page 16)

Color Print 1.16. Malaria, net protection. (see page 18)

Color Print 1.17. Handling vipers. Milking venom for the production of an antivenin. (see page 22)

Color Print 1.18. Beyond the help of human hands. Paul is the second man standing from the left. (see page 26)

Color Print 1.19. Hospital water brigade. (see page 35)

Color Print 1.20. Gwatin Home at Guinter Memorial Hospital, tub bath. (see page 36)

Color Print 1.21. Clinic visits to Pero during the rains did not allow for Land Rover travel. (see page 9)

Color Print 1.22. Dr. Faust conducting a baptism in a dammed stream; Wurkumland, 1953. (see page 54)

Color Print 1.23. Sierra Leone, West Africa. (see page 57)

Color Print 1.24. Train wreck . . . seven years later with her mother. (see page 60)

Color Print 1.25. The local tavern where the palm wine is sold. (see page 62)

Color Print 1.26. Deliveries: "Julius Caesar." (see page 81)

Color Print 1.27. Kombe being led to the hospital. (see page 92)

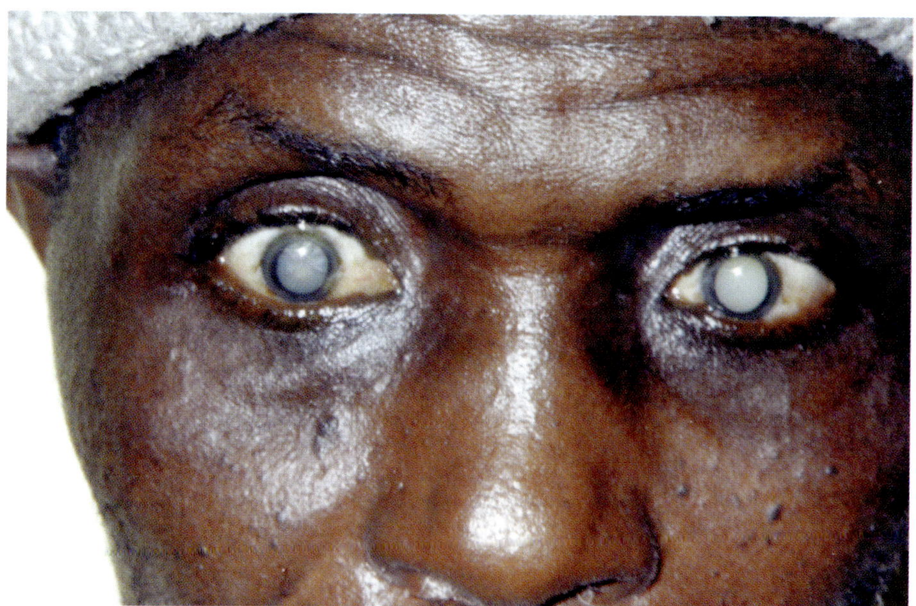

Color Print 1.28. Bilateral blindness from mature cataracts is common. This picture was taken at Rotifunk when we were doing our first cataract extractions. (see page 92)

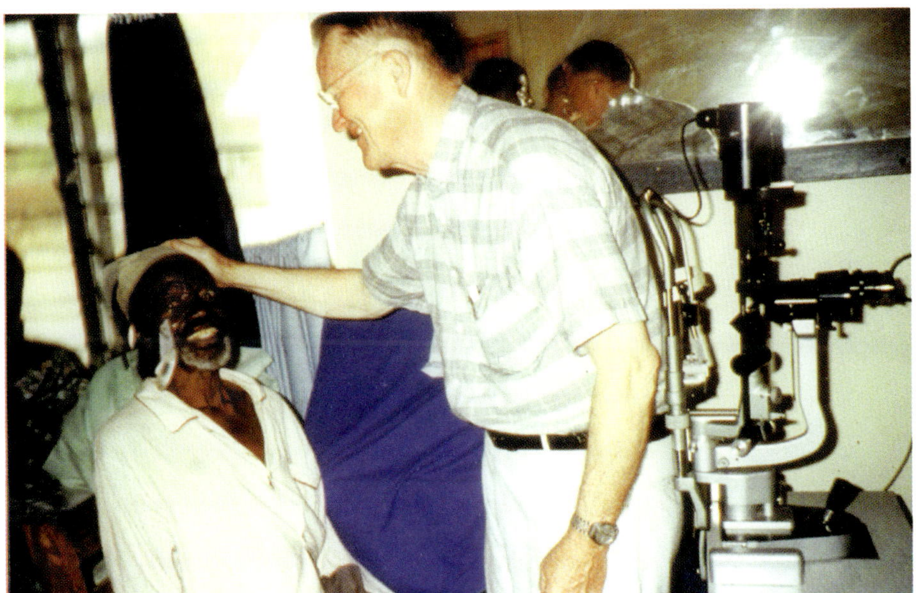

Color Print 1.29. Kombe. (see page 93)

Color Print 1.30. No longer blind after his operation. He now walks without being led. (see page 94)

Color Print 1.31. "Ma Ami" really sees again. (see page 94)

Jaw Dislocation

A woman was presented to us at the hospital with a dislocated lower jaw. Spouse abuse occurs in Sierra Leone like other nations in the world. The history revealed that there had been an altercation with her husband two months ago, and the blow had literally dislocated her jaw. Eating and speaking were difficult. Examination revealed little movement of the mandible. An attempt was made to reduce it, but without anesthesia it was not possible for her to relax sufficiently for the repositioning. Under anesthesia we learned that it would not have been possible to reduce it without surgical intervention. On exposing the temporal mandibular joint it was found that there was tissue in the way which prevented the condyloid process from being repositioned in the fossa. Following successful surgery the woman was again able to talk and for us she had smiles that were very appreciative. At a later check, she continued to have smiles, and had gained weight.

Deliveries

Caesarean sections are sometimes referred to as "Caesars." It was obvious that a young mother with a cephalo-pelvic disproportion would not be able to deliver her baby normally. Several times in her presence, the term "Caesar" was mentioned.

The fact that thousands of mothers die each year in childbirth is common knowledge. When told that she would need an operation, she readily agreed.

The next day the mother was up and even had a smile. While cradling the newborn in her arms, Ruth asked the mother what name she was giving to her son.

She replied, "Julius Caesar."

One day Ruth was confronted by a breathless runner who informed her that an expectant mother was on the way to the hospital. He declared that she was not going to make it in time. Ruth dispatched four men with a litter. They returned shortly with the little newborn lying on the stretcher. The mother was walking behind.

A woman in her early forties developed a large abdominal mass. At

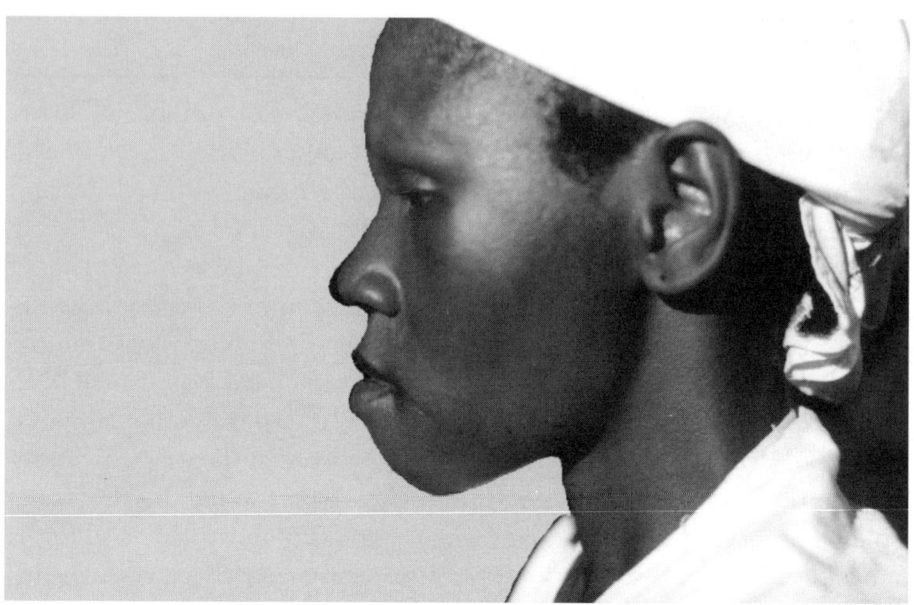

Figure 2.6. Jaw dislocation.

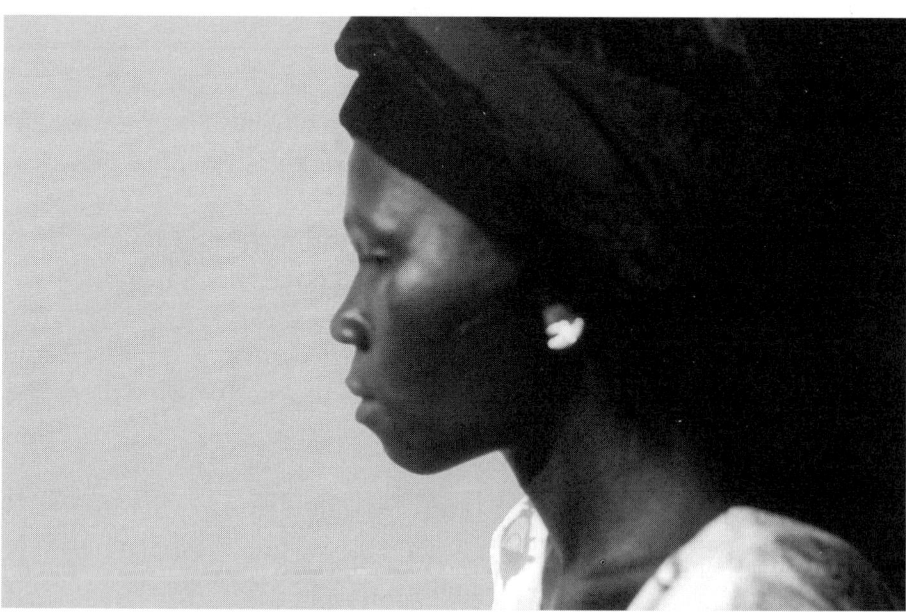

Figure 2.7. Jaw dislocation repaired.

surgery it was discovered to be an ovarian cyst the size of two basketballs. Fortunately it was dissected without being ruptured. After placing it in a bucket, the contents were examined and found to be hundreds of putty-like balls surrounded by fluid. On the way to the latrine for disposal, it was glimpsed by a school boy who sped screaming into the school. Believing witchcraft to be involved, the students scattered in all directions and the entire community was upset. The nurse assistant transporting the specimen also became paralyzed with fear as he was concerned about the reaction toward the patient. We immediately contacted Pastor W. B. Clay who used his stature and his booming voice to explain the "growth" allowing all to return to their normal activities. The students, however, did not return to school.

A missionary couple elected to have a home delivery for the birth of their third child. A doctor with special training in obstetrics was in attendance. All went well and a healthy baby girl was born.

After the doctor left to return to her home 90 miles upcountry, complications developed. Ruth and I were only 40 miles away serving at the Taiama general and eye clinic. We received an urgent message to come as no one knew how to reach the attending doctor on her return trip. The message stated that the baby had been born but post partum bleeding had developed. We hurriedly gathered obstetrical instruments, medications, and intravenous fluids and dashed down the road.

In spite of an enlarged uterus that simulated an intact pregnancy, the patient's vital signs were stable. Crede produced a large quantity of clotted blood. To maintain the contracture of the uterus, the husband's strong hands successfully compressed the uterus to keep it small. The bleeding stopped. We waited while the exhausted mother slept for several hours. Only later after sighs of relief and a light supper for all, including the patient, did we return to our station singing all the way and glorying in God's mercy and protection to His missionaries so far away from home.

The maternity staff at the Rotifunk Hospital under the direction of nurse-midwife Betty Beveridge, was solicitous and considerate of the doctors who occasionally were asked to participate in difficult deliveries. Often the doctor would be called from his sleep only at the last moment when everything was in readiness.

One night, half asleep, I staggered over to the hospital and was pre-

Figure 2.8. Deliveries. "Julius Caesar."

sented a patient who had been brought in a lorry from Taiama more than fifty miles away. Dr. George Harris had stopped at Taiama on his way to Bo. He advised transferring the patient to Rotifunk for a possible Caesarean section.

Examination revealed the head of the baby to be in the birth canal. I reached for a forceps that was on the surgical tray that had been set up for the operation. Returning to the patient, I discovered that the baby's head had disappeared.

Instinctively I grabbed the scalpel and made an abdominal incision from the umbilicus to the pubis. Up popped the baby free in the abdominal cavity. Two large Kocker clamps were placed on each side of the uterus to stop the copious bleeding of the mother. The umbilical cord was clamped and the baby handed to Miss Beveridge.

The uterus was shredded preventing any possible repair. The mother already had five children.

A hysterectomy was performed after Dr. Mabel Silver had been summoned to administer a general anesthetic.

The next day when the mother was asked about the original incision that allowed for the baby to be rescued before suffocation, the mother replied, "I thought it was another labor pain."

Three Hours of Artificial Respiration

Sometime after midnight a patient was brought to the Rotifunk Hospital in severe pain. A hernia which had been troubling him for several years suddenly incarcerated. This time he could not reduce it. With subsequent swelling it was on the way to strangulation, which if unattended could lead to death. He was aware of the sequence of events in his problem, and was wild eyed with pain. Non-surgical reduction was no longer possible. Arrangements were made for surgical intervention.

I was always most comfortable when Ruth administered the anesthetic. As husband and wife our communication was good, but now at 2 a.m. in the morning she needed to stay at home with our children. Another nurse was called to give the non- inflammable chloroform, since the procedure would have to be done with lanterns because the hospital generator had been torn down for repairs. The substitute nurse thought I was teasing about having her count out loud the drops being placed on the mask. She had never used chloroform before and simply poured it on as though she were using ether. In several minutes the patient was "out." More than that, he stopped breathing. With such profound relaxation, the incarcerated hernia was able to be reduced by manipulation, and we breathed for him with the EMO anesthetic machine. Three hours later, as the sun was coming up, he opened his eyes and spoke to us. His hernia was definitively repaired at a future and convenient time.

Few patients have ever had a continuous prayer being said over them for three hours. His awakening was like the stone being rolled away at Easter.

The surgical team is so important. Multiple steps are involved in creating sterile instruments and field. Many people participate in surgical procedures. Each has to be strictly honest about maintaining an inviolate technique. I have had the joy of performing over 15,000 cataract procedures with only two serious infections. One patient lost his eye, the other received normal vision following treatment. This success rightly reflected the meticulous team approach. Faulty or ill-prepared equipment causes disasters. Six successive patients became involved in a chemical, not bacteriologic, insult. None were left without sight, thankfully, because of the good vision in the other eye.

I cannot help but reflect that a long Christian testimony can be destroyed by a single instance of letting up on one's strict moral principles. With the invited presence and guidance of the Holy Spirit, a strong team effort wins the day.

From Death to Life

In the line of patients I noticed the limp body of a small girl tied to her mother's back. It was apparent that the child was not in a normal sleep. Suddenly I became aware of a foul, putrid odor.

The mother loosened the unconscious child, laid her on the tying-cloth, and lifted the makeshift bandage from the left leg. From the knee down, the extremity was in shreds of rotting flesh.

Usually people take patients away from the hospital when we confide to their relatives that there is nothing more that we can do. In this case, the mother was bringing the child after everyone knew that the leg was beyond repair and that she was only moments or a few breaths away from death.

Ordinarily I would have said a quiet prayer over the patient and then moved on. However, the mother knelt in front of me with pleadings in Temne, a tribal dialect. A nurse interpreted that she wanted me to use

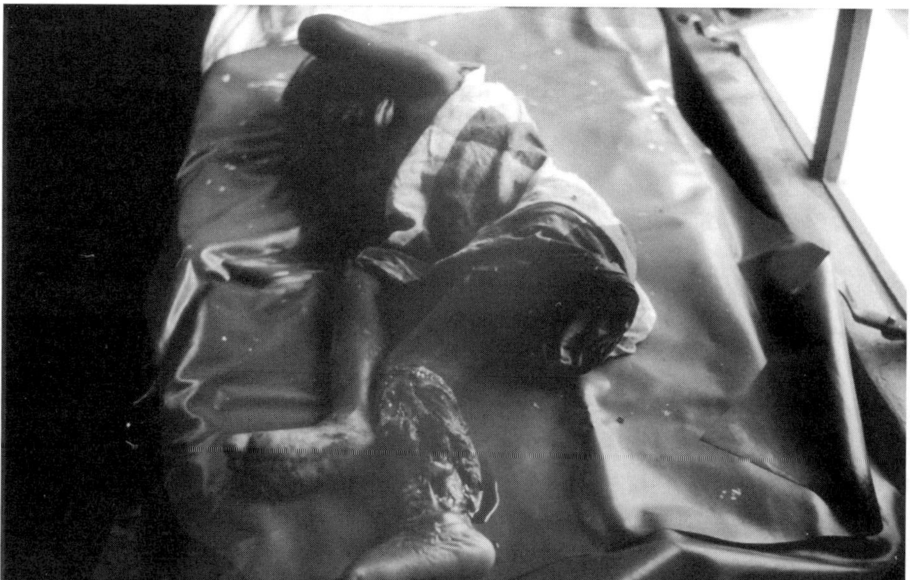

Figure 2.9. From Death to Life. A preoperative picture of the little unconscious girl with the offending left lower leg.

Figure 2.10. From Death to Life. Another patient who moved from death into life.

the "knife" – meaning to do surgery. To this very day, I do not understand my reaction in that moment. Apparently the thought flashed through my mind that where there is life there is hope. Although the little girl was not conscious, she was breathing and her heart was beating. Swiftly the nurses bathed her and positioned her on the operating table.

We made sure that she was still alive before applying antiseptics to prepare the lower extremity for amputation. The toxicity of the decaying lower leg was poisoning her entire system. A tourniquet was applied mid-thigh.

We had taken the precaution to start an intravenous administration of fluids in the event that some supportive measures might be necessary. Lidocaine was used to infiltrate the area, but there was no movement or reaction to the injecting needle. Massive antibiotics were given. A standard operative procedure was done in less than ten minutes.

The fluid replacement effectively brought back consciousness a short time later. We were able to feed her a nutritional diet. Within a week, the accompanying photograph was taken of a sweet and winsome little darling. A prosthesis for the left leg was later successfully adapted.

Glory to God.

Crocodile

Occasionaly our family would picnic on weekends. The children loved to jump into the Land Rover and drive to the swamp along the Benue River. Almost always wildlife was seen. On one occasion we went all the way to the Benue, and arranged for a cruise in a large dugout canoe. We intended to see the wildlife along the banks, which would include large birds and animals which had come down to drink. Above all else, we anticipated seeing crocodiles sunning themselves on sandy bars.

During the course of the trip the children were not very comfortable, and there was some complaining the entire trip. Each time there was some wildlife that could be seen and the children could be directed in the proper direction, the wildlife would have disappeared into the bush if it were a deer, or into the water, if it were a crocodile. The sun was high and it was very hot.

On the return to the beach the children begged to have a little time of splashing in the water. None of the children ever gave a thought to the fact that the waters might be dangerous and it wasn't until possibly twenty five or thirty years later that our oldest daughter Mary, learned

Figure 2.11. Crocodile.

that at the time of this swimming her father sat nervously on the bank with a loaded high-powered rifle at the ready with the safety off. Perhaps if I had known at that time how silently crocodiles could approach the shore and spring out for their prey, I would have been less willing to allow the children to have their swim in the Benue River.

In later years we learned of a missionary teenager who, while attempting to swim across a river, was dragged to his death by a crocodile. The canoe in which he and his father were cruising down the river, capsized with the loss of their gear, including their firearms. They ended up on opposite shores. The boy, a strong swimmer, jumped into the water to join his father on the opposite side. As he was in midstream, the father noted a swirl in the water upstream. Before his son could climb the bank, the crocodile grabbed him and dragged him out into the deep water, leaving only claw marks on the sand. Without a gun the father was only able to run into the water and splash in a futile attempt to prompt the crocodile to let go of its prey. The boy's body was never recovered.

When I visited with the boy's mother several years later, I was to learn of acceptance that is only possible by the grace of God. The parents were confident in the promise that "In all things God works for the good of those who love Him, who have been called according to His purpose." **(Romans 8:28 NIV).**

First Eye Surgery

The first eye surgery I performed was in 1958 at the Hatfield Archer Hospital in Sierra Leone. I had been sent to the Rotifunk Hospital to assist in the general surgical program. Dr. Mabel Silver had labored at that hospital for more than twenty years. Her successful treatment of patients made Rotifunk famous and actually was one of the four premiere hospitals in Sierra Leone. However, Dr. Silver declined to do surgery.

After a two-year residency in general surgery at the Akron General Hospital, Akron, Ohio, my family and I were posted at the Rotifunk Hospital to work with Dr. Silver. The program soon became so busy that Dr. George Harris and his family were also brought to Rotifunk. This

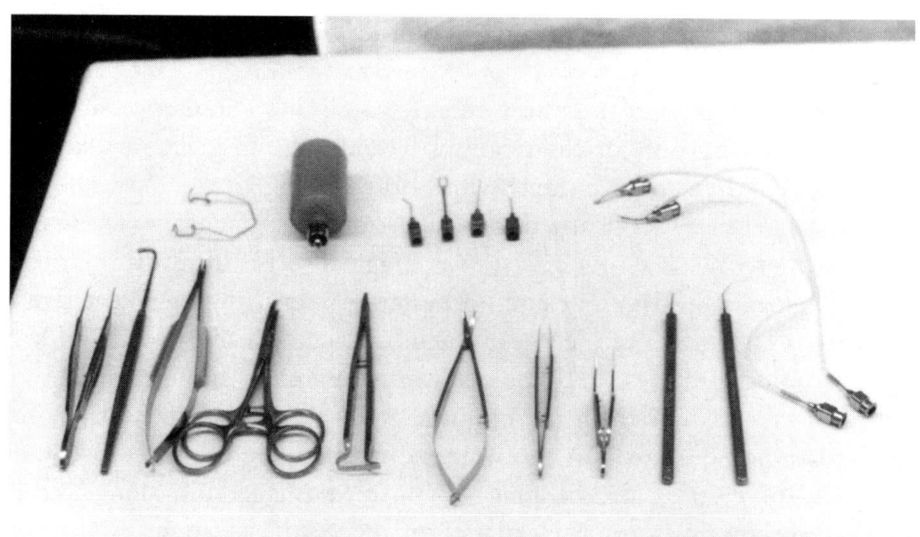

Figure 2.12. Eye instruments.

allowed me to do some oversight as the Board of Mission's field representative while still engaged in the growing surgical ministry. Dr. Harris and I did the full compliment of surgery, but herniorrhaphies and C-sections demanded a great deal of our time. Dr. Harold Adolph in *Today's Christian Doctor,* Summer 1999, notes that in Africa only one in twenty women needing a C-section for obstructed labor can get their operation. Only 15 percent of patients with hernias in Africa can get the operation they need during their lifetime, even if their hernia is strangulated.

It was troubling to see so many patients come to the hospital who were blind and receive no treatment. We began praying for them, which can be dangerous. Sometimes when we pray for others, the Lord may turn it around, and rather than asking others to do what needs to be done, places the responsibility on us. I mentioned our concern about the blind to an ophthalmologist friend of mine in Akron, Ohio. It was a surprise some months later to receive a set of eye instruments and a book of "how to" regarding cataract surgery. I devoured the book and had some practice runs with the surgical assistants using beef eyes. I reasoned that my knowledge of general surgery might help me to at least try to do the demanding ophthalmological procedure and give blind patients a chance for vision. Unless blind people could see where to go for food, they would become thin and malnourished. Without natural resistance, they became diseased and died.

The day came when arrangements were made for the first eye operation. Three totally blind people were selected. It was hoped that possibly one out of the three might obtain some vision. I asked Dr. Mabel Silver if she would come and participate in the occasion – especially to pray. She prayed in Temne. The patients followed her prayers with arms extended, hands open, as was their custom.

It was at this point that I nearly panicked. How could I have come to such a place as this, a farm boy from Paynesville, Minnesota, where my main activity had been cultivating corn with a team of horses that needed special expletives to make them go? I had never opened an eye before except in the cadaver room as a freshman medical student. In a few moments, I was to cut open a living eye. It would bleed. The opaque lens would have to be removed if the patient were to see.

With the support of Dr. Silver's prayer, I set about doing the task at hand. It was I who was doing the praying now, "Lord, help me do this effectually with precision, that there may be the blessing not only of physical sight, but also of spiritual insight into your love as revealed in Jesus Christ."

In a wonderful way, the Lord blessed and healed these first patients. All three were thrilled with new sight. They wanted to dance. The success of these opened the floodgates for other blind patients in Sierra Leone. As word spread, the blind were brought to us from every corner of the country.

The day came when the executive secretary of the Board of Missions, Dr. Carl Heinmiller, visited the Rotifunk Hospital. Noticing the many blind people sitting around, he inquired as to what was being done for them. It was explained that they were waiting for their surgery as time allowed between the regular general surgical cases. He declared that something had to be done about this situation. He would secure an ophthalmologist and send such a specialist to meet this tremendous need.

Months passed and no ophthalmologist was found. He then asked if I would be interested in training as an ophthalmologist to help all these people. Ruth and I made this a matter of prayer, realizing that it would mean going back to school again for another three year period. The need was real so we made preparations for a residency in ophthalmology.

At that time in history, openings to residencies for ophthalmology were almost non-existent. Some doctors were waiting for one, two, or more years trying to get into an eye residency. Wanting to be near my parents in Minnesota, application was made to the University of Minnesota eye program. Dr. John E. Harris was sympathetic with the story that was told of the need in Sierra Leone and made available a place for me in the program. Later on, I was to learn that Washington University School of Medicine also had accepted me in their eye program, but plans already had been made to go to Minnesota.

Following the residency in eye training, we were posted back to the Hatfield-Archer Rotifunk Hospital in Sierra Leone. After about six months, the Sierra Leone conference moved the eye program at Taiama. It was there that a new facility was built, especially for the eye program. I had been known as a general surgeon when last seen in Sierra Leone; now in addition to eye patients, strangulated hernia and obstructed labor cases were occasionally brought to our Taiama facilities. We could not abandon these critical conditions; and so we did some herniorrhaphies as well as C-sections during the scheduled eye program.

After a period of time, the eye program was next established at Bo, the eastern provincial capital of Sierra Leone. The description of the ministry there is told in an article written by Esther Groves titled *Where Hope is an Eye Clinic in Bo.*

Today the Kissy UMC Eye Hospital in Freetown is the center of the church's evangelistic eye ministry. This is a corporate venture of the Sierra Leone Conference of the United Methodist Church, the United Methodist Church's General Board of Global Ministries, the Central Global Vision Fund, and the Christian Blind Mission International.

Kombe, From Begging to Praising

"What do you want me to do for you?" Jesus asked Bartemaeus. The blind man said, "Rabbi, I want to see." "Go," said Jesus, "your faith has healed you." Immediately he received his sight and followed Jesus.

Mark 10:51,52 (NIV)

Kombe was a totally blind pagan who daily begged for alms at the gate of the Taiama United Methodist Church in Sierra Leone.

Compassionate Christians raised money for his trip to the Rotifunk Hospital for remedial surgery.

Following the usual pre-operative prayer and while waiting for the local anesthetic to take effect, I visited with Kombe, as he spoke English well. I said, "Kombe, we are happy that you are here at the hospital, that you are submitting to surgery in order that the Lord may give you new sight. Remember, we also prayed that you might accept the Lord Jesus Christ in your heart. Renewed sight will pass away again some day, but to those who give their lives to Christ, to those who know Him, they see forever." It was at this point that I raised the question that if he had the choice, would he rather be a new person in Christ for eternity or have new vision for the rest of his physical life? After a slight hesitation he replied, "I would rather be a new person in Christ!" There were some smiles behind the surgical masks. No one really believed him. He was just saying the respectful thing, as he knew he was being ministered to in a Christian hospital. Then after another short pause, he quietly added, "I want to see again, too."

Our prayers for him were answered. Following successful surgery, he made preparations to return to Taiama. He was busily moving about, no longer being led by other people. He could see and was now independent. He joyfully left the hospital, walking without being led. Actually, he walked out of our lives, and we gave no further thought to him.

A year later I was a guest preacher at the Taiama United Methodist Church, referred to as "The Cathedral in the Bush." It was a vibrant church pastored by the Rev. B. A. Carew. People from the cottage (hut) prayer groups in surrounding villages would be in attendance for Sunday services. The women and men had strong organizations, the latter conducting a large Lord's Acre project. At the close of the service, Communion was to be served. Pastor Carew announced that those who had committed their lives to Jesus Christ, those whose love and loyalty were to the Lord, were invited to come and kneel for Holy Communion. Several hundred baptized members out of the congregation of a thousand responded. At the last table, as I was passing the bread, I noticed a man, healthy looking, well dressed and wearing glasses.

Thick "cataract type glasses" were unusual for someone in this far off place. Returning with the cup, he took it, raised his face, and smiled. My heart leaped within me. I was looking into the face of Kombe. He really meant what he said when he desired to become a "new creation in

Christ."

Once he was a beggar. His clothes now indicated that he was gainfully employed. Once he knew constant hunger. No longer thin, it was obvious that he could buy adequate food. Once he was a lonely man, now he was experiencing the fellowship of the Christian church. Once he was without faith or hope. Now by his kneeling at the communion rail he was laying hold of the Lordship of Jesus Christ and the promise of eternal life. "If any man is in Christ, he is a new creation; old things are passed away; behold, all things are become new." (**II Corinthians** 5:17).

Loving God,
We thank you for the joy of sight.
Thank you for the revelation of new insight into your love as revealed in Jesus Christ.
Do for us as you did for Bartimaeus and Kombe.
We ask in Jesus' name. Amen.

Ma Ami Really Sees Again

Ma Ami was slowly starving to death because she was blind, and there was no one to care for her. She was regularly seen at the marketplace and kept alive only by the generosity of people who would share food and pennies with her. Among her benefactors were some of her Muslim faith. However, it was the Christian concern and compassion of the people of Calvary Church at Taiama that resulted in money being raised for her operation, transportation and care during her hospitalization at Rotifunk.

Following the operation on her first eye, she was overjoyed to be able to get about and be active again. She considered it a privilege to sweep the floors in the church, and the eye clinic. She also encouraged others to come to the hospital for aid. Before long she was regular in her attendance at worship services at the church as well as the women's activities.

The day came when Pastor B.A. Carew counseled with her, and she was accepted into the fellowship of the Christian church. Ultimately her second eye was operated on, and she was thrilled beyond words when one day she was fitted with an appropriate pair of glasses made available

Figure 2.13. Survivor of the Massacre.

by an American organization, New Eyes for the Needy. Ma Ami not only had received the physical sight that would last for a few more years, but also received the eternal life of which Jesus spoke when he said "I am the resurrection and the life."

As Christians we hold within our grasp the most powerful force in the world today – the resurrection power of the Lord Jesus Christ, who not only heals bodies and minds, but also the spirits and souls of people until "all things are new."

Survivor of the Massacre

C. V. Rettew, one of the schoolboys who was at Rotifunk during the time of the 1898 massacre of missionaries, later became a pastor. Several times while visiting with me he would recount the circumstances surrounding the death of the missionaries, whom he referred to as "those beautiful people." Tears would course down his cheeks as he described the death scene – each missionary being surrounded by out of control and screaming groups of men, who beheaded each of their victims. He lived with a remorse that no action was taken to protect the missionaries from this terrible fate. Like all the other students, with the coming of the rebels, he fled into the bush for protection.

Pastor Rettew and his wife were faithful witnesses of Jesus Christ all the days of their lives. During the time that Ruth and I served in the eye clinic at Taiama, we would often hear the tinkling of a little bell. We would smile to each other, knowing that Mrs. Rettew was on her rounds in the village proclaiming the good news of salvation, open to all who confess their sins and accept Jesus Christ as Lord and Savior. In a letter from Pastor Rettew in 1961, when he was retired and infirm, he wrote: "Three things are essential for all followers of the Lord Jesus Christ; humility, indiscriminate love for all persons irrespective of color and condition, and a genuine faith in Christ." By running into the bush for protection on that fateful day in 1898, Pastor Rettew was given the privilege of leading hundreds and thousands of people to Jesus Christ as their Lord and their Savior. His destiny was not one of martyrdom but rather of life that he might be instrumental in bringing new life to others during the life that he was given.

Martyrs

In January, 1898, a session of the West African Conference convened at Shenge. Already rumors of imminent tribal wars were circulating throughout the country. The Howards, Kings, and Miss Eaton left for the United States soon after the conference. The other workers returned to their stations. By April the situation grew worse, but the work went on in spite of the rumblings of war.

During the last week of April, 1898, Mr.Ward left by rowboat for Freetown to secure cash to pay the workers. Many workers came to Rotifunk to await Mr. Ward's return and attended services in the church. Soon after the service several Sierra Leoneans came to town half naked and extremely frightened. All the Sierra Leonean women left town Sunday afternoon. Boarding pupils were sent home. In the evening the booming of guns was heard as the war boys were attacking the Kwellu barracks. A watch was kept that night and no one was allowed to sleep. At this crucial time Dr. Hatfield arrived in a hammock from Taiama prostrate with her illness.

Figure 2.14. Mende Wunde warriors.

Monday morning, preparations were made for the missionaries to escape by boat, including the Rev. T. F. Hallowell and his family. While waiting for the incoming tide, news came that the war boys had captured Mr. Coker, trader and church member. He was brought to Bendasuma and murdered. This crushed all hope of escape by river. The missionaries quietly made their way into the bush with Dr. Hatfield still in a hammock. The raiders came to town and three policemen escaped. About 1 p.m. the mission laborers confided to Rev. Hallowell that they had taken oaths to help in the massacre of the missionaries and unless he did likewise he too would be killed. The Poro Society was important and strong, especially in the lives of Mende men. He told them he had to consult his boy first with the intent of stalling for time. He went to Rotower and returned early in the morning with his boy. He then went to the hiding place of the missionaries to see how they were faring and advised them to get on towards Freetown. They sent Pa Hallowell with another mission boy to get the records in the mission house. On the road the missionaries were violently arrested and brought to town by screaming groups of men.

During the three hours of the missionaries' captivity, grizzly events took place. Mr.Cain and Dr. Archer were shot. Miss Ella Schenck fled to the boy's home where she had gone for shelter. When found, she was stabbed to death. Another account was that she was taken to the Frontier Police Barracks where she was raped and murdered. Mrs. Cain reportedly ran into the burning mission house, dying in the flames, rather than being subjected to abuse. The Rev. Walter Schutz, mission superintendent at Rotifunk in the early 1920s, was told that Mrs. Cain was killed in the barracks and did not commit suicide. Dr. Hatfield, too ill to move, observed the tragic scene, silently standing with folded hands in prayer until the moment of being stripped of her clothing and beheaded.

In Taiama the McGrews were held captive for several days. On May 8, 1898, they were taken to a small stony island in the Tai River where they were beheaded and their bodies thrown into the river never to be recovered.

Dr. Marietta Hatfield had arrived in Sierra Leone in 1891 and Dr. Mary Archer in 1895. Working with Dr. West, the medical program had expanded wilth new facililties at Rotifunk. Nurse Ella Schenck was engaged to be married. Her intended was on his way to Rotifunk from Freetown at the time of the tragedy. As his boat entered the mouth of the Bumpeh River from the Atlantic ocean, he was informed of the Rotifunk massacre in which all the missionaries had been killed. He reversed his course, returned to Freetown, and no further word was known about him.

Rev. Ira N. Cain was a strong and energetic man in possession of firearms. He refused to use them for his defense, explaining that he had come to help and to save, not to kill, the people of Sierra Leone. In recounting this incident, Bishop J. S. Mills, writes:

> *I have elsewhere said and now repeat that the law of sacrifice is the first law of the kindom of God. The life of the Master illustrated this fact, for even 'the Son of man came not to be ministered unto, but to minister, and to give his life a ransom for many.' From the beginning obedience to this law has been the condition of human progress. The mother gives her life for her child, the patriot dies for his country, and the missionary dies for his King.*
>
> *When Brother Cain refused to fire on the black mob ready to slay the little party of whites, I have no doubt that when he consulted his noble comrades, they said, 'Let us lay down our lives for Africa, even as*

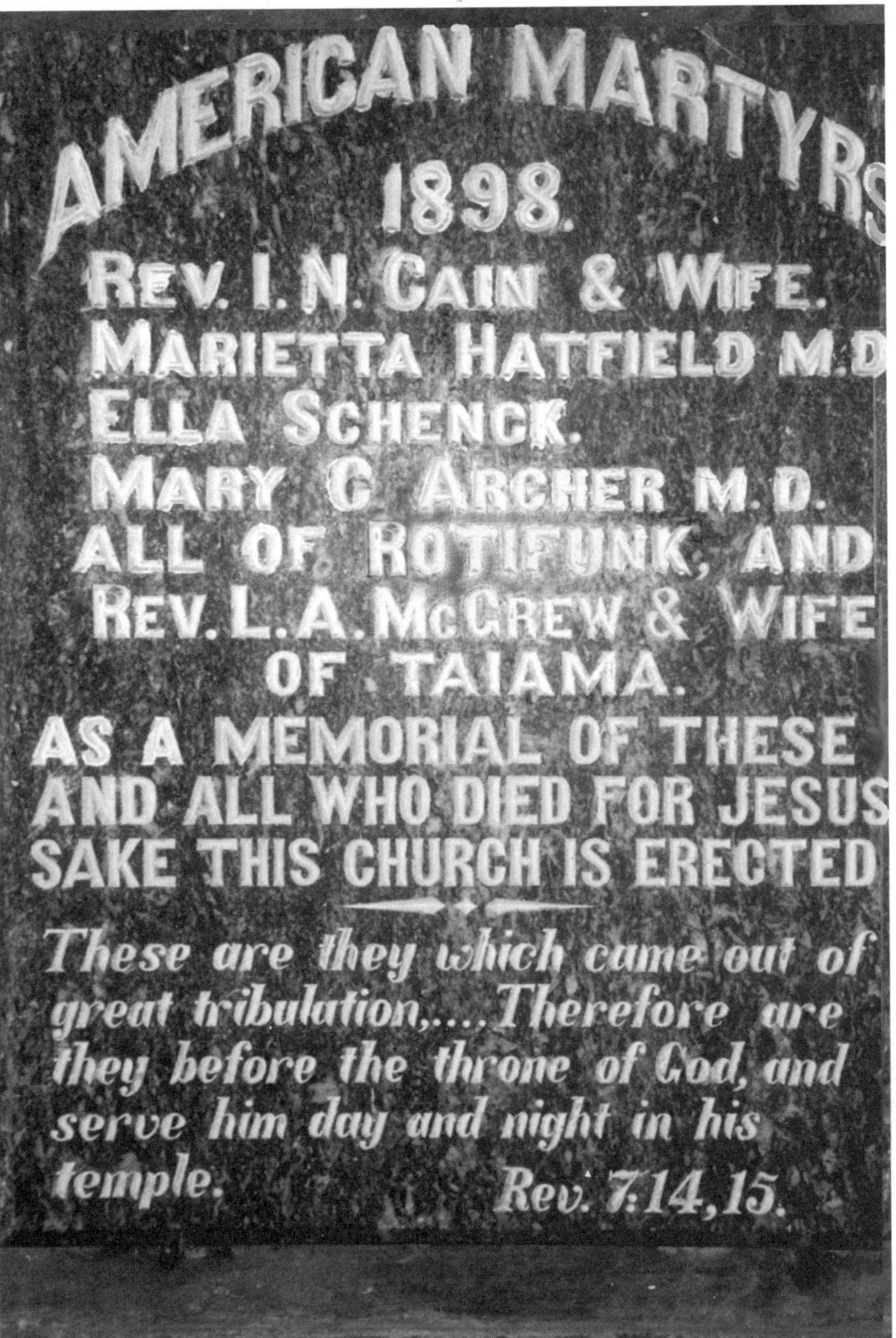

Figure 2.15. Martyrs.

> *our Saviour did for us.' And they were at once enrolled in the great army of martyrs, who counted not their own lives dear unto themselves. The redemption of Africa goes forward by such service. The graves of Christian missionaries and explorers are the steppingstones across Africa. It has pleased God to give our church the honor of furnishing a glorious band, who by this high offering of sacrificial service has done so much to redeem Africa.*

The list is long of other missionaries, who for their faith, paid the supreme price by laying down their lives in deadly climates with untreatable diseases. Jesus gave His life willingly even though His prayer was, "Father, if you will, take this cup away from me." (Luke 22:42, Good News for Modern Man). No missionary ever wants or intends to die,but their commitment often places them in harm's way. The fact that these ambassadors for Christ all died in the line of duty did not diminish the response of others to "go into all the world" and fill the ranks of those chosen for the high calling of Christ to preach the Gospel. Because of Chief Thomas Neale Caulker's friendship with missionaries and the government, he was killed along with many hundreds of others.

The likeness of Bai Bureh, 1840-1909, brilliant strategist of the Hut Tax War, appears on the 1000 Leone note. Reportedly he did not plan or condone the murdering of missionaries. Those killed in the Temne

Figure 2.16. UMC Sierra Leone Conference historian Mr. Henry J Williams (right) with his wife.

country were with the fighting forces. The English missionaries were at his mercy at Ro-Gbere, but they were in no way molested beyond being detained. The Rev. W. J. Humphrey lost his life in his over-solicitude for his people, who were perfectly safe. Bai Bureh killed Mack, Humphrey's murderer. The historian A.B.C. Sibthorpe stated that there were upwards of 200 tried for being implicated in the Protectorate massacres, of whom thirty-three were executed.

When the fighting stopped, Bai Bureh remained illusive for a considerable time. Ultimately he emerged from the bush, giving himself up with the words, "the war done done." The government did not want to punish him as he had fought bravely without killing defenseless people. They did not dare to release him for fear that he might start another war; so they deported him to Ghana. In 1905 he was allowed to return to Sierra Leone and ended his days in his own chiefdom. Never again was the British authority challenged.

In unpublished notes, Mr. Henry J. Williams makes enlightened statements about the Hut Tax that caused the rebellion and the impact that it had on the growing Christian church in Sierra Leone. He begins by saying:

> *It is reasonable to think that a cause as self-giving and considerate as was the Church Missionary enterprise, would be received with open arms; that a benevolent government whose purpose was to maintain law and order, provide schools, open roads and promote the common good would be accepted and respected.*

But progress and change never come without the shuffling off of old casts and the abandoning of old ways. Man does not make such changes readily. They are usually accompanied by strain, suffering and revolution, and in many instances, death.

Loss to the Mission

Seven lives were destroyed at Rotifunk and Taiama. Added to them was the loss of eighty thousand dollars worth of property and furnishings including churches, schools, dispensaries, industrial buildings and the boat house at Shenge.

Reconstruction Must Go On

The United Brethren Church laboured and prayed to propagate the Gospel and establish a Christian community (church) in Sierra Leone. Three hundred thousand dollars had been invested in personnel, travel, property and furnishings. An African church of some five thousand members had been organized, with trained African leaders. Schools enrolled nearly a thousand pupils, and a medical centre was started. Now all seemed lost. The most important concern then was the native church. It was important, Dr. A. W. Drury said, because it was the main consideration of the missionary's going to Africa.

The horror of the martyrdom of the missionaries soon subsided and the Boards began to lay plans to press the evangelization of Africa with new zeal and purpose. "There is no thought of abandoning our work in Africa," Bishop J. W. Hott declared, "Our sisters and brothers have mingled their blood with the soil of that land, more sacred to us now than ever before. What would our crucified Lord and Master think of us as a church if we faltered now and deserted the many there who have proven faithful to Him?"

Educational Institutions of Higher Learning

Coincidentally, the decision to erect the Harford School for Girls and Albert Academy at Moyamba and Freetown was taken shortly after the arrival of Rev. and Mrs. J. R. King on October 7, 1898, who nobly once more faced Africa and its problems. The trustees of the Missionary Association with undaunted courage and full of compassion for privileges lost by the girls in 1898, transferred them to Moyamba at a total cost of four thousand dollars to be trained as teachers, itinerants, interpreters,and for the future marriage to the native workers with bright examples in Christian homes showing the light. The school which was dedicated in 1900, began with the following girls who were professed and baptized Christians. They were Jessie Murrel (formerly Jessie Yoko) first girl to be offered by Madam Yoko, Clara McGrew Williams (Henry William's mother), May Funderburgh (mother of the Karefa Smarts), Elma Bittle, Catherine Lawrence, Laura Meredith, Ruth Keister and Maggie Hallowell. Financial assistance and clothing came from some kindhearted friends in America.

With an initial donation of five thousand dollars from Ralph

Lenninger, a wealthy citizen of Brooklyn, and cousin of Rev. Ira E. Albert, the Albert Academy was to be erected and named after him. He died by drowning in the Bumpeh River on November 6, 1902. The school was opened on October 4, 1904. From the original five the number is now over a thousand in enrollment. Both schools have produced students in all faculties of education in Africa, Europe, Canada, and the United States. Harford School and Albert Academy have produced ambassadors in the persons of Mrs. Shirley Gbujama and Dr. W. H. Fitzjohn. Mrs Alice Fitzjohn was one of the first women to be ordained in the Sierra Leone conference of the United Methodist Church.

Also in the political field two excelled exceedingly: Sir Milton Margai, Sierra Leone's First Prime Minister, and the Protectorate's First Medical Officer. The highest position ever attained was that of Dr. Siaka P. Stevens, Executive President of the Republic of Sierra Leone, whose awards are G.C. R.(S.L.)D.C.L.(S.L.,D.C.L) (Lincoln).

Two products of the school became its principal. Dr. R. E. Caulker, 1940-1959; Mr. A. Max Bailor, M.A., P.G.C.E, 1961-to recent years.

Two bishops trained at Albert Academy: Dr. B. A. Carew, O.B.E., was consecrated in February 1973, the Rt. Rev. T. S. Bangura, M.A.,C.R., on February 21, 1979.

The Gospel in the Provinces – Church Growth

After the 1898 incident, the church assumed a new dimension which continued at a meteoric rate. The Martyrs Memorial Church in Rotifunk was dedicated in 1904 as was the Hatfield-Archer Dispensary whose structure gave way to the magnificent hospital at Rotifunk which was dedicated in February 1951.

It has been stated that the church down through the ages has been built upon the blood of martyrs, whether in the Roman arena or in the outposts at Rotifunk and Taiama in Sierra Leone, West Africa. Before the year was out, as noted by Mr. Williams, replacements were on their way for Africa. The church did not end with Calvary.

Rotifunk in Review

Rotifunk, 1957

Following two years of residency in general surgery at the Akron General Hospital, Akron, Ohio, we were ready with our seventeen barrels and six crates to return to Sierra Leone in West Africa. On the way we bought cowboy hats for the children and on our trip to the Boston airport we were stopped by a traffic officer for speeding 52 miles an hour in a 40 mile an hour zone. Our driver was the Rev. Richard Kunz who showed great composure in dealing with the officer. When the officer expressed surprise at the five children wearing cowboy hats and all the luggage in the car he inquired about us. After learning that we were medical missionaries on our way to West Africa, he was quiet for a few moments and then shifting his hat, he dismissed us without writing a ticket.

Once on the plane we began to relax until we realized that we weren't moving or taking off. After what seemed an interminable ten minutes the pilot announced that we were ready for takeoff. He explained that the delay was necessary to burn off fuel as we were overloaded. The psychology of that report had a devastating impact on the passengers. We were starting out over thousands of miles of oceans and he was burning up the plane's fuel before we even got off the ground. Thankfully we landed safely at Santa Maria in the Azores on the long leg of our flight.

The Thanksgiving dinner in Freetown, November 28th with the Theuers, Galows, Phelps, Esther Megill, and Metra Heisler had a special significance as did the December 1st dinner arranged by Rena Karefa-Smart, wife of Dr. John Karefa-Smart. On December 2nd, Don Theuer, Theodore Tucker, Tim and I traveled to Rotifunk and then on to Moyamba, home of Harford School for Girls. In Taiama we visited with nurse-midwife Lois Olsen and Pastor B. A. Carew, before going on to Bo for visits with Charles and Bertha Leader, as well as Les and Winnie Bradford. Then it was back to Freetown.

A cablegram from Dr. Carl Heinmiller on December 5, decided our future. We were to go directly to Rotifunk without any delay for language study. However, I did attend a leprosy conference directed by the famous Dr. Robert Cochran at Ganta Hospital in Liberia December 7-19. Dr. Cochran had also been the director of the Kano, Nigeria, work-

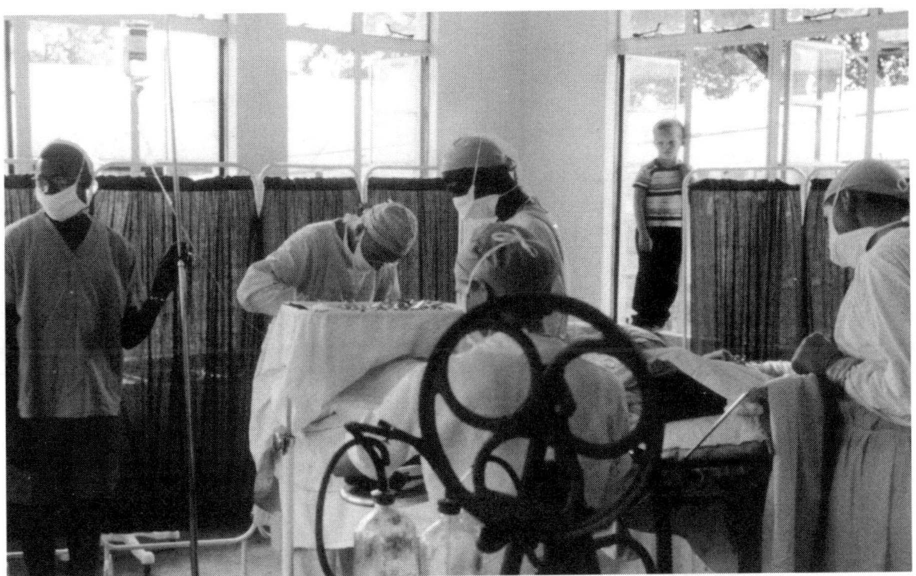

Figure 2.17. Our son, John, standing in the window of surgery asking when Ruth would be coming home.

shop that I had attended three years earlier.

Returning to Freetown and my family, I spent December the 21st at the quay trying to locate our luggage which had been shipped as ocean freight prior to our departure on the plane. While observing the loading of the steamship *Accra* which was leaving for England, I noticed one of our steamer trunks going up on the hoisted platform. It contained all the clothes for our family. I frantically stood there waving my arms trying to gain someone's attention and finally was permitted to go on board where arrangements were made for the off-loading of this important trunk.

On December the 30th we arrived at Rotifunk. This was to be our home for the next three years.

Rotifunk, 1958

1958 at Rotifunk was a busy and demanding year. Following the two year surgical residency at Akron General Hospital, I was assigned to meet the patients' surgical needs at the Hatfield-Archer Hospital in Rotifunk, Sierra Leone. The staff had not been trained in surgical sterilization or techniques. It was important that items dropped on the floor not be replaced on the sterile surgical table. Successfully putting on sur-

Figure 2.18. Rotifunk Hospital, 1957.

gical gloves without contamination took many days of practice. Ruth played an invaluable role during this period of training as well as administering the general anesthesia when spinals wore off or were not effective. The newly developed EMO machine was designed especially for use by personnel not trained in anesthesia programs. Our children sometimes would find their way to the surgical wing and stand in the open and screenless windows asking when mother would be coming home. Eventually, remodeling produced a more secure amphitheater.

The suction machine was of ancient vintage, but it created a vacuum for mucous aspiration. It also was successful in draining amebic liver abscesses which on occasion amounted to 1600 cc.

The first surgery was a hernia repair for Samuel, a fifteen year old student, February 7, 1958. The gloves had been overcooked in the sterilizer and were not strong enough for handling. Some packaged new ones that I had brought along were used. The first assistant had the misfortune of contaminating his gloves and gown. The second assistant also suffered a break in technique. The first operation was done solo.

The surgeries were not the challenge that they had been in 1953 at Bambur, Nigeria. Complicated obstructed and incarcerated herniae, as well as fractures, now were routinely addressed. Little stress was noted when I did an abdominal exploration and repair of a jejunal laceration,

Figure 2.19. Sir Milton Margai, the first Prime Minister following independence in 1961.

again from a stab wound similar to the first surgery I had done in Bambur, Nigeria. Ulnar stripping was a commonly done procedure for leprosy patients who developed enlarged ulnar nerves that compromised the function of their arms. The stress that was involved, however, was trying to minister to blind people by doing cataract extractions for which I had not been trained.

One might say that the greatest stress of all was generated outside the surgical theatre with the countless hours spent on hospital records, book reports, correspondence, ordering supplies and instruments, and finally the receiving of a telegram April 30, 1958, which read, "Dayton requests Gess serve as executive secretary until January, 1959."

That January date was to come and go so that it was actually not until August 13, 1959, when the field representative correspondence was turned over to Clyde Galow. With this new role of leadership, numerous meetings were involved with the missionary personnel at the various mission stations as well as with the indigenous leaders of the Sierra Leone conference which had been formed in 1958. As early as 1950 the Sierra Leone West African Mission had been authorized to send one delegate to General Conference. Now delegated as a field representative, my interests were not centered solely on the hospital at Rotifunk. Representation was made to Albert Academy, Harford School for Girls, community development programs such as that initiated by Pastor B. A. Carew at Taiama, by Donald Pletsch at Yonibana, by Les and Winnie Bradford at Manjama, and the Bo Bible Training Institute, where Donald and Tusalene Wonnie served so effectively in the wake of outstanding names such as Dr. and Mrs. Charles Leader, Vivian Olson, Joseph C. Humper, Laura Kandeh, the Gilbert O. Olsons, the DarEll Weists, and others. Visits were made to churches and places of which I had never heard.

Being ordained, I was called to preach nearly every week, and sometimes twice. I enjoyed hearing great preachers such as Dr. S. M. Renner, B.A. Carew, J. K. Fergusson, Crispin and Eustace Renner, J. B. Vandy Rogers, David Caulker, Dr. F. B. Davies, David Bockarie, Alfred N.N. Karimu, Dawda, W. B. Clay, and other dedicated pastors in the Sierra Leone conference. My favorite pastor was C. V. Rettew. His earnest and practical messages included, "The Sower," where he described four kinds of people coming to church, "The New Birth," "Naama," in 2 Kings 5, and one of his most famous, Psalm 17:15, based on "I Shall Be Satisfied, When I Awake With Thy Likeness." He declared that man goes up, down, and out but is not satisfied. Missionaries are not satisfied at home – they come to Africa with the Gospel. David, the Samaritan woman, and others were not satisfied. Only Jesus Christ satisfies – the Altogether Lovely One, the Finest of 10,000.

Pastor C. V. Rettew especially appreciated missionary Walter Schutz who served at Rotifunk in the 1920s and 1930s. Paramount Chief A. G. Caulker of Rotifunk was a drunkard when the Rev. and Mrs. Walter Schutz arrived in Rotifunk in 1923. The chief had been a student at the Mission Shenge school and obtained to the fifth standard. When he was made the chief of the Bumpeh chiefdom (of which Rotifunk is the capital), he began to drink heavily. Rev. Shutz would go to his compound every Sunday morning to hold a 6 a.m. service for the court messengers and the strangers who came for medicine or fish and who came to tell the chief Ho-do. The chief had a spite against the mission because of its stand against drink, polygamy, etc. For about 11 months Rev. Schutz faithfully held services at the court. The chief did not show much interest because of his spite against the mission but still wanted Rev. Schutz to continue with the services. The account then continues in Rev. Schutz' own words:

> *One day a small leopard was killed. Stanley, our son, was just about 6 weeks old. The chief was proud to have a white boy in his country. He wrote me a note asking that I come and that he would give me the skin of the leopard if I would tell Stanley when he grew up that Chief A. C. Caulker had given it to him. I thanked him and we continued watching the dance put on because of the leopard being killed and during the ceremony honoring the hunter. The Chief in his talk referred to the "strict interpretation" the mission put on the use of alcohol. I told him I would like to talk this over with him privately. He invited me to his inner court and with a shush of his right hand dismissed the messengers that were with us. He then talked over the matter of drinking. At first the chief had all the kinds of arguments to present, even quoting St. Paul advising Timothy "take a little wine for thy stomach's sake." I told the chief that the tragedies from alcohol were without number and that I stood by the stand that our church holds on drink. I further told him that from what I have seen of chiefs taking*

to drink, I would prophesy that before ten years were over he would no longer be the chief of his chiefdom if he continued as he had been doing with liquor. I told him that the British governor had made the observation that all too many men, when they become chiefs, die of strong drink. The reason was that they soon became alcoholics and burned out their stomachs. We must have talked for two hours or more when I suggested we take this to God in prayer. We both knelt down and he made one of the finest prayers I have ever heard, asking God to forgive him and heal him from this curse. When we got back on our feet he said to me, "I want to make a promise to you, I'll never drink another drink of any strong drink as long as I shall live, by the grace of God." I told Chief that was a wonderful thing and I was sure God would help him to stay sober. I went home and prayed that God would help him in his new life.

The wonderful change that came over the chief was truly remarkable. He began to take an active part in the church, sent boys for schooling, paid a pound every Sunday to the church, and his example became widely known. Ultimately he was chosen the first chief to the executive committee on the legislative council of the government. He was widely used by the government as an assessor chief and would be called to help install new chiefs in many parts of the country. He became a trusted chief by everyone. He persuaded many to leave drink alone and when the governor had a cocktail party for the legislative council, he asked the server dishing out the drinks for lemonade or any soft drink. The colonial secretary, Mr. Brutt, was sitting next to him. He asked the chief if it were really true that he does not drink. The chief told him that it was. To this the colonial secretary replied that he was glad to meet an African chief who does not drink.

Chief A. G. Caulker outlived all the other chiefs who were crowned around him during that time. He served many years longer than most of them. He was highly respected by the government and the Sierra Leone people for his fine character.

With the coming of Dr. George Harris, his wife, Norma, and children, March 21, 1958, my world suddenly improved. Following language study he was ready for duty June 19th. We spent the entire night helping a patient to breathe. The patient had gone into shock from blood loss. The blood of our head dispenser Ernest and mine were the

Figure 2.20. Dr. George Harris (left) checking the watchman's clock.

only ones that were compatible for the patient. Since I was doing the technical work, Ernest offered to be the first to donate through the cut down we had going on his leg. Thankfully Mr. Kai rallied and came through his ordeal – and ours.

Four days later, George pulled his first tooth. This reminded me that three years earlier the first procedures that Dean Olweiler did at Bambur, Nigeria, involved extractions of teeth. George became expert at onchocerciasis nodulectomies, and soon began doing more of the regular surgeries. In early June when I was away for meetings, he was faced with an incarcerated hernia where a loop of bowel protruded from the abdominal cavity and its blood supply was put in jeopardy. Untreated, the obstruction can lead to the death of the patient. Surgery is imperative to relieve the obstruction.

Lois Olsen in *Contentment is Great Gain* relates this incident as told to her by George himself:

> *The patient had arrived at the hospital at Rotifunk shortly after George's arrival. He was the only doctor at the hospital at the time and felt he was not capable of doing the surgery. He decided to take the patient to Connaught Hospital in Freetown; an arduous trip, part of the way over a dirt road. There was also a ferry to cross. Eventually,*

he got the patient admitted to the hospital. He stayed in Freetown overnight and in the morning went back to see the patient. To his amazement the man had been discharged without being treated. With a great deal of effort, George searched the city, found the man, and brought him back to the hospital. This time he waited until the man was seen by a doctor and was sure that the patient would have the necessary surgery. After that, George was no longer hesitant to attempt surgery at Rotifunk.

Many different types of surgery were done. The scheduled cataract extractions might be followed by an abdominal hysterectomy, incarcerated hernia, or a vesico-vaginal fistula repair. Even a tonsillectomy and adenoidectomy was done August the 31st, 1959 on Mervin Bailor.

Mention was made about cataract surgery because in 1958, we no longer could ignore the plight of so many blind people around us. After receiving eye instruments and a "How to" book from Dr. Korsmo in Akron, Ohio, I began "operating" on cow's eyes in preparation of the first cataract operation to be done on a patient. By the end of the year, December the 3rd, George was operating on "cow's eyes." Two days later he did his first successful human cataract extraction.

Within several weeks of each other two young people came down with appendicitis. Samuel Pieh, son of Pastor Pieh at Taiama, became acutely ill. He did well following the operation, and today is in important leadership as Executive Director of Mid-South/Africa Link, as well as utilizing his Master of Public Health Degree and Master of Science Degree in Biology and Science Education. He was asked to coach the Mende dialogue in Steven Spielberg's famous movie, "Amistad."

On a visit to Rupp Memorial School in Kabala, we found Hope McQuisten, twelve year old daughter of missionaries Jim and Nancy, not feeling well. Examination revealed possible appendicitis. On the return trip to Rotifunk we met Jim and Nancy on the road as they were planning to visit Hope at the school. They turned around and proceeded with us back to Rotifunk. With laboratory studies, appendicitis was diagnosed, and with the studied approval of Dr. Silver and Dr. Harris it was decided that Hope needed surgical intervention. Three days later Hope was well enough to attend church services in Rotifunk.

During one session in surgery we were honored by the visit of Dr. John Karefa-Smart. A decade earlier he had been the surgeon doing the procedures in this very room in which we were visiting. He had been appointed to the Rotifunk Hospital in the early days when Dr. Silver was directing the medical program. Presently he was working with the World Health Organization, based in Switzerland. Again several decades later a visit was made by Dr. Karefa-Smart to the Kissy UMC Eye Hospital in Freetown, Sierra Leone. He has been in political leadership in Sierra Leone for many years.

Figure 2.21. Visit of Dr. John Karefa-Smart.

1958 was a proud year for Rotifunk. The church, school, and hospital were reaching out in love to "our neighbors" even as our Lord had commanded us.

Rotifunk, 1959

1959 at Rotifunk was even more busy and demanding than 1958. The appointment as field representative in Sierra Leone by the Division of World Mission necessitated much travel. Frequent trips were made to Freetown for committee meetings. The return to Rotifunk might not be until late in the evening. The next day would find the surgery schedule as usual involving scrotal amputations secondary to filarial infection, abdominal or vaginal hysterectomies, extraction of teeth (occasionally as many as seven patients in one day), herniorrhaphies, (sometimes "sliding," sometimes obstructed, and sometimes incarcerated), urethral dilatations (later it was found necessary to have a special clinic day for these procedures), thyroidectomies, vesico-vaginal fistulae repairs, and complicated oncocerciasis nodulectomies.

Executive committee meetings were held frequently in Freetown and Bo, with Rotifunk, Moyamba, and Taiama occasionally in between. On one occasion Gertrude Bloede and Betty Esau were being harassed by an officious doctor in Koidu. The nurses simply shut down the Jaiama Clinic. It took a day and a half to travel to Jaiama to learn the "stories" from both sides. Maternity patients apparently preferred to go to the American midwives in Jaiama rather than the government hospital in Koidu. Some egos were involved but the complaint that surfaced was "the nurses keep the patients too long before they seek help or arrange for referrals."

The nurses were in full agreement and appreciated being able to make referrals, but they realized that sometimes these patients never got to see the doctor and then did not receive any care that the nurses could have provided at Jaiama. Changes in the government staffing righted the situation within a short time.

The original message was "Dayton requests Gess serve as executive secretary until January, 1959." However leases and other official duties were still being signed in the fall of the year. I also found myself dedicating churches such as Foindu and Lalehun. There were many baptisms, including Kurt Arthur Harris and Linda Marie Phelps. Sermons and speaking engagements averaged one or more each week.

A summary of highlights of 1959 included: the birth of Kurt Arthur Harris, May 23, 1959; the birth of Andrew David Gess, September 11, 1959; and the Kayima Mobile Trek in which we faced the near tragedy of losing a patient in surgery. However the receptiveness of the people at the evening services where there was singing, praying and testimonies, was most encouraging. A number of people raised questions about beginning the Christian life. It was especially thrilling to share with Chief Fasulaku the joy that is found in accepting and serving Jesus Christ. Another highlight was the Saima and Masakunda trek described elsewhere. There were the visits to Rotifunk of Sir Milton Margai, Dr. John Karefa-Smart, and other notables. One visitor did not come under his own power. Dr. Rolf Holst Ronness, prominent dentist and acting ambassador from Norway, and his wife, June, a medical doctor and one time mayor of Freetown, were socializing with Mr. John Akar, whose parents operated the largest retail facility in Rotifunk. Dr. Rolf came down with an overwhelming attack of malaria. Parenteral fluids and appropriate medication restored him.

John Akar was well known as the director of the internationally noted Sierra Leone dance team. They performed on numerous occasions in Europe as well as in the United States. His artistry included authoring the words of the Sierra Leonean National Anthem:

High we exalt thee, realm of the free,
Great is the love we have for thee.
Firmly united ever we stand,
Singing they praise, O native land.
We raise up our hearts and our voices on high,
The hills and the valleys re-echo our cry,
Blessing and peace be ever thine own,
Land that we love, Sierra Leone.

One with a faith that wisdom inspires,
One with the zeal that never tires,
Ever we seek to honour thy name,
Ours is the labour, thine the fame.
We pray that no harm on thy children may fall,
That blessing and peace may descend on us all.
So may we serve thee ever alone,
Land that we love, our Sierra Leone.

Knowledge and truth our forefathers spread,
Mighty the nations whom they led.
Mighty they made thee, so too may we,
Show forth the good that is ever in thee.
We pledge our devotion our strength and our might,
Thy cause to defend and to stand for the right.
All that we have be ever thine own,
Land that we love, our Sierra Leone.

We had the pleasure of doing Kombe's other cataract. Substituting his name "Kombe" for "Paul," I shared Acts 9:17, "Brother Kombe, the Lord Jesus, who appeared to you on your way here, has sent me so that you may regain your sight and be filled with the Holy Spirit." By the grace of God that actually happened.

Another highlight which was very sad involved the train stopping at the Rotifunk station. The route of the train included Rotifunk on its way to Bo and eventually to Kenema. At Rotifunk passengers alighted and freight was loaded and unloaded. Women and children would offer food and small items for sale to the passengers. The interchange through

Figure 2.22. A mother, with baby on her back, selling cakes to train passengers, 1959.

the windows required their getting close to the train and sometimes standing on the tracks. An unexpected lurching start of the train threw a young woman off balance. She fell beneath the wheels which amputated one of her legs. In the confusion and panic no one called for help. She bled to death within 300 yards of the hospital.

On July 29, 1959, I was called to attend a difficult maternity case. The posterior face would not rotate during the bipolar version and the uterus ruptured. We were completely set up for surgical intervention and rejoiced with a live mother and baby.

Dean Spencer, a teacher in woodworking at the Albert Academy, fashioned a boat which was to be christened *Bumpeh Evangel*, the winning name being submitted by Ruth. Such a launch was needed for medical "trekking" on the Bumpeh River. It was powered by a ten horsepower Evinrude outboard motor. Dean, Momoh Yilla, our guide, and I set sail from Freetown November 27, 1959. On hand for the occasion were Grace and Les Shirley, as well as Dr. A. F. Tuboku Metzger, the Sierra Leone Chief Medical Officer. There were some serious delays because of rain squalls so that the cruising was not as speedy as planned.

Our charted plans were to sail directly across the large bay between Kent and the mouth of the Bumpeh River. Rising winds forced us to head for the shoreline which added three or four times the distance to be traversed. Night fell and at midnight we were on mud flats. With the rain it was cold. But most discouraging of all was that our guide became confused as to whether our boat was above or below the mouth of the Bumpeh River. We became silent with prayers rising. Suddenly we realized that we actually were rising above the mud flats. THE TIDE WAS COMING IN! We were being swept along with it into the very mouth of the Bumpeh River. By 7 a.m. we arrived at Rotifunk to the relief of our families, disembarking as triumphantly as Noah from the ark. On November 29th, the following day, the *Bumpeh Evangel* was officially dedicated to help reach people in inaccessible areas with medical and spiritual help.

Another highlight was seeing Paramount Chief Safili Maturi's architectural plans come alive with the building of another missionary residence on the Rotifunk compound. Norma and George Harris and family were privileged to be the first residents.

A medical missionary and his family in "isolation" was certainly not true for us at Rotifunk. Harford School for Girls was only seventeen miles away in Moyamba. Principal June Hartranft and other missionary teachers often signed our guest book and we theirs. These outstanding and scholarly mentors included: Virginia Pickarts, Elaine Gasser, Lucille Esbanschade (later to be ordained), Mary Alice Lippart, Donna Colbert, Lois Lehman, and Britisher Gwen Darbyshire.

We also endeavored to serve the Sierra Leone pastors and their families as they came through. We encouraged their visits because a healthy and energetic pastor was important in the sharing of the Gospel. Sierra Leone medical and political people came to visit and to be treated. Missionaries of other denominations were often guests at our table. We were part of a Christian fellowship that was dynamic and powerful because we moved forward in the strength of Jesus Christ, the Savior of the world.

Rotifunk, 1960

On January 9, 1960 *The Daily Mail* had a spread on the dedication and launching of the *Bumpeh Evangel*, designed to ply the Bumpeh River waters. The tides are of great magnitude by the time the river reaches

Rotifunk. At low tide launches are not possible. The dedication that took place on Sunday afternoon at 4 p.m. was during low tide. The *Bumpeh Evangel* was not able to move until after the distinguished guests had left. Subsequent sailings proved delightful and useful. Not only was the hospital reaching out weekly to the clinic in Taiama and occasional visits elsewhere, it was reaching out to the people in our own backyard who previously were inaccessible. No one enjoyed the dedication service more than Dean Spencer who lovingly had built it from scratch. The *Bumpeh Evangel* was a joy to behold.

At the height of the dry season, guests easily made their way to Rotifunk. This was also true for the vast numbers of patients who had learned of Dr. Mabel Silver and her expert and compassionate care and the fact that two American doctors (George Harris and myself) were doing the range of general surgery as well as eye surgery.

Besides Dr. Carl Heinmiller and Dr. John Schaefer of the Division of World Mission, visitors included Bishop and Mrs. Boughman, Rev. German, Max Bailor, Thomas Bangura, who needed to have a "penny" removed from his esophagus (Sierra Leone pennies were nearly the size of American dollars), B. B. Cofield from Liberia, Robert and Sue Spencer of *African Creeks I've Been Up* fame, and many others. We were able to see Don and Lilburne Theuer often, either at Rotifunk or in Freetown, because of the business and accounting part of his leadership and her welcoming missionaries from upcountry to the mission house.

During our March 31 visit to Freetown for committee meetings, we were again invited to lunch with Rena and John Karefa-Smart and their children Rosalie, John, and Susan. Frank Karefa-Smart, John's brother, was also there. It is significant that it was not until February, 2000, forty years later, that we would have the privilege of visiting with Frank again.

Perhaps the most cheered visitor, who arrived several times a week, was Don Appelman, occasionally accompanied by his wife, Joyce. The generator was always needing his help as did the water supply and plumbing. His advice was needed on building construction and repair, especially the new leprosy ward where contractors had a hard time getting the footings and walls straight without leaning. Also, he was able to coax our vehicles to keep running if George Harris was too busy in surgery.

In the final months of our three-year term at Rotifunk, significant

Figure 2.23. Mount Bintumani, the highest peak in West Africa.

treks were taken to Kono land. Sanford Price made annual trips to help with buildings and maintenance of property at Rotifunk and Jaiama. We saw him during a trip that was being made to Kurabunla in April of that year. We visited about an advertisement in *Time* magazine touting Rolex watches that had accompanied mountain climbing teams. The thought came to me that perhaps Rolex watch company in Switzerland might be interested in knowing that following a period of surgery in the Kurabunla area, an assault was to be made on Mt. Bintumani, the tallest peak in that part of West Africa. Their advertising often mentioned that their watches had been to the top of places like Mt. Everest, K-2, and other noted peaks. In the letter I asked them if they wanted a wristwatch to accompany us in the climbing of Mt. Bintumani. They generously sent a Rolex Oyster Perpetual Explorer automatic watch officially certified as a chronometer. They mentioned that the watch would not need to be returned to them. Perhaps they had decided this when research by the staff learned that Mt. Bintumani was only 6,390 feet in elevation. Compared to Mt. Everest's more than 29,000, it would not make for dramatic advertising. The watch was eventually passed on to our oldest son, Tim, and to this day is in working condition. It does not need battery renewals and the watch continues to run on and on. Perpetual

Figure 2.24. Surgical safari at the base of Mount Bintumani in the center of this picture.

motion is a great advantage.

We set out for Kurabonla April 20, 1960, after having had a Rupp Memorial School committee meeting chaired by Gareth Wiederkehr. The road proved difficult. David Kindy, Don Theuer, David Johnson our surgical assistant from Rotifunk, and I were in one vehicle. David Rupp carried the others. We did not succeed in reaching Kurabonla because of the serious road condition, and had to walk the final three miles into the village along with carriers who managed our medicines, supplies, and climbing gear.

Patients needing medical and surgical care were waiting for us. On the first day we did three cataract extractions. The second day included more eye surgery but also femoral and inguinal herniorrhaphies. The early morning surgery on April 23rd was canceled because the patient had a violent cough and we were fearful that his eye surgery might be complicated by the cough. Leaving David Johnson to care for the post-ops, six of us set out for Sukurela at the base of the mountain. We had great camaraderie, good meals cooked over an open fire, and "showered" in open streams. As was our practice, Christian times of service and worship were held each day during which the villagers were invited to participate. My appointment was to conduct a Bible study of II Timothy.

Up at 5:15 April 25, we had devotions and a final packing session. Six official porters, one for each climber, accompanied us to the base camp at 4, 900 feet where our camp was erected. On the way, Gene Ponchot missed capturing a bush goat which would have provided meat for the entire party of twelve that night. With the denial of that feast, our spirits sank. However, just before dark, while it was still raining, one of the porters spotted a huge black boar which at first I thought was a buffalo. I was the only one who still was shouldering a rifle. Two porters dashed off with me downwind of the meandering animal. My telescopic sight was useless in the rain, but it was mounted above an open sight so that we had delicious pork that night. The excitement of the hunt was overshadowed by the discomfort of being wet and cold throughout the night.

Having had success the previous day, I stayed in camp to fix it up, fill water bottles with a hand filter, and better secure the tents for a drier night. During that day Dave Rupp captured two red pigs.

The next morning we enjoyed pork steaks and liver for breakfast. All six of us (Russ Birdsell, Don Theuer, Gene Ponchot, Dave Rupp, Ken Rupp, and myself) made the final climb to the summit at 6, 390 feet. We tarried to have pork sandwiches along with tea and then enjoyed a Bible study on top of the world in Sierra Leone. The view was breathtaking. We planted a British flag, since Britian still claimed Sierra Leone as a colony in 1960, independence coming the following year in 1961. I placed a slip of paper in a sealed bottle with our names and the inscription of II Corinthians 4:5, "For we preach not ourselves, but Christ Jesus the Lord; and ourselves your servants for Jesus' sake." After returning to base camp, Dave Rupp went out alone on a hunt to "sneak up on a buffalo." He did, was successful, and beef was added to our menu of pork.

Coming down to Sukurela the next day, we were caught in a raging tropical storm. For over an hour I huddled beneath a banana plant. We hardly considered the pouring rains as we had come upon fresh elephant spore. Baboons were barking on each side of us. Perhaps the baboons were aware of the heavy loads of pork and beef that the porters were carrying. Meat was shared with the chiefs and their people in the area. The people were especially attentive to the witnessing service prior to the distribution of the hunting catch.

Then it was off to Kurabonla which we reached by noon. We were hardly prepared for the excitement that was taking place at our eye camp. David Johnson had been dressing the surgical patients. Especially enthusiastic were the eye patients who had been blind but now could see. We were grateful to have had a part in the Lord's healing.

On our return trip we stopped at Kamron and were graciously received by Jake and Ruth Schierling who encouraged us to tarry and get cleaned up at their facilities. The night was spent at the Monko Resthouse where we concluded out study of II Timothy.

The following morning we finally arrived back in Kabala. It was a joy to see our children, Tim, Mary, and Beth. Another student, Ron Baker, heard us relate the interesting stories of the eye surgery and the mountain climb. More than forty years later when speaking to some premedical students at Huntington College, he related the incident of how these blind patients near the Loma Mountains were able to SEE AGAIN because of a missionary's trek to that far-off place. The impact of these events prompted him to consider medicine which resulted in his serving at a medical missionary in Sierra Leone, Africa, for many years.

We had another school board meeting and then Gene Ponchot, David Johnson, and I set out. We stopped at Magburaka where Wilbur Warner and his wife invited us to share their supper. Finally there were only David and me to continue on to Rotifunk where by God's grace we arrived by 10 p.m. Within ten hours I was back in the Rotifunk surgical theatre.

The final medical trek of 1960 to Kono began June 10th. At 3 p.m. after having completed a total hysterectomy at Rotifunk, a stop was made at Taiama where eight sputums had been prepared for examinations. Five of the eight were positive for tuberculosis. Along with onchocerciasis and the many tropical diseases, tuberculosis was one of the most dreaded diseases in Sierra Leone. AIDS was not on the scene at that time. Going on to Bo and Manjama, equipment was delivered to Les and Winnie Bradford. A warm welcome and a delicious meal was enjoyed with the Ben Clossans.

The following day breakfast was with Clyde and Gladys Galow and then we headed our Land Rover toward Jaiama where we found Tonda Thomas, daughter of Delores and Jack, being troubled with a rash. She had the signs and symptoms of measles.

On beginning the surgical program at Jaiama that had been arranged by nurse Betty Esau, we were met by such procedures as supracervical hysterectomies, cataract extractions, herniorrhaphies, and vesico-vaginal fistulae repairs. On the way to lunch after doing a thyroidectomy, I mentioned to Ruth that some day I might have to face the complication of "nicking" the recurrent laryngeal nerve. The next day I was devastated. The thyroidectomy patient could not talk! After two days of agonizing and self recriminations, the patient greeted me in a normal voice. Edema had temporarily blocked nerve transmission. Along with the patient I was alive again in this dangerous world.

Operations of this type were repeated the following days. The number of surgeries was astounding. On June 16th one of our patients nearly went into a potentially fatal asthmatic crisis. Our urgent prayers and available ephedrine and aminophylline thankfully saved the patient. The final day was spent doing less involved operations such as circumcisions and tooth extractions.

We were humbled when our patient, Paramount Chief Moriya, from Kangama said, "Thank you for saving my life." The reply that came forth from my lips was, "I wish you the blessing of the Lord Jesus Christ." Nothing more was said.

Later in the day Paramount Chief Dudo Bona took Joseph Solo Cole, the surgical assistant, and me to see the mining of diamonds. I could not help but share with him Jesus' story of the Pearl of Great Price – possessing the Lord Jesus Christ as personal savior.

Again the next two days involved only minor surgeries that would not need extended followups. Ruth and I were humbled by the expression of thanks and gifts such as country cloth for Ruth and a gown for me. On the morning of the twentieth, ten days after leaving Rotifunk, we packed the Land Rover which had been sold the day before to Isaac Williams. He allowed us to drive it back to Rotifunk from which he would have his driver pick it up. The evening of July 21 found us in our own beds at Rotifunk. We prayed for the uneventful recovery of the patients we had treated at Jaiama and for Betty Esau, who bravely was serving alone in this most distant of our clinics.

On July 6 George and I responded to an urgent call from Taiama. An eclamptic patient was in serious trouble. We set up for an extraperitoneal C-section which resulted in a mother and baby doing well.

After getting the older children from Kabala and selling Tim and

John's bicycles, we boarded the *Accra*, August 12, 1960, for the ocean voyage to England. The children thoroughly enjoyed the deck games and the other ship activities. Docking in Liverpool we were met by Pat and Nina Flynn. Pat and I were classmates at Evangelical Theological Seminary, Naperville, Illinois. He was doing a pulpit exchange in Birmingham. With a twelve seater Bedford personnel car we visited Keswick, Edinburough, Glasgow, Blantyre, the birthplace of David Livingston, Loch Lomond, the Firth of Forth, Earlston, where Dr. Sloan of the Mission to Lepers spoke so eloquently, Doncaster, and finally London.

On August 17th we bordered the *Saxonia* for our trip across the ocean to Montreal, Canada. The first day on the rolling ship found Andrew taking his first two steps. We traveled up the St. Lawrence River and docked August the 24th. Mother and Dad Gess were at the dock to meet us. We also had the pleasure of seeing my high school buddy, Fred Kobler. Wally, Elsie, and Heather Thomas entertained us in their home. Elsie was Ruth's Canadian cousin. A train trip to Toronto and then to Buffalo, New York, eventually reunited us with my sister June and her husband, Ed Malin, as well as Mother and Dad.

We were on American soil again, but within four years after a residency in ophthalmology at the University of Minnesota, we would be back in Sierra Leone with an eye program at Taiama.

Taiama Eye Clinic.

An Eye Doctor to Taiama

Following the eye residency at the University of Minnesota, we packed our barrels for the return to Sierra Leone. Our stationing was at Rotifunk. We outfitted the previous leprosy building for an eye unit. The busy schedule began.

The main hospital had no surgeon at that time. I was remembered as a general surgeon from 1957 to 1960, and was called upon to do both general and eye surgery. The candle was burning furiously at both ends.

A decision was made by the medical board to transfer the eyework to Taiama, centrally located in the country. It was on the highway with Freetown 118 miles to the west, Bo sixty miles to the East and a railway station eight miles to the south. We were to learn that Taiama was a stopping off place for travelers between eastern centers such as Bo and Kennema and Freetown on the coast.

Since Ruth was an R.N., the medical board reassigned Miss Metra Heisler to another needy area as was done so many times in her life, but always with her understanding and cooperation. Ruth was to care for the general medical problems; I was to do the eye care and Ruth's referrals, especially cardiac patients.

On one occasion, difficulty was encountered on making a trip to Bo for a missionary council meeting. Heavy rains caused a pileup of vehicles near Mano. Stragglers came back to Taiama for shelter. The next day we decided to go a roundabout way adding thirty miles to the trip to Bo. Less than ten miles from Bo another pileup of lorries and cars was met. One lorry stuck in the mud was leaning precariously. The motto printed on the top of its bed was "Help me, I'm falling."

Missionaries from the Freetown area turned around and went back to Freetown. We followed them and enjoyed two days at Hamilton Beach before returning to our busy schedule at Taiama.

The move to Taiama in February of 1965 meant starting all over again with the eye program. The $20,000.00 raised for the new eye facility intended at Rotifunk had been used for the upgrading of the general surgery program. A contingency fund of $1,700.00 was all that remained. By counting blocks, sand, cement, and metal sheeting for the roof, an optical building was put up at Taiama with that amount in less than a year.

During the building, spare rooms at the end of the clinic were set up for examining and refracting lanes. An area was partitioned off in the maternity ward for an eye theatre. A well was dug. A carport was set up. The cisterns were repaired. An old generator which had been on its last legs for several years was repaired. One electric line was strung to the clinic and one to the residence which could be used when the clinic was not using the power. The three buildings were connected by covered walkways to protect the staff and patients from the heavy rains.

Don Appleman, Les Bradford, Les Shirley and other missionaries installed electric wiring, tiled floors, and contributed to the major repairs of the clinic and missionary residence.

The program rolled along with daily increasing numbers of operations, general as well as ophthamological. Obstructed and incarcerated herniae could not be turned away. Ma Abby Johnson and Yebu Smart with their busy maternity program presented patients in need of emergency Cesarean sections. There were many other emergencies. On New Year's Day, 1965, a hysterectomy needed to be done. We had no IV stand. A nurse held up the bottle until the carpenter could put together an appropriate stand. Joe Solo Cole, Alfred Bangura, Willie Williams, and Joseph Sowa handled the flow of eye patients. Mr. Stewart visited us frequently from Njala University and serviced the optical equipment. We began edging lenses and producing glasses as a finished product.

Figure 3.1. Sister Hillary visits.

Slit lamp examinations revealed live swimming microfilariae of onchocerciasis in every second patient. Many patients were already at the end stages of their disease with irrevocable blindness. We began the dangerous treatment of onchocerciasis with Banocide and Antrypol. Severe skin reactions occurred. Some included all mucous membranes.

It was Ruth's challenge to monitor the oral steroids to give protection to the patients. Alfred Bangura became expert at doing the intravenous injections. Urinalyses were done to alert the presence of proteinuria leading to a cutback or temporary discontinuance of the medicine. The wonderful discovery of Mectizan (ivermectin) by Merck, Sharp, and Dome was still not available for the more than twenty million people infected with onchocerciasis, known as river blindness.

It was a busy program working hand in hand with Pastor B. A. Carew and his church across the street known as "The Cathedral in the Bush." Things were coming together and were under control.

We were privileged by the occasional visit of Sister Hillary, director of the Catholic Hospital at Serabu. It was wonderful to talk "shop" with one of the best surgeons in Africa. Her wit and charm made her visits a high point for our children.

Most of our family was together during the summer of 1965 as we had the pleasure of Tim and Mary's visit during a break from their studies at Westmar College, LeMars, Iowa. Tim observed some eye surgery and scrubbed in on a herniorophy emergency for a non-reducible incarcerated bowel. Beth was at the Hillcrest School, Jos, Nigeria, as a junior. John, Paul, and Andrew were with us during their vacation from the Rupp Memorial School in Kabala, Sierra Leone.

. . . THEN IT HAPPENED!

Hepatitis

August 20, 1965. Paul came down with hepatitis. We promptly administered gamma globulin by injection to Tim, Mary, John and Andrew.

August 21. It was too late for John. The following day he developed clinical signs and symptoms of hepatitis. Then I noticed a chill. Was it malaria? Bile in the urine proved that I, too, had hepatitis. Obviously we had been exposed to contaminated food.

August 23. Dr. Sama Banya, physician at Njala University came to attend us. Thirty five years later he was continuing to attend the entire country of Sierra Leone in his position as foreign affairs minister.

August 26. Tim and Mary left Taiama to fly back to the U.S.A. I was unable to leave my bed to see them off. For the next eight days I was too ill to even make entries in my journal. On September 4th, news came of Dr. Albert Schweitzer's death which intensified the depths of my despair. I was getting weaker and more icteric (yellow) by the day. I could not eat.

September 5. Pastor and Mrs. Carew visited. Their prayers were a great blessing. Later in the day Eustace Renner and his wife Zainabu dropped in on their way through Taiama. He, too, prayed, actually kneeling by the bedside. His uplifting prayer was truly appreciated. Except for these prayers, I was at the lowest ebb of my life, wondering if there would ever be a change for the better. I had weakness, liver pain, diarrhea, and the 103 to 104 degree episodes of fever were frightening. This was not typical of the disease. I began to question who constituted the five percent who did not recover from hepatitis. I decided to take chloramphenicol, the same medication that helped our first surgical case in Nigeria thirteen years earlier. It is especially effective against typhoid type diarrheas. Within two days I began to improve in spite of being very icteric.

September 6. Andrew mentioned that he didn't feel well, but he and Ruth set off for the school at Kabala with Mr. James Simpson, his children, and the Spencer's children.

September 7. Andrew and Ruth came back the next day. He was experiencing abdominal pain and his urine was dark. How many more would be affected? Banya dropped in.

September 8. Ate lunch! Urine less dark.

September 9. Allis Ribblett and Clyde Galow here for lunch. It was at this time that the dramatic incident occurred of a snake crawling up onto my bed and over my feet. This is described in another anecdote. Fred and Margaret Gaston brought medicines from Freetown as well as a lawnmower for our large Taiama compound.

September 10. Les Bradford and Les Shirley dismantled the electric generator to take it to Freetown for rewiring.

September 11. Was out of bed today! Jack and Delores Thomas stopped by for a visit.

September 12. Dr. Sylvester Pratt and his nurse stopped in and stayed for supper.

September 13. Les and Grace Shirley, Les Bradford, and Clyde Galow dropped in for a visit to encourage me in my recuperation.

September 15. Am now walking, but weak. Dr. Shadeke dropped in and prayed with me.

September 16. Took the top off the mower to show Ali how to engage the starter gear. Dr. Banya arrived while I was doing this. He laid down the law: "No activity or work for another two weeks."

September 17. Dean and Ramona Spencer, Howard and Mary Mueller dropped in to visit. Mary needed her glasses fixed.

September 19. Virginia Pickerts and Vivian Olson arrived at 4:30 p.m. The Spencers and the Muellers stopped in on their way back to Freetown.

September 20. Les Bradford picked up Andrew to take him to school at Kabala.

September 21. Jim and Cleo Simpson with their children Carol and Tim here for lunch.

September 22. Four mothers delivered from 7:45 a.m. until 11 a.m. Abby Johnson, Yebu Smart, and Gladys are all very busy. Dr. Sylvester Pratt rechecked on me as he journeyed to Freetown. Les Bradford brought the rewound generator and electrical supplies.

September 24. Dressed in street clothes for the first time in three and a half weeks.

September 25. Kurt and Hilda Hein here working on the optical machine.

September 26. Clyde Galow preached at the "Cathedral in the

Bush" church across the street from our missionary residence. His wife Gladys and their son Robbie came along. Robbie accidentally spilled kerosene on our cat which paralyzed it for a short while.

September 29. Clyde Galow, along with Methodists Don and Viola Redman, stayed for supper. The union of the EUB and the Methodist church would take place three years later.

September 30. Jim Beck, Peace Corps, welded our clothesline poles. Vivian Olson arrived 9 p.m.

October 1. Left for Freetown.

October 2. Slept most of the day at Hamilton Beach.

October 4. Returned to Taiama. A new mother had just died with a retained placenta. The nurses were in tears.

October 6. Aggressively began antibiotic treatment for seriously ill Everett Carew, son of Pastor and Betty Carew. A spinal tap revealed cells.

October 7. Did a Swan Scleral imbrication burying a rod of synthetic material on Mr. Wright's superior temporal tear and temporal disinsertion.

October 8. Treated Fred Gaston's chronic ear infection plus rales in his left chest. After the eye cases, I did a right indirect inguinal herniorrhaphy on a patient who was having difficulty in reducing his hernia.

October 10. Fred much improved. He and Margaret stayed for supper. I had slept most of the day following the church services.

October 13. Dr. Willie Fitzjohn, Dr. S. M. Renner, Mr. Max Bailor visited. A little later, dear Mr. Kundaba from Mano dropped in. I thoroughly enjoyed these visits without feeling tired. I must be well. Thank God.

Finally Ruth will receive some needed help with the busy Taiama clinic.

Burn Care

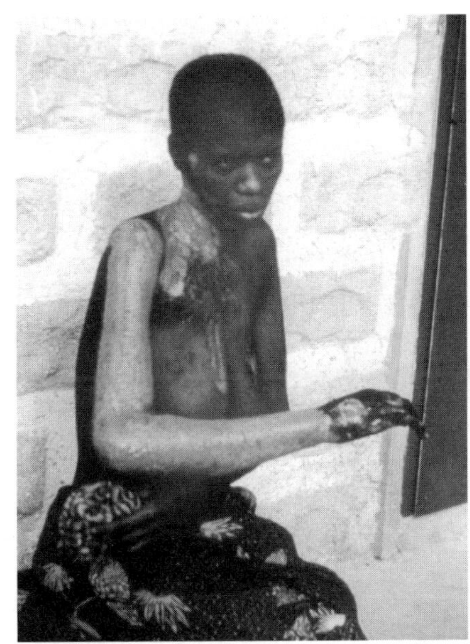
Figure 3.2. Burn care.

During our time at the Taiama Eye Clinic Ruth conducted a general clinic. On one occasion she was presented with an overwhelming burn challenge. It involved weeks of personal intensive care. Ruth tells it in this way:

"The clinic was closed for the day when I was called to admit a severely burned woman. Her right arm and neck were covered with agonizing burnt flesh. She became our special concern for many weeks. Lowell had recently read that a new treatment for severe burns was being investigated using a dilute solution of silver nitrate compresses.

We patiently compressed the patient with this solution day after day. Then came the period of delicate skin grafting, taking pinch grafts from the patient's waist area to her arm and neck. I can still hear her pleading, "Mawo, mawo," which means "Wait, wait," with the changing of the moist dressings. Amazingly the skin grafts took, and she was finally discharged from the hospital.

With the help of Betty Carew translating into Mende, we were able

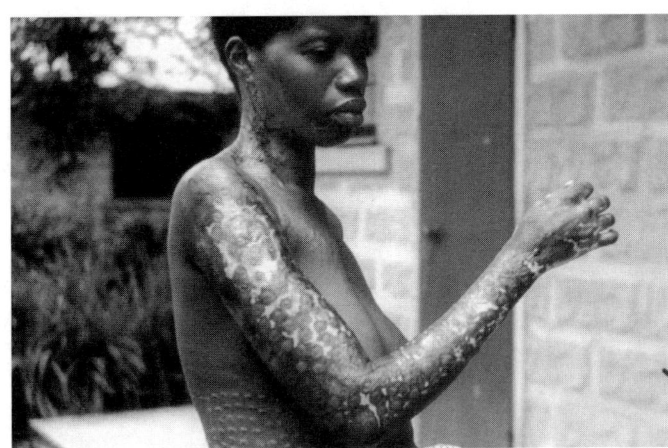
Figure 3.3. Pinch grafting.

Figure 3.4. Burn Care. Marvelous healing.

to share our reason for being in Taiama and the message we brought of God's Son and his love for all.

She came from a distant village and we didn't think we would ever see her again. She did return later wearing a new dress and presenting us with a tray of beautiful rice she had grown. She wanted to say, 'thank you!' What joy!"

Fish Bone Surgery

He was only twelve years old, but like a man, Simeon Thomas stood tight lipped between his father and his uncle. Occasionally an uncontrollable cough erupted with grimacing caused by the pain. The father explained that while eating fish, he began to gag. In spite of vomiting, "it" remained "stuck."

I became especially concerned when I learned that two days had passed before coming for help. The fact that they had come to an eye hospital at Taiama did not deter them. My worry was that the bone may have already eroded into the mediastinum. A dear friend, wife of a trial lawyer, almost died when an esophagoscope perforated the esophagus during a routine examination.

Surgical companies and detail representatives have always been generous in sharing instruments no longer on the front part of the shelves but still of good quality and use. I had been given several esophagoscopes and bronchoscopes with attendant claw forceps up to twenty inches in length that could be directed down the tube. Perhaps I should have given them to other hospitals, but here they were at an eye hospital. I loved good instruments – the very feel of them gave me a measure of delight. I had used instruments of this kind in my surgical residency. (see "The Sword Swallower"). In the back of my mind there was the thought that I might need them someday.

The boy was lying on the operating table. We had invited his father and his uncle to come along into the surgical suite. They were standing on one side of the table, Ruth on the other. As was our custom, we prayed before proceeding. Simeon grasped Ruth's extended hand. "Dear Lord, you made the lame to walk, the deaf to hear, the blind to see. Bless and heal Simeon. In Jesus name. Amen."

Simeon showed no signs of fear. We had learned years before that patients can go into shock from overwhelming pain while still remaining stolid and uncomplaining. He opened his mouth for topical anesthesia and cooperated perfectly in the positioning to introduce the esophagoscope. He did not squirm or fight while the tube was being inched along down into the esophagus.

Suddenly, it appeared – an unbelievably large and jagged fish bone half way down the esophagus. The long grasping forceps was slipped down the tube. It was apparent that the bone was too large to be drawn into the instrument. Trying to control my emotions and with as low and steady a voice as possible, I instructed Simeon not to move. I extended the forceps beyond the end of the tube and grasped the bone. Slowly the forceps and esophagoscope were withdrawn as one. Had the boy jerked or moved, the forceps would have slipped off. In spite of all the pain he did not even move so much as a finger.

Within several seconds we were able to show Simeon the "big fish" he had caught.

Figure 3.5. Our trek to Saiama where children had never seen a white person.

Operation at Saiama

I had never been this far away from the hospital at Rotifunk, in fact it was nearly to the border of the Republic of Guinea. Arrangements had been made by evangelistic missionaries, Jim and Nancy McQuiston, who were familar with that far off corner of Sierra Leone. Ruth and I had previously done volunteer surgery at Kayima. But even this was not as far out and as far away as Saiama. In order to get to Saiama, we had to ford rivers, actually walking through them with water nearly up to our chins and which almost needed swimming. Also we had to climb a very long mountain of pure rock before ultimately getting to the area. Once we entered the village our arrival was announced by the children screaming and running off into the bush. Apparently white people had not been seen in this remote area.

The village elders received us and helped us to set up camp. By that afternoon some patients were seen and preparations made for surgery the following day. There were people in need of surgery, but for the first day there was only one who was presented to us. In order to allay fears all of our preparations were done outside, even the scrubbing of our hands, prior to surgery. Careful attention was spent on providing a ster-

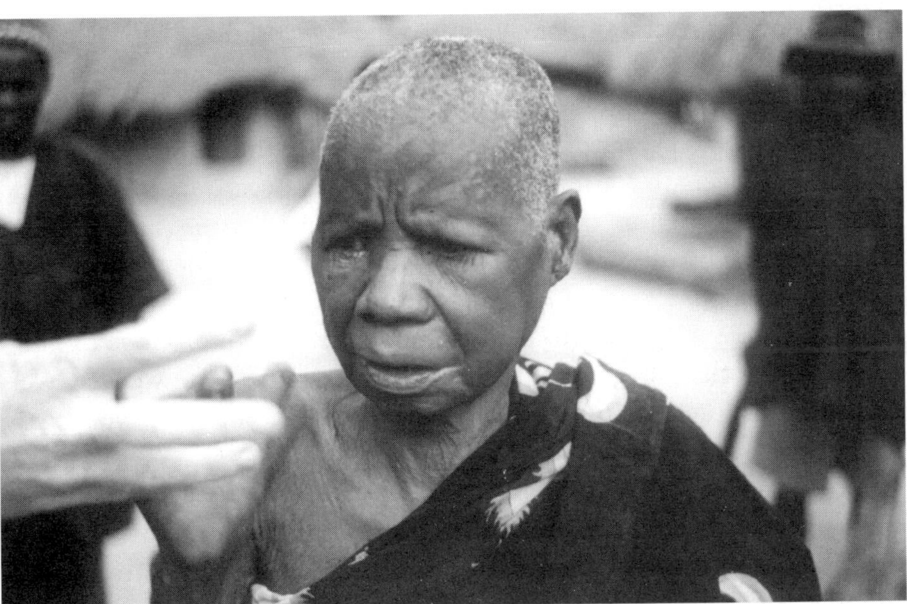

Figure 3.6. The "sacrificed" lady able to see following her operation at Saiama.

Figure 3.7. Rice being sacrificed.

ile field for the operation, and it was done successfully. The following day, at the removal of the bandages, the patient was able to see for the first time in years. A picture taken which depicts the old lady looking at my hands, shows her surprise at being able to see the world.

Later we were to learn that this old lady had been "sacrificed" by the village elders to honor "the white visitors." They felt that little damage could be done by offering an old lady who was entirely dependent, having to be brought food and led wherever she went. With the new found sight, the patient was able to be independent and even productive. The realization of this finally took hold in the community and we were welcomed by the presentation of other patients who needed to have surgery to see again.

It was a time of rejoicing for the people, and we took this opportunity to refer to the way in which the knowledge of Jesus Christ as Savior brings joy into the lives of people. Respectfully they listened to our testimonies. Our far-out visit proved to be as great a blessing to us as well as to the people to whom we ministered. Our only disappointment was that of witnessing a spirit-worship ceremony during which calabashes of rice were thrown into the bush to appease the spirits while hungry children stood by.

The Bridge Over the River Tai

Baptism and the Blood of Martyrs

This tranquil scene depicts a baptismal service. As an ordained pastor, as well as being a medical doctor, I was able to assist in the baptism of 119 people, who were immersed in the celebration of their new found faith in Jesus Christ as the Savior and Lord of their lives. In the background looms the bridge over the Tai River. Its right pillar is grounded on a large and immovable rock. On this rock in 1898, Pastor and Mrs. McGrew were beheaded during the Hut Tax War, a general uprising of the people against the British colonialists who levied the hut tax to institute a source of revenue for political, social, medical and educational development. Many African civil servants who were a part of the British rule lost their lives. All white people, including missionaries, were in great danger. It was to this rock that the Rev. and Mrs. McGrew were taken and killed. At the Hatfield Archer Mission Hospital at Rotifunk

Figure 3.8. Taiama Eye Clinic dedication, 1965.

sixty miles away, an even larger tragedy was taking place. Dr. Hatfield, Dr. Archer, nurse Ella Schenck and evangelists Rev. and Mrs. Cain all were killed.

There is a saying – and not without truth – that the church of Jesus Christ is built on the blood of the martyrs, as it was hardly a year before new and dedicated missionaries came to take up the work. Strong churches evolved where they had been destroyed. The church at Taiama, "the Cathedral in the Bush," was to be one of the largest churches in Sierra Leone.

Dedication, Taiama Eye Clinic, 1965

The day came when Ruth was not expected to run the clinic alone, to nurse me, and to entertain visitors all at the same time. My recovery from hepatitis was gradual but eventually full strength returned. The building and repair projects were completed and the formal dedication took place in December, 1965. Rev. B. A. Carew, conference superintendent, led in the formal dedication and brought the message. Among other guests present were Dr. Moses Mahoi, director in charge of the hospital at Rotifunk, and Rev. Clyde Galow, missionary and field representative of the Division of World Mission.

Optical equipment was provided by Wallman Optical of

Minneapolis, Minnesota, and "Brot Fur Die Welt" of Germany. The Centenary congregation of Steelton, Pennsylvania (through its Carrie Park May Fund) furnished the center. The Division of World Mission of the Evangelical United Brethren Church gave assurance of underwriting current budget items. In the main the program was now self supporting.

Funds to provide a ten kilowatt generator were received from more than one hundred individuals and electric cooperatives in Illinois. A Methodist layman, Arthur H. Peyton, manager of McDonough Power Cooperative in Macomb, Illinois, was on loan to AID of the United States Department of State to make a rural electrification survey of Sierra Leone. In May, 1965 he visited the Taiama Eye Clinic where the urgent need impressed him. His lectures and slides on Sierra Leone resulted in the generator installation in October, 1965. Because of the interest of Mr. Peyton and his wife, Glenna, members of the Wesley United Methodist Church's Fellheimer Trust, further donations were given to the eye program over the succeeding years.

The statistics for the first twelve months of the Taiama Eye Clinic were interesting. 146 major operations were performed, including such procedures as cataract extractions, lid plastics, pterygia excisions, enucleations, eviscerations, retinal reattachments, besides a number of general surgical operations and eight Cesarean sections during the course of more than 150 deliveries in the maternity section. Over 15,000 patients were seen in the general clinic. 5,100 students in the EUB schools were examined during the visual surveys. Complimentary glasses were provided to ordained EUB pastors as well as needy students. Several ministers of the Sierra Leone government came for glasses at the Taiama Eye Clinic, as well as the sister of the prime minister, Sir Albert Margai. It was an honor and a privilege to be able to minister in the name of Christ in this specialized eye ministry.

Typical of the many expressions of gratitude received by the staff at Taiama is the following quote: "Many, many thanks for the spectacles provided....you cannot imagine my joy with their use....words are insufficient to express my gratitude to Almighty God."

Figure 3.9. Scrubbing for surgery in Kurabonla at foot of Mount Bintumani, 1966.

Taiama, Complete Program, 1966

Following the dedication in December, 1965, the program at the Taiama Eye Clinic surged ahead. The fabrication of eye glasses to prescription was especially popular as well as the availability of eye surgery for the blind. The plastic repairs of harelips which were done transformed appearances and personalities.

One young woman who had been overlooked as a bridal candidate was married within four months of her procedure and an eighteen month little girl developed an engaging smile.

Our patients included Mende, Temne, Sherbro, Karonko, and many more people from distant tribes. VIPs found their way to the out-of-the-way Taiama Eye Clinic: government leaders and their relatives (cataract surgery was done on the mother-in-law of the president), doctors, lawyers, Peace Corps personnel, and prominent church leaders. We smiled when we realized that people of all walks of life were stopping at our $1,700 optical building with its sophisticated eye program. We met their needs and unashamedly prayed with them. Ultimately we would send them on their way with "the Lord bless you." Our ministry was in the name of the Lord Jesus Christ to his people.

In April, 1966, mobile eye surgery was made available to the northern reaches of Sierra Leone. Alfred Bangura and Joe Solo Cole packed eye instruments and medications for the trip to the Loma Mountains. On the way we picked up sons John and Paul at the Rupp Memorial School in Kabala. Eye surgery was performed at Kurabonla near the base of Mt. Bintumani. Following the surgeries, a successful ascent was made to the peak of the 6,390 foot mountain by Fred, Dean, and Larry Gaston, Dean Spencer, our sons John and Paul, and myself. We were supplied by game that we captured along the way. It was a sobering moment to have a worship service on the top of the highest mountain in West Africa. Following this mountaintop experience we returned to our work at Taiama.

The most dramatic event in early 1967 was about to take place – the birth of 9 lb. 10 oz. Daniel Harrison, whose parents were teachers at the Sierra Leone Bible College at Jui fourteen miles out of Freetown on the main highway leading upcountry. Even though the Taiama program was officially an eye program, Ray and Arlene Harrison requested that they be allowed to come to Taiama for the delivery of their first child. The Harrisons were aware that, as a general surgeon at Rotifunk, I had been called upon to do many Cesarean sections. For some reason, they were strongly led to want the protection of that surgical procedure if it were necessary. As it turned out, she had a very difficult delivery. It was prolonged and required special help. At the time of the delivery, the baby refused to breathe spontaneously. The stuck valve of the oxygen cylinder could only be turned by the strong hands of the attending father, Ray, who also operated the foot pedal of the suction machine. Attention needed to be given to artificially help with the breathing. Ruth, who was in attendance, then excitedly informed me that the mother was in difficulty. She was continuing to bleed in a way that was descriptive of placenta accretia. At that moment, mercifully, the newborn uttered a beautiful cry and began to breathe. Full attention could be directed toward the mother. A manual removal of the placenta was required. Providentially, the uterus remained intact averting the need for a hysterectomy. A detail never forgotten by the parents was the overwhelming presence of flying ants necessitating the turning off of the lights in surgery and managing with what light came from an adjacent room.

There had been a great loss of blood. The mother was very weak and pale. Compatible blood was not available. Wonderfully, in the succeeding days, Arlene gained strength and she and baby Daniel were able to rejoin Ray, a key professor at the Bible College. I always wondered what had prompted this young missionary couple to so strongly feel that they needed to be near facilities for surgical intervention. They were counseled that in any future pregnancies, they should be near adequate facilities for possible complications of this nature. Her next pregnancy was normal. However, with the third pregnancy, she again had to be helped with this recurring complication. We stand in awe of the protection given to missionaries, who go to far off places and are exposed to extreme dangers, willingly, in order to preach and to share the good news of Jesus Christ to save.

The Closing Months, 1967

In 1967 Dr. and Mrs. Don Megill spent considerable time with us in Taiama helping with the program. Don developed into a skillful surgeon, doing herniorrahphies, C- sections, as well as eye surgery.

On February 17 teacher Francis Gitteh Alli drowned in the Tai River. I was asked to identify his body at the river's edge the next day. I was also asked to fire my gun over the river to frighten away the spirit which they believed had pulled teacher Alli under the water. I was unwilling to reinforce fear and homage to evil spirits. It was difficult seeing so many children with amulets around their necks to ward off the spirits of ill health.

On June 23, brave little Melinda Bradford had her umbilical hernia repaired. She was the sweetest of all our post-op patients.

The last months at Taiama were hectic but not chaotic. Surgery was done whenever there was a pause. While doing some eye work at Kamakwie Wesleyan Methodist Hospital, we had the pleasure of being entertained by Dr. Wilbur and Jane Zike. On our trips to Rotifunk, we usually found patients waiting for surgery, especially general surgery.

The three year period of intense work in both general and eye surgery began to tell. On March 2, 1967, a diary entry expressed "surprise at feeling like an old man at the age of 45." Barrels began to be packed and plans made for a sabbatical. What we did not anticipate was the five year length of time that we would spend at the Quain and Ramstad Clinic in Bismarck, North Dakota, during the college years of several of our children.

Our return to Bo in Sierra Leone finally took place in 1972.

When the Dog Bites

An experience that forever remains vivid for me was the terrifying death by rabies of a young woman in Nigeria, Africa. When brought to the Guinter Memorial Hospital she was in the final stages, writhing and screaming. Supportive treatment quieted her somewhat in her final hours.

Years later in Sierra Leone I again was faced with the possibility of another tragedy involving rabies. Angie Myles, the nurse in charge at Taiama, her four children, cook and nanny, had been bitten by a rabid dog. The account was written up by Katharine E. Matchette of Corvallis, Oregon, entitled *When the Dog Bites, Good News*, March-April/1983, as follows:

> Four children plus a puppy should equal happy times. But for Angie and Joe Myles and their four children, the combination nearly spelled tragedy.
>
> The Myles family brought the pup to their home in Taiama, a small interior town in the West African country of Sierra Leone, on January 1, 1982, a Friday. At first the pup seemed withdrawn and frightened. By the following Tuesday his personality had changed. He began jumping and biting everyone who came near. That day he bit the family cook and the nanny who watched the younger children, as well as Jeffrey, twelve, Madiana, ten, and Andy, seven. Four-year-old Michelle was bitten four times.
>
> Angie, a Jamaican nurse in charge of the United Methodist clinic in Taiama, began to be concerned. "I sent the children, cook, and nanny to the government doctor and he cleaned the wounds," she remembers. "He thought the pup had bitten the children because he was not used to them."
>
> But Angie could not shake her concern. "That night after praying, I decided to lock up the dog and observe him," she says. "On Wednesday I noticed he had torn the mosquito-proof wire netting on the door. I became suspicious that he was rabid, but I was afraid to express my fears."
>
> The next Friday Angie planned to conduct a mobile clinic in a nearby village. Before she left she checked on the pup. "As soon as I opened the door he jumped on me and bit me," she says. "I also noticed that he had not eaten and that he had lost a lot of weight."
>
> When she returned from the village, Angie went to the doctor and told him her fears. They called a veterinarian who came to the clinic immediately. "It definitely looks like rabies," he said when he heard Angie's story and saw the pup.
>
> Only once in medical history has a human being contracted rabies and survived. Angie knew she must find vaccine immediately. "I went to my

room to pray," she recalls. "But the words would not come out. I cried both for my children and for my dog. Then I could hear a voice saying, 'Fear not,' for 'underneath are the everlasting arms.'" (Deuteronomy 33:27).

At 8:30 p.m. she was finally ready to begin the 116-mile trek to Freetown, Sierra Leone's capital. As she left, Angie stopped at the clinic where a prayer group she had started was meeting. "I told them what had happened and asked them to pray," she says. The group stayed until midnight, she learned later.

In Freetown Angie could locate only a few boxes of outdated duck embryo vaccine—not nearly enough for the series of 14 to 20 painful injections each of the seven victims would need. It would be better than nothing, she decided, and bought it. She had hoped to find the newer, more effective, and less painful human diploid vaccine.

Before she left Freetown Angie stopped at the home of Anna Morford, mission treasurer, to seek help. No one was there, so Angie left a note on the door telling of their plight.

"Sad, depressed, and dejected, I made the trip back to Taiama," Angie says. "I prayed, when I could, between tears. Again I could hear, 'Underneath are the everlasting arms.'"

Rabies confirmed

At home in Taiama Angie could only wait and trust. On Sunday the puppy died. "The veterinarian found rabies in both the brain and the salivary gland," Angie remembers. "I was given the opportunity to view the specimens under the microscope. I could not keep back the tears when I thought of my children, cook, and nanny."

In the meantime Anna Morford had returned to her home in Freetown on Saturday evening. She found Angie's note and shared its contents with Dr. Lowell Gess, a visiting ophthalmologist from Alexandria, Minnesota.

Dr. Gess contacted the Peace Corps headquarters in Freetown, where he learned there was no vaccine to spare because a group of new volunteers must receive preventive injections the following day.

Anna attempted to call the mission's area secretary, Pat Rothrock, in New York, but no one answered the phone.

In desperation Anna placed a call to Sherman and Jessie Morgan, old friends from her home town, Philomath, Oregon, late Saturday night (January 10).

"My first reaction was frustration," Jessie recalls. "What can we do?" But the Morgans were determined to try. Sherman and Jessie spent most of Sunday in futile attempts to place an order with a supplier in Miami.

On Monday morning Jessie finally succeeded in reaching Pat Rothrock in New York with Anna's message. Pat said she'd take it from there. Two hours later she called Jessie in Oregon and told her the vaccine would be shipped out of Lyons, France. Everyone breathed a sigh of relief when Jessie called Anna, the mission treasurer in Freetown, and relayed the good news.

Back in Sierra Leone, missionary Keith Watkin had joined the search. On Sunday the Catholic clinic gave him more outdated duck embryo vaccine, so that the Myles family could continue injections.

Anna spent much of Monday canvassing pharmacies in Freetown. Several had supplies of various types of outdated rabies vaccine, but no one carried the human diploid vaccine she sought.

Tuesday passed with no word from France or New York on the promised vaccine. "We should have a back-up supply," Dr. Gess decided.

Anna contacted KLM (the Royal Dutch Airlines) for help in locating another vaccine source. "The manager had once been bitten by a rabid dog in Zaire, so he was very sympathetic," Anna remembers. "He promised he would try to have it on Thursday's plane.

New supply

By Tuesday, Peace Corps officials had completed their preventive injections. When Dr. Gess assured them that the missions supply was *en route*, they agreed to loan their vaccine. Wednesday morning Angie, Joe, Andy, and Michelle came to Freetown for their injections. Angie took medicine for Jeffrey and Madiana, who had returned to school, but the employees had to continue on the old vaccine.

At this point Anna and Dr. Gess had received no confirmation of either shipment. That afternoon the KLM manager called to say that the vaccine would come on Thursday's flight from Amsterdam.

It was Thursday morning before the long-awaited cables from New York and France arrived. Both confirmed that the vaccine was on the Wednesday flight out of France. But when Anna went to the airport it had not arrived. The Paris airport was snowed in. The flight had left Lyons without any freight.

Since most airlines serve Freetown only once a week, it would be another week before the shipment could be sent. Now all their hopes rested on the supply from KLM. They waited and prayed.

The plane arrived as scheduled. On Friday morning Anna picked up the vaccine without incident and repaid the Peace Corps loan.

Saturday, January 16, just a week after Angie left the note, Anna turned the vaccine supply over to Joe Myles. "It was hard to realize that only a week had passed," she says. "It seemed like an eternity."

Anna looks back on that week with awe. "Why was the telegram so slow in coming? Why wasn't Dr. Gess content with one supply source?" she asks.

Angie Myles knows the answer: "God took control," she affirms. "Many friends and well-wishers prayed on our behalf, and Almighty God, our loving and merciful Father, answered all their prayers. God was faithful to His promise. I thank Him for carrying me, my four children, my cook, and my nanny in His everlasting arms."

In later years, Angie Myles and Ingrid Holmgren conducted an extensive care program for handicapped orphans in Sierra Leone, a project underwritten by the Swedish United Methodist Church. Angie completed the requirements for ordination and used her medical background as director of the medical outreach of the United Methodist Church in Sierra Leone. She continues to be a dynamic preacher of the Gospel. Her life of ministry was made possible by helping hands in the form of a prayer group in Taiama, fellow missionaries, friends in Oregon, General Board of Global Ministry personnel in New York, Peace Corp volunteers in Sierra Leone, and a sympathetic KLM Air Lines pilot. Thanks be to God.

The Gospel and Medicine

The year was 1882. The Rev. Dr. and Mrs. R. N. West arrived at Shenge as God's specially chosen to teach, preach, and heal. This was a continuation of the desire of Christians in America in their sending in 1842 the first missionaries with the light of the Gospel to Sherbro land.

Shortly after the West's arrival, they were sent to Rotifunk accompanied by the Rev. Joseph Gomer to succeed Miss Mair, a Scottish missionary with twenty-six years of rich experience in West Africa. Dr. West depended very much on prayer in the undertaking of difficult situations and challenging patients, telling them that unless God blessed the work he would fail. He had few instruments and little medicine with which to work. However the accomplishments of his ministry was a great power for good. Often missionaries would have been driven from their work but for the doctor among them.

Dr. R. N. West and the Rev. I. N. Cain in 1894 approached the capitol town, Taiama, in Kori Chiefdom. In November, 1896 a deed for 100 acres of land was obtained. The Rev. and Mrs. L.A. McGrew began the mission house December 2, 1896. Visiting was Chief Fora Vong's wife. A group of 150 persons sang "All Hail the Power of Jesus Name" followed by prayer and the reading of Psalm 24. In her remarks, the chief's wife mentioned the needs of the people and welcomed the mission. Mrs.

McGrew was the first to turn over the sod, followed by her husband and then the chief's wife. The service closed with the singing of "Throw Out the Life Line."

The martyrdom of Rev. and Mrs. McGrew four years later is best described in the words of Mrs. Henry Williams:

> *Mr. and Mrs. L. A. McGrew were martyred on a rock in the Taia River May 8, 1898. They were beheaded and cast into the water by a cruel, infuriated, superstitious mob as a last effort for the supremacy of heathenism. Truly as in the day of our Master, they knew not what they did. Although it is not pleasant to witness such a horrible incident it was said that while Mr. McGrew was being beheaded, Mrs. McGrew stood in divine strength and then knelt in prayer for her murderers and for Africa before her life was taken. The love of Christ constraineth. What else could stimulate our missionaries than the martyrs of all ages? Blest be God who gives the victory through our Lord Jesus Christ.*

On the bank of the river an appropriate place was provided for a tablet where it could easily be seen and read as a perpetual memory. A hand points to the rock, and the inscription reads: "On this rock the American missionaries Rev. L. A. McGrew, and his wife Clara McGrew, were massacred May 8, 1898. Consultatory words to all missionaries: Africa must be redeemed. Do not forget your part. Linger a little at the McGrew rock, then let thought be intensified and grow into beautiful acts, and our martyrs shall not have died in vain."

It was significant that by February 18, 1910, sod again was turned, this time by the chief of the Kori Chiefdom, for the establishment of the Mission Building in Taiama. Miss M. E. Eaton, missionary in charge, also joined in the ceremony. At the time of the cornerstone laying, sixteen stones were engraved with the names of chiefs and supporters. One stone bears the name of Mr. and Mrs. L. A. McGrew who twelve years earlier had been killed on an exposed island of rock in the Tai River. Their engraved stones had been taken from that rock. More stones later were taken for the completion of the building. "Upon this rock will I build my church." (Matthew 16:18). Truly it was the blood of the martyrs on which the church was built. Work continued with leaders such as Pastor and Mrs. I. A. Inskip, Pastor C. V. Rettew, and Pastor P. Kaister. Ultimately "the Cathedral in the Bush" was built during the ministry of the Rev. B. A. Carew prior to his election as first Bishop of the United

Methodist Church in Sierra Leone. He drew in local congregations once a month and banqueted the leadership. The Lord's Acre was a dramatic act of stewardship.

The medical work at Taiama at first involved mission leadership such as pastors and teachers. Even in more recent years, Pastor B. A. Carew dispensed medications for malarial fevers. Miss M. E. Eaton introduced a clinic for children at Taiama in 1906. However it was not until later years when Dr. and Mrs. LeFourge, as well as Dr. Mabel Silver, that an organized program was established. Nurses often preceded doctors and organized medical programs assuming great responsibility as described by nurse-midwife Lois Olsen in her book, *Contentment is Great Gain.* an exciting and informative account of her midwifery work. Among others Miss Metra Heisler, Mrs. Gladys Galow, Miss Betty Esau, Mrs. Ruth Gess, Mrs. Angie Myles, and Sister Kalon, shared in this ministry.

From the very beginning the church has realized the importance of medical services in the missionary outreach of the church. In pursuit of this, Dr. Marietta Hatfield sailed from the United States to open the United Brethren medical work at Rotifunk in 1891. The Hatfield-Archer Dispensary at Rotifunk was dedicated in 1904 and new buildings dedicated again in June of 1907. It was nearly a half century later, February, 1951, that the premiere hospital was established at Rotifunk. Dr. Mable Silver was followed by physicians such as Dr. John Karefa-Smart, Dr. Moses Mahoi, Dr. Lowell Gess, Dr. George Harris, Dr. Donald Megill, and earlier by tours of service of Dr. Winifred Bradford, Dr. Allan French, and Dr. LeForge. Perhaps the longest term of service as doctor at Rotifunk second to that of Dr. Mable Silver was Dr. Zenora Griggs, who served for nineteen years before leaving in 1919. The importance of the role of medical services can be pointed up by a statement reported following the sailing of Dr. Marietta Hatfield from the United States to the hospital at Rotifunk. The women's missionary association reported the incident as follows: "Medical work has begun in the history of the mission, and has proved an important factor in aiding in the spread of the Gospel."

Jaiama: Medical work was started in Jaiama in 1910 by the Rev. J. Hal Smith. Nurses who developed the medical program included Miss E. J. Ney, Miss E. M. Haigh, and Miss E. M. Hoyle between the years of 1920 and 1928. In 1928 Dr. and Mrs. E. I. Conner came to serve for a four year period. In 1935 Dr. Gladys Huscher began a ministry of ten years. More recently the medical work has been carried on by Miss N. M. Vesper 1951-1954; Miss Gertrude Bloede, 1954-1955, back 1958-1965; Mrs. Joy Thede, 1955-1958; Miss Lois Olsen, 1958 from June to October; Miss Betty Esau, 1959-1960; Miss Metra Heisler, 1961-1962, 1965-1966, 1969-1970; Miss Brunhilde Goebel, 1966-1976; Miss Renate Horn, 1970-1976; and others down to the time of Friederike (Fritzy) Carlsen, 1990-March, 1993. Names appear in a listing in the appendix.

The Church in Temne Land

Just before the end of the 19th century (March 9, 1899), pioneer Rev. Thomas Franklin Hallowell, a teacher from the school in Rotifunk, along with his wife, journeyed into Temne country and started the nucleus of the first church in Makundu. The Rev. Hallowell was an unusual evangelist with great patience who won the affection of hundreds of people leading them to accept Christianity. His ability impressed the mission leadership, especially the Rev. J. R. King. Within seven years on August 17, 1907, a renovated barri at Yonibana was dedicated by the Rev. E. M. Hursh. Mr. Alfred Smart joined the work. A primary and a secondary school were established, the latter in the 1960s. The church eventually became known as the Hallowell Memorial Church. Other fields of service were established at Rokon, Ronietta, Roruks, Kumrabai (a fine hunting ground where Pa Schutz hunted antelope, guinea fowl, and many other animals), Mamilla, Rochen Kamanda, Rochen Malosa, Maryaka, Magburaka, Mamaligi, Rokell, and Mesengbe.

An agricultural and health program was established through the ministry of the Rev. and Mrs. Donald Pletsch. Animal husbandry as well as the growing of pineapples for a cash crop was successfully implemented. A farmer after seeing how much fertilizer helped a rice crop wanted some of that "medicine" for his rice growing. A comprehensive health clinic was operational. Helen and Don well remember Biarri, from Helen's clinic, who had to rest several times while walking the length of a city block before treatment, but who was playing football with his friends some months later. With these programs the church in Yanibana thrived, extending its influence socially and economically as well.

It was at Yanibana that the Betty Carew Centre was constructed and

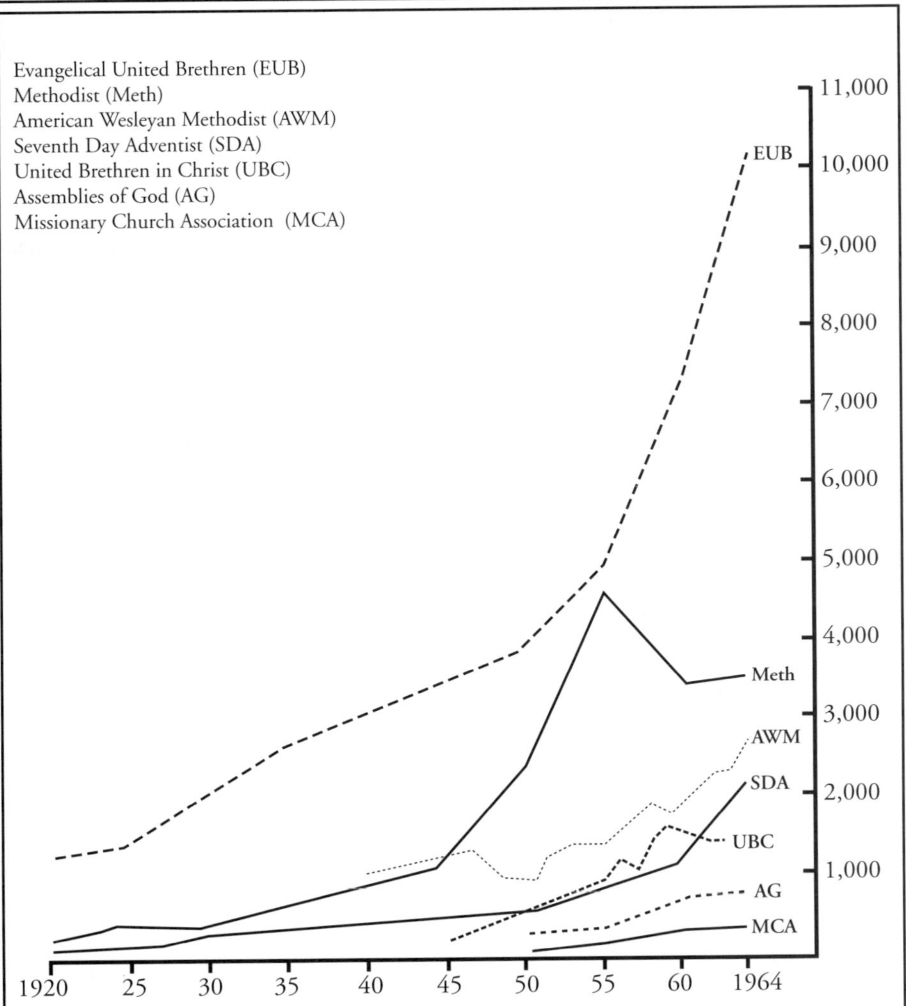

Figure 3.10. These lines show that church growth among the tribes varies greatly from Church to Church. Yet the people among whom the churches work are fairly uniform in their cultural and religious backgrounds. The MCAs have made hardly any impact, while the EUBs have made comparatively great gains. From 1945 to 1955 the EUBs had slow growth – a gain of 1453, or 40.9%, while the Methodists soared – a gain of 3509, or 248.9%. After 1955 the EUBs soared – gaining 5160, or 103.6%, while the Methodists lost – losing 1192, or 25.3%.

established shortly after her death in July, 1971 primarily under the leadership of Ted and Hilda Hebel. It undertakes the teaching of crafts, gara dyeing, and needlework. Women also took their babies to the Centre where there was direction for family life. The literacy work was originally supervised by Mr. A. D. Carew.

The church growth that the Pletches and Hebels witnessed was evaluated in Rev. Gilbert W. Olson's perceptive book *Church Growth in Sierra Leone,* published in 1969. From his findings a striking graph was constructed. The reasons for the dramatic growth, as in the case of the Evangelical United Brethren Church, (now United Methodist Church), or loss of individual church movements, make up the body of his treatise which needs to be read and re-read.

Like Jaiama, Makeni, and other churches in the northern and eastern part of Sierra Leone, the last decade of warring has scattered the Yonibana flock.

The Tragic Death of The Rev. J. Hal Smith
Missionary to the Konos
by **Reverend D.H. Caulker**

The Rev. J. Hal Smith, first missionary to the Konos, died on the 15th of February, 1915, on Monday, at 12:00 o'clock sharp, writes the Rev. D. H. Caulker:

> *The tragic incident occurred in this wise. Soon after morning prayers on that fateful day, Pa Smith heard his chickens making a great noise, and he sent one of the Mission boys to see what was the matter. The boy quickly returned and reported that there was a hawk hovering around with the intention of carrying away a chick. As soon as he heard this, he quickly took his gun and went out to shoot it. Coming near the place, he called me to take hold of his glasses, which I did. He stepped back, and stood on a rock that was near the fowl house, waiting for the hawk to appear. The chickens seeing him rushed toward him, but they were enclosed within a big fence and were unable to reach him, save for one big rooster which got out somehow and began to follow him. In attempting to push it gently aside with the butt of the gun he missed it and the butt struck the ground—immediately going off. He was struck on the right side under the ribs. This happened at eight o'clock in the morning. We took him into the house and sent to call the Chief to arrange to take him down to Freetown. Pa Smith instructed me not to move him at all from Jaiama, because he knew that he*

would not pull through.

I at once dispatched a telegram to Freetown to report the incident. He lingered for four hours and then died. I then sent another telegram to report his death, and we made a nice coffin for him, Pa Momoh and myself. I kept the body for two days waiting for someone from Freetown, but no one came. On the afternoon of Tuesday, the 16th, one Government Officer came to the town, and he came right away to ask if there was anything he could do to help. I told him I would be glad to have him help me in the burial services on the morrow, if no one of our people came to perform the last rites. To this he agreed. On Wednesday, as no one came, both of us went on with the burial service. After the burial, Mr. Bobbridge, as the Government Officer was called, went away on his journey to Yomandu, and on that evening Mr. J. S. Dove got in from Hangha, and in the night about seven o'clock the Rev. J. F. Musselman and the Rev. J. K. Smart came in from Freetown. On Thursday morning we had another service in the graveyard. Mrs. Hal Smith was in America at this time. The tombstone was set on the grave in 1916, June, by the Rev. J. F. Musselman and Bishop A. T. Howard. It reads:

***"God lives and rules and cares"* . . . his last spoken words.**

Figure 3.11. The tragic death of the Reverend J. Hal Smith.

Figure 3.12. Reverend D.H. Caulker in his 113th year.

The Reverend D.H. Caulker

Following the death of J. Hal Smith, the work was in the capable hands of Rev. D. H. Caulker who was forty years old when he travelled with J. Hal Smith to Kono. His faith and devotion to the church and school drew many into the Christian fellowship of believers. He ministered not only to Sierra Leoneans but also to "inexperienced missionaries."

The Rev. and Mrs. Wimmer arrived in Kono in October, 1916 and in 1920 they were joined by Rev. and Mrs. H. H. Thomas and Miss E. J. Ney. Mrs. E. High, a trained nurse, took up the work in 1922. She was joined by nurse E. M. Hiza in 1927, and by Dr. and Mrs. E. I. Conner in 1928. Jaiama became established as a station from which extension programs developed. The Rev. Fred and Margaret Gaston ministered in Kono land for nearly two decades, Fred being in the unusual position of district superintendency on two occasions.

Reports from Fred and Betty Walker noted that they served from 1946 until 1956. When the Walkers were at the central station at Jaiama, other stations in their oversight included Ngandohun, Sefadu,

Yengema, Kangkordu, Keyima, Tombudu, and Hangha. The Walker sons, David and Richard (delivered by Dr. Gladys Huscher) were born in Kono country. Their births and presence were important in opening many hearts and doors to their ministry. Especially appreciated was the faithful and responsible work of Dindi Caulker who served as matron of the girls' home. Being in charge of the boarding homes, the Walkers were involved in the purchase of food supplies, and the preparation and serving of two generous meals of rice and stew each day. Hundreds of bushels of rice were purchased (pan by pan on the back porch) each harvest season and stored in the rice house for daily distribution. At intervals, the rice house had to be cleaned. There were always volunteers for the job. The rats were in demand for evening cookouts by the boys. During their second and third terms of service, the Walkers were involved in extensive building at Jaiama and the Bible Training Center in Bo, besides being acting Executive Director of the field.

As Mr. Caulker related, Mrs. Smith was in America at the time of the accident having been sent home because of ill health. Her interest in Sierra Leone and Kono never waned. We cherished personal letters of encouragement from her especially during the time that I served as Field Representative in the early 1950s.

On February 9-10, 1985, Ruth and I made a special 200 mile trip to Jaiama to visit with Pa Caulker. He was in his 113th year. His countenance was well preserved, his mind quick, and his faith strong. The lady caring for him sang a hymn. We read from II Corinthians 4:5, "For we preach not ourselves, but Christ Jesus the Lord: and ourselves your servants for Jesus sake." We included also the 17th verse, "For our light affliction, which is but for a moment, worketh for us a far more exceeding and eternal weight of glory." In our prayer we thanked God for using him as an instrument of His grace in establishing the church in Kono land.

After several pleasantries, we stepped into our car and returned to Freetown over a bumpy and harsh road, convinced that the long trip was well worth it. We had been in the presence of greatness. Several months later, he died. His soul rests in everlasting peace.

Chapter Four

Bo

Six men (ages 22-40) blind from onchocerciasis (river blindness) being led by a small boy. Merck's medicine, Ivermectin, can now prevent the resultant blindness.

Theologically Proper

During our five year leave of absence from 1967-1972, there was the merger of the Evangelical United Brethren and the Methodist churches. When Ruth and I indicated that we were ready to return to the mission field, we found that a reassessment and a re-evaluation was required. Our early service was with the Evangelical church and subsequently with the Evangelical United Brethren church.

Examination involved medical internists and even a psychiatrist. It was also the procedure that returning missionaries be brought before a panel of jurisdictional church representatives which included youth delegates.

One college student from Hamline University probed deeply as to our spiritual motivation for medical missionary service. The scene was turning into a courtroom drama. Ultimately I paused and I asked her what United Methodist church she attended. Her reply had the effect of a lead balloon which ended the interview. She said, "I am not a United Methodist. I am a Christian Scientist."

We were on our way back to Bo in Sierra Leone.

Methanol Poisoning

During our time of service at the Bo eye clinic in Sierra Leone we had the occasion to successfully treat an eye condition of an expatriate of Russian descent. At a later date we were presented with a gift of appreciation. On opening it, we found a large bottle of vodka. We didn't know quite what to do with it, and so we put it on a shelf in a storeroom. Later on when it was observed by someone, we decided that perhaps there was no real use for it. We "liberated it" by pouring it down the sink.

It could not have been more than three or four months later that we examined a nineteen year old student who was led into the clinic by several of his friends. He was nearly blind. We tried to get a history but were not successful as to the cause of the blindness. Examination showed the pupils to react rather sluggishly and fundoscopic examination showed some hyperemia of the disc. At this point we asked if by any chance he had been subjected to the ingestion of some sort of poison. Ultimately we were to learn that in the laboratory of the secondary school he and several of his buddies had surreptitiously taken a bottle of methyl alcohol, otherwise known as wood alcohol, and had imbibed. More than two hours had passed. We knew that there were real problems ahead for him without aggressive treatment. Visual impairment fortunately can be the first sign which brings the patient to the clinic for what help there is.

We immediately dispatched a runner to the downtown of Bo to try to find some rum or vodka, hoping that we could find something of 75 or at least 50 percent alcohol content. The rationale for it was that methyl alcohol when it is broken down forms formic acid and formaldehyde which produce an acidosis and cause gastroenteritis, pulmonary edema, and retinal ganglion cell and diffuse retinal damage. However, if the patient is given a large amount of ethyl alcohol, the ethyl radical has the disposition to replace the formaldehyde radical and thus prevent the poisoning effect of the methanol. This was the first time in my life that I was encouraging someone to have a "second glass." In fact we encouraged him to take an adequate amount but not enough to make him dangerously drunk.

We were successful in getting an adequate level of alcohol in his system. It must be mentioned that we also treated the patient for his acidosis with sodium bicarbonate and this along with the oral ethanol was successful in that the ethanol competed with the methanol to neutralize it. I am happy to report that within a four week period the patient came to the clinic without being led and eventually was able to read again in spite of the fact that he had lost his central vision in the initial episode. After this experience perhaps we will have second thoughts about "liberating" vodka the next time it is given to us in appreciation for services rendered!

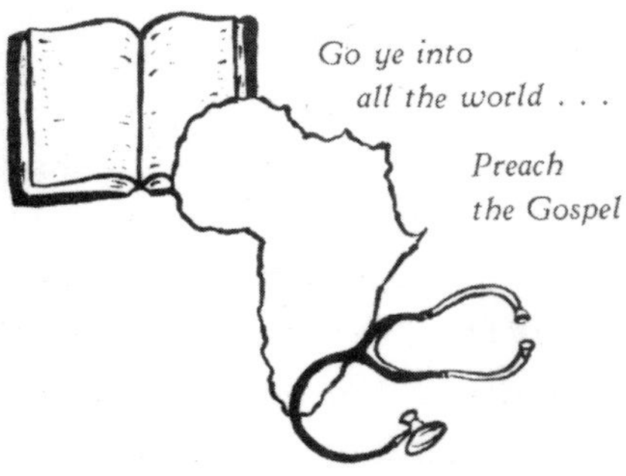

Be ye steadfast, unmoveable, always abounding in the work of the Lord . . . your labor is not in vain in the Lord.
I COR. 15:58

Sudan Interior Mission
164 W. 74th St. New York, N.Y. 10023
405 W. Huron Toronto, Ont., Canada

Dr. Jeanette Troup
S.I.M., Jos, Nigeria, W. Africa

Figure 4.1.

Lassa Fever and a Succession of Helping Hands

Missionaries develop a deep bond of friendship during their ministries so far away from "home," that is, the place of their birth and their concerned families. Over a period of time the relationship with indigenous people become "family." Ruth and I often remark that we have as many dear friends in West Africa as in the United States.

Dr. Jeanette Troup and her brother, Roger, also a physician, were medical missionaries in Nigeria and dear friends of ours in Christ. They medically cared for the members of our family during our time in Nigeria, 1952 to 1955, while we were serving at the Guinter Memorial

Hospital in Bambur. This was also true of the extended missionary family. Roger and I performed a cholecystectomy for Mrs. Ira McBride, the wife of our mission superintendent, Dr. Ira McBride, when gall bladder attacks became unmanagable.

Our next term of service was to be in Sierra Leone, West Africa, following a two year residency in general surgery at the Akron General Hospital. The senior Troups served a church in Akron, and took our family under their wings. We could not believe how kind and helpful they were to us.

In the succeeding years we were to be separated – the Troups in Akron and Nigeria – the Gesses in Minnesota and Sierra Leone.

Suddenly, on the international scene in 1969 there appeared the specter of an untreatable deadly disease, called Lassa fever, a defined group of RNA viruses. The outreak occurred in Jos and Vom. It was characterized as a febrile illness with an ulcerative pharyngitis and hemorrhagic predisposition. Upwards of twenty cases were traced to a single woman admitted to the Evangel Hospital in Jos. We were to learn that Dr. Jeanette Troup acquired the disease and died subsequent to an accidental needle prick while performing an autopsy on a patient who had expired with Lassa fever. We could not believe that such a tragedy could befall one of the most kind, considerate, able and devoted servants of the Lord Jesus Christ.

A massive hunt was mounted to study Lassa fever and to determine the vector. Mice and other rodents were high on the list of suspects. The investigation included Sierra Leone, to which we had returned in 1972 to open up the Bo UMC Eye Clinic. In 1970, Dr. John Frame of the Division of Tropical Medicine of Columbia University searched for patients who had recovered from Lassa fever in Sierra Leone. Being next to Liberia he harbored suspicions that an outbreak might occur in Sierra Leone. He prepared a report outlining the general characteristics of the disease. This report was placed in my hands as Ruth and I were opening the Bo Eye Clinic. In turn I passed it on to other United Methodist mission stations.

It had been five years since we had left the eye program in Taiama. Refractive equipment had been stored during this period at Rotifunk Hospital. We brought it all to Bo and along with John Morlai spent days cleaning it up from the soilings of mice and cockroaches.

In mid 1972, Dr. Paul Goff, a Peace Corps doctor in Freetown, was alerted to a devastating febrile illness occurring at the Panguma Catholic Hospital. Panguma was 17 miles from our Bo Eye Clinic. The memory of Dr. Jeanette Troup's tragic death prompted daily side glances at any febrile patient with malaria. Any treated fever that would go on for more than five days was held as highly suspect.

Research teams traveled to Panguma and tirelessly worked for a month. They systematically set out to determine the vector. Even more encouraging for us was the fact that they brought along plasma with Lassa fever antibodies that was life saving.

From their research it was finally determined that the deadly virus was carried by a wild field rat, whose urine, when dry, released the virus into the air along with other dust particles. This discovery brought a marked relief to us, as well as to Dr. Justin and Marge Sleight who had joined us for a year of volunteer eye surgery at Bo. Just knowing from where the virus came, made us breathe a little easier and deeper.

While the research began in Nigeria and ended in Sierra Leone, the best minds and medical practitioners came from great distances including the United States and Britain. Much has been learned in subsequent years on how to treat and manage Lassa fever. A new treatment regime has reduced the fatalities tenfold. In July, 2000, four persons including a doctor, died in Freetown of Lassa fever. The doctor had been treating four of his relatives for the disease. Also, a British volunteer in Sierra Leone contracted the disease, and in spite of state of the art treatment in England, could not be saved.

More helping hands will continue to be needed in the 21st century.

Schistosomiasis

Extrusion of the eye (proptosis) always presents a challenge for diagnosis. Our patient with proptosis of his left eye was a twelve year old boy. A mass could be felt in the orbit. No longer could he move his eye and double vision was incapacitating. We elected to remove the mass or at least biopsy it.

At the time of surgery the mass was found to extend deep and wide in the orbital cavity. Removal would certainly damage essential eye, muscle, and nerve structures. A biopsy was taken and sent to the Armed Forces Institute of Pathology in Washington D.C. Over the years Dr. Zimmerman had helped us with diagnoses. On one occasion we received a large bill for the preparation and examination of a tissue which we had sent them. When I wrote a letter mentioning that Dr. Zimmerman had done this gratuitously in the past, I received a canceling invoice.

Dr. Jakobiec's examination produced a ripple effect at the Armed Forces Institute of Pathology. To their knowledge after reviewing the literature, this proved to be the first case of Schistosomiasis involving the orbit of an eye. This notoriety led to the publication of *Granulomatous Dacryoadenitis caused by Schistosoma haematobium*, Archives of Ophthalmology, Feb. 1977, Vol. 95, pages 278-280, Jakobiec, Gess, Zimmerman.

From my youth up, I had been aware of "swimmer's itch" caused by a schistosome species carried by migratory birds. Lake Koronis was host to this malady and for a week or two each year prevented campers at the Lake Koronis Assembly Grounds from really enjoying a dip in the lake. Careful toweling prevented most of the pruritic papular dermatitis.

Schistosoma haematobium was something else. It could cause blood in the urine and also occasionally damage to the liver.

It was understandable that the inflammation and fibrosis around the eggs created the mass behind this boy's eye. A urinalysis revealed the spiked eggs of Schistosoma haematobium. Following treatment with a trivalent antimony compound, the mass melted away. The eye returned to its normal position and moved easily and correctly again.

"Thou, O Lord, art a God full of compassion." **Psalm 87:15**

Popeyed

He was cupping the left side of his face with his hands. At the command of his father he removed his hands. I couldn't believe my eyes. The boy's left eye was extruded onto his cheek. He was not crying, but his companion, another 11 year old boy, had tears streaming down his cheeks. While roughhousing with sticks the friend's stick had gouged out this boy's left eye.

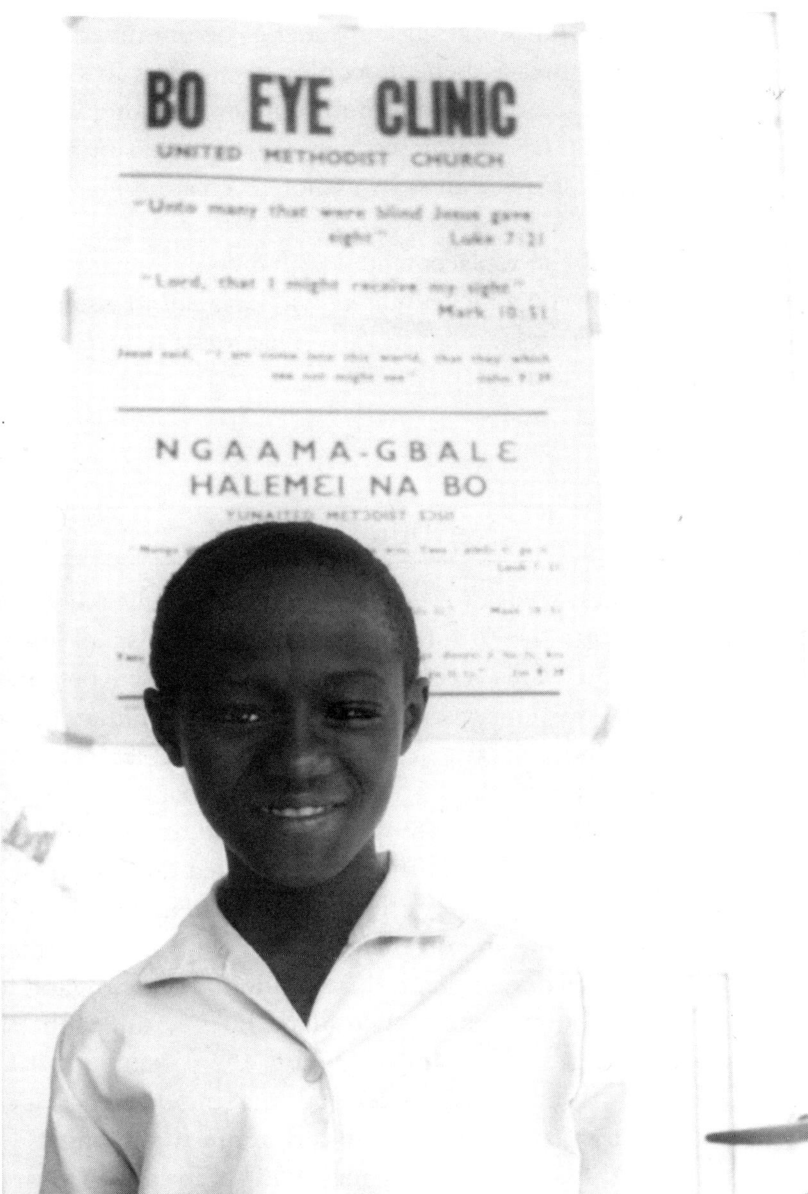

Figure 4.2. "Popeyed."

Immediately we took him to surgery. After applying a topical anesthetic, we simultaneously prayed and irrigated the eye and socket with a sterile isotonic sodium chloride solution. A peribulbar anesthetic was done. It was surprising not to have more bleeding. The vessels to the eye were intact. The s-shaped optic nerve had straightened allowing the eye to come forward. The eye itself appeared to be uninjured.

A wire speculum spread open the conjunctival edges in the orbital cavity. Holding the eye between my thumb, index, and middle fingers, I gently reposited it. The conjunctiva was only loosely sutured to the limbal areas in the four quadrants, so as not to create a pocketing for infection.

After the relief of the replacement, I offhandedly remarked to Dr. Justin Sleight, "I'll bet you a nickel that he will have 20/30 vision or better in a few days." Justin later confessed, "That was the first bet I ever enjoyed losing."

River Blindness

One of the saddest scenes I ever witnessed in Sierra Leone was that of six men, ages twenty-five to forty-five, being led by a small boy. All were irrevocably blind. This was happening in a country where in our early days of medical missionary service the medical community declared that river blindness did not exist in Sierra Leone. And yet, these blind men were representative of the 25 to 30 million people in the world afflicted with onchocerciasis, commonly referred to as river blindness. The culprit is a microfilarial worm that is transmitted during the bite of a small black fly, the simulium damnosum, that breeds in fast moving streams where people bathe and do their laundry. The adult worms can attain a length of six inches and reproduce millions of microfilaria for a time of up to fifteen years. These microfilaria burrow under the skin, causing intense itching to the point of making the patient suicidal. If they invade the eye, an inflammation develops that in 50 percent of cases results in a secondary glaucoma (increase of eye pressure), which if left untreated destroys the eye. These six men had received no treatment. My heart went out to them for they were at a stage at which I could be of no further help. It was too late for the harsh and dangerous treatment with diethylcarbamazine and suramin, the commonly used medications in the 1970s. The World Health Organization (WHO) was trying to help countries in Africa eradicate the black fly by spreading insecticides over the streams with low flying airplanes. Surely there should be some

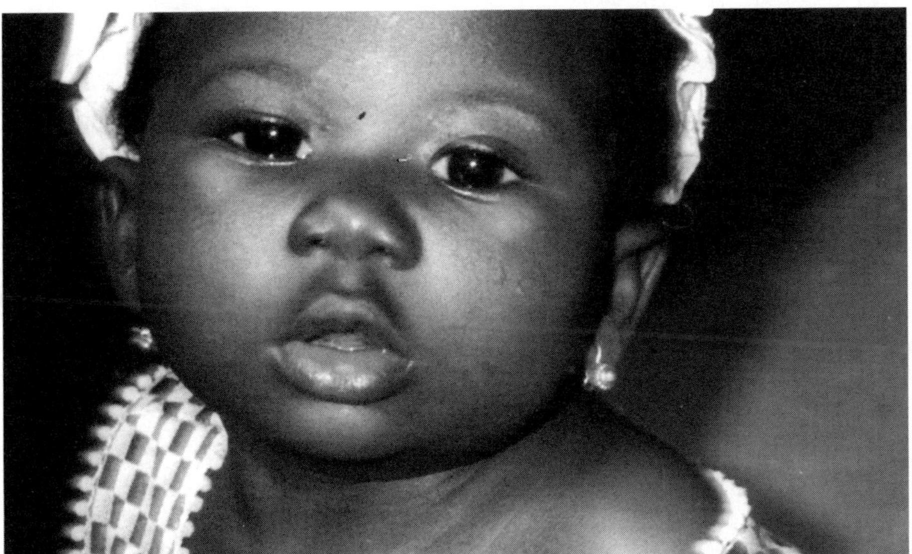

Figure 4.3. Congenital glaucoma unrelated to river blindness causes the eyes to enlarge; a condition that requires surgery to correct.

way that this tragic blindness could be prevented. It became a matter of serious prayer.

It was at Bo that special attention was given to especially secondary glaucoma from the inflammation which was the primary cause of the fifty percent blindness of patients infected with onchocerciasis. Pioneer work by Doctor Cairns in England produced a new procedure called trabeculectomy which incorporated the formation of a protective scleral flap. However, we found success in only about thirty percent of our cases. The plight of the remaining seventy percent was a matter of intense prayer. Was there some way to prevent so many and so young people from becoming blind? Consulting the surgical text books in my possession, an old method of creating a tongue of iris tissue as a path for drainage as suggested by Dr. Stollard became of interest. Instead of smoothing the iris tissue out flat and then having the scleral edges closed over it, the thought came to allow the tongue of iris tissue to curl up on itself with the pigment layer lining the formed tunnel. Theoretically it should stay open as the iris pigment was known to not stick together or grow (heal) to itself.

Permission was granted from new surgical candidates for this untried procedure. It soon became apparent that for secondary glaucomas asso-

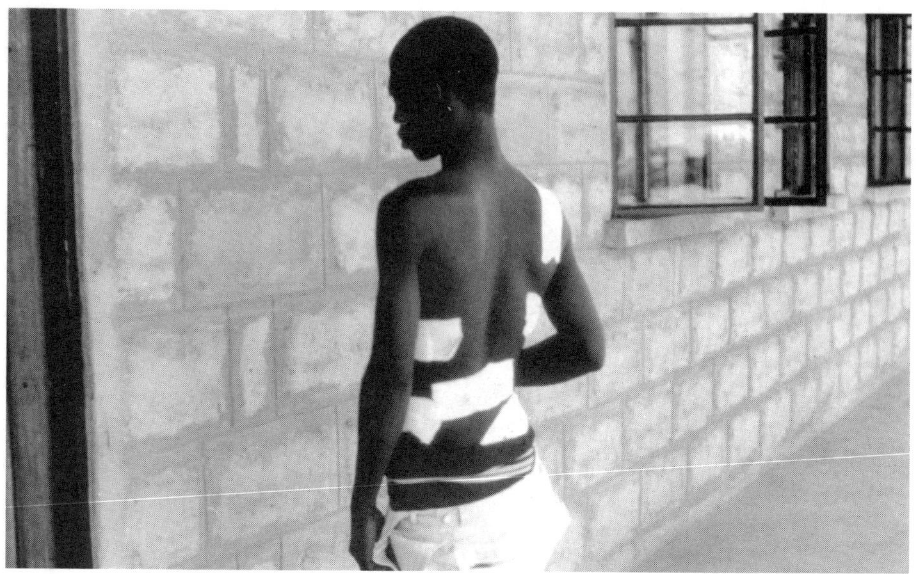

Figure 4.4. Noduclectomies for onchocerciasis.

ciated with onchocerciasis we were beginning to achieve a success rate of over eighty percent!!!

Subsequent series were done at Lunsar Eye Hospital by Dr. Eleanor Koeth and Dr. Ingrid Graelle. I did a study of fifty Caucasian patients. Success rates were in the high eighty percent to low ninety percent for control of the elevated intraocular pressure even without the need for additional glaucoma medication. A subsequent series by Dr. Robert Barbe did not show a statistical difference in this new approach, but Dr. Norval Christi doing a series of 5000 in Pakistan had the impression that it was beneficial. A full description can be found in *Trabeculectomy with Iridencleisis*, British Journal of Ophthalmology, Vol. 69 No. 12, pages 881-885, Dec. 1985.

The real breakthrough came when Merck & Company, Inc., a prominent pharmaceutical company, developed ivermectin (mectizan) which has the capacity to reduce the microfilaria more slowly with a significant reduction in systemic and ocular reactions. Treatment needed only to be repeated at six to twelve month intervals.

To have developed a drug that can save the sight of these millions of people around the world, must have been elating for Merck & Company. The financial rewards would be tremendous. At this point there was soul-searching going on at the company headquarters. The patients who needed ivermectin were poor and indigent. There was no way that they could pay for the medicine. In one of the truly ennobling decisions sometimes made by management, Merck & Company offered ivermectin free of charge to the World Health Organization (WHO) if they would manage its distribution.

In Sierra Leone at one time, slit lamp examination would reveal microfilaria swimming around in the anterior chamber of eyes of patients looking like wiggling silver threads. About half of all the patients examined would have these little worms. A decade later I was able to go an entire day without seeing these deadly microfilaria. Nodulectomies also helped to reduce the source of their production.

It has been a joy to treat patients with river blindness at the present time, and assure them that they need not go blind from the disease. Always in the background of my mind is the decision that Merck & Company made to make it available to the world without reaping great financial gain. Their helping hand exemplifies the wealth of good will that still can be found in the world today.

Enucleations

Eye infections in Africa often progress to the point where the eye can no longer be saved. An inordinate number of enucleations and eviscerations need to be performed. This destructive procedure was mastered by members of our surgical team to give adequate room for the placement of prostheses which looked normal and had movement.

Twelve year old Momoh needed to have such an operation. He was mischievous in nature, but learned quickly how to care for his "false eye."

In school when things became quiet or dull, he sometimes enlivened his classmates by removing his "eye" and tossing it up and down.

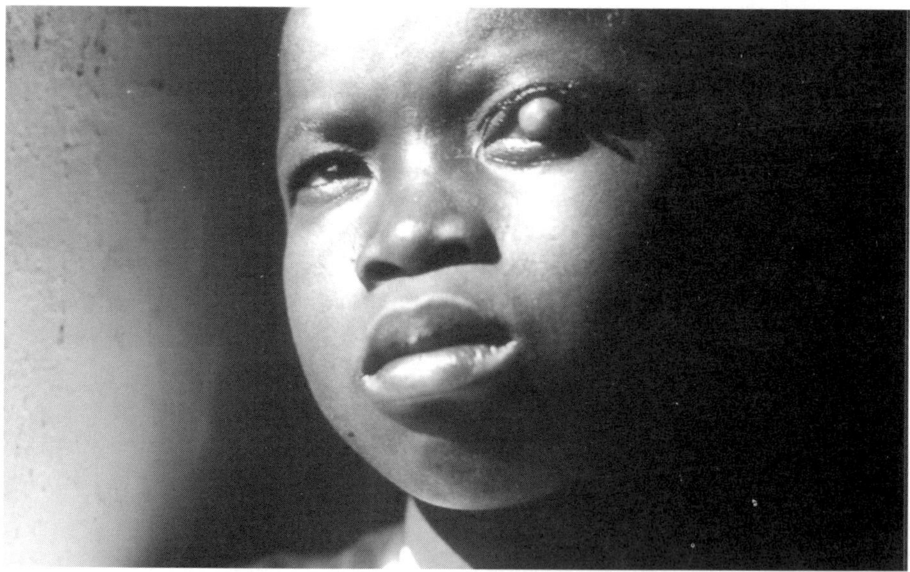

Figure 4.5. Growth on a sightless eye.

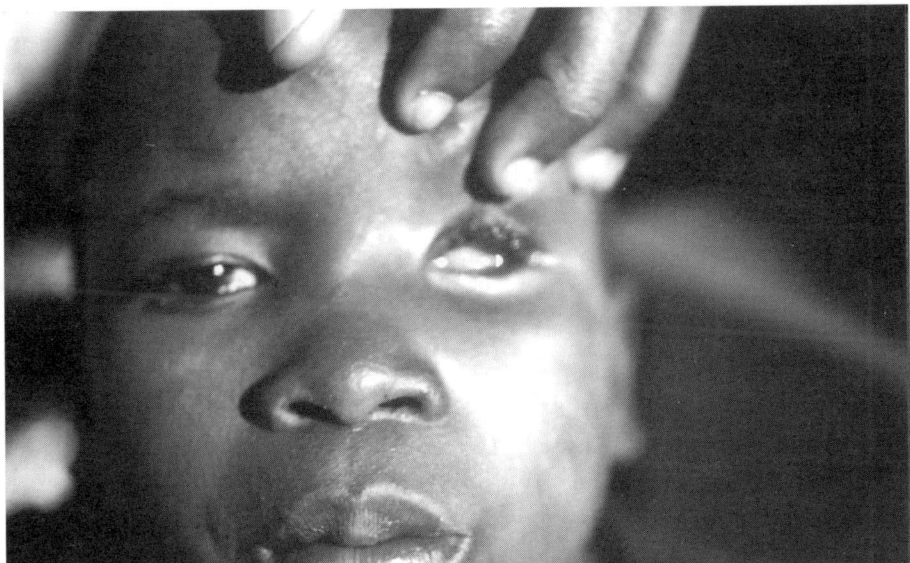

Figure 4.6. Healing following an enucleation.

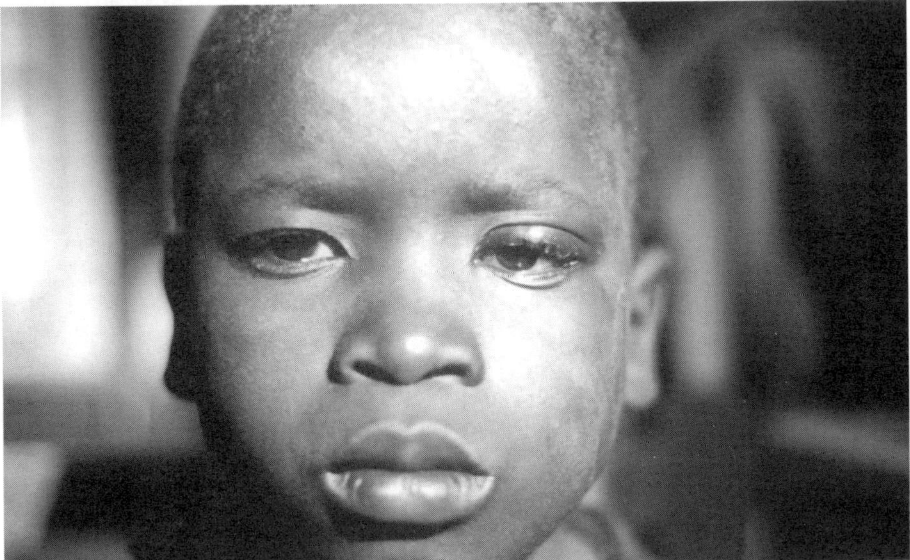

Figure 4.7. A prosthesis in place.

When Hope is an Eye Clinic in Bo – 1974 – Esther Groves

The middle-aged African woman lies face up on the surgical table as missionary ophthalmologist Lowell Gess observes, "If no one intervened, this patient would go completely blind with glaucoma. What we will do is make a hole in her eye to serve as a sort of overflow. If we were just starting work here in Bo, we would not do this operation because it may or may not be successful. One cannot have reverses in the beginning or people will say the place is not worthy. Now they trust us and we can do it."

A young African assistant, Andrew Josiah, swings the surgical tray into position above the patient. The masking cloth is fitted over her face with only her eye showing through the oval hole in the center. The lower edge of the cloth is attached to the tray so that she can breathe easily. There is no oxygen.

Seated behind the patient's head Dr. Gess separates her eyelids with a lid speculum as assistant John Morlai, fly-swatter in hand, scans the room for any insect that may have accompanied patients into the clinic.

Gess now incises the cornea at the top and with forceps removes a speck of iris. It leaves a hole that can be seen as a tiny dark spot. As he

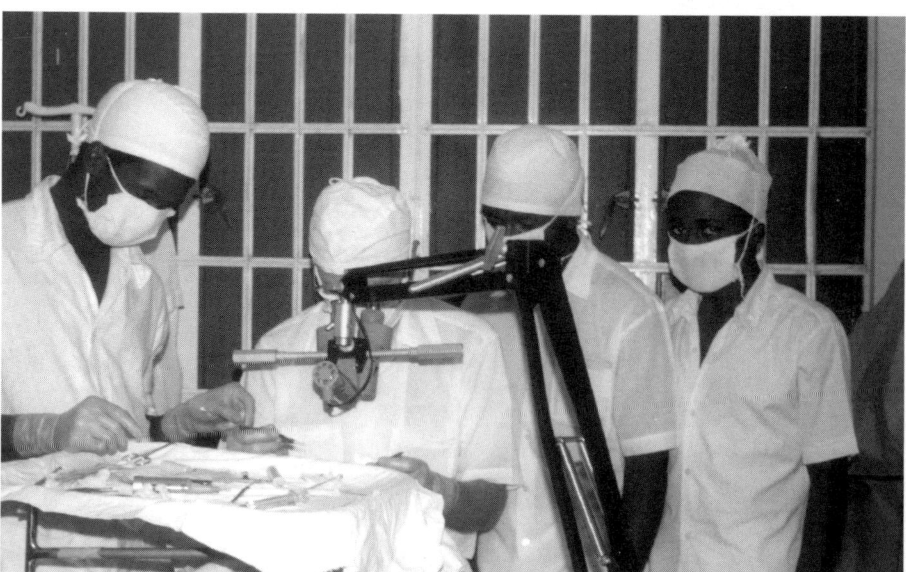

Figure 4.8. Surgery setup at Bo.

sews up the incision saline is inserted, creating a balloon that rests on the pupil, a sign of watertight closure.

"For the rest of her life we will want to see that bug (the tiny dark spot). It's her lifeline to sight. Let's see how she does with this before we do anything to the other eye." As it turns out, the operation is successful.

This is what the Bo Eye Clinic means to West Africans – the difference between blindness and sight. Only a year ago many blind persons sat in darkness listening to a world of sounds. Some were babies and children with congenital cataracts, some were adults with worms in their eyes. They were led here and there by relatives, they went to native doctors, they experimented with native medicines, sometimes with dire results. A few lived in pain.

Then in September of 1972 Sierra Leonians began to hear that a puumoi (Western) doctor had come to Bo. They began to show up at the clinic before it was officially open, so United Methodist Missionaries Lowell Gess and his wife Ruth, a nurse, paused in their preparations to treat them. Soon the first white eye patches were seen in bush villages.

The Gesses took on five Christian high school graduates to train as assistants. When the clinic opened on October 20 this training contin-

Figure 4.9. Bo Eye Clinic staff, 1973.

ued in and around eye examinations, treatments, and surgery; gradually skills were sharpened and the work gained momentum. News spread that the blind could see and before long patients filled the clinic and overflowed onto the front verandah.

A day at the clinic begins between 7:30 and 7:45 a.m. as the assistants (there are now six) come to work. Patients are already entering the T-shaped one story concrete building and taking places in the front room that serves as waiting room, office, and optical shop.

At the rear door a white Land Rover Cruiser pulls up with the Gesses and Justin and Marge Sleight. Dr. Sleight is an ophthalmologist with a private practice in Lansing, Michigan, here for one year of voluntary medical service at his own expense. Marge Sleight helps with secretarial routines. Both couples live in the same duplex and arrive every morning in time for 7:45 devotions with staff and patients.

Almost before the last note of the closing hymn has died away the staff is in action. Francis Boyo makes out number slips for patients, John Morlai asks a youngster, "Are you a patient?" and Ernest Kroma checks the vision of a young woman in traditional handkerchief, tie-dyed top and wrapped skirt. Other patients watch so that they will know what to do in turn.

The two doctors and the other assistants, Andrew Josiah, Joseph Mosima, and John Fornah go to the five-bed ward to look at post-surgery patients and change dressings. The ward is the right wing of the four-room T, the surgery room the left wing. In the center is the room with examining and refraction lanes. Limited space has been used well; refraction lanes normally 20 feet have been halved to 10 feet with mirrors and reverse-letter eye charts.

Now seated by his slit lamp, Gess examines quickly and carefully but shows friendly interest in the person before him ("And how is so-and-so?"). Constantly busy, neither doctor seems hurried, and the patients respond with trust. Gess is looking at a thirty-four year old man totally blind in one eye and almost blind in the other. "Pressure out of control here – iris plastered against the lens – bleeding in anterior chamber." Perhaps with an operation the man will be able to see well enough that he won't have to be led around.

By this time the doctors and their wives are the only light faces in a sea of brown. Sleight looks at the growing crowd and observes dispassionately, "It's going to be a wild day." Four persons are visiting relatives in the ward, which holds male patients one week, female patients the next.

Dr. Sleight is examining a little girl, Fatmata Gbondo. "This began as a measles complication," he says. Measles complications are not unusual in Africa; children frequently die of measles here. "Most places would have thought this eye completely lost. She was given antibiotics to protect the inside of the eye and medicines for the outside, and the eye was patched to give it support. The eye broke out but the perforation is healing. Yesterday when she was tested she had 20-50 vision. That eye will be saved."

"An unusual case," Gess comments as he looks at a small boy. (Sleight points out later that most cases here are unusual compared to the States. People with cataracts are in their 40's and 50's compared to 60's and 70's in the States, and the cataracts are more advanced.) "The cornea is deteriorating and losing its thickness. At this rate the eye will open, the inner contents extrude, and the iris will plug the hole." Gess sketches the little boy's condition on the patient card as Joseph Mosima tells the mother, "Only for the left eye, four times a day." The eye drops cost four leones; Gess decides the patient can be charged two leones and shows the mother how to apply the drops.

In the background the air conditioner hums quietly under a steady rhythm of low-pitched voices – doctors talking, assistants translating, patients answering. Occasionally Marge Sleight comes to ask about a patient card or invoice, or Ruth Gess to consult about a letter or telephone call. Ruth shuttles between rooms like a weaver drawing many strands together, catching loose ends and working them into place. Between them the women make possible a steady flow of patients and free the doctors of nearly all business and housekeeping chores.

In the surgery room assistants Andrew Josiah and John Fornah prepare to operate on a white-haired woman with nodules on her hip. Such nodules contain worms that cause onchocerciasis ("river blindness," so called because the fly and worm breeding cycle occurs partly in fast moving water). The progeny of the worms migrate under the skin to the eyes, so nodulectomies are routinely performed even though they are not eye operations. Andrew and John have been trained to handle them except for nodules on the chest wall or in a critical area of nerves.

Andrew makes two light cuts over the nodules. As John pulls back the edges of the incision with speculae, he snips around the increasingly visible nodule and brings the whitish lump into the open. A few more snips and it comes free. The young surgeon probes the incision, locates two smaller nodules and removes them, sews up the incision and moves on to another lump, repeating the entire process. A large nodule the size of a plum is removed, then a smaller one. Soon the two young men help the old lady sit up and she walks out by herself as Andrew removes his cap, mask, and gown. Not bad for a high school graduate!

Ruth Gess is treating a man who has what looks like goose bumps on his chest. A patient with onchocerciasis needs hetrazen and eventually antrypol injections to kill the worms under the skin. The body reacts to the presence of dead worms with fever and other symptoms – the patient becomes ill. Then Ruth performs a delicate balancing act, giving the patient just enough steroids to provide relief until his body adjusts so that higher dosages of medicine can be given.

By this time the waiting and examining rooms are more crowded than ever. Marge Sleight is busy with invoices for glasses that have just arrived from London. Charges need to be refigured in leones and people notified by mail, phone, or friends that their glasses have arrived. Gess explains to a young man that his new glasses are mostly a gift from the clinic. What he does not say is that the balance must be made up by gifts. ("I like to think the Lord provides.")

Mohammed Tholley, a 21 year old from a village 96 miles away, sits down by Sleight's slit lamp. He has had pain in his eyes for nine years, has permanently lost the sight in one eye, and has a cataract in the other. He can barely distinguish light from darkness. Sleight will operate on him this afternoon but the chance of sight is remote; even though the cataract is successfully removed, the retina may be found to have been damaged. But Mohammed is still a young man and he has begged to take the chance.

The doctors discuss his case and operation. "We will lift the iris off the lens before we penetrate the lens," Justin Sleight decides. Lowell Gess says to Joseph, "I wonder if Andrew knows that it's an aspiration first?" and Joseph goes off to tell Andrew, who is assembling packs to be sterilized for each operation.

Gess looks at Kalu Tullah, an older man led in by a relative. "Ruth, this will be the second patient for this afternoon's surgery." He does not – cannot – promise Kalu Tullah sight, only: "We will try." Sleight is examining seven year old Posch Komara from Freetown, 167 miles away. Both of her eyes are completely involved with congenital cataracts. She is told to come back at 1:30. If the first two operations go well they will operate on her, too.

The two doctors look at a middle-aged Lebanese who had sought medical help in Lebanon to no avail. They detect lid-lag, a retraction of the upper lid that is a sign of a thyroid condition. "It takes an opthalmologist to detect this!" says Lowell with a twinkle. "We know what's wrong with you but we don't treat this here. You need to go to the hospital." Ruth takes notes for a letter to be sent with the man and goes off to type.

Now a dark trembling old lady is lowered into the chair by Sleight's slit lamp. "I think maybe she can see a little bit today," Justin says, holding a glass lens in front of her eye. She does see, and laughs a little, then relaxes as the doctor gently swabs her eye and administers drops. Justin and Joseph apply the new dressing like one man with four hands, so smoothly does the gauze, shield, and adhesive go into place.

A tiny bald-headed boy is led in wearing a makeshift pair of glasses so large for him that the handles curve around his ears and back past his cheeks. Joseph brings the new little pair of glasses and tries them on him; the child's mother smiles to see her son's improved appearance. A minor adjustment is made and the docile little fellow tries them on again, fingering the tortoise shell frames and looking about through the thick lenses.

Assistant Ernest Kroma has become proficient in grinding prescription lenses by hand. A semi-automatic machine now does the work but Ernest's skills are still needed. On occasion the clinic has even provided a pair of prescription glasses in the chosen frames an hour after the examination!

By 1:30 p.m. Mohammed Tholley is on the operating table, taking his long chance, covered to the chest with a white sheet. He hears a prayer in his own tongue, Temne. Dr. Sleight is seated behind Mohammed's head and Andrew is ready as scrub nurse.

The cornea is slit deftly and the eye flooded with saline. Justin reaches under the cornea to the cloudy mass in the center. Andrew, steady as a rock, holds the pediatric scalp vein needle in place in the eye with one hand while reaching with his other hand for the next instrument needed. The milky mass in the center of the eye is grasped and moved; it fluctuates with the injection of more saline but the nucleus is stubborn and will not come out. Gess, entering in cap and mask, agrees with Sleight that a larger incision is needed.

Andrew is sponging the eye with a homemade swab – a cotton-wrapped toothpick. ("We roll our own," says Gess, "It's cheaper and the others aren't always available.") Sleight laces the cornea further back, reaches in, seizes the pale mass, and begins to move it out. Another instrument. Then the cloudy mass yields and it is drawn out, and the stitching up begins.

The patient's eye with the lids drawn back seems as large as the eye of an immobile giant staring upward. Fingers move in and out of the bright pool of light, weaving the fine strong filament like a spider magician, and the incision is closed. Next comes the dressing and shield. Assistants help Mohammed Tholley sit up and he puts on his sandals and walks between them to the ward. The operating area is cleaned up and the next patient prepared.

Now it is Gess's turn. He addresses Kalu Tullah as "Pa," the term of respect for older men. "Pa, we are going to give you a small shot." He injects the local anesthetic and John Fornah prays in Temne. Quick, sure cuts bring the cornea away from the eye. Gess threads loops with a curved short needle and Andrew snips the ends. Then a slender white cylinder of frozen carbon dioxide is touched to the lens, which freezes to it. Out comes the oval lens intact. A saline bubble falls into place above the pupil as the incision is closed. "In the States they use freon," says Gess, "but in Europe they use carbon dioxide because it is cheaper and so do we. We do have freon on hand, and if we had to do this on two patients in a row, we'd use freon for the second."

Other assistants, finished with duties in the outer rooms, don caps and masks to watch the third operation. They are keenly interested in their work, even borrowing books to study eye pathology in the evenings. Their interest and high morale is due partly to the Gess' thorough training, partly to the Christian ideal of service-with-love that the missionaries personify and teach. Together they can provide translation in nine languages, an indispensable service.

Andrew carries in Posch Komara and lays her gently on the table. Her black crinkly hair is braided neatly in cornrows; gold-color earrings pierce her ears. She lies quietly under the sheet, eyes closed, a lovely little girl.

"Tell her she will feel only some pricks but nothing else," Lowell says to John Fornah. "The main thing is to get her to accept the injection." But at the first injection Posch cries, "Mammy! Mammy!" and begins to turn her head before the needle is withdrawn. They talk soothingly to her, Justin and John hold her, and when the rest of the injections are given she whimpers only a bit. John takes her hand and prays.

Gess inserts the pediatric scalp vein needle, Andrew holds it in place, and Sleight controls the saline flow. (With a child you float out the cataract.) Like the two before, this will not be an easy operation.

Gess says, "I'm going to make just one little opening here, (to Sleight) that chamber is beautiful, you're doing a perfect job – I can't get it off all the way, I'm going to stop." Then everything comes loose and Lowell hands up the tube with the cloudy nucleus at the end of it, suctioned out. He is looping stitches into place when Ruth appears at the doorway and asks, "Was she good?"

"Yes, she's nearly asleep – Doctor Sleight's sleeping potion!" Lowell says as an afterthought, "I saw on the box that it cost 20 leones."

"It's worth every penny of it," Justin replies. Posch, though conscious throughout, has not moved once during the operation thanks to the special anesthetic from the U.S.A. She cannot afford it but perhaps some gift will cover the expense.

By this time the room is very hot and everyone is sweating. Ruth and Justin discuss the possibility of an exhaust fan in the surgery room that would draw in cooled air from the centrally located air conditioner in the examining room. But that would take money, and medicine and glasses come first.

John carries Posch to her bed on the ward. It isn't women's week but the arrangement will work with little Posch. One of the assistants is on duty with patients all night, tending to their needs and dozing in between.

After the operations Mr. Bangura, who has a hole in his head, shows up for his daily check and change of dressing. For years he went from hospital to hospital with an infected draining right sinus that cost him his right eye. Gess saved the other eye by making a hole in his forehead that brings drainage outside. Today as usual the sinus is irrigated with hydrogen peroxide and freshly dressed, and Mr. Bangura goes off in comfort with his young, attentive wives, each one, however, already a grandmother.

A young girl also comes in for a check, wearing a false eye that is absolutely undetectable. Justin Sleight had fashioned a prosthesis to fit, an eyepiece resembling a specially built up contact lens which fits over the useless eye and turns with it.

At last the day is at an end. Four weeks later Mohammed Tholley's long chance has paid off. He can actually see somewhat. His eye is being kept quiet with steroid medications. Kalu Tullah had not received much hope from the doctors beforehand because of the pathology in his eye. His eye is slowly – very slowly – clearing. Little Posch is coming along well and will have her second operation in a little while. It had not been an easy afternoon, but Lowell Gess and Justin Sleight and their supporting staff can feel happy about the day. Perhaps – one can always hope – other ophthalmologists like Justin Sleight will volunteer anywhere from six months to a few years to help keep the clinic running. Because for Mohammed, Kalu, Posch, and many, many others, hope is an eye clinic in Bo.

Bo, 1972

On September 1, 1972, we docked at Freetown, Sierra Leone. Happy to be back in the land of his birth, our youngest son Andrew kissed the ground. Ten days later he became a teenager. Within a few more days he was attending the Rupp Memorial School in Kabala, a six-hour journey away.

Our eye program was to operate in Mende country. Bo was the second largest city in Sierra Leone. Our mission compound bordered the main road leading in and out of Bo. A small headquarters building was altered and adapted to house the Bo Eye Clinic of the United Methodist Church. The optical equipment that had been used at Taiama and stored at Rotifunk, was brought up to Bo. John Morlai helped Ruth and me clean and restore items that had been tucked away in boxes in which mice, cockroaches, and lizards had felt comfortable. Even while the clin-

Color Print 2.1. Dr. W.H. Fitzjohn and wife Alice. (see page 103)

Color Print 2.2. The quay that greeted us on our arrival in Sierra Leone, November, 1957. (see page 104)

Color Print 2.3. John and Paul in the surgical window waiting for mother to come home. (see page 106)

Color Print 2.4. The Ribi Ferry was not working. A canoe was needed if we were to return to Rotifunk. (see page 105)

Color Print 2.5. EUB Sierra Leone pastors, 1958. (see page 108)

Color Print 2.6. Dr. and Mrs. (Norma) Harris arrive March 21, 1958. Nurse Betty Esau (Wight) is in the background. (see page 110)

Color Print 2.7. Historic picture of the beginning of the Surgical Program at Rotifunk Hospital, Sierra Leone. Standing from left to right: Lowell Gess, M.D., Mabel Silver, M.D., George Harris, M.D., and nurse assistants David Johnson, Joe Solo Cole, and Maxwell Carew. The sophisticated equipment was portable making possible surgical procedures on treks to remote areas such as Kayima and the Loma Mountain regions. (see page 112)

Color Print 2.8. Ruth being escorted to hospital by Dr. George Harris. (see page 114)

Color Print 2.9. Ruth being transported home following the delivery of Andrew, September 11, 1959. (see page 114)

Color Print 2.10. Dedication of "Bumpeh Evangel," the boat built by Mr. Dean Spencer while teaching at Albert Academy. (see page 117)

Color Print 2.11. Mobile surgical trek and assault of Mount Bintumani. (see page 119)

Color Print 2.12. On top of West Africa's world; Mount Bintumani at 6,390 feet. (see page 121)

Color Print 2.13. Bible study on top of Mount Bintumani. (see page 121)

Color Print 2.14. Surgical trek to Jaiama (over 250 miles from Rotifunk Hospital) during the time of nurse-midwife Betty Esau Wight, 1960. (see page 122)

Color Print 2.15. Escorted by Paramount Chief Dudo Bona to view diamond mining. (see page 123)

Color Print 2.16. Dr. Sama Banya, my physician during my hepatitis illness. (see page 128)

Color Print 2.17. Bishop B. A. Carew and his family, except for the oldest boy, George, now a Ph.D., 1973. (see page 128)

Color Print 2.18. The Bridge Over The River Tai. It's right pillar rests on the stone on which Rev. and Mrs. McGrew were martyred, 1898. This scene witnesses 119 new Christians being baptized. (see page 136)

Color Print 2.19. Taiama Church "Cathedral in the Bush." (see page 137)

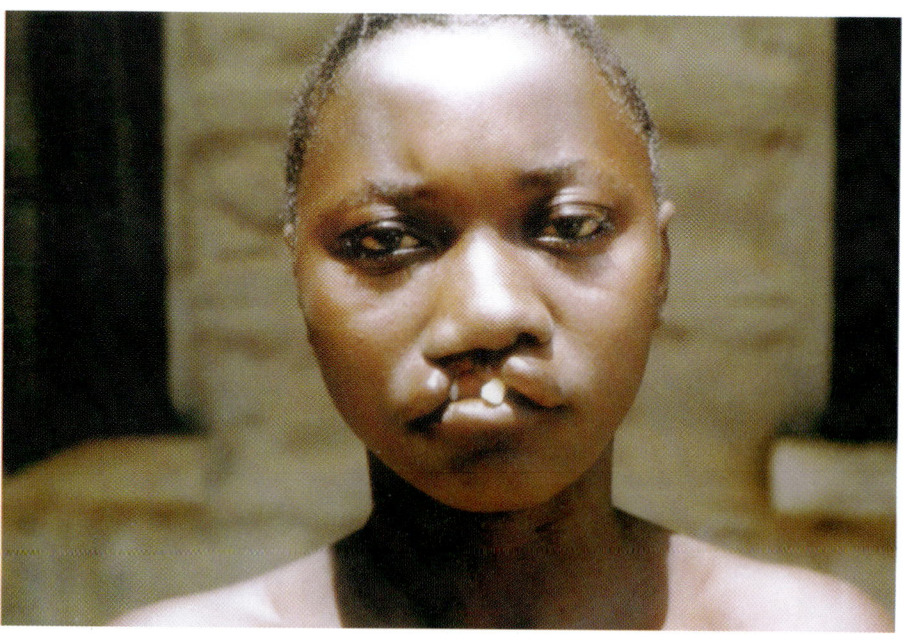

Color Print 2.20. Preoperative plastic repair, 1966. (see page 139)

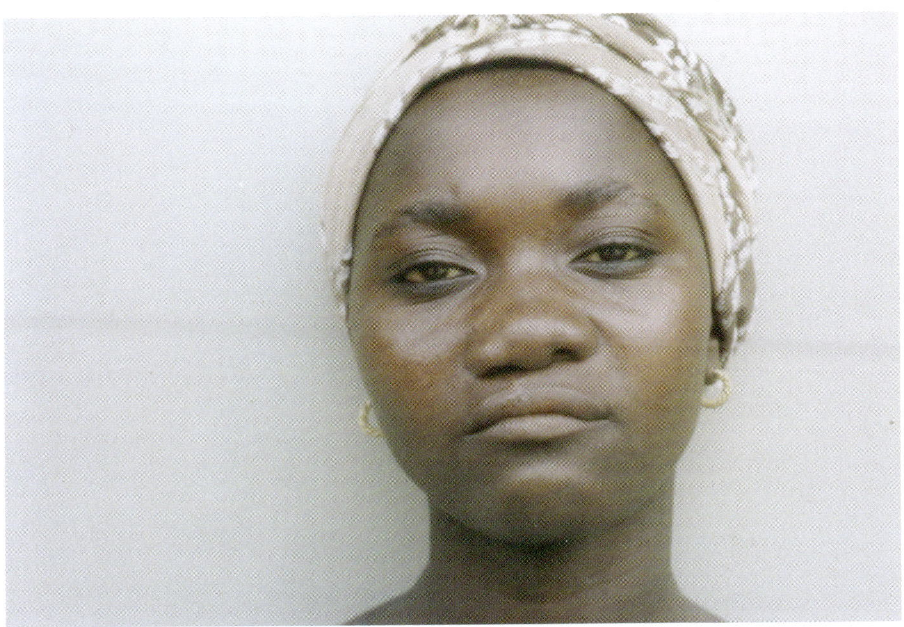

Color Print 2.21. Plastic repair, postop. (see page 139)

Color Print 2.22. Mrs. Ray Harrison holding their fourth son, 1966. (see page 140)

Color Print 2.23. Angie Myles with family members. (see page 142)

Color Print 2.24. River blindness (onchocerciasis). Six men aged 25-40 irrevocably blind. (see page 162)

Color Print 2.25. Justin and Marge Sleight, Ruth and Esther Groves. (see page 170)

Color Print 2.26. Outstanding staff: Bo Eye Clinic, 1972-1975. (see page 169)

Color Print 2.27. Justin and Marge Sleight leaving after their year's volunteer service, 1974. (see page 171)

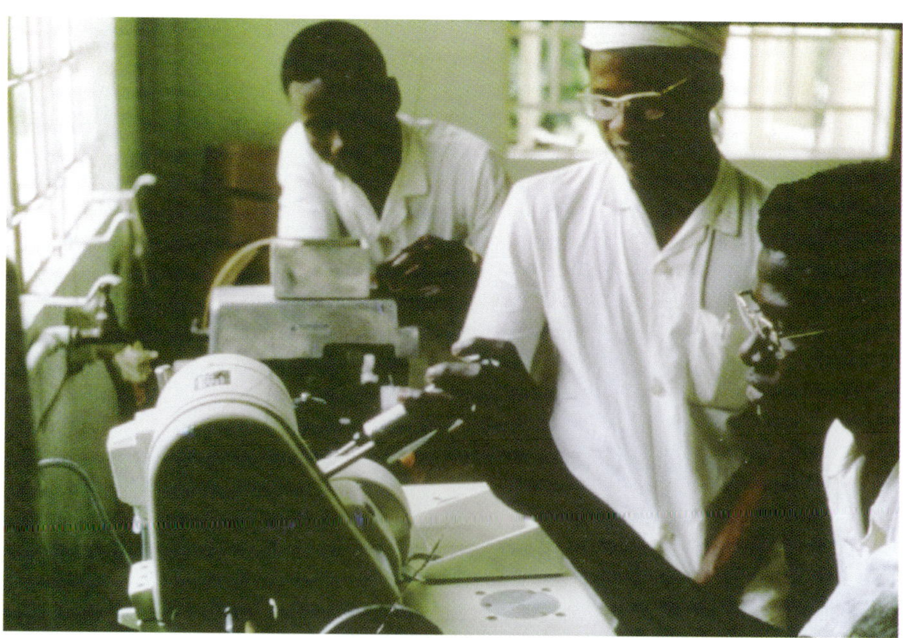

Color Print 2.28. Edging glasses. (see page 173)

Color Print 2.29. A previously blind mother has her first glimpse of her baby. (see page 174)

Color Print 2.30. Mr. Bangura. "When Hope is an Eye Clinic in Bo." (see page 175)

Color Print 2.31. She isn't heavy ... she's my sister. (see page 193)

ic was being set up, we could not refuse eye treatment to many disparate eye conditions.

Still without a staff, we made a tour of medical facilities in the southern and eastern regions of Sierra Leone. We visited Jaiama where Brunhilde Goebel and Renate Horn were doing a marvelous maternity work; Yekior where Fred and Margaret Gaston were pioneering a new area and doing first aid on the side; Segbwema Hospital with its long and historic impact on health care in Sierra Leone; Dr. Sama Banya with his important work at Kenema; and Kamakwie where Dr. and Mrs. James Tysinger were engaged in a tremendous program. He was making plans to pursue an eye residency. In later years he returned again and again to Kamakwie to do sophisticated eye surgery using phacoemulsification and then placing intraocular lenses.

On our return to Bo we extended contracts to Mr. Ernest Kroma, Andrew Josiah (later to become a physician's assistant in California), John Morlai, Joseph Mosima, Jonathan Kamara, Francis Ndema, Samuel Coker, and John Fornah, who presently heads up the Kissy surgical program. Dr. David Stayer and his wife, Irene, of Irving, Texas, helped us with the starting up of the program. They underwrote an optometric training period for Alfred Bangura who had been with us in the eye program at Taiama. The training in the United States was in Houston, Texas.

Officially the Bo Eye Clinic was ceremonially opened November 1, 1972. The first patient, Pastor J. B. Vandy Rogers of the large Centenary United Methodist Church was discovered to have glaucoma. Medicine and surgery were used to protect his vision for the next twenty-eight years. Air service within the country of Sierra Leone allowed patients from Freetown and elsewhere to speedily get to the Bo Eye Clinic. One of our favorite patients whom we met at the airport from time to time was Mrs. S. M. Renner. She, too, needed management for her glaucoma.

The Bo Eye Clinic was honored with the visit of the General Board of Global Ministry's Dr. Isaac Bivens. Within an hour's time Dr. Bivens was given a complete eye examination and fitted with his first pair of reading glasses at no charge.

In the early days while trying to get set up, we were frequent guests at the table of Gilbert and Beverly Olson. Helen and Stan Trebes often had exciting occasions at their house which included hair permanents,

Shanghai (the missionary game), and the enjoyment of Andy Williams records, played over and over in bemusement but always with appreciation.

The Thanksgiving potluck took place at the Olson's. In attendance were missionaries Clyde and Gladys Galow, Ted and Hilda Hebel, Don and Helen Pletsch, Fred and Margaret Gaston, and nurse Brunhilde Goebel.

Ultimately the Bo Eye Clinic became well established. Early on the patients attending would rarely exceed fifty for this small facility, but with increasing numbers we were prompted to not only see patients each day but also to include a surgical schedule each day. Little did we dream that as many as 166 patients would eventually be seen and treated on a single day. Everyone pulled together to meet the challenge. The African staff worked long but effective hours. On one "work day" we had:

Rollie Crandall fixing the fan
Jeanne Crandall typing seven of my dictated letters
Taking care of Sue Crandall who had the misfortune of a fishbone lodging in her throat
Dan Humphreys fixing the sterilizer, lensometer, and diamond edger
Stan Trebes fixing the desk drawers
Barbara Humphreys, Beverly Olson, and Ruth sewing drapes.

We looked forward to a new and full year at the Bo Eye Clinic but we did not anticipate how eventful and sometimes dangerous it could be.

Bo, 1973

In February, 1973, the United Methodist Church, Sierra Leone Conference, consecrated the Rev. B. A. Carew as its first bishop. Bishop Maynard Sparks, from the General Board of Global Ministries participated, along with Dr. S. M. Renner, Dr. J. K. Fergusson, and other council members. The new Bishop Carew had a history of an unusually successful pastoral ministry. As bishop, his wise guidance was to lead the United Methodist Church in Sierra Leone to new achievements.

Before they were captured, members of a Black September gang terrorized the Bo area. Twice the United Methodist Church Bo compound was invaded. Our two watchmen usually were found to be asleep whenever we checked on them. The people in our area took matters into their own hands with the robberies and captured one thief whom Gil Olson delivered to the police. Sadly, another thief was the object of the people's fury and was beaten to the extent that he subsequently died.

As a delegation we went to the police to inquire about protection for the Bo Eye Clinic and the Bo Bible Training Institute, as one of our members was severely harmed during one of the break-ins. Several days later I was called from examining an eye patient and was presented to the Sierra Leone chief of police and the director of the CID (Criminal Investigation Department) from Freetown. They sat down and visited about the trauma suffered by our missionaries and gave assurances that they would do all in their power to prevent further happenings. Within several weeks we learned that the loot had been found and the gang apprehended and sentenced.

We were to see a number of Moorens ulcers in the years to come. The first one had a deadly impact on me and the staff. Chali Bangali was a youth of 18. He was popular at school and a good student. He was brought to the eye clinic by a member of our staff and was assured that his painful eye could be helped. One look with the slit lamp confirmed a diagnosis of Moorens ulcer. This was also the first viewing of a Moorens ulcer for visiting opthalmologist, Dr. David Stayer. The marginal ulcer had already excavated tissue at the limbus a quarter way around the cornea. It did not respond to antibiotics, corticosteroids, or surgical excision of the limbal conjunctiva. Relentlessly it completed its encirclement and destroyed the eye. Our only constructive service to him was the fitting of a prosthesis which looked and fitted very much like a normal eye. Sue Robinson, area representative from the General Board of Global Ministries had only two weeks earlier brought a set of appropriate sizes and colors.

The optical shop made great strides. Ernest Kroma on some days fabricated as many as eight prescription glasses. Brot Fur Die Welt helped financially to furnish the needed frames and lenses. Christoffel Blinden-mission made available a Weco diamond edger. We were grateful for the practical help of Christians in Germany. Also at this time, a Christian ophthalmologist, Wilmert Harms, with whom I had studied for several months at Harvard, sent a ticket to enable me to attend the 1973 Academy of Ophthalmology meeting in Dallas, Texas. He understood how important it was to keep up on the latest trends in the fast changing world of ophthalmology. During the meeting several of us missionary doctors including Dr. Darrel Parker and Dr. Inder Bhar and I were royally entertained in Dr. Stayer's home. While in the USA, I also had the opportunity to visit four of our children who were in graduate school at that time.

In July of 1973 we had the pleasure of entertaining Ray and Arlene Harrison and their children, including Daniel, the eldest, who was born at the Taiama Eye Clinic. Gareth and Treva Wiedekehr, with their sons Wayne and Wes, also dropped in. We were shocked and saddened later to hear that Wayne sustained an animal bite (squirrel) at the school in Kabala and was overwhelmed with the toxicity of this trauma before help could be secured. Few tragedies can be as deep as to have a small son die in his father's arms while on his way to the hospital.

July 18, 1973, was a red letter day when Dr. Justin Sleight and his wife Marge, arrived. He had arranged a year's sabbatical leave from his practice in Lansing, Michigan. Their participation in the program was of inestimable help. A brief description of his participation in the program is found in the anecdote entitled, "Hope is an Eye Clinic in Bo."

We also had the help of a long time, dedicated missionary, Dr. Jenny Gibson, who would come over and give general anesthesia for our pediatric patients from time to time. However, I noted a number of weeks later on July 15, that I finally had figured out a way to do anesthesia for children. May 7, 1974, mentions ketamine being used for anesthesia.

Trips to Freetown were made frequently as the 118 miles were paved. On one occasion I was called upon to give a paper to the Sierra Leone Medical and Dental Society on the topic of onchocerciasis. Sometime later doctors in Freetown were made "believers" that onchocerciasis did exist in Sierra Leone.

Another trip was for a missionary retreat. During these times the missionaries were removed from routine schedules on their appointed places and allowed to visit with others to know of successes as well as failures. Also included in this fellowship were Sierra Leone leaders such as Rev. Francis Tommy, Dr. F. B. Davies, H. R. N. Jusu, and Cris Williams, our dynamic women's movement leader.

The Christmas 1973 visit of our four sons was special. As a quartet they sang several times in church services. The day after Christmas the family journeyed to Yifin to do eye clinics. This was a remote place at the base of the Loma mountains, where Dr. Hugh and Muriel McClure from Canada were conducting an eye program. They were wonderful hosts. The boys would go hunting while I did the eye clinics.

A never to be forgotten incident occurred when, with their rifles on their shoulders, the boys sauntered past the gate of President Siaka Steven's Yifin retreat. There were armed guards at the gate and our boys were armed. Without breaking step, greetings of "Kusho" were exchanged. No one realized the tenseness of the situation.

The following day the missionaries were entertained by President Stevens for tea. Mrs. McClure presented him with a birthday cake. The President was most cordial and emphasized to this select group, that he didn't feel alcoholic beverages were necessary for social gatherings. "A fruit juice would do," he said.

Bo, 1974

Early in 1974, I took in an eye workshop in Liberia while Justin Sleight minded the store at the Bo Eye Clinic. Our sons, John and Paul, assisted in some of the school surveys at Jaiama (1300 students) and Yengema (1200 students). Students were discovered who were in dire need of glasses. Other pathology was also uncovered for further handling at the Bo Eye Clinic.

While there was much gaiety during the visit of "our four sons," they were productive as well. Utilizing the optical equipment, both John and Paul had the experience of examining patients and fabricating glasses. Without television to occupy their time, it was rewarding to know that besides family devotions and prayers, John read C. S. Lewis's *The Great Debate*, and Paul read William Barclay's *Ethics in a Permissive Society*. On their return flight to the U.S.A. they stopped off at Francis Schaefer's LeBrie for a short visit. This entire three month visit was underwritten by the General Board of Global Ministries to help keep families together. It was a great blessing.

The eye program had developed to the extent that even with Justin's help, we were being unduly pressed to accommodate the numbers of patients for glasses and medical problems as well as keeping up with the surgery. Retinal reattachments were being addressed along with a host of trauma patients.

Alfred Bangura, who had received optometric training in Houston,

Texas, with the support of Dr. and Mrs. David Stayer, played a significant role in the examination of patients. It was a great disappointment that he was unable to obtain his official degree in optometry. However, the Sierra Leone army was happy to have his commissioned eye service. With the developing civil war and the continued encroachment of the rebels, Alfred was pressed into combat leadership. Tragically he was killed in this bitter civil war.

Another stark tragedy happened to Dr. Yilla, our friend and fellow physician in Bo, who was referred to a London hospital for neurosurgery of a slipped disk. During the operative procedure, the surgeons were concerned about some "white thread-like structures." The anesthesiologist reminded them that Dr. Yilla was from Sierra Leone, West Africa, possibly suggesting Guinea worm infestation. A biopsy was taken. Analysis revealed aberrant spinal nerves. Dr. Yilla never walked again.

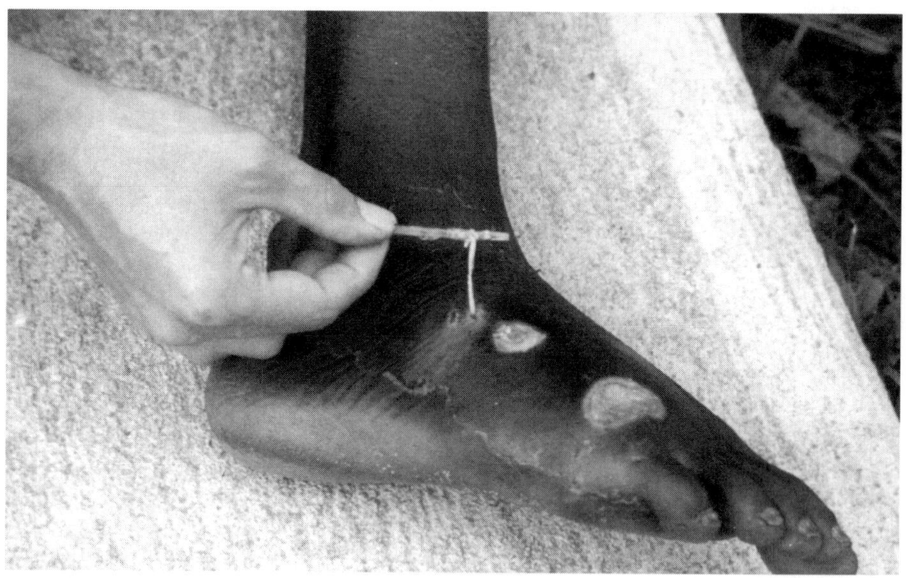

Figure 4.10. Guinea Worm Disease, 1974.

Guinea Worm Disease

Regardless of specialty, a "doctor" can be presented any number of challenges in Africa.

Dracunculiasis, or guinea worm disease, is a disabling infection caused by the nematode parasite dracunulus medinensis. We were presented with this disease even while conducting an eye care program.

People become infected when they drink water containing tiny crustaceans, called copepods or "water fleas," that act as intermediate hosts of the organism and harbor infective larvae. When the ingested copepods are killed by the digestive juices in the stomach, the larvae are released and move to the small intestine. They penetrate the intestinal wall and migrate to the connective tissue of the thorax, where male and female larvae mature and mate sixty to ninety days after infection. They grow to two-three feet in length and slowly migrate to the legs in ninety percent of cases.

About a year later the mature female worm approaches the skin and forms a painful papule in the dermis which blisters and allows the worm to be exposed and discharge swarms of motile larvae. The larvae are ingested by copepods in stagnant water. Drinking this contaminated water which has not been screened, filtered, or boiled, renews the cycle of Guinea worm disease.

Ruth's Trips to the USA

It had been two years since Ruth had seen "her girls" with their babies. A windfall estate gift enabled Ruth to make a special trip back to the USA. During the visit she needed to consult a physician about a "pain" in her back that kept recurring. She was reassured by phone and subsequently returned to Bo in Sierra Leone. Within six weeks she became violently ill with gall bladder signs and symptoms. The General Board of Global Ministries promptly authorized passage for her as well as for me to accompany her for treatment. We intended to go to Frankfurt, Germany. The cost of the tickets were comparable to those which would take us all the way to the United States. We stayed on the plane and with the help of pethadine injections to handle the pain, we arrived unannounced at John F. Kennedy International Airport, New York, New York. Bob and Connie Dietrick, UMC missionaries who served at the Kissy UMC Urban Centre and who were waiting for the arrival of Rob's brother from South America, happened to see us disembark. We were unable to contact the GBGM office because of its being a holiday and also we were unable to contact any other individuals. The Dietrick's took us to their home and then transferred us to the Newark airport where we took a direct flight to Rochester, Minnesota and the

Mayo clinic. Surgery was promptly done and within two weeks Ruth and I were back at our posts in Bo, Sierra Leone.

Bo, 1975

The years of service at the Bo Eye Clinic went by very rapidly with such an absorbing schedule. It was never anticipated that the patient load would exceed fifty or sixty a day but as noted earlier it often was more than 160 during the latter half of the tour. Surgeries were done four or five times each day. During January and February our son Tim lent a hand. He helped with every aspect of the program and on January 27, 1975, recorded his first complete cataract extraction procedure. By the end of February he was doing four or more cataract procedures each day as well as the occasional glaucoma operation (trabeculectomy).

The spiritual tone of the community of missionaries was a special blessing at Bo. Prayer meetings were held together and were life directing. Chalky and Elaine Cox, Phillip Dean, Jenny Gibson, Richard and Carol Jackson, and David Griffeth, represented Protestant, Catholic, and other independent persuasions, but during prayer times all hands were raised in praise and supplication to God. It was a foregone conclusion that the baptism of the Holy Spirit could and would happen.

Following one season of prayer, a package of cigarettes was tossed into the middle of the circle. The owner declared, "that is the end of it." Several weeks later he demonstrated to the group how his fingernails had changed. The distal parts were yellow with the past nicotine, the proximal or newly formed nails were clear.

Preparation for our departure from the Bo Eye Clinic was an involved process. Paul, who had not as yet started his work at Fuller Theological Seminary, flew out to help with the packing. Most of the instruments and technology were our own. We donated some to the Lunsar Eye Clinic where the Sierra Leone Baptist Church was beginning an eye clinic. Our trained staff was transferred as a body to this new work at Lunsar.

When the packing was completed, nineteen barrels and four crates were ready for shipment. Admission has to be made that while some crates contained slit lamps and other optical equipment, one crate held the dismantled parts of a Honda trail mini-bike from which Andrew could not be separated.

We do not know how we could have managed without Paul's help. I was going day and night trying to minister to all the people who sought help before the Bo Eye Clinic closed its work. The above mentioned Christian fellowship with prayers for one another, kept us healthy and sane.

The Bo Eye Clinic years were to contain some of the deepest spiritual experiences of our lifetime.

Family Volunteers

While still in medical training, our son Tim had the opportunity of visiting us at the Bo Eye Clinic. He flung himself into the program which served as many as 166 patients a day. It was a defining experience which led to his first cataract extraction January 27, 1975. Before the end of February, he was doing as many as four cataracts a day along with the occasional trabeculectomy for glaucoma patients. Following his marriage to Joanne Anderson, the two of them served for six weeks doing volunteer eye surgery at the Lunsar Baptist Eye Clinic.

In the 1970s it was the policy of the General Board of Global Ministries of the United Methodist Church to underwrite visits to the field for family members whose parents were under appointment. Ruth and I had been at the Bo Eye Clinic for over a year and a half when it was our pleasure to welcome a Christmas visit that included our four sons. It created quite a stir when these four young men appeared with long hair and beards. Ruth and I had determined not to blink an eye at their appearance. We were just happy that they chose to visit their parents rather than head out for the hills as so commonly was being done by college students in that day.

Since John and Paul had spent a large portion of their lives in a mission situation, it was easy for them to move about to do hunting or to help in the eye clinic as they desired. Both became expert at fabricating glasses – edging lenses to size and then fitting them into appropriate plastic frames. Simple refractions were done for patients who had good distant vision, only needing presbyopic corrections for reading.

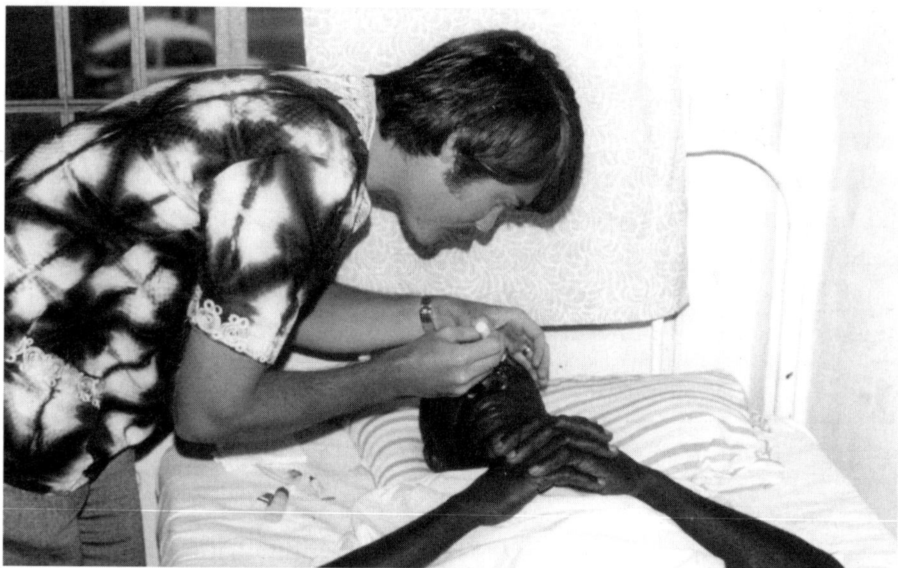

Figure 4.11. Tim Gess preparing patient for surgery.

One morning while John was hunting, Paul came to the clinic early and examined a patient that fitted the above description. He measured the patient for glasses, did the edging, placed the lenses in a plastic frame, and sent him off completely happy in less than ninety minutes. The examination included a glaucoma tonometer check by brother, Tim, and a funduscopic exam by me. Significant is the fact that Paul returned to his graduate study at Fuller Theological Seminary and qualified as a family counselor. The absent John pursued an optometric career and refracted patients and fitted glasses as his life's work.

Twice in recent years Andrew has been able to accompany us during our visits to Sierra Leone. It was a joy for him to visit the country where he was born on September 11, 1959. He was able to renew boyhood friendships at Rotifunk, Taiama, Bo, and Freetown. Andrew participated in the devotional time of the staff as well as with the patients whether it was at the Lunsar Eye Clinic or the Kissy UMC Eye Hospital. The high point of each day was the hearty hymn singing, scripture reading, testimonies, and praying. It was exciting to have a new congregation each day which numbered over 100 people. Especially helpful was the expert VCR filming that Andrew did of the eye hospital patients, facilities, program, and staff personnel. Donors are encouraged when they visually witness the lively and extensive program in Africa.

Manjama Health Centre – Box 121 – Bo

Narrative Report January - November, 1984

Manjama Health and Maternity Centre started in the early 1950s as a self-help project with the permission of the late Dr. Milton E. S. Margai, the first Prime Minister of Sierra Leone. Rev. J. B. Vandy Rogers, the District Superintendent of the UMC (then EUB) Conference, supervised the construction of the first wattle mud building.

Dr. Winifred Bradford served in the wattle mud building until she and her husband and children left finally for the USA in 1968. Mr. Lester Bradford had established a forestry and agricultural program along with animal husbandry and the construction of a fish pond. Mrs. Horton, an English qualified Sister, worked for one year 1968 to 1969.

The Conference handed over the clinic to Rev. J. B. Vandy Rogers, and he and Mrs. Laura Sackey worked together. The old wattle mud building collapsed. The present building was put up by Rev. J. B. Vandy Rogers, District Superintendent, supervised by Mr. Daniel Humphreys, a former American missionary who taught at Leone Secondary School, Bo. The new Health Centre was dedicated about 1970 by Bishop Carew, and officially opened by Hon. Lamin Gobio. In 1974, Joseph A. Sackey, a laboratory technician, joined his wife on the staff.

Manjama Health Centre is governed by a local committee composed of church and community leaders, which reports to the United Methodist Conference Board of Medical Services. The local committee is being expanded to handle wider aspects of development, especially agriculture. Manjama does not seek external funds for the recurring budget, since experience shows that the principle of self-help and self-support is a sounder basis for future development of this type of health work. There are, however, some needs which can be met only by outside well-wishers. Support continues from the community, the Bo-Pujehun Rural Development Project, the United Methodist churches in the USA, and the Swedish Methodist Church, which had presented a van.

In the villages the staff work with local committees, following the recommendations of the World Health Organization for bringing primary health care to the greatest number of people with their own active participation.

Manjama staff cooperated with government health services, in one case even furnishing supervisory and immunization services to a government Health Centre at the request of the Medical Officer.

Manjama is an active member of the Christian Health Association of Sierra Leone (CHASL) to which Mrs. Morgan contued to give many years of distinguished leadership.

Since our reason for being is service for our Lord Jesus Christ, we open clinic sessions with devotions. With respect for all persons, we encourage our Muslim patients to recite their own Al Fatiha prayer. We assist the evangelist in the work of the local Manjama village church, taking turns at conducting the Sunday evening services.

In the 1980s, Miss Dorothy Gilbert, nurse-midwife, a UMC missionary veteran of many years in Zaire, joined the staff. The work expanded into other villages in an outreach program. The antenatal and under-five clinics grew dramatically especially after immunizations were begun in 1983.

The philosophy of a community development program was to expand to other clinics in succeeding years.

Overlooking Freetown

Overlooking Freetown

The Building of the Kissy UMC Eye Hospital

I have overlooked the city of Freetown, Sierra Leone, West Africa, many times from varying heights, but there was one experience that I have not – and perhaps will not ever – forget.

It was 1976, and I was on my way to do eye surgery upcountry at the Lunsar Eye Hospital. My road circled Mount Leicester. At the highest point, more than a thousand feet above Freetown, I stopped at the side of the road where it met the mountain. On the other side there was a perilous drop. At this elevation, thick, enveloping clouds often made it impossible to view the surrounding country.

On this day it was clear. As I moved to the open side of the road, I could see the bustling city lying at my feet with traffic movement resembling little ants. During the dry season the backdrop is brown, but with the rains, greenery springs up everywhere.

After viewing the breathtaking scene for a period, I was suddenly struck with the realization that there were a million people at my feet. Along with the more than ten million people of West Africa, they needed modern eye care. In that moment I felt a Christian compassion that

Figure 5.1. Kissy UMC Eye Hospital.

prompted a resolve to continue a yearly volunteer eye ministry to Sierra Leone for as long as the Lord would lend me breath. "To this very day (25 years later) I have been helped by God, and so I stand here giving my witness to all..." Acts 26:22 Today's English Version (Good News Bible).

With the completion of our three-year tour of service at the Bo Eye Clinic in 1975, we retired as medical missionaries. We established a practice in Alexandria, Minnesota, but could not forget the continuing need for eye surgery in the country of Sierra Leone. With the encouragement of the Douglas County Hospital and the community in general, Ruth and I continued to return to Sierra Leone for approximately three months each year – the months of January, February, and March. Local patients were willing to wait for their eye surgery until our return to Alexandria.

During the initial returns to Freetown we had a temporary facility set up at the Kissy Urban Centre. The term "Kissy" represents an area of eastern Freetown predominantly settled in early years by members of the Kissy tribe from upcountry. Between visits, we would store slit lamps, operating microscope, and refractive equipment. The Annual Conference of the United Methodist Church in Sierra Leone ultimately felt that a more permanent facility should be built. Mr. Henry R. N.

Figure 5.2. The five original volunteers from Central UM Church, Milbank, S. Dakota: Arvid Liebe, pharmacist; James Mundwiler, mortician; Loren Ebsen, contractor; Floyd Bohn, accountant; Roger Reiners, contractor.

Jusu and Ms. Anna Morford encouraged this. Mr. Jusu made available an architect, and plans were drawn up for an eye hospital. The building was to be fifty feet wide by eighty feet long, which would accommodate all that was needed for a comprehensive eye program. A second floor above the surgical wing was to be built as an apartment for visiting ophthalmologists. Over the years forty ophthalmologists have spent from one to three or more months doing volunteer eye surgery at the Kissy UMC Eye Hospital.

The money to underwrite the building of the hospital was to come from the General Board of Global Ministries. However, the $70,000 allocated was not adequate for the entire building. To supplement that amount, a letter of need was prepared. Women from the Missionary Society of the Alexandria United Methodist Church mailed copies to over 10,000 ophthalmologists in the United States. The letter challenged eye doctors to help build the Kissy UMC Eye Hospital in Freetown, Sierra Leone, West Africa. It was suggested that the receipts from a single intraocular lens implantation procedure be donated for this hospital. Surprisingly and wonderfully, a number of doctors responded, and the hospital was completed.

It is a thrilling story as to how the hospital was built. The Reverend Walter Erdman, a pastor in Milbank, South Dakota, had invited me to speak to his church about medical missions. After the presentation, he mentioned that he had some men in his congregation who were enthused about missions and might be challenged by a project such as building a hospital in West Africa. In less than four months, five volunteers from his congregation were on their way with the supplies and equipment needed for the hospital. Interestingly, there were only two contractors among the five, Loren Ebsen and Roger Reiners. The other three gentlemen were Floyd Bohn, an accountant, Arvid Liebe, a pharmacist, and Jim Mundwiler, a mortician. Others also came repeatedly to help with the construction and repair of the eye hospital such as John and Frances Rebstock. Not only have these helpers and volunteers actually laid block upon block, but down through the years they have continued to pray for the work and to contribute financially to the ongoing program. Many people, including individual doctors, churches, and interested people have shared in the ongoing expenses of this eye program. It continues today as the premiere eye care center in that part of West Africa. We thank God for the concern and compassion of so many people for the eye needs of people in that part of the world.

Now twenty-five years later, I look back with gratitude for that vision while overlooking Freetown and the call to continue to do all in my power that the blind might see and many learn of God's love.

Kissy UMC Eye Hospital Background

During the 1976 to 1982 period when Ruth and I made our annual three-month pilgrimages to Sierra Leone, there were many open avenues of service. Visits were made to Rotifunk, Taiama, and Bo, but the principal opportunity was at the Lunsar Baptist Eye Hospital. The surgeon, Dr. Eleanor Koeth, was well trained in ophthalmology and was quick to develop surgical skills for cataract and especially glaucoma procedures. Some years later Dr. Koeth, Dr. Ingrid Graelle, and I published an article titled Trabeculectomy with Iridencleisis, *British Journal of Ophthalmology*, Volume 69 No. 12, (December 1985), pp. 881-885.

Dr. Graelle became adept at intraocular lens implantation. Her hus-

Figure 5.3. Dr. Ingrid Graelle, Ruth Gess, R.N., Dr. Eleanor Koeth.

band, a pastor, taught at the Jui Bible College where he started his writing career which eventually led to successful publications in Germany.

The Lunsar administrator, Sister Ursula Schwemmer, made Ruth and me welcome during our visits. It is hard to understand how she would share choice foods sent as gift boxes from Germany, rather than keep them until a time when sharing would not be necessary. She was a master builder of staff houses and hospital wards. Building suppliers were invariably prompted to give her unusual discounts. Sister Margaret Breitling was one of the best surgical assistants with whom I ever had the privilege to work.

Dr. Herb Friesen, accomplished and dedicated eye surgeon to Pakistan and Afghanistan, and his wife Ruth, spent time at Lunsar developing further the surgical program prior to the arrival of Dr. Jan Stilma, surgeon extraordinaire. Dr. Stilma did extensive research in glaucoma and onchocerciasis (river blindness). Dr. Robert Barbe, Dr. William McElroy, Dr. Richard Wilson and Dr. Ralph Buhrman made significant contributions, especially in the education field which Dr. Barbe initiated and oversaw for a number of years. It was a privilege to work with these outstanding skilled and Christian motivated medical missionaries.

After Lunsar was moving ahead with the development of their program, I spent more time in Freetown. Some surgery was done at the Connaught Government Hospital where Dr. E.B. Ceesay and Dr. Dennis Williams conducted the program, but more and more work was being carried on at the Kissy Urban Centre. We did examinations for pastors and lay persons at King Memorial United Methodist Church during the Annual Conferences. Glasses were provided. Eventually we were given accommodations at the Kissy Urban Centre main building which included a waiting room for patients, a surgical prep room, and a small six by ten foot room for the surgery. An air conditioner was supported in a small window which made the close quarters livable. Dr. James Foulkes and his wife, Martha, of Kasempe, Zambia, visited us for a period. He took extensive notes and participated in some of the procedures. On his return to Zambia he developed an eye clinic and became proficient in cataract extraction with intraocular lens implantation. In recent years, besides doing volunteer general surgery in the Sudan, he has given instruction and oversight for eye procedures.

The response to the medical and surgical care of eye patients at Kissy was overwhelming. It was obvious to the United Methodist Church Conference leadership by 1981 that an eye program was greatly needed. It was at this time that Mr. Jusu engaged Ms. Muhleman, a qualified architect, to draw up architectural plans. Three lovely mango trees were sacrificed for the hospital plot. The foundations were begun January 15, 1982, and the walls began to go up. Later in the year the five volunteers from Milbank arrived. Before they returned to South Dakota, a roof was in place.

Some nine months later the original five volunteers were joined by other volunteers. The hospital rooms and the apartment above surgery were outfitted. Patients then were seen and surgery begun. In January, 1984, the Kissy UMC Eye Hospital was dedicated.

Kissy UMC Eye Hospital Dedication

Following the heroic and expert building of the Kissy UMC Eye Hospital by the Central Global Vision Fund workers from the Central United Methodist Church in Milbank, South Dakota in 1983, the hospital was ready for dedication February 18, 1984. Bishop Thomas S. Bangura officiated, assisted by Bishop Arthur F. Kulah from Liberia with

Figure 5.4. President Siaka Stevens cutting the ribbon at the Kissy UMC Eye Hospital Dedication, February 18, 1984. {*left-to-right:* Bishop Arthur Kulah, Vice President Kamara Taylor, President Siaka Stevens, Bishop Thomas S. Bangura, Dr. Frank B. Davies.}

future Bishop Felton E. May in attendance. The President of Sierra Leone, Siaka Stevens, cut the ribbon. The scripture noted at the entrance was taken from II Corinthians 4: 5, "For we preach not ourselves but Christ Jesus the Lord, and ourselves your servants for Jesus' sake," (KJV). This verse was etched in the framework. Almost twenty years later it was finally made public for all to see as they enter the hospital.

The selection of a staff was of primary importance. Deference was made to Mrs. Gess for this responsibility as she had been responsible for the business management down through the years. She chose Leticia Williams as administrator. John Fornah and Ernest Kroma, who worked with us at the Bo Eye Clinic, were drafted from the Lunsar Eye Clinic. Mr. Fornah headed up the surgical department and Mr. Kroma the refraction. With the growth of the hospital, twenty-three people have become a part of the continuing staff.[1]

When the rebels threatened to overrun Freetown in 1997, Mrs. Williams and two of her daughters escaped to live with her relatives in

1. **Present Staff:** Dr. Ainor Fergusson, eye surgeon; Mrs. Leticia Williams, administrator; Mrs. Hannah Koroma, assistant administrator; Mr. John B. Fornah; Mrs. Elsie Fornah; Mr. James Koroma; Mr. Jonathan Bendu; Mr. Mohamed Rogers; Mr. Ernest Kroma; Mr. Sahr Andrew Alpha; Mr. Joseph Sesay; Mr. Bossy Kamara; Mr. Aba Turray; Mr. Paul Tarawally; Mr. Malcolm Albert; Mr. Bob Conteh; Mr. Adams Bangura; Mr. Sheriff Kargbo; Mr. Abduli Conteh; Mr. Lamin; Mr. Johnny Sawyer.

Figure 5.5. Kissy UMC Eye Hospital staff.

Gambia. The assistant administrator, Hannah Koroma, and her three daughters were caught in the onslaught. One of the daughters was kidnapped. It was to be nearly a year before her whereabouts were known and arrangements made for her release.

The Year of Dedication, 1984

With the dedication of the Kissy UMC Eye Hospital, the eye program expanded. The early surgical emphasis was continued and enhanced by surgical volunteer specialists coming for one to three months at a time. The first surgeon in 1984 was Dr. Russell Boehlke accompanied by his wife, Donna. Seven times over the next sixteen year period they came with valuable medicines and supplies to do surgery and clinical work.

The second volunteer was Dr. Hal Bryan and his wife, Greta. At customs the listings of the items they brought totaled over $80,000.00. They returned in 1985 and again in 1992.

Other 1984 volunteer eye surgeons were: Dr. John S. Dunn, Dr. Winston T. Cope, Dr. Ricky Russell, and Dr. Frank J. Cerny who, besides doing eye surgery, played the organ for services at the Brown Memorial United Methodist Church located on the same compound as the eye hospital.

The handling of this complicated program was well managed by Mrs. Leticia Williams. Her previous training in the UK assisting in eye surgery was extremely helpful. She possessed administrative skills that brought leadership to a disparate band of newly hired staff.

The Sierra Leone Conference of the United Methodist Church took an active role in guiding the new eye program. Dr. F. B. Davies, pastor and general practitioner, gave leadership as chairman of the Conference Medical Board. It was at this time that he and his family suffered the tragedy of having their son killed in an automobile accident.

There were other causes for disappointment in the early part of 1984. On January 5, 1984, Mr. Ernest Kroma was given the responsibility of protecting eye equipment on the veranda that had not as yet been moved into the main building. A pellet from his warning shot aimed above intruders struck one of the would-be thief's left eye and an enucleation was required. Subsequently the patient was fitted with a prosthesis which appeared normal but disappointingly provided no vision. Mr. Kroma was incarcerated by the CID for nearly a week's time. When released he gave his testimony at the Brown Memorial United Methodist Church January 15th, in which he told of sharing Christian songs and witnessing during the time of imprisonment.

In January and February, 1984, the Milbank volunteers completed cabinets in the hospital as well as in the living quarters above the surgery. They completed a highly efficient kitchen, living room, two bedrooms, and two baths in the apartment that housed volunteers. The team consisted of Roger Reiners, Bernice Ankeny, Rev. John and Fran Rebstock, and Rev. Ralph Dunn. Other volunteers from Tennessee came to serve in the dentistry program.

During the latter part of February, I needed to make a trip to Cairo, Egypt, where I presented a paper on trabeculectomy with iridencleisis. During my absence Ruth awoke one morning to see that our Toyota Corona station wagon was resting on stones minus all four wheels, the battery, and its tools. The philosophy of some in West Africa is that if property is not appropriately guarded it is fair game for the community to appropriate.

This thought was underlined one night when Ruth and I were awakened by scratching on the screen in the living room. Getting out of bed and investigating, I saw a hand reaching in through the cut screen grasp-

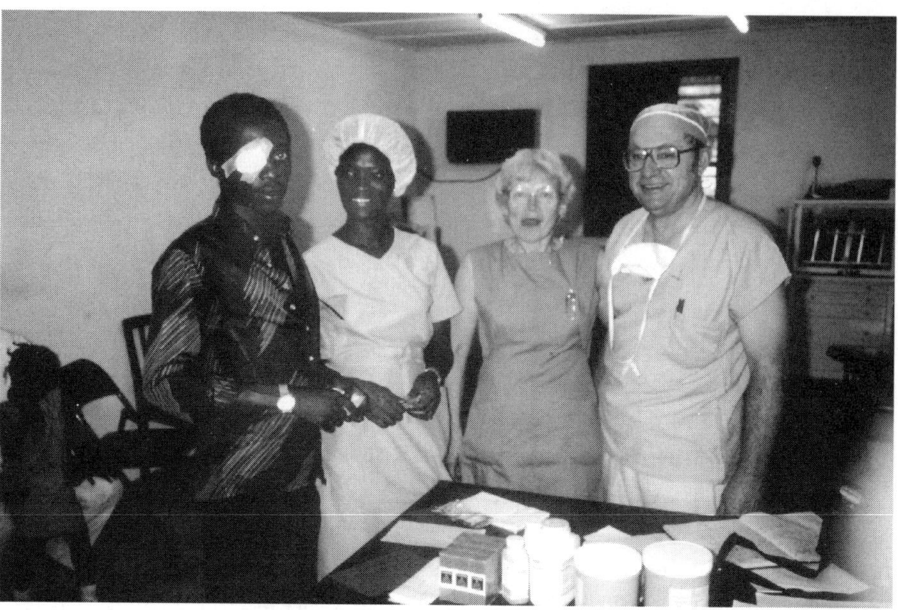

Figure 5.6. Dr. and Mrs. Russell Boehlke with Lettie Williams and patient.

ing the radio that had been resting on the desk close to the window. With a forceful vocal rebuke the hand released the radio and the body plummeted to the earth and sped off in the darkness.

Tragedies and Triumphs in 1985

By 1985 the number of patients seen and operated upon mushroomed. Dr. and Mrs. Justin L. Sleight revisited the eye program after having spent a year with us at the Bo Eye Clinic in 1971. He was to return again in 1989. They opened their home to Mr. Ernest Kroma for an extended period in East Lansing, Michigan, while Mr. Kroma qualified for a dispensing degree.

Dr. and Mrs. Boehlke came to do volunteer surgery again. Other volunteers were: Dr. Knute N. Guldjord, Dr. Larry J. Gerbens, Dr. John C. Roberts, and Dr. Frank Moran.

Early in the year the mission was privileged to have a visit by Mr. Spurgeon Dunnam who was the reporter/editor of the *United Methodist Reporter*. His visit to the Kissy UMC Eye Hospital took place at a time when Dr. Knute Guldjord was present. Dr. Guldjord's practice was in Bremerton, Washington. He had arranged to spend a month away from his private practice in the United States to join in the work at Kissy. Now he was dealing one by one with a long line of patients with eye problems and was enjoying the fellowship with them at the time that Mr. Dunnam interviewed him.

Dr. Guldjord was not present at Kissy as a part of any structured mission. He had met me at a medical convention and agreed to come as a volunteer. He spoke appreciatively of the clinic's equipment and facilities. He said that he was happy to be a part of ministering to the need of people in West Africa when they had so few opportunities for treatment. When he was asked why he responded to the invitation to come to Kissy, he said, "We all like to feel we are doing something worthwhile in life and doing God's will. I feel a very deep relationship to God as I use my talents here among these people."

It was a privilege to welcome Dr. Ingrid Graelle, an ophthalmologist living at Jui, while her husband taught at the Bible and Theological College. She had not had the background of intraocular lens implantation, but during her visits to the Kissy UMC Eye Hospital she readily took up this new modality and became most expert at it. On one of her visits she was aware of the subdued tone of the hospital where on the day previous an unusual tragedy had occurred. Mrs. Fattu Jalloh, while having a cataract extraction, went into an asthmatic crisis with respiratory failure. In spite of successful intubation and medical treatment, Mrs. Jalloh could not be revived. She was to be the only eye fatality of many thousands of patients in West Africa.

During the second week of February, 1985, one of the most significant trips in Africa was taken as Ruth and I set out to visit Rev. D. H. Caulker in Kono country. On the way during this 200 mile trip a stop was made at the Lunsar Eye Hospital where we visited Sister Ursula Schwemmer and Dr. Jan Stilma. They told of their tragedy when they described the death of Mr. Joseph Ngeba, one of their most promising nurses in training. He had been struck and killed by lightning as he crossed the road in front of the Lunsar Hospital to buy bread. Joseph was especially adept in English partly because of his exposure as a close friend to our sons John and Paul Gess when we served at Bo.

Our visit with Rev. D.H. Caulker (described in Chapter 3) was one of the most inspirational we had ever experienced. In his 113th year, his love for the Lord's work was undimmed.

Our return to the Kissy UMC Eye Hospital February 14, 1985, was especially important because I received a lovely Valentine from Ruth which was to be the same Valentine that I was to receive each year for the following twelve year period. In the midst of tragedies and death there is the living love that we have for others who have a like love and loyalty to Jesus Christ.

1986 – The Eye Program in Full Swing

The year 1986 was to be a banner year. More volunteer ophthalmologists participated in the Kissy UMC Eye Hospital program than ever before. Early in the year, Dr. Albert H. Bryan, better known as Hal, returned with his wife Greta, to do his intensive surgery, sometimes doing as many as fifteen to twenty intraocular surgeries a day. He was followed by Dr. Robert Searle, Dr. Jack A. Aaron, Dr. Hillmer A. Fonken, Dr. Norman F. Woodlief, and the revisiting of Dr. and Mrs. Russell R. Boehlke. Dr. Richard A. Yook brought his entire family with him. This struck a responsive note with the Kissy staff. Their visits were always anticipated. Ms. Vivian Olson volunteered seven months at the hospital doing clerical work with the proper balancing of books. She had been an appointed missionary for over thirty years and was well known for her Christian compassion. Many people came to the hospital with the intent to see "Miss Olson."

The year was one of political stability but inflation was beginning. Ultimately the devaluation of the leone was to assume such a proportion that a large amount of currency needed to be carried in a handbag to pay for purchased items. With this handling of large quantities of leone notes, a practice developed where waiters and clerks would announce that the payment that was received after being counted by the cashier was short – never was it reported to be in excess. To deal with this, customers made it a practice to have a second person count the money before giving it to the waiter or cashier. If the report was that the amount was short, the reply was simply, "Oshe" (sorry) and the customer would take his leave.

It was an important time at the Kissy UMC Eye Hospital when the Zeis OMPI-6S microscope arrived. It had all the recent improvements in optics as well as zoom features and x-y movement. Controls were from a foot panel. This instrument along with the Yag Laser, five Haag

Streit slit lamps, a DBR 310 Ascan, and B & L phoropter, impressed visiting volunteer eye surgeons. It was a pleasure to be able to use excellent instruments and instrumentation in this faraway place in West Africa.

Ruth and I were informed early in the year of a serious automobile accident involving several United Methodist missionaries. One of the passengers, Miss Metra Heisler, was brought some thirty miles to Freetown for care. Ruth and I were made aware of her presence at the Nethland Hospital by Rev. Joseph Humper and Rev. David Caulker. Immediately we visited her and found that she had been hospitalized for nearly a day and a half and had yet to see a physician. She had a serious leg injury and she complained of chest pain. We prevailed on the administration of the hospital to allow us to care for Miss Heisler at our Kissy UMC Eye Hospital. We stopped on the way for X-rays of her chest which were read as normal. In bed, she needed to be propped up on a chair in order to breathe. It was obvious that the rib cage was compromised in spite of the negative X-rays. On her return to the U.S.A., she was found to have a hemothorax and five fractured ribs. We thank God that she was able to hold steady until such time as definitive treatment was made available.

On January 30, 1986, Ruth and I had the pleasure of being presented to his excellency Dr. J. S. Momoh, President of Sierra Leone. The

Figure 5.7. Shaking hands with President Dr. J.S. Momoh, 1986.

occasion was one of recognition of volunteer services of people coming to Sierra Leone. When asked to respond, I reminisced about shaking hands with the past president Siaka Stevens in 1956. It had been thirty years since that handshake and I asked that a new handshake be done today with the hope and prayer that President Momoh would have strong and sturdy shoulders to assume the mantle of leadership for Sierra Leone.

Following this service we were invited along with Rev. Susan Messenger and Rev. Franklin Messenger to have dinner with Rev. Crispin Renner and his wife Theresa, an excellent cook. Over the years they repeatedly invited us to their home to share a meal, as well as bringing food to us while we worked at the Kissy UMC Eye Hospital. The Christian fellowship with this family was one of the high points of our repeated visits to Sierra Leone.

Holiday Spirits or Eye Medicine

On our return trip to Kissy UMC Eye Hospital the second week of December, 1986, we were transferring planes at Chicago's O'Hare airport. We were informed by a KLM official that they would not be able to take along all of the seventeen boxes of eye medicines that we were carrying as excess baggage. Previously KLM had been helpful and supportive in graciously accepting our many boxes that weighed up to seventy pounds each. We at once realized that if the boxes did not accompany us to Amsterdam and then on to Freetown, we would not have the use of the medicines and supplies during the early week or two of our visit. We explained this to the officials of KLM, but they insisted that the cargo was more than KLM could manage.

Smitten and dejected, we returned to our seats trying to understand the events that were happening. Suddenly it came to me – Christmas was only a week away. There just might be some confusion with cargo because of extra baggage in relation to the celebration of Christmas. Innocently I went up to the baggage department and asked for the person in charge. I explained to him again the great need that we had for the medicine, that it must accompany us, in order for us to give sight saving operations in West Africa. And then out of the blue I said, "If by any chance this eye medicine is being bumped because of the need to carry holiday spirits on the plane, it would not be a very good story for the press." Letting it go at that I returned to my seat.

It was hardly ten minutes before a new high ranking official came to visit Ruth and me. He explained that KLM was making arrangements to take our excess baggage with us in order that we might continue our work. We had a very pleasant flight and a most rewarding time of surgery in Africa over the holiday season.

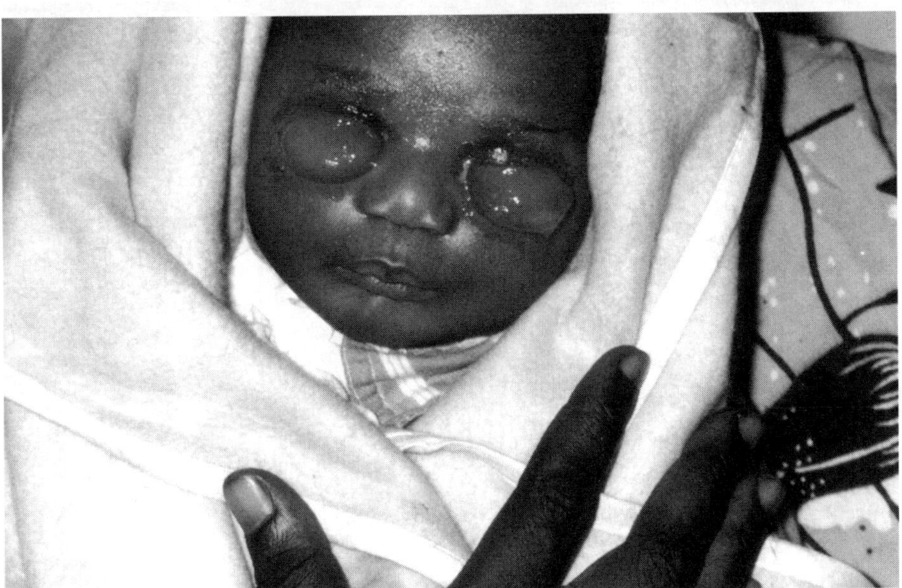

Figure 5.8. Newborn with everted eyelids.

Kissy, 1987

Shortly after arriving at the Kissy UMC Eye Hospital for our time of service in 1987, there was brought to us a newborn whose upper eyelids became everted during the birth process. There was great swelling of all the tissue, not only of the eyelids themselves but surrounding tissue. It was frightening to the mother and local attendants. Witchcraft was believed to be involved. The infant was presented to us by a sympathetic neighbor not related to the family. In this case surgery was needed to restore the lids to a normal position, unlike a similar case we had wit-

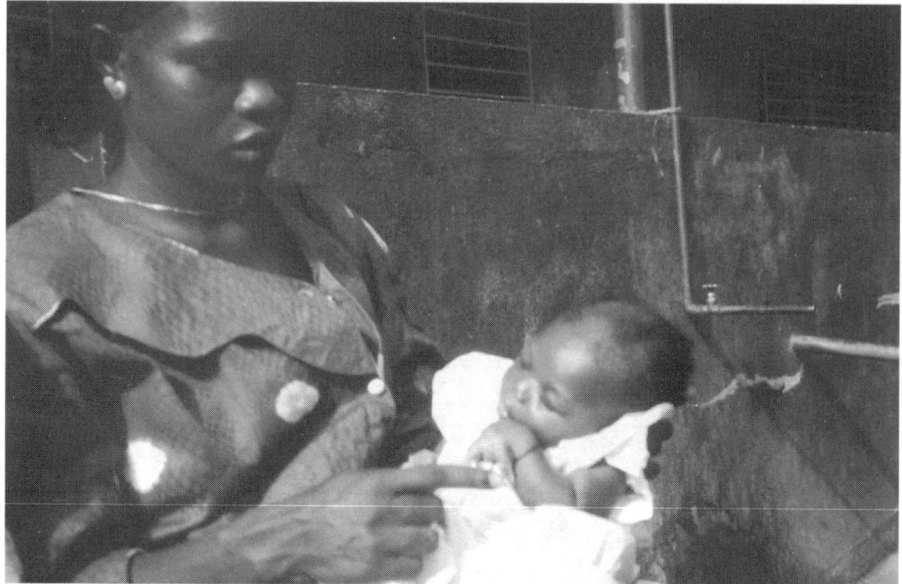

Figure 5.9. Eyelids restored to normal position.

nessed in Abak, Nigeria, where the head nurse was able to remedy the problem without anesthesia.

This incident acquired some notoriety, with Dr. F. B. Davies learning about it and making reference to it in his church where he was senior pastor, Baughman Memorial United Methodist Church. The church actually was on the opposite side of Freetown but the story that came to him was that there was a child needing surgery at the Kissy Eye Hospital, who they named "Dr. Lowell Gess."

1987 proved to be a stellar year. Dr. Edward P. Hurst made his first visit to Sierra Leone. There were Minnesota ophthalmologists, Dr. Allen K. Larson, and Dr. Wesley D. Sonddreal, as well as Dr. L. Ray Cain, who was impressed by the needs of the people of West Africa and continues to keep in touch with the Kissy program.

It was wonderful to have Washington University School of Medicine classmate, Dr. Wm. G. Prater, come with his daughter to lend a hand. Mrs. Margaret Gaston, who was overseeing the eye program for a six month period, tried to make their stay comfortable but the ordinarily reliable Freetown water supply had broken down. Years later Dr. Prater was still referred to by the staff as "that fast surgeon." Dr. Russell and Donna Boehlke visited and were hailed as usual by the appreciative and excited staff.

The year was rounded out by Dr. Arland K. Faust. We had worked under his father's leadership in Bambur, Nigeria from 1952 to 1955. His father possessed not only a Bachelor of Divinity degree but also a Ph.D. His mother, Mrs. Aletha Faust, worked tirelessly in women's work. The Zumuta Mata is a powerful women's fellowship until this present day. With Dr. Arland Faust's missionary background, his time of service was especially well done.

The time of service was not without excitement. During one night I was awakened by a strange noise below our bedroom. I knew that trustworthy and honest Bossie Kamara was on duty as guard and dismissed the thought of following up on this incident. The next morning we were to learn that thieves had made their way through a window and actually lifted out our Honda generator. It was inconceivable that a machine of such size and weight could be handled so deftly.

We were happy to have the services of Dr. Justin Sleight again in 1987 and along with him we were thrilled to have volunteers coming to put the finishing touches on the hospital structure in the persons of Loren Ebsen, Jim Mundwiler, Floyd Bohn, Bernice Ankeny, Ed Reiners (father of Roger who was one of the original contractors), Daryl Stengel, and Al Pay. Their three week period dressed up the hospital to look and function first class. Unfortunately, Al Pay needed to have hospitalization for a heart condition that required the expert treatment of Dr. F. B. Davies. It was necessary for Mr. Pay to return to the U.S.A. before the team had completed their mission.

It was always a pleasure to have people visit the Kissy UMC Eye Hospital not only as patients but also as supporters. Visitors included Vivian Olson, David and Nancy Forster, Dr. Ken Jones, a dentist doing volunteer service in Sierra Leone, Rev. Dale Eppel accompanied by his wife Evelin and children Edward and Irene, Pete and Mary Shearer, and prominent Sierra Leoneans including Bishop T. S. Bangura, Rev. David Caulker, and George Carew, with whom we were happy to celebrate his appointment as deputy ambassador to the Court of St. James in England.

Figure 5.10. Installation of generator by volunteers.

Kissy, 1988

As we were about to make tentative arrangements for our annual trip to the Kissy UMC Eye Hospital, I visited my 92 year old father in the Faribault Rest Home. Since he was not doing well, I mentioned that Ruth and I would skip our visit to Africa this year. He nearly bolted out of his bed declaring, "I'll not be responsible for blind people in Africa not receiving their surgery. I insist that you go."

We made our trip to Africa but our premonition proved correct. With my sister June at his bedside, he slipped away February 13, 1988. The news of his passing came to us by cable several days later, written by our son Tim. It read, "Grandpa went to be with Grandma February 13 at 12:10 p.m." The severe frost that winter in Minnesota delayed his burial for a number of weeks. By then we had returned and were able to participate in the committal service at historic Salem Evangelical Church four miles north of Paynesville. Mother's death had preceded his by five years.

Kissy UMC Eye Hospital saw Dr. and Mrs. Russell Boehlke and Dr. Hillmer A. Fonken return again with great enthusiasm on the part of the staff. They were followed by Dr. Robert E. Jardinico, Dr. John P. Ritchy, and Dr. Royce O. Hall with assistants Cheryl and Sue, who proceeded to do great numbers of eye procedures. Dr. Hall was to return another two times before he and Cheryl proceeded to Tanzania to work with the Tutsis. The establishment of his hospital facilities in far off Tanzania did not escape the notice of the Rolex Awards Committee.

The Kissy UMC Eye Hospital was established by many helping hands, some who only appeared for a day or two never to be seen or heard from again. Such was the situation with Charles Maddox and Scott Music who, seeing our need to have our new generator positioned and electrically installed, set about to the task of accomplishing that deed.

We also cannot forget the immense thrill that we had as a staff when a Fulani couple presented themselves to the hospital. Both the man and woman were tall and regal with striking good looks. I can say that perhaps there was never a more beautiful African woman that had visited the hospital. She was totally blind and had been so for fifteen years. Following her cataract operation and intraocular lens implantation the following day, she took her first steps without being directed after that long period. The husband was perhaps even more thrilled than his wife. He had been lovingly solicitous all these years and now she was able to resume her responsible place in their home.

We shall always remember Ayub Fawaz, a Lebanese merchant in Freetown who developed cataracts subsequent to his diabetic condition. He realized the risks involved in surgery but did exceedingly well developing better than 20/20 vision in each eye following their surgery. In his enthusiasm he was our greatest supporter in bringing patients to the hospital. On one occasion he brought Major Momoh, brother to President Joseph Momoh, and along with them the First Vice President, A. K. Kamara and his wife.

It was during 1988 that Paul Tarawally and I had the thrill of setting up the new OPMI-6S operating microscope with the x-y and zoom functions controlled by foot panel. We also set up a brand new 900 series Haag Streit slit lamp.

Figure 5.11. Wonderful volunteers. From left to right: Enid and Loman Young (artist), Everett (Pete) Shearer (well digger), Joyce and Richard Reeves (volunteers to Sierra Leone and African University, Zimbabwe).

Volunteers continued to come to help in the program. Dick and Joyce Reeves along with Pete Shearer spent days fixing many items. Mrs. Reeves set about sorting a large supply of lenses. We were unbelieving that she would stick to this arduous task in such heat. The Reeves also were greatly interested in the African university in Zimbabwe and spent much effort and time in seeing that it came into being.

Tremendously significant was the visit of Wilko and Virginia Schoenbohm. When they learned of the inconsistency of the electric energy from the city of Freetown, they offered to underwrite the expense of solar lighting through their home church, Hennepin Avenue United Methodist Church in Minneapolis. Helping the unfortunate was second nature to the Schoenbohms as they were responsible for the establishment of Camp Courage in Minnesota. It was at this time that Chrostoffel Blindenmission presented the program with a 30 KVA generator which became the lifeline of our program since the city electrical supply was intermittent. It also was capable of wide swings of voltage which at one time caused the replacement of thirty light bulbs.

Selection of staff members was usually done by Mrs. Gess. A very bright and promising young man applied for work in the surgery department. Mrs. Gess was not happy about taking him on. We could not understand her position as he was the one person who was needed in the expanding surgical program. Within a week we began to notice the disappearance of IV administration sets as well as IV solutions, not dreaming that this capable new employee would be at the basis of this. Ultimately it was discovered that many items were being "liberated" by this gentleman. The discovery of his thievery was made by another member of our staff. It was sad to have to let this promising young man go. Happily we learned later that he turned completely around, and was gainfully and responsibly employed.

It was in 1988 that we were honored by a visit by Dr. Randolph Nugent of the General Board of Global Ministries of the United Methodist Church. He was making his visit especially during the time of the Sierra Leone Annual Conference. On his visit to the Eye Hospital we ceremonially had him start the new generator that had been installed the previous day. Whenever I turn on the generator thoughts often go back to Dr. Nugent's visit to the Kissy UMC Eye Hospital. Over the years the General Board of Global Ministries has been most supportive of the eye outreach. They have underwritten Dr. Ainar Fergusson as a PIM (Person In Mission). Also they have made available the Advance Special which is a fund to which individuals and churches can give toward the eye program. This fund has enabled the purchasing of medicine, equipment, and supplies.

Our flight in 1988 to Sierra Leone involved excess baggage of nineteen seventy pound boxes. Northwest and KLM Airlines were especially helpful in making possible the transportation of the many needed items for the hospital discounting the cost of over half of them. The Kissy UMC Eye Hospital has been the recipient of tremendous good will over the years.

A Unique Situation, 1989

The Kissy UMC Eye Hospital under the administration of Mrs. Lettie Williams, had no regular ophthalmologist in residency. Mrs. Gess and I would return each year for January, February, and part of March. The remaining months would find other volunteer eye surgeons coming to address the eye needs of Sierra Leone and neighboring countries. In 1989 new ophthalmologists were Dr. Marc Sirota; Dr. Michael H.

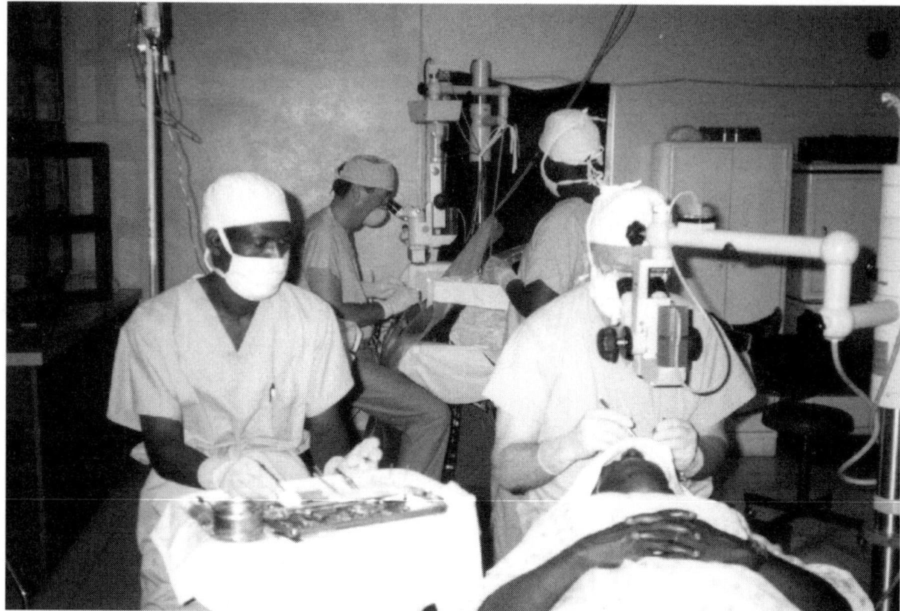

Figure 5.12. Volunteer eye surgeon Dr. Charles Carter using the Zeiss OPMI-6S in the background.

Cunningham, who returned a second time within the year; Dr. Michael Gottner, who returned again two years later; and Dr. Charles B. Carter, who usually made his volunteer trips to Haiti. Dr. Carter made return trips and for years has strongly supported the outreach of the Kissy UMC Eye Hospital with prayer and generous tangible financial gifts to this present day. Other returning ophthalmologists were Dr. Richard Yook, Dr. Royce Hall, presently engaged in a wonderful program in Tanzania, and Dr. Justin Sleight, who with his wife, Marg, have yearly remembered the staff at Christmas.

It is a source of constant amazement that an excellent and high quality eye program could be carried on by volunteers coming and going. Over the years sub-specialists have done retinal work, strabismus care, and corneal transplantation in addition to the usual cataract extractions and intraocular lens implantations.

Every effort was made to ensure the capabilities of visiting eye doctors. Usually checks would be made with other doctors about their expertise.

At one time I received a sobering call from a Florida ophthalmologist who learned that an acquaintance was scheduled to do eye surgery at Kissy. He told me that the doctor in question had had no training in intraocular lens implantation. To my dismay I learned that the doctor had already set out for Freetown. Emails and faxes were not available in those days. The hospital had no telephone for trans-Atlantic calls. There was no way to warn the staff.

I learned later that the surgical assistants at Kissy UMC Eye Hospital realized immediately the unique situation that the doctor was not trained in intraocular surgical procedures. They intercepted the scheduled patients and the following day removed the operating microscope, table, and other equipment and began painting the ceiling and walls of the surgical theatre! During the remaining time the doctor did an excellent job in patient evaluation of eye diseases in the clinic.

Don and Lilburne Theuer arrived February 23, 1989, to spend several months upgrading the hospital's accounts and general program. While in Sierra Leone, Don was asked to do an extensive evaluation on the Rotifunk Hospital related to its future growth and development. More than a decade later visitors still were using the highly polished and varnished platform in the apartment showers that the Theuers had designed. Their past appointment as mission accountant and mission host and hostess enabled them to understand the West African way of doing things upon which they built.

Highlights occurring in 1989 included:

1. Coming to know Arlene Hache who was bravely carrying on in isolated Taiama.

2. Fellowshipping with Lunsar Baptist Eye Clinic Drs. Barbe, Stilma, and Wilson. All were unusually expert in surgery. During his time at Kissy Hospital in 1990, Dr. Wilson was especially adept performing glaucoma surgery, doing as many as five trabeculectomies as well as four intraocular lens implantations in a single day.

3. Seeing the onchocerciasis research program at Njala University, directed by Dr. Gbakima.

4. Reeling from the sparkle of a six carat diamond ring on the finger of one of our intraocular lens patients. Ordinarily we assumed that people with means would travel to Europe or the U.S.A. for elective surgery. But here he was with his ring as well as a diamond studded watch.

5. Commiserating with Ruth following the theft of her purse which contained the keys to the clinic.

6. Sharing the pleasure of Augustine McCauley's proficiency in learning the art of refraction and operation of the lensometer.

7. Visiting with Dr. William Simcoe and being able to tell him how important to the world was his development of the irrigation aspiration cannulae system. Sometime later a similar visit was possible with Dr. David McIntyre, whose innovative cannulae and later phacofracture technique made possible the manual handling of cataracts prior to IOL implantation.

8. Reveling in the high moment of being asked to say the post communion words at King Memorial United Methodist Church – reminiscent of the role usually given to the Rev. J.K. Fergusson during the active years of his ministry.

The Coming of Dr. Ainor Fergusson

In the early 1990s Ainar Fergusson, MB, Bch.Do., MD, was employed at the Abha Eye Hospital in Saudi Arabia. While visiting relatives during his leave to Sierra Leone, Desert Storm erupted. He and his wife, Cassandra, decided to remain in Sierra Leone because of that conflict. Interest in eye care drew him to the Kissy UMC Eye Hospital. Volunteers were not always available. Dr. Fergusson made himself useful and within a short time was invited to be part of the staff. His medical degree had been secured in Cairo, Egypt; Diploma Accreditation in Ophthalmology in London, England followed. Time was also spent at the Wills Eye Institute. His original eye training was not in surgery but Christoffel Blindenmission made available a training period in India.

As the civil war intensified in Sierra Leone, volunteer doctors from the USA and Europe were not able to come. Dr. Fergusson stayed on despite occasions that were life threatening. The heavy load of surgery was placed on his shoulders. He rose to the occasion and for years has been the only eye doctor routinely doing cataract extraction with intraocular lens implantation in West Africa. He has done surgery at Conakry, Guinea, as well as Guinea Bissau.

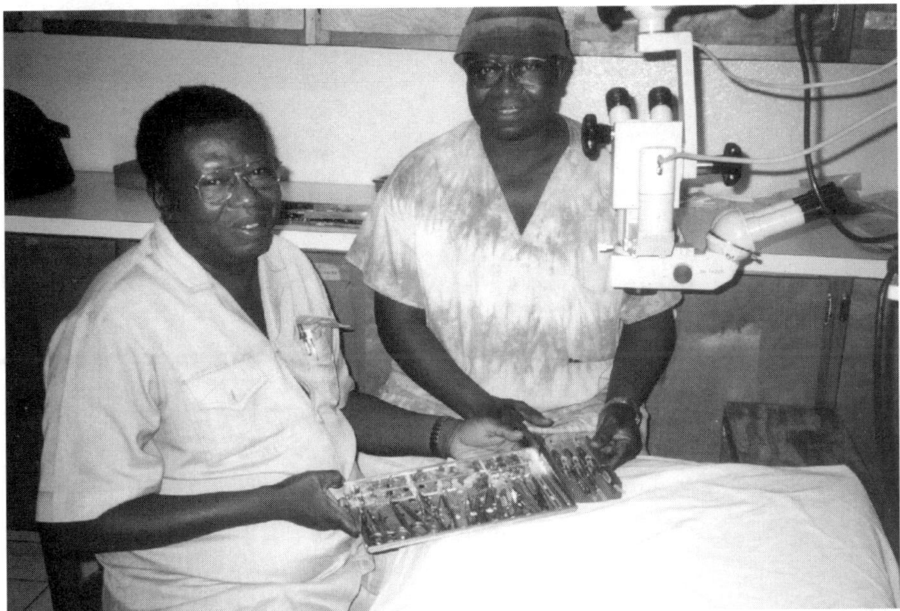

Figure 5.13. Dr. Ainor Fergusson, ophthamologist in residency at the Kissy UMC Eye Hospital with John Fornah, surgical nurse.

Dr. Fergusson has been joined from time to time by Christoffel Blindenmission appointed doctors. The first was Dr. Richard Lockwood and his family from Ohio. The second CBM appointment was Dr. Nick Cook and his family who came from England. Both Dr. Lockwood and Dr. Cook and their families were caught up in the tragic civil war and were evacuated under emergency conditions. They were the last appointees until the year 2000. Ruth and I have been able to return from time to time, the last visit being in October and November of 2001.

The First Year of Retirement, 1990

January 1, 1990, was like any other winter day except that I did not need to go to the office. Official retirement had taken place at midnight December 31, 1989. By January 11, Ruth and I were back in our beloved Sierra Leone. One of the first persons we met was Mr. Joe Skasko, a policeman from Pennsylvania. He had a love and concern for orphans and their care and was helping Ms. Ingrid Holmgren in her wonderful work at Pa Loko which took place even in the midst of hostilities. Joe's interest in Sierra Leone continued to grow over the years.

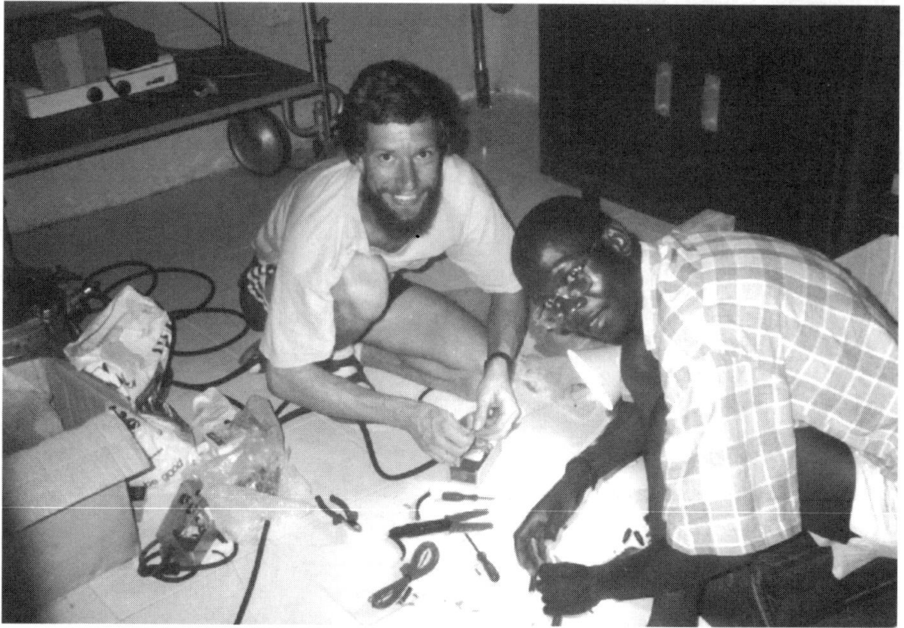

Figure 5.14. Solar lights installation by Dieter Monninger and Paul Tarawally.

He became a personal friend of the Sierra Leone ambassador to the United States, Mr. John Leigh. He made a special trip to Sierra Leone to bring back a young person needing advanced surgery, and while there made arrangements for a forty-foot container that he packed at the St. James Presbyterian Church in Mechanicsburg, Pennsylvania. It contained a wealth of supplies for the care of orphans as well as medicines and surgical equipment for the Kissy Health and Maternity Centre and the Kissy UMC Eye Hospital.

The following day Mrs. Joy Winter, wife of Dr. Frank Winter, past chair of the ophthalmology department at Stanford University in California, came to do research on surgical procedures that might give background to their Christian eye ministry being established in Ghana. This outreach expanded due to the efforts of Dr. and Mrs. Herb Billman. Dr. Billman later established the Emanuel Eye Hospital in Accra, Ghana. A new facility underwritten by the Christian Eye Ministry was established at Cape Coast under the leadership of Dr. Peter Egbert. Volunteers are usually pleased to work with the Christian Eye Ministry, a part of International Aid because of the excellent provision for travel and housing and for surgery made possible by Ms. Faye Kragt and Mr. George Wood. In his retirement Dr. Billman has continued to provide viscoelastics and medicine, not only for the work in Ghana, but also for the Kissy UMC Eye Hospital in Sierra Leone.

While 1990 saw two new volunteers coming to Kissy in the persons of Dr. Thomas Walker and Dr. Drew Logan, it was this year that set a record for returnees, FIVE. They were Dr. Edward P. Hurst, Dr. Richard H. Yook, Dr. Royce O. Hall, Dr. and Mrs. Russell R. Boehlke, and Dr. and Mrs. John P. Ritchey.

Figure 5.15. A singing baptismal testimony.

It was like "old home week" with all these past volunteers who had become "family" to the Kissy staff. Now with their past experience they knew what to expect, what medicines and supplies to bring, and how to plunge into the work without needing a prolonged period of orientation. An interesting statement by one of the doctors was, "there are no uncomplicated cases in Africa."

Besides doctors, help came from people such as Wally and Ginger Schwam. Our flight to Sierra Leone on one occasion had taken us by way of Robert's field in Liberia. This necessitated a transfer of our excess baggage to a different plane. An exorbitant charge was stipulated for which we lacked funds. The ensuing hassle was delaying the flight. Wally slipped up to the airline executive offices. Word promptly came for the baggage to be loaded. No extra charges were made.

In the clinic we were grateful for the refraction help of Mrs. Hillary Faye Cope. Her husband was a teacher at Fourah Bay College which is at a considerable elevation above Freetown. She made no complaints about descending to sea level and the intense heat that enveloped her each day at the Kissy Eye Hospital.

Truly significant in 1990 were the solar lights installed by Dieter and Martin Monninger and Paul Tarawally. The lights were financially underwritten because of the interest of Wilko and Virginia Schoenbohm and the support of the Hennepin Avenue United Methodist Church. The Schoenbohms were also instrumental in providing help for compound improvement at the hospital involving ditch repairs and replacement of the roof.

Following the cataract extraction and intraocular lens implantation of Mrs. Regina Bangura, wife of Bishop T. S. Bangura, I shall always remember the statement she made as she left the hospital. It was "'fraid for nothing," following which she strode out the clinic door.

Memorable were the Rev. Eustace Renner's arrangements for Ruth and me to have an audience with President Momoh. It was a friendly visit during which he expressed appreciation for the presence of the Kissy UMC Eye Hospital. It was apparent that his brother, who had undergone a cataract operation with IOL a short time before had briefed him on the hospital's ministry.

The most memorable occasion was attending the Rev. Angie Myles' church in Kossoh Town. She had invited the Rev. Moses Massaquoi to preach. He used Luke 18 which gives the account of the blind man. I was given the privilege of conducting the baptismal service. A fifteen year old young lady presented herself after having accepted Jesus Christ as her Lord and Savior. Some consternation had been involved in this because all her people were Muslim. And yet her decision was final. At the baptismal service she asked that she might give a testimony. It consisted of her singing, beautifully, "I have decided to follow Jesus." Angie Myles was always helpful to people in difficult situations and at one time was in charge of a large group of orphans being cared for by the Swedish United Methodist Church working in Sierra Leone.

Trouble on the Horizon, 1991

Our first trip to Kissy UMC Eye Hospital in 1991 began on New Year's Day. On landing in Freetown we were met by Rev. Angie Myles and Larry and Marge Chambers. The Chambers were spending a year at Rotifunk restoring the hospital.

We flung ourselves into the work at Kissy. Involved was the orienting of Dr. Kai Lewis, an eye doctor who trained and practiced in Liberia. Liberia was going through the throes of a civil war. Dr. Lewis and his family escaped to Freetown, Sierra Leone. His services at the Kissy UMC Eye Hospital were sought by the Sierra Leone Conference of the

Figure 5.16. Volunteer and appointed United Methodist missionaries in 1991; in 2001, there were four.

United Methodist Church and the General Board of Global Ministries of the United Methodist Church in New York. However, in a short time he made plans to leave for the United States to further his training in preventive eye care.

During the month of January, 1991, the three day Gulf War erupted. During this time Dr. and Mrs. Ainar Fergusson were in Freetown on leave from their work at Abha Hospital in Saudi Arabia. They chose not to return to Saudi Arabia because of the conflict and cultural differences. Knowing of the Kissy UMC Eye Hospital in Freetown, Dr. Fergusson's interest and commitment led him to the hospital first as an observer, then as a helper, and finally as the staff doctor who was to continue for at least another decade.

During the Gulf War, we were careful not to share political views as some of our Muslim patients heartily supported Saddam Hussein. On one occasion, we were invited to a meal with a Muslim family just prior to the active three day hostilities. With the defeat of the Iraqi aggressors, mention of Hussein's role was never again broached.

The Rev. Bodo Schwab, predecessor to Mr. Thomas Kemper, general secretary of the German Mission Board, visited Sierra Leone and gave

Figure 5.17. Ruth's white hat.

encouragement. The German United Methodist Church invested heavily in personnel and finances in the Jaiama Nimi Koro Medical Clinic. Miss Brunhilde Goebel and Miss Renata Horn did extensive tours of service. The last German supported nurse was Ms. Fritzie Carlson whose life was miraculously spared time and again during the rebel incursion. She lived through these terrible times only to die in childbirth several years later in her own homeland. Her children along with her husband, the Rev. H. Van Jollie, a pastor, continue to live in Poland.

Besides being involved in the training of two eye doctors during the year, I also had the privilege of tutoring Madianna Myles, daughter of Joe and Angie Myles. Madianna was preparing for acceptance into a registered nurses degree training program. In spite of the war and the political collapse of the country, she eventually attained her degree, following in her mother's footsteps.

Our second trip to Sierra Leone began on April 23rd. Excess baggage cost over one thousand dollars (which on one occasion on a previous trip had reached $1700.00). Shortly after our arrival we were invited to the investiture at the statehouse to receive the "Office of the Civil Division of the Order of the Rokel" in recognition of service in Sierra

Leone over the past thirty-eight years. The Rev. David and Mammi Caulker along with Mrs. Regina Bangura, represented the United Methodist Church at this occasion. In anticipation of this august meeting, Ruth had bought and brought a white hat. It had been several decades since she had purchased a hat.

Three days later we finally made the promised trip to Rotifunk to see the repairs that Larry and Marge Chambers had accomplished at the Hatfield-Archer Hospital where we had served from 1957-1960. It gave us immense pride to see the hospital restored again. Little did we realize what was happening at Kissy while we were away those two days.

Plans had been made to stay overnight in Rotifunk with the Chambers' which allowed us time to visit Rev. W. B. Clay and walk through his plantation of fruit trees. This plantation was two and a half miles from Rotifunk, but he made this trip by foot each day. We also had a chance to visit with Laura Kandeh, daughter of Rev. and Mrs. C. V. Rettew, prominent early Christian leaders in Sierra Leone. We were surprised also to be able to see Bossie Koroma with whom we had worked more than thirty years before.

The following morning on our way back to Freetown we stopped at Taiama to treat the eye patients who had gathered for our announced visit. We also had the opportunity to see friends that we had known during our 1964-1967 time of service there.

On arriving home at Kissy we were met by somber faced Lettie Williams, Angie Myles and David Caulker. During the night thieves had broken into the hospital making their entrance through our bedroom which providentially we were not occupying because of our trip to Rotifunk. They carried off the recently delivered medicines and supplies that we had just bought. They also took the refrigerator, TV, VCR, radio, typewriter, tools, and Ruth's new white hat.

Losing those items was not the serious part of the incident. Volunteer ophthalmologist Dr. John Barker and his daughter Susan were terrorized in their upstairs apartment. The thieves threatened to break down the door, but Dr. Barker placated them by passing all the money that he had through a hole in the barred window screen. He threatened them by saying that he would call the police. They laughed and taunted him saying "we *are* the police!"

After hurriedly taking their loot, gunfire took place. The hospital guards had been tied. One guard was able to free himself from the wire bands that were cutting into his wrists and eventually made his way to the police station. The police investigation turned up one of the thieves who had been shot dead. He still was cradling the radio I had purchased just days before at Schipohl Airport, Amsterdam. The police identified the corpse as a repeat offender who only recently had been released from prison. I never was able to reclaim my radio as the police "needed it for evidence."

We rejoiced with returning surgeons Dr. Charles Carter, Dr. Michael Cunningham, and Dr. Michael Gottner. New was Dr. Richard A. Bowers with his wife Miriam Rader, who extended their stay to several months. They took to their hearts the people and staff at Kissy and in return the people and staff took them to their hearts. Like Dr. Charles Carter they have continued to be supportive of the program over the years.

Besides Dr. John S. Barker and Dr. Jerry D. Harrel, the other new volunteer was a retired Air Force ophthalmologist, who has served more than a decade at the Lighthouse for Christ, Mombassa, Kenya. In subsequent years he often referred to the meaningful prayers that were offered preoperatively for the patients at Kissy, often by John Fornah.

1991 was the year that storm clouds appeared on the horizon. Foday Sankoh, following his covert training in Libya, adopted Charles Taylor's tactics that were being carried on by usurpers in Liberia. Initially he kept to the jungles near the Liberian border, but by the end of the year he became a threat to the democratically elected government headed by President Joseph Momoh. This was the beginning of one of the harshest, most brutal, and cruel civil wars the world has ever seen.

Humper Elected Bishop, 1992

The important event in the life of the United Methodist Church Sierra Leone Conference in 1992 was the election of a new bishop following Bishop T.S. Bangura's retirement. The Rev. J.C. Humper prevailed over the Rev. David Caulker for this important office. Bishop Humper took his early training in Sherbro Schools. He attended the Bible Training Institute as well as the Teacher's College in Bo, and then Fourah Bay College. In the United States of America he received degrees at Union Theological Seminary and Garrett-Evangelical Theological Seminary. Being chairman of the Inter-Religious Council in Sierra Leone during his tenure as Bishop gave him an important role in the peace process.

Following the April 29th coup, life in Freetown stabilized. The National Provisional Revolutionary Council (NPRC) under the leadership of Valentine Strasser established a once-a-month Saturday morning clean up day which was monitored by armed forces. Strasser headed the military government for four years until being ousted by Julius Maada Bio in early 1996.

Except for the return of Dr. Hal and Mrs. Bryan in March, prior to the coup, the coming of volunteer ophthalmologists was not encouraged for the remainder of 1992.

Over the years Christoffel Blindenmission has been helpful in the eye care outreach in Sierra Leone. As far back as 1973 they provided a beta-radiation, Strontium 90, an instrument used to deter the regrowth of pterygiae. In 1992 they made available the services of Dr. Richard Lockwood with his family by providing for their support. In a major way they provided medicines and supplies as well. Their strict rules of financial accountability has kept Kissy from being put under a proviso. They have gone the extra mile by covering the costs of a financial accountant checking the books of the Kissy UMC Eye Hospital each month. We thank God for CBM's personnel such as Mr. Carl Becker, Mrs. Ute Norman, Dr. Allen Foster, Mr. Simon Bridger, Mr. Siegfried Wiesinger, Mrs. Magdalena Wiesinger, Mr. P. Gerhard Weiland, Dr. Joe Taylor, and other dedicated people in Germany. In the U.S.A. the Christian Blind Mission International is located in Greenville, South

Carolina. Mr. Alan Harkey and Mr. Brian Piecuch continue to keep faith with the ministry of the Kissy UMC Eye Hospital. They have avidly supported it throughout the difficult times in Sierra Leone. CBM is a hallowed and respected name in the halls of the Kissy UMC Eye Hospital.

Coup, April 29, 1992

In April, 1992, I was in Sierra Leone alone. Ruth and I had been there earlier in January, February and the first part of March. Now, on April 18th, I was delivering some additional medicines and supplies. I immediately became immersed in the busy surgical practice. Dr. Richard Lockwood and his family were still at the Kissy UMC Eye Hospital. We were training Dr. Ainor Fergusson in some of the procedures at that time. On the 29th, a Wednesday, we were in the midst of surgery when suddenly there was a loud report as though a bomb had exploded. It turned out to be an anti-aircraft gun which had been fired along the main highway entering into Freetown just a half block away. This was the beginning of a coup which toppled President Joseph Momoh's regime. There was much confusion. Dr. Lockwood and most

Figure 5.18. Destruction accompanies coup.

of the staff left immediately.

The shift in power from President Momoh to junior officers was the result of an unhappy situation where the soldiers felt they were not being treated well at the front lines of the civil war. They revolted and took over the leadership of the country. President Momoh escaped to Guinea.

The following day anarchy existed. Roaming bands looted houses and businesses. There was a great amount of destruction and burning. The large Datsun dealership just a block away from the hospital was ransacked with all the cars taken and the supplies damaged. The building itself was severely damaged. This also took place at the Honda dealership five blocks away. They destroyed equipment and items such as stoves and refrigerators. The supplies of rice from a storage dock two blocks away were all taken by roaming bands of looters. No one was safe.

At the door of the hospital I was met by a former patient who had had a corneal transplant done by Dr. Donald Doughman the year before. He had been trying to protect his home when looters burst through the door and manhandled him, damaging his operated eye to the extent that the retina and ciliary body of the eye were extruding from the scleral shell. It was necessary to eviscerate the eye. In spite of the mayhem, we decided to keep the doors of the hospital open rather than have them broken down. We were aware that on all four sides of the hospital, houses and garages were being broken into and vehicles taken. By keeping the doors of the hospital open we were able to care for patients who presented themselves with gunshot and grenade injuries. One man had a live grenade go off in his hand. The hand was severely damaged, and his whole body was bloody. Somehow the shrapnel missed vital organs, and he did not bleed to death. One of his eyes was completely shredded. We needed to remove that eye, but the other eye was less damaged and was salvaged. In the days and weeks to come we were happy that he not only lived but was able to see and move about independently.

Thoroughly exhausted, I finally left surgery and climbed the stairs to our apartment. On looking out the window I realized that there was not a single light to be seen in the entire city of Freetown with its population of one million. I quickly turned off the solar light, not wanting to be a target for a flying missile.

For four days and nights we continued the policy of not locking the hospital doors. Everyone cowered in their homes. While I did sleep in my bed, it would have been wiser to have been under the bed because of the flying bullets. The former President, Siaka Stevens, literally sought refuge under his bed during a period of unrest. It was wise not to turn on any lights and give occasion for someone to shoot through the window. The nights were long. I remembered Psalm 91: 5-11, "Thou shalt not be afraid for the terror by night; nor for the arrow (bullets) that flieth by day; for he shall give his angels charge over thee, to keep thee..." I took comfort in Isaiah 26:3, "Thou shalt keep him in perfect peace whose mind is stayed on Thee." In spite of being all alone I truly tried to keep a positive attitude. Nights don't last forever, as "weeping may endure for a night, but joy cometh in the morning." (Psalm 30:5).

Food was a problem. I only had two boxes of corn flakes and some powdered milk and the occasional orange or banana slipped through the window. No one was on the streets as there was a strict curfew. Somehow a messenger got through to me with a note instructing me to report to the U.S. Embassy downtown. This was almost impossible to do because of roadblocks but I dutifully got into my car and went from roadblock to roadblock. Because my skin was white apparently they didn't feel that I was a threat, and allowed me to pass through the barricades. When I got to the embassy, it was completely boarded up. No one was around. I saw one man standing near the corner. I asked him, "Is there anyone here at the U.S. Embassy?" He whispered, "Oh yes, there are marines inside, but they are not showing themselves." I asked him, "Is it possible to report, as I was asked to come down?" He apparently was out there officially and said, "No, there is no way in which they will open the doors."

I returned to the Kissy UMC Eye Hospital. The next time I ventured out I had the good sense to take along with me my passport as well as a few personal items. I went to the Bintumani Hotel which was deserted. I retreated to Wilberforce to see if Ted and Rosemary Townsend were there. Happily I met a number of missionaries who, when they saw me, said, "Where have you been?" They had been trying for several days to find me to tell me that we were all being evacuated in the morning. I stayed that night at the Townsend residence and left my vehicle in the garage we had built several years ago. When I got to the Mammy Yoko Hotel, I met several hundred people, mostly expatriates. At least a hundred missionaries were being evacuated. During the time of signing up, I felt that since I was able to freely go through roadblocks, I should stay and complete my work. There were a number of post-op patients who would need to have care over the next few days. At the last moment I took my name off the list and prepared to stay.

It was Sunday and I returned with my 1987 Honda Civic to the King Memorial United Methodist Church. A policeman had asked to ride along. With him by my side, barricades presented no problem. An enthusiastic worship service was in progress. My appearance caused some surprise because it had been assumed that all the white people in Sierra Leone had been evacuated. I later learned that the evacuation that did take place was to warships as well as to the airport from which people were delivered to the neighboring city of Conakry in Guinea.

After a week things began to stabilize. The patients were doing well; I prepared to go on to Ghana for the planned visit with Dr. Herb and Ruth Billman at their eye clinic in Cape Coast. When I got to the airport to take the Ghana flight it was explained to me, "Oh we're very sorry but the Ghana flight flew over Freetown. They didn't want to risk landing." That meant that I was isolated. I saw on the runway a small plane with the propellers turning. I asked where that plane was going. They informed me that it was leaving for Monrovia, Liberia. I frantically asked, "Is there any room on it?" The man at the counter, the only man present, took my small bag and went out with me. I was able to get the last seat on the plane which was located next to the pilot. With that, the plane took off for Liberia. I transferred and eventually got to Accra, Ghana, where I was met by Dr. and Mrs. Billman. I enjoyed the stay with them for six days, and then had the wonderful experience of returning to Alexandria. Finally I was home with my loved ones. On getting into bed that night I heard no shellfire around me. Be it ever so humble!

Repeat Surgery After 37 Years

While changing the dressing of an elderly patient, who the day before had undergone a cataract extraction with intraocular lens implantation, she turned her head and looked into my eyes with the joy of newly restored sight. "You don't recognize me," she said demurely with

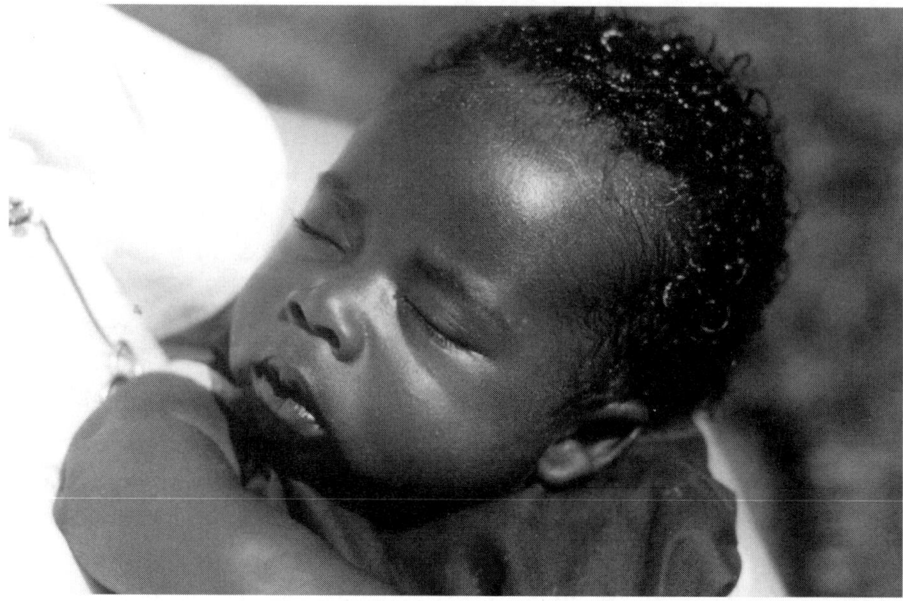

Figure 5.19. Repeat surgery after 37 years. Fatu's baby delivered by C-section.

a winsome smile. "Thirty seven years ago when I could not deliver my baby, you helped with an operation (Caesarean section)."

In the following moments the events were reconstructed. It was in the middle of the night (1957) that I attended the patient who was now sitting before me. Following a prolonged labor in a nearby village she was brought to Rotifunk hospital to have the surgery.

"That baby boy you delivered had the opportunity to go to school and presently is a professor at Fourah Bay College. His name is Lowell," she said.

That I had been involved in two such different operations needs an explanation.

Following the four years at Washington University School of Medicine and a year's rotating internship at Ancker Hospital, St. Paul, Minnesota, Mrs. Gess, a registered nurse, and I were appointed as medical missionaries to Bambur, Nigeria.

Surgical procedures were done almost daily during those first three years of our missionary service. On an extended furlough of two years, I took a surgical residency at Akron General Hospital. Knowing a little more about general surgery, I returned to West Africa, this time to Rotifunk, Sierra Leone. It was then that this patient had been assisted in the birth of her baby.

During the three years at Rotifunk we were overwhelmed by the numbers of blind people. An ophthalmologist could not be found. The General Board of Global Ministries of the United Methodist Church inquired if I would be interested in addressing this need. Following a three year residency in ophthalmology at the University of Minnesota, we were back in Rotifunk, Sierra Leone, West Africa, doing eye care but also doing occasional surgical procedures such as incarcerated herniorrhaphies and Caesarean sections.

It had been thirty-seven years between these two operations. During those years tens of thousands of people had been served, representing meningitis epidemics, the cruel curse of malaria, parasitic diseases, overwhelming infections, malnutrition, and countless surgical emergencies and elective procedures. Of the 30,000 surgeries performed, at least half were on the eye.

In times of reflection we realize that many of these people may not have survived had Ruth and I not responded to the missionary call to serve in that needy part of the world. We are grateful for our health and count it a privilege to be able to minister to others in their time of need.

Dr. Richard L. Lockwood, 1992 – 1993

With the support of Christoffel Blindenmission, Kissy UMC Eye Hospital was honored to have Dr. Richard Lockwood and his family appointed for service between January 1992 and September 1993. The term of service would have been extended had it not been for the forced evacuation of missionary personnel from Sierra Leone.

Dr. Lockwood states:

My work at the Kissy UMC Eye Hospital was definitely a high point in my life. In this environment I had the opportunity to work with a staff consisting of dedicated and skilled Sierra Leonean nationals in providing eye care in a greatly underserved region. During this time we were told that the United Nations did a survey of countries around the world to determine the relative standard of living in each of the countries. Different factors were taken into consideration including per capita income, infant mortality, health conditions, services available, and so forth. I was told that of all the nations in the world Sierra Leone was the most needy. The eye hospital was definitely located in an area of great need.

A typical day would begin with devotions including singing of hymns and choruses and the presentation of the Gospel message. The clinic was always busy with many patients presenting for treatment each day. They would come from great distances. We saw patients from Guinea, bordering Sierra Leone on the north and east, and I recall seeing at least one patient from as far away as Nigeria. Patients would generally come with a family member. On many occasions they were led because of being blind. The most common cause of their blindness was cataract. Patients blinded by cataracts usually were older but quite often were middle aged people as well as even some infants. These patients could be helped with surgery. Likewise, many patients were in the process of becoming blind from glaucoma. These patients usually were treated with surgery. Patients were seen with various forms of eye injuries as well as injuries caused by the use of "traditional medicines." Some patient needs were met by the prescription of eye glasses. Others were treated with medicines, reassurance, and prayer. It was a joy to work with these patients because they could be helped.

The clinic and operating room were extremely well equipped for this part of the world. There was an abundant supply of intraocular lenses to be used to replace the focusing power of the eye which was lost when the cataract was removed. These were, in most cases, provided complimentary from various companies where they were manufactured. All in all it was as one doctor expressed it, 'Kissy UMC Eye Hospital is the best thing that ever happened to Sierra Leone.'

I went to work in Africa to help provide for the eye care needs for people in a very needy environment. I went with a desire to bless these people. In the end it was I who was blessed having the opportunity to work at the Kissy UMC Eye Hospital with all the dedicated staff and have the opportunity to work with Dr. and Mrs. Lowell Gess.

Figure 5.20. Dr. Richard Lockwood with his wife Lucinda and their children.

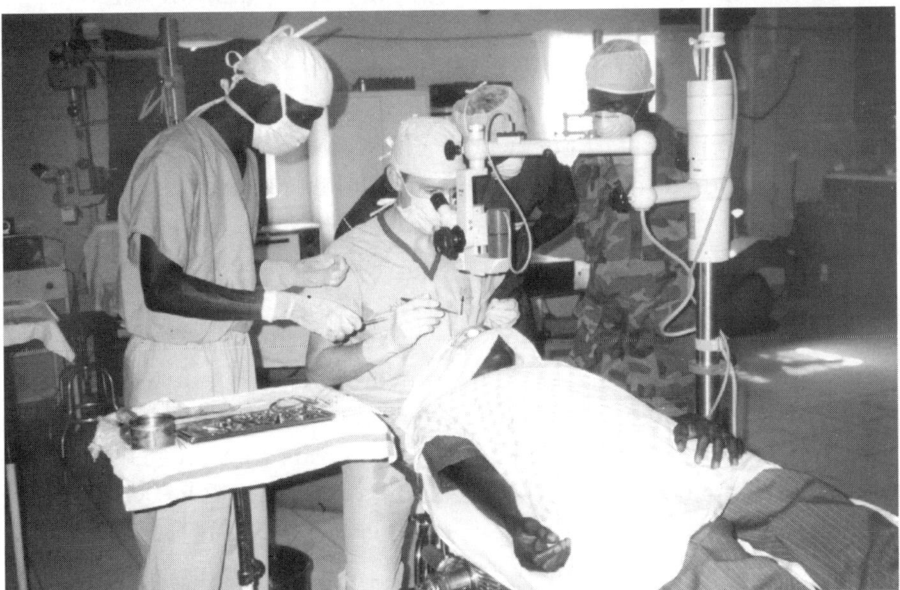

Figure 5.21. Dr. Richard Lockwood's surgery being viewed by the patient's relatives.

A Banner Year at Kissy, 1993

With the relative political stability present in Sierra Leone in 1993, the hospital truly had a banner year. A concerted effort was made to address the many corneal conditions that affected West African people. Dr. Donald Doughman of the Department of Ophthalmology of the University of Minnesota, brought more than a dozen cultured corneas for transplantation. His expert anterior segment surgery gave the hospital added status.

On one day during his visit, we had four ophthalmologists doing surgery at three operating microscopes. Dr. Bill McElroy came to join Dr. Rich Lockwood and myself. It was great fun to have outstanding help in a faraway place on the earth. An international flavor was added to this assembly of volunteers when Dr. Anne-Liese Lauffemburger from Switzerland arrived.

Popular Dr. Charles Carter and Dr. and Mrs. Russell Boehlke served in February and May respectively. Dr. Nick Cook and his family came under the auspices of CBM in August. On September 5th at the Brown Memorial United Methodist Church there was a recognition service led by Pastor Alfred Karimu for Drs. Lockwood and Cook, the mantle being transferred from Richard Lockwood (Elijah) to Nick Cook (Elisha) with a plane being used to rise into the air instead of a chariot.

Of special significance was the October-November volunteer service of Dr. and Mrs. Russell Boehlke. They had been the first volunteers to Kissy Eye Hospital in 1984. Their 1993 visit was to prove to be the last volunteer visit of an ophthalmologist other than myself until the present date of writing (2001). The uncertainties produced by the Revolutionary United Front (RUF) precluded safe travel.

During the year Ruth and I made two visits to Sierra Leone. We were met January 2nd by Dr. Richard Lockwood. The Mercy Ship *Anastasia* was docked at the Freetown quay. Drs. Bob Dyer and Bert Souryal were on board. It was a privilege to fellowship with them at Christian Ophthalmology Society meetings with outstanding ophthalmologists such as J. Lawton Smith, Mike Siatkowski, and Brad Ferris.

On January 10th I fulfilled my promise to Pastor Coker of Bombara Town United Methodist Church. I had agreed during our 1992 September-October tour to preach at his church. It was fortunate that I

Figure 5.22. *Anastasia* docked at Freetown, Sierra Leone. Volunteer ophthalmologist Dr. Bert Souryal is standing on my left.

had two months to prepare for my topic, "I Will Build My Church" as I was surprised to see Bishop and Mrs. J. C. Humper in the congregation. Ordinarily, he would be doing the preaching and I would be in the congregation.

Farid and Wilamenia Hassib, like Crispin and Theresa Renner, were so helpful over the years. Between visits they would store our ophthalmic preparations in their air-conditioned drug storage area. Often we would fellowship over a meal. On one occasion when Farid was chairman of the Freetown Rotarians, he arranged for me to be inducted as "an honorary Rotarian." On my visits around the world I was always proud to be able to say to local Rotarian clubs that I was an "honorary Rotarian." I was also able to say that I was an "honorary Lion" – that honor being given to me by the Alexandria, Minnesota Lions Club. Both of these clubs have been of immeasurable help in meeting the world's eye needs, as well as having other emphases.

A high point of the year was the visit of our son Andrew on September 11, 1993, born exactly 30 years earlier at Rotifunk, Sierra Leone.

The low point came on a return trip from Zimbabwe where we had been working in Karanda with Dr. Daniel Stephens. Our booking home took us by way of Johannesburg, South Africa, Sydney, Australia, the Fiji Islands, the Hawaiian Islands, and then Los Angeles. It was on the last leg of this trip from the Hawaiian Islands to Los Angeles that Ruth became seriously ill with a developing stroke. It was to be diagnosed as an infarction of the left posterior cerebral artery which resulted in a complete right lateral homonymous hemianopsia and some nominal aphasia. Thankfully recovery was rapid, allowing Ruth to return to Africa within a year's time. The Lord is kind.

Three Visits to Kissy, 1994

Still recovering from her stroke, Ruth was unable to accompany me on January 1, 1994. Instead our grandson Christopher Boehlke, a junior at Macalester College majoring in philosophy, used Ruth's ticket. Chris is the son of our daughter, Mary, a practicing clinical psychologist, and her husband, Steve, a consultant to corporate management. The exposure of Chris to medicine and the mission outreach was to be a turning point in his life. The original intention of his going with me to Africa was simply that of offering a strong back in the management of eight boxes of medicines and supplies, each weighing up to seventy pounds. He was an old pro at carrying eye instruments, for at the age of thirteen he carried a heavy portable yag laser for several blocks on its way for servicing. It was at a time when he was just recovering from a recent illnes and was not at his peak strength.

Once at the Kissy UMC Eye Hospital, Chris participated in the flow and care of eye patients. His outgoing personality enabled him to become an integral part of the staff. Not at all squeamish, he observed cataract surgery and IOL implantation through the assistant scope of the operating microscope. We had the opportunity of doing some community-based eye care trekking that took us to places where his mother had lived as a girl – Rotifunk, Taiama, and Bo. It was at Bo that we met with Dr. Dennis Williams and observed the remarkable program and facility of Sight Savers (the Royal Commonwealth Society For the Blind). The visit at Rotifunk found us treating over fifty patients. It was a pleasure to work in the restored hospital, the result of the year of volunteer service of Larry and Marge Chambers. Also it was thrilling to be with Tator

Carew, Julia Caulker, Marian Caulker, and Nancy Judy with whom we had worked in years past. Eventually I was privileged to help restore Nancy Judy's eyesight with IOL implantation in both of her eyes.

Chris and I could not visit the Kabala Rupp Memorial School as the distance was great and there was the problem of political instability and the activity of the Revolutionary United Front (RUF). Chris was an innovative chef and was hard to beat at Shanghai, a game popular with missionaries. Our common interest in philosophy, in which we both hold majors, brought up topics and personalities such as Socrates, Plato, Aristotle and especially Augustine and Kierkegaard. His exposure to the role of missionary medicine in meeting the needs of people was determinative in his interest in a medical career. He saw that patients at the Kissy UMC Eye Hospital were not only receiving physical sight for independence and productivity but also spiritual insight of lasting worth. His background and interest has enabled him to place high in his medical class standings. Two other grandchildren are presently doing premedical subjects as college juniors. Debbie Gess is attending Westmont College, Santa Barbara, California, while Adam Gess is at Wheaton College, Wheaton, Illinois, where he is also enjoying a high status in swimming.

Especially touching was the concern of our Sierra Leone friends in their inquiries about Ruth's health. One of the most meaningful prayers I have ever heard and experienced was that of Angie Myles for Ruth's healing. There were also the wonderful prayers of Bishop Humper and David Caulker for the Rev. Ken Green, hospitalized in Connaught Hospital. He was hanging on to life by a single thread of faith, being beyond further help from the doctors. In God's time, he was to return to the pulpit as one of the most effective preachers in Sierra Leone.

During this first visit it was possible to go to Njala University and witness the research in onchoceriasis that was being carried on by Dr. Aiah A. Goakima.

We helped a fellow colleague, Dr. Moses Mahoi, with whom I had worked at Rotifunk Hospital during our 1957 -1960 tour. He needed cataract surgery. His entire career had been spent doing general practice in Sierra Leone. I last visited with him in October, 1998. Most of the doctors had fled the country because of the insecurity of the times. He continued to spend his efforts and his days helping those in need in the

Figure 5.23. Dr. and Mrs. Tom Foy with nurses at Kissy Health and Maternity Centre.

Lumley area of Freetown. Some people traversed the entire distance of the city in order to get to his care. He himself was crippled with arthritis of his upper and lower extremities. He used an assisstant to record his findings and directed the treatment after someone else had placed his stethoscope on the patient's chest. Mentally he was sharp. His spirit was at peace with the assurance of forgiveness for what he referred to as his faults and hurts to others during his life. Several months later, while his country continued to be torn apart in the vicious civil war, he was laid to rest.

During our second and third visits of April 15 to May 15 and September 15 to October 23, we were delighted to see the progress of Dr. Ainor Fergusson's surgical techniques.

Volunteers Tom and Faye Foy completed their work at Kissy Health and Maternity Center. Mr. Lee Weaver dug wells on the Kissy Urban Centre Compound, and the Canadian ophthalmologist, Dr. Ralph Buhrman, encouraged the use of IOLs at the Lunsar Baptist Eye Hospital. The Rev. Joe and Carolyn Wagner were very much involved in having Operation Classroom renew the medical program at Kissy Health and Maternity Centre.

These were the highlights of 1994.

Figure 5.24. Lee Weaver operating a well digging machine brought out by Pete Shearer.

Kissy UMC Eye Hospital Ten Years After Dedication, 1994

The Kissy UMC Eye Hospital was dedicated February 1984. During this past decade forty volunteer ophthalmologists have shared their time, tithe, and talents with the people of West Africa. Of the nearly 10,000 surgeries performed, 85 percent were cataract extractions with intraocular lens implantations and 10 percent were glaucoma operations. A list of the surgeons appears in the appendix indicating the month and year of service with a list of addresses and telephone numbers.

The Kissy facility has been upgraded with tile floors throughout the building. The well-constructed shelves and cabinets by Loren Ebsen, Roger Reiners and the other volunteers, continue to be useful. Painting has taken place inside and outside. Of special mention is the 102 foot drilled well completed by Mr. Lee Weaver who took over the well-digging equipment from Mr. Pete Shearer. On occasion the entire city of Freetown is without water. Now at Kissy, surgical patients' relatives no longer need to bring along buckets of water so surgery can proceed.

Equipment: On entering the front door to the waiting room one sees three lines of patients: (1) those being registered; (2) those having

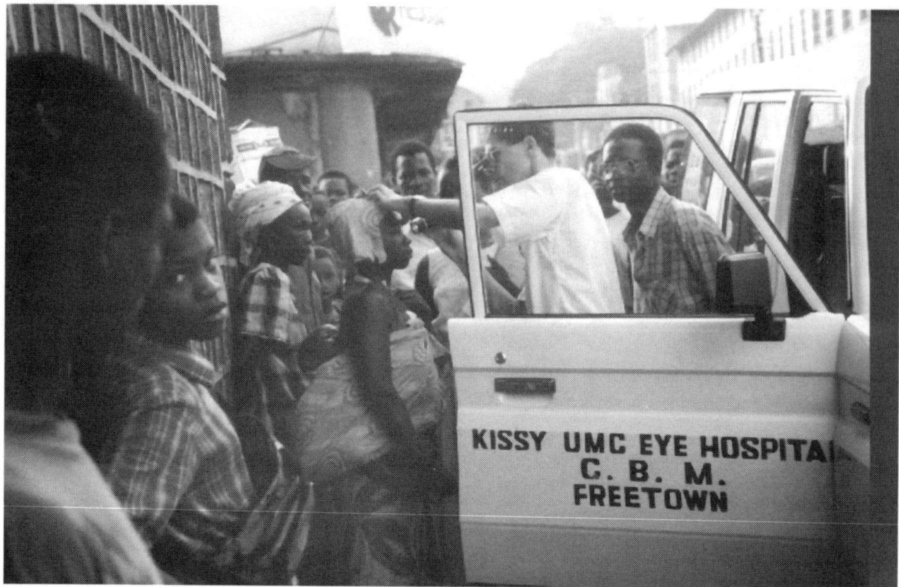

Figure 5.25. Dr. Cook examining a queue of beggars as they congregate on Siaka Stevens St. at 7:30 a.m..

their visual acuities tested; and (3) those at the auto-refractor. In the refraction room there are five Haag Streit slit lamps that are manned for examination and Goldmann tonometry as well as a refraction lane with each slit lamp. The left middle room has two beds for postoperative patients who choose to rest for a short while after surgery. The right middle room is used for A-scan measurements, keratometry, as well as having another Haag Streit slit lamp and refraction lane. Surgery is well supplied with IOL's due to the generosity of optical houses. The three Zeiss operating microscopes are clean and in good repair because of Carl Zeiss Corporation's special concern for the program. We also have a O degree assistant scope to aid in the teaching program that included West African eye doctors from Nigeria, Cameroon, and Ghana.

April 29, 1994, marked the second anniversary of the leadership of the NPRI (National Provisional Ruling Council). They made strides in improving Sierra Leone but were hampered by a costly and devastating rebel incursion into the eastern and southern regions, and ultimately into the northern. The American Peace Corps volunteers were withdrawn because of the political instability in those areas.

Staff: Our administrator, Mrs. Lettie Williams, was in London, England, participating in a program emphasizing community based

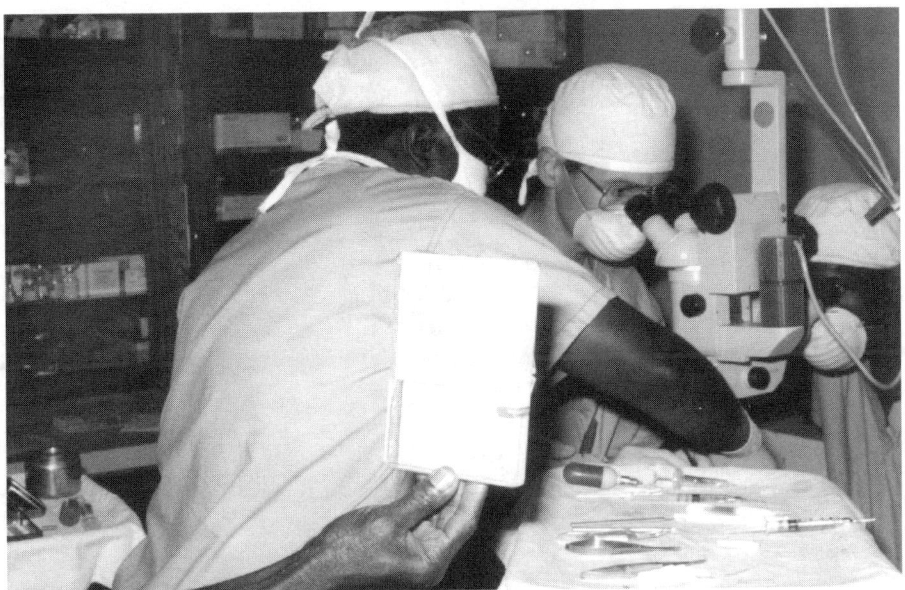

Figure 5.26. Dr. Nick Cook in surgery.

health. She returned to Freetown before the end of June. Mrs. Hannah Koroma did a good job, stepping into Lettie's shoes for this period. Augustine Macauley on occasion does up to thirty refractions a day. He is now being helped by James Koroma, Paul Tarawally, and Mohamed Rogers. They also do some of the fabricating of the spectacles. John Fornah continues to run a tight ship in surgery with the help of Mohamed Rogers, Jonathan Bendu, and Andrew Sahr Alpha. Joseph Sesay, Joseph Squires, and Malcolm Albert organize the patients for examination. Mrs. Elsie Fornah receives the payments and schedules the surgery. Our three watchmen are delighted to welcome the return of Lamin Bangura, who has been loaned to the hospital by the CID, along with his AK47. Bossie and Abu do the cleaning and washing chores. Mr. Adams tends the grounds. We are especially happy to have Dr. Ainor Fergusson, a native Sierra Leonean, active in the program. He was doing about three extracapsular cataract extractions with intraocular lens implantation each day, four days a week. Dr. Nick Cook, a British ophthalmologist underwritten by Christoffel Blindenmission, did four or five. At age thirty-two he was a human dynamo, well respected by the staff and patients. He did an extensive evaluation of the causes of blindness, in particular the extent of treatable blindness, amongst street beg-

Figure 5.27. Dr. Cook leading a devotion with gathered patients.

gars in Freetown, Sierra Leone. He completed his two year stay during the summer of 1995.

It is a thrilling experience to have 100-150 patients present each day when the staff leads a service of hymns, scripture, prayer, and testimony. I am sure that the angels are impressed by the staff's choruses which many of the patients know and in which they are quick to join. Often quoted is Luke 7:4: "Unto many who were blind Jesus gave sight." We are happy when people like Yateh Glulah, who had his sight restored a year ago subsequently accepted Jesus Christ as Lord and Savior. Ruth and I count it a privilege to minister in a program of healing in which people receive sight both physically and spiritually.

The Lord has blessed and is continuing to bless this eye ministry. Kissy UMC Eye Hospital is the only facility for surgical eye care for Freetown and the surrounding area. This is comparable to taking care of half of the four plus million people in the state of Minnesota. Patients also come from the neighboring countries of Guinea and Liberia. With God's help and that of the staff, the General Board of Global Missions of the United Methodist Church, Christoffel Blindenmission, optical and pharmaceutical houses, and many churches and interested individuals, the prospects for a compassionate and complete eye care program for Sierra Leone have never been brighter.

To quote Lettie Williams – "We are thankful to God that the Kissy UMC Eye Hospital is an organization that is highly interested in the spiritual development of people's minds as well as caring for their eyes."

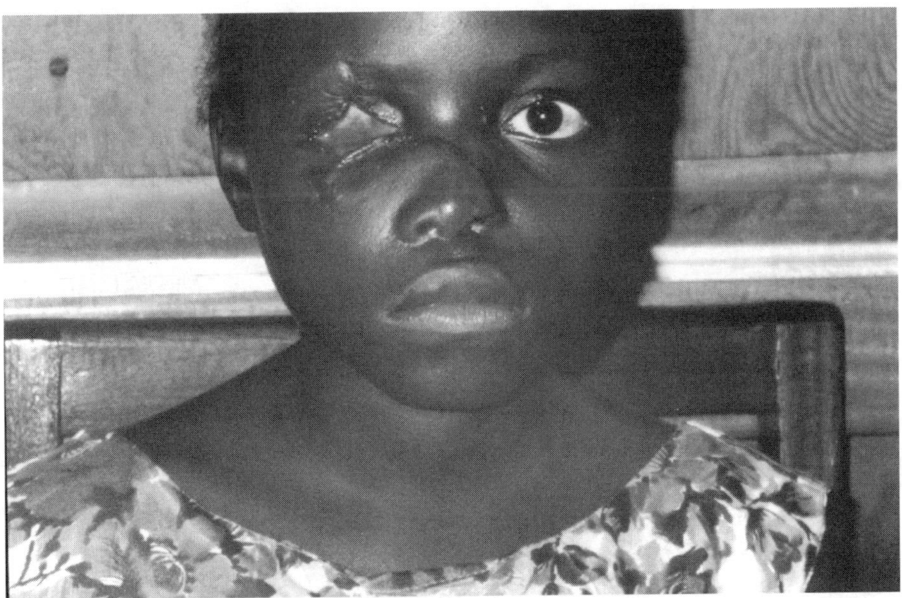

Figure 5.28. Destroyed right eye from a rebel's machete.

A Daring Trip, 1995

By mid-March, 1995, I was the only American missionary left in Sierra Leone. Being conspicuous by my white skin, help was given me at every turn. I have never had such royal treatment. Baggage, immigration, and security checks were expedited in an unbelievable way.

Sierra Leone was in the greatest crisis in its history. This once beautiful and cultural jewel of West Africa was in the throes of an internal war. The rebels, known as the Revolutionary United Front under Foday Sankoh, step-by-step were taking over rural Sierra Leone as Charles Taylor did in Liberia five years earlier. They moved from place to place at will killing village leaders and then burning their homes. By intimidation they forced children and teenagers to join their ranks who then are caught up in the ritual of killing and destroying. They kept themselves supplied by looting.

It was never known how often their AK47's are real and functional. In the attack on Bo it was learned that most of the arms were imitation – with only ten of the more than fifty attackers actually having real armament.

It is inconceivable that the insurgent rebel forces could use such brutal tactics on the young and old to bring subjection of the populace. The amputation of limbs and other disfigurements became a ritual. Pictures of a child with a stump for his arm and a little girl with her eye destroyed by a machete seem unreal. Children, God's gifts, are to be loved and protected.

In the wake of what has happened to the thousands of maimed people, how is it possible to live with the perpetrators of such evil acts? Is forgiveness possible – is it necessary? Can a truth and reconciliation commission actually become a reality?

Jesus' parable of the good Samaritan speaks to this problem. In spite of the wounded and dying man being his enemy, the Samaritan's compassion prompted the care which saved the man's life. The prodigal's father was able to forgive his wayward son, even though the brother could not. The Christian cannot risk chronic hostility and unforgiveness without being destroyed. Stress of this nature is destructive to the spiritual life as well as to the cardiovascular system. Forgiveness means accepting what has happened and deciding not to seek or take revenge. "...if anyone is in Christ, there is a new creation: everything old has passed away, everything has become new." (II Corinthians 5:17).

The day before I flew out of Sierra Leone the rebels attacked Moyamba, killing and burning. Paramount Chief Madam Gulama's compound of houses was entirely destroyed. I had examined her eyes to provide glasses just forty-eight hours prior to this catastrophe.

Most leaders crowded into Freetown. All hospitals and health centers upcountry were closed. The UMC Clinic at Jaiama was especially hard hit with all its equipment and large supply of medicines looted by the rebels. The Kissy UMC Eye Hospital was in operation in Freetown, along with the Connaught hospital and several small private ones. It is fortunate (providential) that the Board of Global Ministries had placed Dr. Ainor Fergusson, a Sierra Leonean eye doctor, under salary as a Person In Mission. He has developed into a competent eye surgeon and is now the only hope for surgical eye care in that part of West Africa. In

March, 1995, while the civil war was raging in Sierra Leone, Dr. Fergusson was doing four to six cataract extractions with IOL implantation each day. More than one hundred patients were daily cared for at the hospital.

Many peace overtures were made but the rebels refused to negotiate. Earnest prayers are needed for this besieged country.

The day before leaving I ministered to a pastor who narrowly escaped death and who had family and church members killed or maimed at the hand of the rebels. He had lost all of his possessions, even his glasses. The villages of his parish had been looted and burned. He was a sober person, not the usual ebullient, outgoing, cheerful person we had known before. The war is creating havoc in Sierra Leone that may take generations to erase.

Amidst this tense situation the church stands firm in the faith that God in his love will prevail. While some maintain that "hell isn't bad enough" for the rebels who kill and maim innocent men, women and children, most are willing to put their Christian convictions on the line and "pray for them that persecute." (Matthew 5:44). What stability is left in this devastated country is due to the faith of Christians that God's righteous people will prevail, and that peace will follow the present tragedy.

The Islamic community in Sierra Leone is largely of the Sunnei background rather than the radical Shiite fundamentalism. Regardless of our own religious persuasion, Ruth and I have sought to obey the Lord to love and serve whomsoever was and is in need of health, healing, and the restoration of sight – physically and spiritually. We are happy to be a part of the outreach of the United Methodist Church in its medical work in addition to its emphasis on agriculture, education, and evangelism. The Church is feeding the hungry, giving water to the thirsty, taking in the stranger (refugees), clothing the naked, and visiting the sick and imprisoned, especially those imprisoned in the chains of superstition and sin.

My going to the Kissy UMC Eye Hospital at such a precarious time as this might be questioned by some as an illogical death wish. It definitely was questioned by the U.S. State Department. They learned of my presence in Sierra Leone, and I was required to register with the embassy even though I was scheduled to make my return flight to the

U.S.A. several days later.

My trip had a practical side to it. I delivered seven seventy pound boxes of medicines and supplies. Other shipments had been held up. Saving the eye sight of patients – especially children – was of utmost importance.

Secondly, it was important that I do surgery with Dr. Fergusson, who was still new in the field of intraocular lens implantation. With the use of videotaping during surgery, further skills were added to his technique.

And thirdly, my being there when other expatriates had been evacuated was of great encouragement to the staff. As native Sierra Leoneans, they were caught in this tense situation. They had nowhere else to go. My willingness to spend some time with the staff meant a great deal. I will never forget the firmness of their faith and the depth of their Christian convictions. It was I who was inspired by them.

> *If my people, who are called by my name, shall humble themselves, and pray, and seek my face, and turn from their wicked ways; then will I hear from heaven, and will forgive their sin, and will heal their land.*
>
> **II Chronicles 7:14**

On the Way to Abak, Nigeria, 1995

Later in 1995 (September 2-17), on our way to Abak, Nigeria, Ruth and I again delivered medicines and supplies to Kissy. We were able to assist in the clinic and surgery for only a short time in this continuing tense situation.

That we would come to Sierra Leone at a time when there were no other missionaries present, prompted the staff and Medical Board to have a special time of Christian fellowship at the UMC Conference offices. Ruth and I wondered who the people were that were being presented with such overtures of appreciation for years served until we learned that it was "us."

It was important for us to acknowledge, in their presence, that we were constrained by the love of Christ to minister in His name, but that we were happy that it was among these wonderful Christian leaders and people in Sierra Leone.

Prolonged Amsterdam Visit, 1996

Our return trip to Sierra Leone in January, 1996, was not without incident. A delay of 2 1/2 hours in Minneapolis while a cabin door was being repaired resulted in our missing the KLM connecting flight, Amsterdam to Freetown, by ten minutes. As a consequence of those few minutes we were to spend five full days in Amsterdam waiting for the next flight. Mrs. Kootje Stilma, wife of Dr. Jan Stilma, took us in hand and made our stay pleasant. Dr. Jan was presently spending a sabbatical of six months teaching in Harare, Zimbabwe. At KLM's expense we were billeted at the Victoria Hotel. We attended an English church service in a nearby Catholic church, had tours of Amsterdam, followed the Desert Storm war on television, and witnessed diamond cuttings. We wondered whether or not the diamonds being worked upon were from Sierra Leone. The world was to come to know the strategic part that diamonds were playing in the Sierra Leonean civil war. Rebel forces were able to purchase arms and ammunition with diamonds. By the year 2000, a ban was placed on Sierra Leone diamonds except for those legally processed through government agencies.

By February 1st we arrived in Freetown. Miss Ingrid Holmgren and Mr. Joe Skasko were busily engaged in helping orphans and other abandoned children. We learned of the present political and economic situation from Dr. June Holst Ronness, a general practitioner and former mayor of Freetown. Her husband, Rolf, a dentist, was the ambassador to Sierra Leone from Norway.

At Kissy UMC Eye Hospital we were faced with an emergency – no water. People scheduled for eye surgery were required to have relatives bring three buckets of water as part of their pre-op regime. Adequate pressure would be assured if we were to tap into the pipeline leading to the brewery. Pastor Alfred Karimu of Brown Memorial United Methodist Church judiciously and delicately dealt with the personnel involved in the hookup. We had no conscience about taking some of that water as our supply ran through a meter which allowed Gumma Valley Authority to be paid for the water used.

Kissy UMC Eye Hospital moved right along with the expanding computer technology of the world. An excellent IBM compatible unit had been donated by lawyer Bob Swenson and his wife Bea. Cassandra

Figure 5.29. Sister Kalon, stalwart United Methodist nurse (left).

Fergusson, wife of Dr. Ainor Fergusson, was a computer expert who taught computer courses. She set up the computer in the hospital and in a short time Mohamed Rogers and Elsie Fornah were successfully using it. Unfortunately, during the rebel intrusion into Freetown, it was destroyed. The happy ending to this story is that the Swenson's donated a replacement which is being used today.

Sister Kalon, a prominent nurse in the UMC program had previously been in charge of the clinic in Taiama before being driven out by the rebels. Now she was at the Kissy Health and Maternity Centre. Decreasing vision made her work difficult. A cataract extraction with intraocular lens implantation returned her to 20/20 vision. She decided to postpone her other blurred eye for a later date. A sterilizing mishap at that later date occurred during the procedure. For a time it was feared that she might lose the sight of her second eye, but mercifully her good health and the power of prayer led to useful 20/30 vision.

As we prepared to fly home from the Lungi International Airport, February 23, 1996, we witnessed the arrival of ballot boxes to be used in the forthcoming democratic election. We wondered whether or not such an event could take place during all the present political instability

– happily it did. Pressure had been brought by civilian groups to establish a duly-elected leadership rather than the militarily led present government.

What the male dominated parliament could not achieve was achieved by the brave and determined women of Freetown. They repeatedly marched through the streets in great crowds. It was obvious that they would not be placated. Elections were scheduled.

The election was close between Mohamed Tejan Kabbah and Dr. John Karefa Smart, who had served at the Rotifunk Hatfield-Archer Hospital years earlier. Dr. Smart had been prominent in political affairs down through the years. Tejan Kabbah, however, had a long term of service at the United Nations representing Sierra Leone, and prevailed in the election.

President Kabbah has had a stormy career. Within several months of his election, he was forced to flee to Guinea for his life when the Armed Forces Revolutionary Council (AFRC) coup took place. Called back within a year, he presided over many crises including the Lome Peace Accord and the imprisonment of RUF leader Foday Sankoh. Enduring great setbacks, he has held steady.

The Precariousness of Life and Sight, 1996

The fall of 1996 visit proved again how close to death we were in dealing with some patients. At the end of a congenital cataract procedure on a two year old child there was an aspiration. Thankfully the procedure had been completed with the eye securely closed with nylon sutures. This enabled us to lift the child up by his feet, slap him on the back, and use an aspirator to remove the occluding mucous. He promptly cried like a newborn and in our relief and joy we cried along. I missed the presence of Ruth who usually monitored these delicate anesthetics on infants and children. During this visit, she had remained at home.

A number of pediatric patients required surgery for congenital cataracts and glaucoma. Kwitkow's direct, external goniotomy was used on two patients whose corneas were too opaque for standard goniotomies.

There were scenes of joy for patients, relatives, and eye staff when patients who had been blind were able "to see." Especially moving was

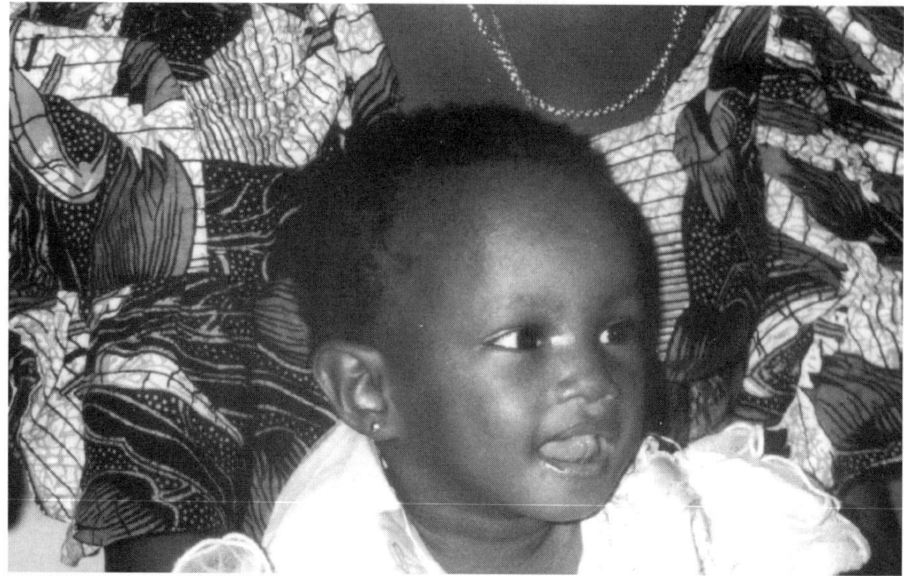

Figure 5.30. Happy child after congenital cataract extraction.

twenty-nine year-old Safia whose Christian faith was willing to accept blindness but prayed for a miracle. She brought an audio cassette to be played in the surgical theater during the operation. She and her church had recorded the hymn, "There is Power in the Blood." Only the eye to be operated on had light perception behind the complicated cataract. She obtained hand motion vision for a period of time but eventually the world closed in on her again. Her unshakable faith did not waiver for she had true insight into God's love.

Another patient was a blind beggar who daily sat in front of the mosque begging. Now he was begging us for help. We told him we would gladly help him and requested that he bring a friend to accompany him during his postoperative care. We understood that he had no money but believed that someone with Christian concern would provide the money for help to him as a Moslem.

The day after surgery he came into the hospital triumphantly saying, "IT ME – I SEE!"

We were able to share with him that the eye hospital was here because many Christians felt "sorry heart" for him and his blindness and wanted him not only to have new vision but also the knowledge of God's Son who loved him and died for him.

Figure 5.31. Ruth's special patient.

The End of a Surgical Career?

I was on my third cataract extraction with intraocular lens implantation when it happened. I could not release the mosquito forceps holding the superior rectus suture. First assistant John Fornah came to my rescue.

I had been experiencing pain in my right hand recently – especially the right thumb. While putting up the Christmas tree, I over-exerted tightening the base. I thought the discomfort would go away in a few days.

It was now six weeks, the pain was still there, and I was lacking strength. The delicate maneuvering of eye instruments was not a problem. I only needed help for heavier instruments during the three week period of surgery.

I was aware that on occasion the distal phalanx of my right thumb would "snap" on moving it up or down. During the night following my last scheduled surgery, I was awakened out of a deep sleep by a sharp pain in my right thumb. The distal phalanx had snapped down and would not go back. It took considerable force to replace it to its normal position.

The terror that night was not about pain. It was the thought that perhaps I would not be able to wield instruments in the future. Agonizingly I prayed, "Lord, is it over? Will I be able to help the blind in the future?"

I did not want another episode of "locking" of this trigger finger. The thumb was splinted during our packing to return home as well as on the trip itself. In Alexandria Dr. David Larson graciously and promptly had me come in immediately for an examination. The next day I was in surgery.

Healing was complete. Today I cannot imagine that I ever had a serious brush with being incapacitated for doing eye surgery. To use one's hands for health and healing in the name of Jesus continues to be a great joy.

During the completion of packing just hours before leaving, I had the opportunity to visit with Pastor Matthew E. L. Philie. Our friendship extended back for more than thirty years. I respected him as a preacher who was always concerned about the spiritual and physical welfare of his congregation and family. I was impressed by his being a master tracker and hunter. Whenever possible, we would team up to hunt.

The most dramatic incident we had together was going after a buffalo. We were aware that these wily and dangerous animals sometimes would circle and come up to the rear of their tracker for a fatal surprise.

In thick bush the buffalo we were tracking sped off away from Pastor Philie. He got off a shot from his shotgun. The ammunition he used was prepared by himself with extra powder and a single slug. It was apparent that he had hit his mark as a trail was able to be picked up that showed blood on tall grass and bushes.

At this point the other mem-

Figure 5.32. Dangerous buffalo.

bers of the party decided to call off the hunt. They knew the danger of trying to follow a wounded buffalo. One of their friends just months before had been mauled by a buffalo but had lived to tell the story.

Since I had the high powered rifle it was my role to proceed first. I sensed the danger of the animal in front and of another loaded gun behind. We came to the small draw of a dry stream and followed the trail across it. Once on the other side, we realized that it turned around and went right back at an angle. With my hair standing on end I wheeled around and there it was, the buffalo in a crouched position. Reflexively I fired. The animal shook with the impact of the missile but did not change his position. Pastor Philie's first shot had caused the buffalo to bleed to death, while in an upright and crouched position.

Suddenly everyone in the area was willing to help. Pastor Philie's congregation had a great church supper; the community rejoiced; and the staff at the eye hospital enjoyed steaks.

Now in the midst of the Sierra Leone civil war I was prompted to do away with my shotgun. I wanted to give no appearance of being armed. Already my powerful 300 H and H Magnum rifle bored by Weatherby had been "loaned out."

Would Pastor Philie allow himself to possess a firearm in these tense days? When offered the gun, he was overwhelmed with emotion. His handling of the pump action shotgun was almost that of caressing. Always he had made do with a single shot firearm. He left me with the gun under his arm in a daze. A few minutes later he returned, and with composure, expressed thanks for being given the type of gun that he had hoped for during most of his hunting career.

We were living in perilous times, witnessing perhaps the lowest point in the history of Sierra Leone. On May 25,1997, a coup led by AFRC Chairman Major Johnny Paul Koroma replaced the democratically elected government headed by President Ahmad Tejan Kabba. Instead of hiding upcountry RUF rebel soldiers were brought into Freetown to join the junta, which was universally condemned by the UN Security Council, ECOWAS (the 16-nation Economic Community of West African States), the European Union, and the UK Commonwealth. Under the primary leadership of ECOMOG, sanctions were enforced with embargoes on arms and oil. Food supplies dwindled and became expensive as did the fuel supply. The country's infrastructure crumbled.

Hundreds of thousands fled the country. Law and order broke down. People existed in apprehension and fear. Hooligans had their own way robbing, looting, raping, and dispossessing people of their homes by simply moving in and forcing the owners to leave. At Rotifunk 300 homes were burned to the ground. We learned of ghastly tales of barbarism where beheading often climaxed rituals of torture. All this was happening in Sierra Leone, the pearl of West Africa, to which other countries in the past sent their gifted young people to study at Fourah Bay University – the Athens of West Africa.

In the midst of this chaos, the staff of the Kissy UMC Eye Hospital continued to minister to patients. It was not unusual for them to have twenty to thirty refugee relatives in their homes. It was difficult to provide food for such numbers. Dr. Ainor Fergusson and I often did more than ten surgeries a day during the brief time of our visit. Most of the surgery was cataract extractions with intraocular lens implantation, but we made a special effort to surgically help glaucoma patients as glaucoma medications often are not available, their cost prohibitive, and compliance is poor. Twenty trabeculectomies were done with the hope that vision would be preserved. A fourteen year-old boy underwent successful strabismus surgery. His straightened eyes gave him a new confidence and composure.

Working with administrator Mrs. Lettie Williams, Ruth helped with the smooth running of the hospital. The staff remains enthusiastic about their work. It is challenging to face a new "congregation" of over a hundred patients each day in the waiting room. Members of the staff take turns being in charge of the hymn singing, the reading of Scripture, the testimonies, and the prayers.

Ruth and I support in prayer these brave people who are confident that right will prevail and that there will be peace again.

Unplanned Trip, June 1998

An unplanned trip June 24, 1998, was made to the Kissy UMC Eye Hospital, Freetown, Sierra Leone. A container arranged by Mr. Pete Shearer had docked one week earlier with a cargo of rice and other food products and clothes. It also carried medicines and supplies for the Eye

Hospital.

Dr. Ainor Fergusson already had arrived in Freetown to begin doing eye surgery for a backload of over a hundred patients needing cataract surgery. That was only the tip of the iceberg. Along with Mr. Samuel Coker, whom we had taught suturing and basic cataract techniques a year and a half earlier, surgery was restarted. Together we did 207 intra ocular lens implantations in a four-week period. I had planned to do no surgery the day before I left but relented and actually did five more.

It was wonderful to set foot on Sierra Leonean soil where Andrew, our youngest had been born. The welcome was overwhelming. No missionary had been seen for over a year. During that year, the Kissy staff and the people of Sierra Leone had lived and died through some of the worst brutalities in the history of West Africa.

When the junta (the AFRC-Armed Forces Revolutionary Council) took control May 25, 1997, they freed all criminals and political prisoners and invited the rebels (RUF-Revolutionary United Front) to join them in a new administration, supplementing the democratically elected President Ahmed Tejan Kabbah. The anarchy spilled over into 1998. Augustine Macauley, our previous optician, recounts being stopped by an eleven year old with an AK47 demanding sweets. An altercation was taking place a few feet away. The boy moved over and executed one of them. People were afraid to appear on the streets during the day and spent sleepless nights awaiting the invasions of their homes.

A ploy often used was to come to a home and offer protection if the people would care for them – which they did. When ready to move on, certain people were ordered to pick up slips of paper with instructions written on them. They read: "cut off right hand," "cut off left arm," "kill this one," "let this one go," "cut off right ear," "put out left eye."

There are 2000 amputees in Sierra Leone. It is estimated that only 20 to 25 percent of those suffering atrocities were able to seek help before they died of complications. The UN established a sixty bed hospital in Freetown for amputees. The USA has donated millions toward primary care and future prosthetic fittings.

My great surprise was to see as many buildings standing as there were. However, along Kissy Road there were many houses and businesses with only naked, burnt out walls.

Kissy UMC Eye Hospital was in the direct path of the ECOMOG

Figure 5.33. Burned out church.

and AFRC/RUF confrontation. Miraculously, the hospital did not sustain a direct hit. The roof had to be replaced because of damage from shell fragments, but the Zeiss operating microscopes, four of the six Haag Streit slit lamps, the keratometer, and the A-scan were left intact. Lunsar Eye Hospital was not so fortunate. Buildings were burned to the ground, and eye equipment (including a Zeiss OPMI-1) was willfully damaged rendering them inoperable.

I have in hand individual reports from the staff. Some were able to flee to remote places upcountry while others went to Conakry, Guinea Bissau, and the Gambia. Those remaining in Kissy would go three to four days without food. While this was debilitating, their greatest fear was being summarily and randomly executed.

Rev. David Caulker was a pillar of strength during these terrible days and months before the February, 1998, liberation of Freetown by ECOMOG forces. Although he preached the truth in love, he was not arrested or thrown into jail with the thousands of others who refused to support the junta in their reign of terror. He stated that it is difficult to preach compassion for the captured junta and the rebels who brought death and destruction. He asked me to preach on July 5, 1998. I shall never forget facing a congregation of about 1000 worshipers who filled King Memorial UM Church to the rafters. I was led to preach on Luke

Figure 5.34. Pastor David Caulker.

10:33 where Jesus has the good Samaritan showing compassion and offering help to his enemy. As followers of Christ, He might expect us to do the same.

Bishop Joseph C. Humper was singled out for arrest and herded with others into a mosque. He and several others discovered a side door and slipped out and found cover. The captors returned shortly and executed the remaining people .

The deep faith and Christian commitment of the people of Sierra Leone and the Kissy staff are undimmed. They are willing to be exposed on the front line. It is a privilege to prayerfully and financially support them in bringing sight to the blind and the spiritual insight of God's love as revealed in Jesus Christ, our Savior.

Attending the Blind in the Midst of War, October-November 1998

The airport was eerily subdued. Peter Conteh, a security officer and friend of long standing, did not have his usual smiling face. The normally busy and hectic scene was unusually quiet. Forty-eight hours earlier, twenty-four officers and men of the former junta ruling party were executed, including Peter's brother and a cousin. Also condemned to

Figure 5.35. The two men sitting in the middle (Peter Conteh and Ishmael Jabbie) are wonderful friends and expeditors at Lungi Airport, Freetown.

death were fourteen civilians who had abetted the junta (Armed Forces Revolutionary Council and Revolutionary United Front).

The war still goes on in the provinces with the rebels controlling the rich diamond mining fields. These resources allow them to purchase military supplies and ammunition.

After being checked three times under military scrutiny, I was able to join Paul Tarawally for the trip to Kissy UMC Eye Hospital which earlier had been caught in the middle of the original clash between ECOMOG and AFRC forces. It remained standing as it did not sustain a direct hit. However, windows needed to be replaced as well as the shell-fragmented roof.

The staff had made elaborate plans to have the hospital in tiptop shape with supplies ready for surgery to start at 7 a.m. the next morning. Along with Dr. Ainor Fergusson, the resident ophthalmologist, we usually did nine to ten procedures each day – most often cataract extractions with intraocular lens implantations. Since the visit was to last less than two weeks, surgery was also done on Saturday.

Besides the surgery, many repairs were needed for the hospital. A repaired operating room table was installed and a Zeiss OPMI-6 operating microscope was brought out by the Operation Classroom. This third operating microscope allowed Dr. Fergusson and me to have our own microscope as well as leaving a third for Mr. John Fornah to do lid procedures, pterygia, and enucleations. Mr. Mohamed Rogers and Mrs. Isatu Sesay, surgical assistants in training, helped the ophthalmologists. Later in the day a new computer was set up with no parts missing!

After checking the eight post-ops from 7:30 to 9:00 Sunday morning, I was on my way to the Brown Memorial United Methodist Church. I had not left the veranda before being met with a patient suffering from a rock injury to the right eye. Applanation tonometry revealed an intraocular pressure of 64 mm Hg. Not being a total hyphema, timoptic and diamox were administered to see if the pressure could be lessened without surgery. The day before, I was to attend a 3:00 o'clock meeting with the UMC Conference treasurer, but again on the way out of the hospital, I was met by a five year old child with a stick injury to the right eye. Under ketamine and local anesthesia it was discovered that the right globe had been ruptured with the eye eviscerated by the trauma. John Fornah did the enucleation and completed the lid repair. We still made it to the meeting. The Conference treasurer, however, had forgotten about it; so the hurried trip was only used to purchase some supplies for the hospital.

Forty-two surgeries were done before the return trip was made to Lungi Airport. The ferry had broken down; so the trip was made in a hovercraft. The rain came down in sheets and the wind whipped up the waves, but wonderfully this seagoing craft skimmed over the ocean with hardly a shake.

The joy experienced by patients once blind and then able to see again always makes the planning and expense of volunteer eye surgery worth while. Most important of all is that patients are then given opportunity by the Christian staff of gaining insight into the love of God as revealed in Jesus Christ – a "sight" that is not temporary but of eternal worth. There are those who find it.

In the Wake of January 6, 1999 – "Soldier Boys"

The civil war in Sierra Leone had been going on for over six years. Internet news reported a peace initiative between President Kabbah and the rebel leader Foday Sankoh during their meeting in Togo.

The eye ministry at Kissy had been active in spite of the war. In 1997 Dr. Ainor Fergusson was targeted for imprisonment or execution by the revolutionary junta. He escaped with only the clothes on his back to Conakry, Guinea. Christoffel Blindenmission transferred him and his family to Bissau in Guinea Bissau. In June, 1998, CBM provided a plane ticket for him to do some eye surgery at Kissy as ECOMOG forces had stabilized Freetown. While in Freetown, Guinea Bissau had a coup. His family was rescued by the UN and brought back to Freetown. I worked with Dr. Fergusson in October and November of 1998. We did 122 surgeries in less than a three week period.

On January 6, 1999, the rebels stormed into Freetown. Dr. Fergusson and the other twenty members of the Kissy staff were holed up in their homes for two weeks before ECOMOG forces drove the rebels out of Freetown.

Bishop Humper noted the following statistics:

- 6500 people lost their lives between January 6 and 28th.
- 2500 houses were burned.
- Post office and police stations were burned.
- 300 police officers were killed.
- More than 350 suffered amputations and other serious atrocities.
- 40,000 displaced people took refuge at the national stadium.
- Over 2000 women were raped.
- Some churches and mosques were burned down.
- No UMC pastors were killed; some church members were killed.
- The 18 year-old daughter of Kissy's Assistant Administrator was abducted and had not been returned.

At the Kissy UMC Hospital:

- Three members of the staff had their homes burned down.
- The hospital was broken into by rocket launched grenades which damaged the newly replaced roof .
- The $40,000 YAG laser was destroyed.
- The vehicles were taken.
- The apartment was stripped.

- Medicines and supplies were taken.
- Massive looting occurred.
- Total losses come to over $100,000.00.

We pray that the plight of the people in Sierra Leone might be recognized and helped by other caring nations. ***To date unofficial estimates include the following figures:***

- Persons killed in Kosovo 10,000 – in Sierra Leone 70,000
- Refugees in Kosovo 200,000 – in Sierra Leone 1,200,000
- Contributions by USA to Kosovo 15 billion dollars – to Sierra Leone 15 million dollars

In spite of all the dangers, the Kissy staff remained committed to the eye program with a deep Christian compassion. We joined them in prayers for peace.

Another urgent prayerful matter is for the "Soldier Boys." Thirteen year old boys are exuberant and playful, like those in the picture, splashing about in the water from the overflowing Kissy UMC Eye Hospital tank. Not at all like these boys was the thirteen year old sullen youngster I was fitting with an ocular prosthesis. A rocket propelled grenade

Figure 5.36. Sierra Leone boys are playful, not maimers or killers.

Figure 5.37. Soldier boys.

had malfunctioned in the launcher. He was fortunate to be alive with only the loss of one eye. We were happy to say to him, "We can help you." After the fitting procedure, he was placed before a mirror. All agreed that he looked handsome. Yet he stood there quiet with no smiles. The next moments were sobering to all of us. We saw that tears were coursing down his cheeks. I turned to John Fornah who had been helping with the selection of the prosthesis and asked him what was troubling the boy to the extent that this supposedly hardened soldier was crying. John explained – "He thought that he would see with it."

It is a dreadful, appalling story. Children in the Sierra Leone civil war, ages ten, eleven, and twelve years, are kidnapped for the war. At first they are used as carriers as well as for the performance of other menial tasks. Eventually under great intimidation they are taught how to handle and operate weapons. To prove their manhood they are forced to take lives, sometimes even of family members. Failure to comply means their own deaths. Boy soldiers are easy to feed and clothe. In their innocent bravado they make up the advancing line exposed to enemy fire. Under the influence of drugs they recklessly plunge themselves into the battle seemingly unaware of the dangers. Graduation comes when they carry out grisly amputation of limbs and other parts of men, women and children. Even infants are not immune from this barbarism.

Kofi Anan of the United Nations acknowleges the "difficult moral dilemma" of prosecuting children:

> *More than in any other conflict where children have been used as combatants, in Sierra Leone, child combatants were initially abducted, forcibly recruited, sexually abused, reduced to slavery of all kinds and trained, often under the influence of drugs, to kill maim and burn. Though feared by many for their brutality, most if not all of these children have been subjected to a process of psychological and physical abuse and duress which has transformed them from victims into perpetrators.*

Child soldiers are denied the normal schooling afforded to others in their age group. Their only families are other child soldiers and the commandants. However, after carrying out terrorist acts, they are no longer welcome back in their own families or villages. They are a lost generation devoid of education, social, and ethical graces.

What was true in Sierra Leone in the year 2000 was also the situation in the Congo, Angola, and other places in Africa, Asia, Latin America, and Europe.

According to U.N. Special Representative for Children and Armed Conflict, Olara Otunnu, there are an estimated 300,000 child soldiers involved in the fighting of wars. He said the international community must exert greater pressure on governments not to enlist children into their armies, and more money must be provided to demobilize and rehabilitate child soldiers and to reintegrate them into society. He also pointed to the need to educate local communities about the suffering endured by child soldiers.

> *Don't forget, the person who comes back is no longer a child because they now have gotten used to violence. In many cases, they were used cynically to commit atrocities. Some of the worst atrocities in Sierra Leone were committed by young people often under the influence of drugs.*

He said such children had to be viewed as victims and healed, not rejected by their communities. "Save the children" has a new meaning at the beginning of the 21st century.

A Sleepness Night, September 5, 1999

It was an eerie feeling driving along the main streets of Freetown. Hundreds (I understand thousands) of homes, businesses, and public buildings had been burned. I saw the charred remains of churches – Anglican, Baptist, and non-denominational. King Memorial UMC was torched but failed to burn. The reason for the church burnings was that "the enemy," – defenseless women and children – were taking refuge in them. Amputations were a part of the invasion, again including women and children.

With the signing of the peace accord July 7, 1999, people would be facing soldiers who killed and maimed their families and friends. How far can peace, forgiveness, and reconciliation go? Especially difficult was the child soldiers' plight. Many would not be able to return to their villages and families where they had been forced to kill by their adult commanders. They were usually placed in the front ranks as they were more reckless and daring in the assault. They took less food and were more easily managed. Often they fought with no particular allegiance – some of them fighting at some time on one side then the other.

It was exciting to arrive at the Kissy UMC Eye Hospital and see it standing. The rocket propelled grenade destruction to the doors, windows, and roof was glossed over with makeshift repairs. The staff was there with a warm Christian welcome. Their faces did not betray the fear, anguish, and deprivation they had experienced day and night for several months. None of the enrolled staff had been killed. Several had their homes burned. All of them lost most, if not all, their personal possessions. They had gone for extended periods without food while they were in hiding. And yet here they were, greeting me with phrases such as "Kabo, how da bodi!" "We tank God" (We welcome you! Are you well? We are thankful to God.)

It was hard for them to understand that I was only there for overnight before going on to Ghana where I did thirty-five sight restoring surgeries at the Cape Coast and Sunyani eye clinics of the Christian Eye Ministry. In a series of meetings with the Kissy general staff, Rev. David Caulker, Rev. Angie Myles (Medical Program Coordinator), Lettie Williams (the administrator), and Dr. Ainor Fergusson (the resident ophthalmologist), important issues were decided.

All this was done with a sense of urgency as everyone had to be off the streets by the 9 p.m. curfew. I was then left with Mohamed Rogers to survey the damage. He actually stayed all night as a sentinel.

The three boxes of medicines and supplies in my luggage did not arrive with me as they had erroneously been shipped to Lome, Togoland, rather than accompanying me to Freetown, Sierra Leone. The next morning on the way to the airport, arrangements were made at the Ghanaian airway office for the return of the boxes to Freetown. Customs clearance offices assured me of prompt and duty free passage. This took place within a week.

After everyone except Mohamed had slipped away, the tour of the facilities was begun. Manhandled, the $17,000 Nikon Automatic Refractor no longer gave accurate digital readings. Lens sets had been

Figure 5.38. Before looting of January 6, 1999.

Figure 5.39. Our apartment over the surgical wing after the looting.

scattered and broken. Some were missing. The trial frames were all gone except one. Trial frames were later seen being worn on the streets of Freetown. The spectacle loops of my Keeler indirect microscope had been torn away leaving only cords and the transformer. All the ophthalmoscopes were gone. Lenses, frames, and equipment in the store and optical room had been emptied from their drawers and strewn about with some breakage. Only one operational fan of five was left. The drug room had been cleared of valuable medicines, supplies, and financial receipts. The surgical theater was in complete disarray at the time of the siege. The staff went to great efforts to restore to proper places surgical supplies, including the intraocular lenses. Parts of the video equipment were missing as was the video camera that attaches to the Zeiss operating microscopes. Headlamps were destroyed, but the three operating microscopes were operational. The $39,000 YAG laser had maliciously been destroyed. No one knew how to open the sterilizer which contained two complete sets of eye instruments with a total value of over five thousand dollars.

The final survey was done in the upstairs apartment. Looted were optical and surgical equipment, mattresses, sheets, towels, kitchen articles, maintenance supplies, tools, sofa cushions, etc., etc.

Dexamethasone, gentamycin, and viscoelastics stored in one of the rooms were scattered with many of them taken away thoughtlessly since they would be of little use to people unqualified in their medical usage.

I spent until 3 a.m. sifting through the debris to salvage usable optical parts. The bed Jonathon had prepared with a net secured felt so good. Lettie had been able to find a mattress. I don't know who contributed the sheets and pillow.

Up at 5:30 a.m. I found the washrooms to be in good shape. The hot shower dared not be used as electricity flashed as it was turned on. The staff all agreed that the most important item not destroyed was our 30 KVA generator, in spite of the fact that the three vehicles had been taken and all other equipment looted.

Astutely the staff had pieced together equipment. The medical and surgical program would resume in full force with the arrival of the boxes of medicines and supplies.

The spirit of the staff was high with a deep commitment to the Lord Jesus Christ. They have compassion for the plight of the many blind people who have been waiting, hoping and praying that someone would come and spring them into the new light of day; so they once more can live normal, independent, and productive lives.

Those of us who are concerned about the outreach of the eye program need to continue in supportive prayer and finances. Repair and replacement costs were itemized at $119, 332.00. Great numbers of people have been blessed by the Kissy UMC Eye Hospital. The staff considers their vocation there as a Christian calling, and by the grace of God, they continue.

Consultation on Sierra Leone Wuppertal, Germany, December, 1999

I was honored to be able to participate in the Partnership Consultation (U.S.A., Germany and other countries in Europe) with regard to the Sierra Leone Annual Conference of the United Methodist Church in the wake of the July 7, 1999, Lome Peace Accord. The brutal, vicious, and barbaric civil war had brought destruction to many properties and infrastructures bringing to a standstill the various ministries of the

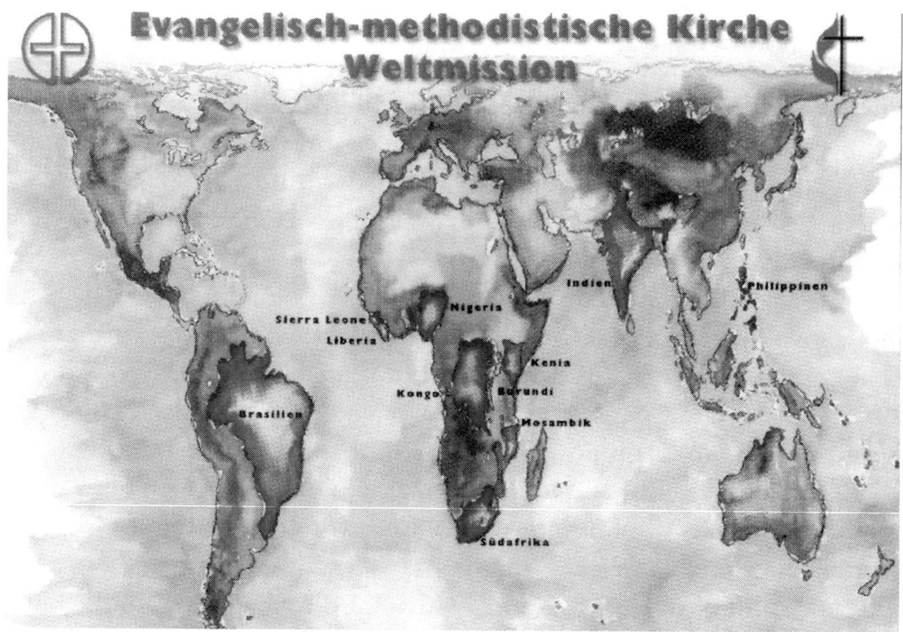

Figure 5.40. The Mission Outreach of the EmK-Weltmission, Germany.

church in Sierra Leone. General and committee meetings engaged in plans for rehabilitation, reconstruction, resettlement, and relief programs and projects of the Conference.

Chaired by Bishop Walter Klaiber, the consultation was conceived by the Rev. Joseph and Carolyn Wagner of Operation Classroom and Mr. Thomas Kemper of the Evangelical Methodist Church World Mission. It received the broad report of Bishop J. C. Humper of war damages and the need for $9,000,000 to establish or rebuild churches, chapels, parsonages, schools, health centres, conference buildings, trauma and HIV/Aids counseling centres, women's training centres, the Bo Bible Training Institute, camp and retreat centres, and other ministries. Prominent leaders were in attendance from Europe. The General Board of Global Ministries of the United Methodist Church was represented by Dr. Zebediah Marewangepo, Dr. Paul Dirdak of UMCOR, and Ms. Maxine West of the Women's Division.

Involved in medical missions for over four decades, I have a deep love for Sierra Leone. While serving as the General Board of Global Ministries' field representative, I had the opportunity of crossing the country from Freetown to Bunumbu and Koidu and then down from

Kabala to Shenge, visiting the churches and schools of the United Methodist Church which shaped the lives of people such as Sir Milton Margai and others. Albert Academy, Harford, and the other 212 primary schools and sixteen secondary schools mean much to the development of Sierra Leone. I can still remember the Christian witness of our school at Kayima where for the first time I heard students heartily sing the song, "They crucified my Savior, and laid Him in the tomb," and then ring out with the chorus, "He rose, He rose, He rose from the dead, and the Lord shall bear my Spirit home."

The thrust of the 93,000 membership of the United Methodist Church with its churches, classrooms, and clinics must be rekindled as reconstruction is anticipated for Sierra Leone. The seventy-five active itinerant elders, the 106 evangelists, and the 197 teacher-evangelists are deeply committed to Christ and the Church's renewal. Operation Classroom under the leadership of Joe and Carolyn Wagner is heaven sent as is a sister Operation Classroom led by Lovelle Meester in my native Minnesota. Through Paul Dirdak the resources of UMCOR are being channeled to help meet the desperate needs of present day Sierra Leone.

Bishop J. C. Humper and the Rev. Angie Myles are vitally interested in a renewed evangelistic and medical outreach of the twelve hospitals/clinics. Outlying clinics have ceased functioning. Destruction has

Figure 5.41. Bishop Walter Klaiber of Germany and Bishop Joseph Humper of Sierra Leone.

Figure 5.42. School being conducted under a tree.

been widespread. The wonderful outreach of Jaiama is missing – the facilities decimated. Pa Loko suffered the same fate. The Kissy Urban Health and Maternity Centre and the Kissy UMC Eye Hospital were in the direct path of the RUF advance January 6, 1999, and suffered extensive damage. An itemization of the Kissy UMC Eye Hospital revealed a $119,832.00 replacement figure. That amount cannot be addressed unless some special (Millennial) funds are made available. However, the program has restarted and up to twenty major surgical procedures are being done each week by Dr. Ainor Fergusson.

Administrative finances must be addressed. It is hoped that they may be included in the Conference budget underwriting the expenses of the program and medical coordinator rather than attempting to raise monies from the income of struggling clinics. Donors react negatively if it is learned that a percentage of clinic income is taken away rather than being used for the replacement of medicines and supplies.

We are praying that the German Conference will renew the ministry that they have underwritten at Jaiama for the last several decades. We pray that the Swedish people will again take up the wonderful work at Pa Loko and include a clinic there. We are encouraged by the way in which Operation Classroom has come to the support of Kissy Urban and

Maternity Centre in addition to their widespread school support. And finally we pray that the General Board of Global Ministries will renew their support for clinics at Rotifunk, Moyamba, Manjama, and others.

The twentieth century saw a marvelous growth of the Church in Sierra Leone. We look to the twenty first century (the new millennium) with great expectations as it is in the hand of God when every knee shall bow and every tongue confess to the Lordship of Jesus Christ.

Back in Our African Home, February, 2000

With the intensity of the savage civil war in Sierra Leone, visitation to the Kissy United Methodist Church Eye Hospital is not always possible. A window of opportunity, however, was presented during February and March, 2000, with the deployment of over 13,500 peacekeepers from Nigeria, India, Ghana, Kenya, and Guinea.

Mrs. Gess and I arrived at the Lungi International Airport in Freetown along with our four large boxes of medicines and supplies. We were given a VIP reception in an air-conditioned room. Attendants took our passports, tickets, and vaccination records and completed our clearance. Every effort was being made to make Lungi International Airport as updated as possible.

While waiting to take possession of our luggage, pandemonium suddenly broke out. A baggage handler's hand had become enmeshed in the gears of the conveyor, and he was being drawn into the mechanism. Before the machine could be stopped, his hand and lower arm were shredded. Uniformed workers hurriedly carried him outside for transportation to the nearby government branch hospital.

Ishmael Jobbie, our airport friend of over twenty years, arranged for our $40 helicopter flight tickets to Mammy Yoko heliport where we were met by Paul Tarawally. He was driving a brand-new four-wheel drive Toyota Hilux, a gift to Kissy UMC Eye Hospital outreach from The Christoffel Blindenmission (Christian Blind Mission International). The two hospital vehicles and our Honda Civic had been burned and destroyed in the wake of the January 6, 1999, rebel invasion of Freetown.

On arrival at the Kissy UMC Eye Hospital we were relieved to see it relatively intact. Doors and windows had been repaired and the roof was in the process of being replaced. The damage had been done by rocket propelled grenades.

Our living quarters above surgery had been ransacked and looted, but Lettie Williams, the hospital administrator, had again supplied it with kitchen utensils, and beds with mosquito netting, even curtains on the windows. A delicious joloff rice meal was waiting for us to enjoy. We were home again. We collapsed into the beds for a good night's sleep.

The next day (Monday) Ruth managed to get the gas-stove working and water flowing in the filters. I went down to the clinic and arranged the slit-lamps for the imminent invasion of up to 150 patients. Very soon the waiting room and the verandas were filled – some of the patients being totally blind. Dr. Ainor Fergusson and I prepared to do up to ten surgeries a day with the help of four surgical assistants. Our entire staff numbers twenty-three which includes the trained ophthalmic assistants as well as three watchmen.

During our two week visit, forty eight operations were done, most of them being cataract extractions with intraocular lens implantation. My last surgery was a difficult "complicated" cataract. His other eye was not amenable to surgery. We were overjoyed the next day when with the removing of the bandage, his face lit up with true surprise and joy. He could see – and see well. We watched him leave the hospital stepping out in front of the family member who had been accustomed to leading him for years. We had counseled the patient that we could not predict the success of the operation. All thanks were given to God.

It was a wonderful experience for Ruth and me to be with our hospital staff for two weeks. In spite of all the fears and dangers, they had remained at their posts rendering the only continued eye care in the entire country.

We also had the opportunity to see our friends of many, many years, because during the last week, the Sierra Leone Annual Conference of the United Methodist Church met at the Brown Memorial United Methodist Church adjacent to the eye hospital. We were showered with African food and words of appreciation for bringing sight and healing to the blind and making provision for needed eye glasses for pastors, many of whom had lost all of their possessions in the recent war.

Our flight home from the Lungi International Airport involved a helicopter ride across the bay from Mammy Yoko Hotel where our dri-

Figure 5.43. Dr. Craig Cameron, orthopedist, flanked by his pastor and an assistant, 2000.

ver, Mr. Paul Tarawally, introduced us to an elderly woman with a left arm amputation and a young man with both arms missing following rebel attacks. Also present was Mr. Mark Kindy with whom some of our children had attended the Rupp Memorial School in Kabala. He had been working with volunteer members of the project Limbs of Hope established by World Hope International. We had the opportunity to visit with Dr. Craig Cameron, an orthopedist, whose account of his visit is reported in *Focus on the Family Physician*, March/April, 200l. During his participation with the team, 147 patients were fitted with prosthetic limbs of the Socketless Mounting Platform type. After learning how to use the prostheses, the victims of this horrible abuse were able to put on and take off their own limb, wash, dress and feed themselves, light a lantern with a match, prepare food, carry a bucket of water, and shovel and hoe in a garden. The new-found independence and productivity gave them hope for a better tomorrow.

Included by Rev. Etta N. Nicol in her article published by the *United Methodist Women Response*, May, 2000, is the heart rending picture of three year old Memuna Mansaray playing with her brother at a camp for war-wounded and amputees in Freetown, Sierra Leone. Her right arm

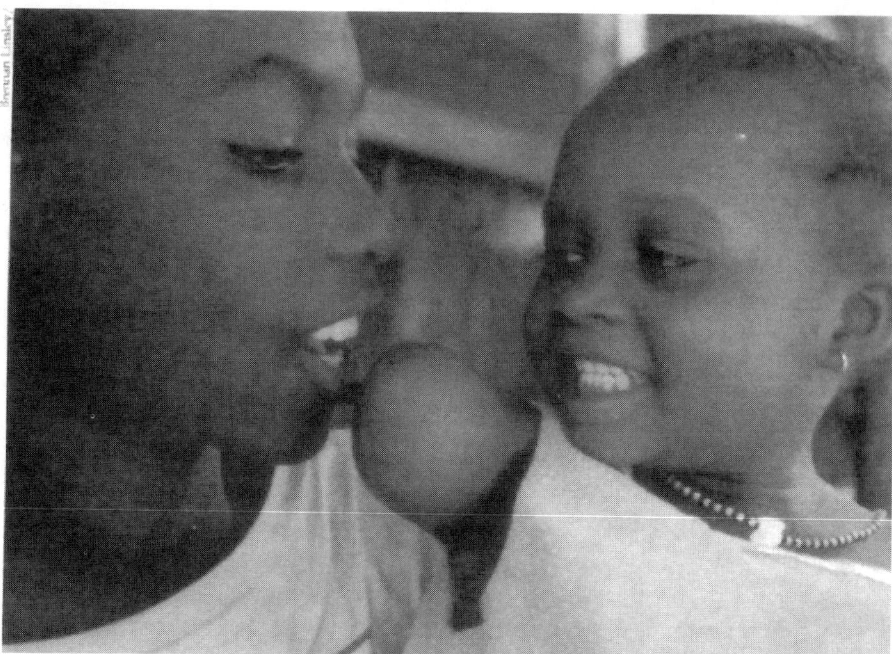

Figure 5.44. Memuna Mansaray, a child amputee victim, 2000.

had been severed by soldiers. A forceful reminder of the tragedy of the civil war took place when at a peace overture meeting with rebel forces, President Tejan Kabbah cradled Memuna in his arms.

While Ruth and I were at Kissy UMC Eye Hospital for such a short two week period, it was heartening to know that so many people could be helped. We thanked God for the good health and safety that we experienced in this politically unstable land. We prayed that true peace may soon be realized – especially the "peace that passeth understanding."

Kissy UMC Eye Hospital Visit
February 16 – March 5, 2001

The Ghana Airways plane set down at Lungi International Airport, Sierra Leone, Sunday evening February 18, 2001, after several hours of delay in its flight plan. On board the plane we sat next to Mr. Kamara who was returning from New York where the Rotary Club had arranged for prosthetic fittings for his double amputation. He remains a proud man unwilling to let his disability destroy his life. This is true also for the more than 2000 amputees who survived. At least that same number died following these forced grisly and vicious amputations often performed by child soldiers not strong enough to do a clean single machete or ax stroke. Only worse were the victims whose eyes were intentionally blinded.

The ferry from Lungi to the government wharf was in service which allowed us to cross the bay by water instead of by helicopter. The apartment over the surgical wing at the Kissy UMC Eye Hospital had been cleaned and made comfortable for our late arrival. The security of a mosquito net over our bed was comforting.

On Monday morning it was a glad reunion with our staff of committed Christians still at their posts after having their lives threatened and their property and personal possessions destroyed. Mrs. Lettie Williams had administratively held things together. Dr. Ainor Fergusson each week had been performing twenty or more cataract extractions with intraocular lens implantation. They welcomed our four seventy pound boxes of medicines and supplies. Mrs. Hannah Koroma, our assistant administrator underwent cataract extraction during our stay. With her absence in the clinic Ruth filled in for her in handling the flow of patients.

Together Dr. Fergusson and I performed seventy-one eye operations; sixty of them cataract extractions with IOLs and eleven trabeculectomies for out of control glaucoma. Unusual conditions of some eyes were encountered for which we could provide only partial improvement. One volunteer eye surgeon who did surgery for a month several years ago stated that he never did a really "normal" cataract extraction in all the time that he was at Kissy.

The need for eye care is great. Kissy UMC Eye Hospital is the hope for millions of people in West Africa. In spite of the continuing standoff between the democratically elected government of President Mohamed Tejan Kabbah and the RUF (Revolutionary United Front) people try to live normal lives under the heavy protection of over 10,000 UNAMSIL soldiers. There are indications that the RUF is weary of the continuing conflict which recently had spread from Sierra Leone to neighboring Guinea. As many as 135,000 refugees from Sierra Leone and Liberia were thought to be caught up in the "parrot-beak" area between the warring factions and have been without food or medicine for as long as three or four months. At the present time they seem to have dispersed into the bush and jungle areas as the refugee camps are nearly empty. A UN representative recently on the Internet called the state of affairs in this area "the greatest humanitarian crisis in the world today." We continue to pray for peace in our beloved Sierra Leone.

Our return flight to Accra, Ghana, from Freetown was not a delay but rather a cancellation. Two extra days were involved with working our way home back to Alexandria, Minnesota. Home was never more sweet. Ruth and I feel privileged to have been able to minister to a destitute people and country in these trying days in Sierra Leone, West Africa.

Figure 5.45. White sandy beaches in Sierra Leone.

When we are in Africa for extended periods, we sometimes watch the sun set over the ocean to the west where our families are located, visualizing their faces, but our "warm" arrival home occasionally involves digging our house out of the snow.

Figure 5.46. Our home in Alexandria, Minnesota.

Visit to Kissy, October, 2001

It had been six months since our last visit. Freetown now is the site for the largest concentration of United Nation troops in the world. Refugees flood the streets bringing traffic to a near standstill for periods of every day. The short distance from downtown to Kissy UMC Eye Hospital normally requiring 10 to 15 minutes often lengthens to two to three hours.

Our Hilux four wheel drive vehicle donated by Christian Blind Misssion to asist in mobile eye clinics throughout Sierra Leone threaded through the mass of humanity crowding the streets. Thankfully no pedestrians were injured during our passage. We were happy to arrive at Kissy UMC Eye Hospital after our trip from Alexandria, Minnesota, via Amsterdam and Accra, Ghana. Members of the staff were there to greet us and help us with our luggage which included 350 pounds of medicines and supplies. Alcon Laboratories and S.E.E. International had generously supplied us for our three week stay of volunteer eye surgery which included 106 eye operations. Eighty-five percent were cataract extractions with intraocular lens implantations with the remainder consisting of trabeculectomies and procedures for pterygia and lid alterations.

During the following days of a busy clinic and surgical schedule, we continued to be amazed by the upbeat attitude of the staff. They consider their work as God's calling for them. They take turns in the reading of scripture, prayers, witnessing, and hymn directing once the hundred or more patients are registered for the day. Their deep Christian commitment is a challenge to Ruth and me. Without exception they have returned to their posts at times of great dager. None were killed, but some lost all of their personal possessions. Three had their homes burned during the rebel intrusion into Freetown.

Being able to help blind patients is a soul inspiring experience. Many were bilaterally blind making them dependent on others to lead them. Their joy at being independent and productive vicariously is experienced by the surgeons and staff. Dr. Ainor Furgusson, a native Sierra Leonean, not only does eye surgery four days a week at Kissy but occasionally flies to Guinea Bissau to help in the CBM sponsored program there.

While I was thrilled to be a part of renewed sight for these blind patients, it was a special event to do a second intraocular lens implantation on Mr. Josef Caulker, a radiant Christian, who on March 4, 1984, received a personally designed Alpha Omega intraocular lens. Seventeen years later, he sees "perfectly" with that left eye but wanted to have the blind right eye restored as well. His hopes and prayers were realized.

Isata Kamara had been blind for several years. Because of the nature of her condition, she required an anterior chamber intraocular lens. Thinking that she might not have much vision we did the other cataract extraction five days later – again requiring an anterior lens. A few days before returning from our visit to Kissy, Isata walked through the door, followed by her daughter who was carrying a baby on her back. Previously the daughter had to lead the mother. The daughter explained that before coming to the clinic, she found her mother in the market having a wonderful time. Along with the many smiles, there were a few tears... of joy.

Samuel Kamara, a soccer standout, realized that something was wrong with his sight. The eye examination revealed only hand motion in his left eye. Vision in the right was drastically constricted. Since eye medications are not always available in West Aftrica, he chose to undergo a trabeculaectomy on his better eye. Postoperatively his anterior chamber was dangerously shallow. Mr. Conteh, who originally diagnosed the glaucoma, prayed for Samuel. Two days later the chamber returned to a normal depth and pressure. Malcolm Albert broke out with this beautiful baritone voice singing the doxology. A half dozen others joined, including the patient.

I cannot help but strongly encourage ophthalmologists and other doctors to share their time and skills as volunteers to a needy world. The December Kissy visit of ophthalmologist Dr. Cathy Schanzer is being anticipated along with Dr. Samuel Pieh and other members of the Mid-South Aftrica Link team who are including Taiama in their volunteer work schedule. Other organizations around the world are gearing up to bring to fruition Allan Harkey's vision of sight for the world by 2020. A doctor is never the same again after participating in the service of love.

While going from Jericho to Jerusalem, two blind men pleaded with Jesus to help them regain their sight. In compassion He restored them. The wonderful ending to this incident was that after their healing, "they followed Jesus." There are patients attended to at the Kissy UMC Eye Hospital who also receive not only physical sight, but spiritual insight into the love of God as revealed in Jesus Christ.

Chapter Six

Trips to Underserved Countries

Great Wall of China

Helping Hands are Extended Beyond West Africa

It was in the fall of 1989. With my next birthday I would be in my seventieth year. A prominent doctor on the surgical committee at Douglas County Hospital happened upon an article in *Medical Economics* describing a difficult situation in which an elderly surgeon, past his prime, needed to be rescued from poor decisions and performances. He refused to give up his practice or his hospital privileges.

It seemed wise to review the ages of staff doctors at the Douglas County Hospital and have a special meeting to prevent such a tragic situation developing in Alexandria.

I was enjoying my practice and surgery with little thought of retirement. The possibility of being censored came as a shock. I could not see myself standing before a committee of my peers and having them decide whether or not I was to do intraocular lens implantation following cataract surgery – a procedure I had pioneered in the upper Midwest.

Ruth and I were stunned. Was the Lord telling us something? Should we shift our practice to Sierra Leone, Africa, where there was no completely trained ophthalmologist? Along with primary surgery we could also teach and upgrade other doctors in the underserved world.

The following day we drafted a letter of resignation and made preparations to close our practice as of midnight December 31, 1989. We made a presentation of over 15,000 charts to our sons, Timothy, an ophthalmologist, and John, an optometrist.

We did this fully aware of the challenges that were inherent in doing volunteer eye surgery in other needy places of the world. The first consideration was the expense of travel and supplies, even though pharmaceutical and optical houses were generous in providing needed items. Secondly, adjustments need to be made to new time zones, which is enervating and tiring. Weeks are needed to get back to a normal sleep pattern. Thirdly, risks are involved. At a moment's notice the country in which one is serving may develop political instability with its inherent dangers. There are tropical diseases to consider, chief among them malaria, which is still the world's greatest killer. And finally the world's AIDS epidemic is a constant threat. In Africa there are over twenty-two million people with HIV, the virus that leads to AIDS, compared to 1.5 million Americans. AIDS deaths have orphaned 13.5 million African children, as noted in *World Magazine,* September 9, 2000.

Suffering tugged at the heart of Jesus. He healed all manner of diseases and disabilities. My commitment to Jesus Christ prompts me to walk in his steps, to do the things that he did, and to teach the things that he taught. The plight of a blind person was of great concern, rousing a compassion ("sorry heart") which energized me to ask, "Need this be?" To be blind, when there is a prevention or a cure, was unthinkable.

Recent statistics number 5,506,000,000 people in the world today of whom 40,000,000 are blind. Eighty percent of these live in poverty-stricken areas of Africa, Asia, and Latin America. Christian Blind Mission International indicates that seventy-five percent of these blind could have been rescued with preventive and curative care. It is hard to believe that 400,000,000 suffer from trachoma, the "Egyptian eye disease." Twenty million are infected with onchocerciasis, known as "river blindness." One hundred thousand small children lose their eyesight each year because of Vitamin A deficiency. Measles takes a dreadful toll.

We ask about the causes. Malnutrition and poor hygiene aggravated by lack of water stand at the top of the list. There is insufficient education and lack of medication. And finally there are shortages of eye doctors, eye hospitals, and instrumentation. Consequently, there are vast areas in Asia where one out of four people is blind and one out of two people suffer from an eye disease. There are many villages in West Africa where up to fifty percent of the adults are blind because of the complications of onchocerciasis. The happy ending to this story is that a cure has been found. The pharmaceutical company, Merck, Sharp and Dohm has made available Ivermectin, also known as Mectizan, to the World Health Organization for free distribution to countries needing it. This wonder drug has protected millions of people from the threat of blindness.

The very size of Africa, which is 2 1/2 times larger than the United States and with its 650,000,000 people using over 1,000 different languages, accounts for special difficulties in reaching the curably blind. Only one in ten people who are blind from cataracts in Africa ever undergo the surgery. Africa has only 500 ophthalmologists for their fifty-six countries. In contrast the U.S.A. has 15,000 ophthalmologists for an area less than half the size of Africa.

It is understandable from the above statistics that a retired ophthalmologist still healthy and willing to serve, should seize the opportunity to be a blessing. No other answer would do than – "Here I am, Lord, send me."

January and February 1990, found us at the Kissy United Methodist Church Eye Hospital, Freetown, Sierra Leone, West Africa, which we had founded in 1983 with the encouragement and support of the Sierra Leone Conference of the United Methodist Church. Twice more during 1990, we spent several months at Kissy. In the years that followed, besides serving in Sierra Leone, we accepted invitations to do and teach surgery in thirteen other countries of the world, particularly during times of political unrest and instability in Sierra Leone.

On to Zambia – 1990

The Christian fellowship with other missionaries is wonderful and precious. I first became acquainted with James Foulkes while we were doing general surgery residencies at Akron General Hospital, Akron,

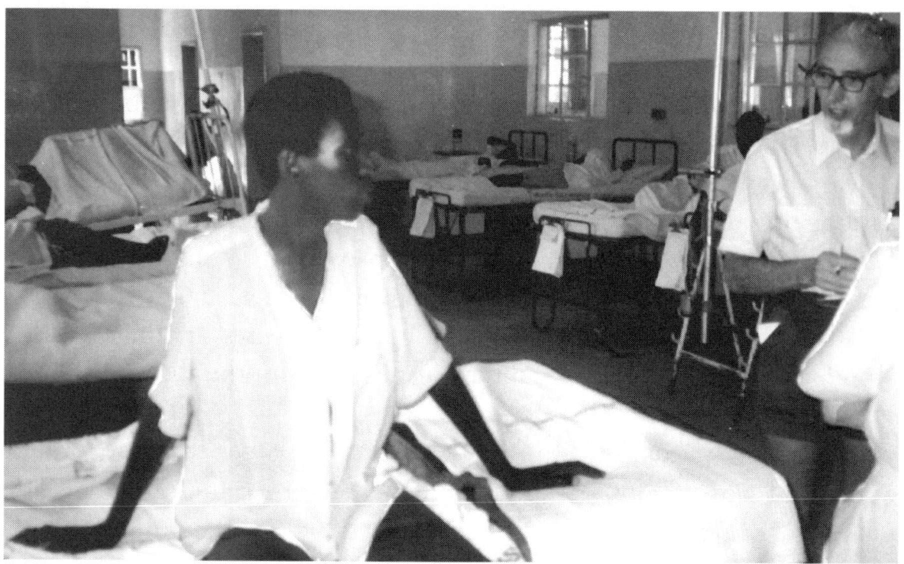

Figure 6.1. Compassionate care for AIDS patients in Zambia.

Ohio, in 1956. Each of us had been drawn there through our relationship with Jeanette (of Lassa fever fame) and Roger Troup. The senior Troups were helpful in finding a place for us to live in Akron and were our spiritual counselors. A group of residents and interns at the Akron General Hospital who were training for overseas missionary service loved to be in their company.

Both Jim and I were involved in general surgery on the field. The presence of blind patients over the years unsettled each of us. Eventually I added an ophthalmologic residency to my training. Jim and his wife, Martha, stopped at Freetown, Sierra Leone, on their way back to their work in Zambia. He absorbed everything he saw at the Kissy UMC Eye Hospital and took careful and accurate notes. He also did some eye procedures.

On his return to Mukinge, he developed an eye program. He constantly upgraded his techniques, even visiting prominent eye surgeon Dr. James Gills in Tarpon Springs, Florida.

In 1990 Jim and Martha invited me to spend three weeks with them at their hospital. Jim became comfortable with the Haag Streit slit lamp and the attached Goldmann tonometer. We worked together at the operating microscope, which had an assistant scope, giving each of us a perfect view of the operative field. His previous surgical skills made the next step of introducing intraocular lenses forthright and successful. In the succeeding years he incorporated eye surgery in his missionary career with its wonderful benefits. He admitted that the immediate results of eye surgery gave him pleasure as well as the patients who were grateful for their restored sight.

My experience at Mukinge was a great blessing to me. I was impressed by the selfless service of Doraine Ross, Mary Hartstein, Paul Bosson and his doctor wife, Alison, and all the other staff who came from such diverse places in the world as Australia, England, and the USA. Daily they were in intimate contact with HIV positive patients. One entire ward was given over to AIDS patients waiting to die – but dying in the presence and ministry of Christian and compassionate care givers. This was my first visit to an African country for volunteer eye surgery other than Sierra Leone.

My return flight to the Minneapolis-St. Paul (Lindberg) Airport was on Sunday afternoon, June 3, 1990. Soviet leader Mikhail Gorbachev emerged from a military airplane; I from a Northwest International flight that had begun in Zambia. Although Mr. Gorbachev represented a potential threat to the American people, thousands turned out for his arrival. I had just completed three weeks of eye surgery in Kasempe, Zambia, and posed no threat, only help. I was met by one person, my wife Ruth.

On to Maua, Kenya – 1990

On August 29, 1990, Ruth's and my trip to Maua Methodist Hospital in Kenya had a nice start. We were upgraded from tourist to cabin class on our flights, which increased the comfort of our travel. However, I was brought down on the day of our arrival in Nairobi, Kenya when I had the misfortune of colliding with another gentleman while running to get out of the heavy rain. I sustained a rib fracture. It was not to affect my surgery, but Ruth needed to help me move the microscope for its positioning, and it was difficult getting in and out of bed.

We were chauffeured to the Maua Methodist Hospital by Ms. Lois Olsen who was teaching midwifery. She introduced us to Dr. John and Sharon Harbottle. He had been medical superintendent of the hospital for a number of years. We also had the pleasure of meeting and visiting

Bishop Ismathie and Duncan Spurgeon, who was visiting Maua at the time.

We set about setting up the surgical instruments and arranging for the examination of patients. The new eye and dental facility which Dr. John Cooksey had raised funds for had not been completed. We used the hospital's x-ray room as a temporary eye clinic. The driver of the hospital van served as the circulating nurse. It was a pleasure to use the Zeiss OPMI operating microscope provided by Dr. Cooksey. We had brought along a Haag Streit slit lamp, an A-scan, and a keratometer. To have the use of sophisticated instruments added to the satisfaction of doing eye surgery in this remote area bordering Somalia.

We performed surgery every day, trying to keep up with the numbers of totally blind people who were presented to us. Often two people occupied the same bed as there were never enough beds to go around. This was not without merit, as the nights were unduly cold at this elevation of four to five thousand feet. This cool temperature was in spite of the fact that on our journey up to Maua from Nairobi we crossed the equator.

The house provided for us was comfortable and allowed us to do our own cooking. It was not uncommon in the evenings to have a blanket wrapped around our legs because of the cool temperature. I enjoyed Dr. James Gill's *The Unseen Essential* during our stay at Maua. Frequently we were invited out for meals to the homes of Dr. Lynn and Sharon Fogleman and Dr. John and Sharon Harbottle.

Mrs. Harbottle conducted services on Sundays at the Meru National Park. We were invited to accompany them and on the way were thrilled to see an abundance of wildlife. Just after entering the park we observed three cheetah, usually an elusive animal, simply looking at us as we passed along the road. Other animals included zebra, waterbuck, giraffe, warthog, Grant gazelles, elephants, ostriches, kudu, impala, and more than 100 buffalo in a menacing herd. We were relieved that our vehicle did not sputter and die at that particular moment.

Ultimately arrangements were made for us to return to Nairobi following a very successful volunteer eye surgery experience. The transport was what was referred to as a "speed taxi." We were to know what that meant when at one time I noticed the speedometer reading 150 kilometers per hour! We wondered whether or not I would be able to accept the invitation of Bishop Charles Makonde to preach the following day.

Figure 6.2. After volunteer eye surgery at the Maua Methodist Hospital in Kenya, a trip to see the animals.

During our stay in Kenya we also had the opportunity to visit the Lighthouse for Christ at Mombassa. We were met by Dr. Jerry and Betty Harrel and Dr. Dean and Carol Larson. I cannot say how much I was impressed by the devotion of these two couples in their extended services – Dr. Harrel following a career with the Air Force and Dr. Larson following a successful private practice in Glendora, California. Each were expert surgeons offering state of the art care that included intraocular lens implantations following cataract extractions. I accompanied Dr. Larson on a safari during which eleven surgeries were done and 191 patients examined, all in the course of an afternoon's work.

Besides the eye program with the twenty-eight Kenyan staff, Tim and Toni Ghrist oversaw as many as twenty pastors who ministered in churches that were extensions of the Lighthouse for Christ. Volunteer eye surgeons were always welcome to participate in this well equipped program.

While at Mombassa it was unusual to be able to meet Dr. Robert and Carol Wenninger who were visiting the Lighthouse for Christ. They are coworkers with Dr. James and Martha Foulkes at Mukinge, Zambia. Somehow missionaries find one another in the far reaches of the very large continent of Africa.

Before leaving Kenya it seemed appropriate that we visit the world famous Masai Mara Reservation. In addition to those animals seen at the Meru National Park, we observed duiker, hartebeast, topi, baboons,

Figure 6.3. After volunteer eye surgery at the Maua Methodist Hospital in Kenya, a trip to see the animals.

monkeys, and a total of sixteen lions feeding on two kills made during the night, from the safety of our safari vehicle. No one uttered a sound as we drove up to within twenty feet of these kings of the beasts.

Our guide was a genial and efficient leader. As he dropped us off at the United Methodist Conference Center in Nairobi, he wished us the Lord's blessing in our volunteer surgical ministry. He wanted us to know that he was a committed Christian.

On to Cairo, Egypt – 1991

Following our time of service at Kissy UMC Eye Hospital September 27 through November 2, 1991, Ruth and I began our return trip to the USA by way of Egypt and Israel. I had been in Cairo in 1984 when I presented a paper on "Trebeculectomy with Iridencleisis" at the International Eye Foundation, Society of Eye Surgeons Fifth World Congress. Since Ruth was not with me, I resolved not to visit the pyramids until such a time as she could share such a momentous experience.

Now, eight years later, we landed in Cairo for that visit to Cheops, the largest of the pyramids, and Sagjara, the oldest, reaching back five thousand years. We purchased a rug picturing Nephertiti.

After guided excursions, plans were made for our trip across the Sinai desert to Jerusalem. An armed Egyptian police guard took us to the Suez Canal. From there Israeli police escorted us to Jerusalem. Fellow United Methodist missionary Romeo L. del Rosario, who was stationed in Jerusalem, made arrangements for our visits to Old Jerusalem, the markets, Gethsemane, the Mount of Olives, Bethlehem, and St. John's Eye Hospital. At St. George's Cathedral we ran into a Lutheran pastor from Minnesota who knew of the Gess Eye Clinic in Alexandria, Minnesota. The visit would not have been complete without going to Jericho, the Dead Sea, Masada, Tel Aviv, Nazareth, Tiberius, the Sea of Galilee on which we had a boat ride, and the remains of Capernaum.

We were impressed by the compression of geography. Israel is not a large country. Israelis and Palestinians constantly rub shoulders with each other. We pray for that day when Jews, Muslims, and Christians obey the great commandment: "Thou shalt love the Lord thy God with all thy heart, and with all thy soul, and with all thy strength, and with all thy mind; and thy neighbor as thyself." (Luke 10:27 KJV).

Figure 6.4. Pyramids of Egypt.

On to Ghana, 1992

After the April 29, 1992, coup in Freetown, there was a massive evacuation of expatriots arranged by the U.S. Embassy to waiting planes and ships. I requested that my name be removed from the list as I had a number of eye patients who had just had their operations and needed postoperative care. I was scheduled to fly on to Accra, Ghana, in a week's time to participate in volunteer eye surgery at the Cape Coast Eye Hospital. During this time I did emergency care of people wounded in the recent fighting.

Arriving at the Lunge International Airport on May 10, I learned that my scheduled flight to Accra had been canceled. The airport was locked and nearly deserted, but a guard who knew me opened the gate and allowed me to enter the terminal. There was only one man in the ticketing area. When I inquired about passage to Accra, he told me that there was a small plane that was ready to take off for Monrovia. There another flight might be arranged for Accra. He grabbed my small travel case, and we hurried out to the plane. They gave me the last seat, next to the pilot.

At Monrovia a transfer was successfully made to a Ghana Airlines flight to Accra. Again I was given the last seat on the plane.

The days spent with Dr. Herb and Ruth Billman were rich days of Christian fellowship at their Cape Coast Clinic. The patient and surgical load was heavy. Preaching on the veranda was effective. I enjoyed immensely the reading of Ruth Billman's autobiography, *Wrap Me.* Later the Billman's were to establish in Accra the Emanuel Eye Center, one of the most accomplished eye outreaches in West Africa.

On to Vietnam, 1993

An exciting and rewarding trip was taken to Ho Chi Minh City, Vietnam, April 10-18, 1993. The planning of this had been done essen tially by Dr. Harry and Baillie Brown of Surgical Eye Expeditions International located in Santa Barbara, California. They did all the arrangements of the visas and tickets. The day came when I arrived in Los Angeles and met up with Dr. George Biernbaum, the leader of the

Figure 6.5. With Vietnamese women eye doctors.

expedition and the partner with whom I was to work in Vietnam. He was from Tennessee and had been on SEE trips before. The Browns had done a very good job of packing supplies. All we needed to do was open up a certain pack and everything would be ready to do the surgery. Everything, that is, except the instruments which would be sterilized just prior to the procedures.

On our way to Vietnam we were surprised at the length of the flight – fourteen hours. When we arrived at Hong Kong, we were ready for bed. The dawn brought Easter. We found a church not too far from our hotel, and although it was conducted in Japanese, we were made to feel welcome. We then flew on to Ho Chi Minh City and were caught up in the flurry of trying to clear all our large boxes. Suddenly we were aware of some help from people outside the customs area. Two of the leading ophthalmologists from the Ho Chi Minh City Eye Hospital were there to intercede with the customs officials. Things went very smoothly from then on and we were taken to our hotel.

The following day we were transported to the main hospital, and on arriving there, we were met by a group of eye doctors who presented us with flowers. After the exchange of formalities, we were escorted to the clinic where we began to examine patients to determine which patients would be receiving surgical treatment. It was quite overwhelming to see the number of patients that they had garnered. They were not just straight ordinary cataracts. They had saved some difficult cases for the "foreigners" to talk over with them. Fortunately, there were two slit lamps, and they also had a keratometer. I had my A-scan portable unit so that preparation could be made for the extracapsular cataract extractions and the implantation of the proper powers of the posterior chamber lenses. We saw over fifty patients that day and then retired to prepare for surgery the next day.

On Tuesday, April 13th, I lectured on the use of intraocular lenses and then did six surgeries. With three of them I demonstrated how they could be done without viscoelastics using air for insertion.

Dr. Biernbaum's lecture was on kerato refraction. The twenty-three Vietnamese eye doctors were eager to be introduced to new procedures. Later that day, Dr. Biernbaum and I stepped out from our hotel and visited the business district to see what shopping was like and had the experience of almost being robbed. We made a hurried retreat back to the hotel.

The next day Dr. Biernbaum lectured on complications of the placement of intraocular lenses. I lectured on trabeculectomy. It was very interesting to be shown how instruments were made in Vietnam. In fact, the person who was making instruments presented me with a state of the art needle holder that she had just fashioned in the hour or two before our visit. I have it to this present day.

On the following day, April 15th, after doing more intraocular lens implantations, we were feted to an evening meal on a floating restaurant. While there we ran into some Sierra Leonean women who were observers for the United Nations in Ethiopia. They were just passing through Ho Chi Minh City on their way back to Sierra Leone.

The following day we were taken on a tour to be shown the various hospitals. One was a communicable disease hospital. We were quite impressed with the number of patients that are seen and the very basic care that is given. Later on we were taken to a porcelain factory and shown how they make these items for export.

Before the end of the visit, three of these twenty-three Vietnamese doctors had placed intraocular lenses.

On April 17th we packed to return home. We were showered with gifts from our patients. Dr. Van, Dr. Chilon, Allie and Tulzzett took us to the airport. Our bags were readily taken care of with these important

Figure 6.6. Some of the patients in Ho Chi Min City (Saigon).

people to intervene for us. We boarded the plane and had the most delicious chicken fricassee that I have had since I dined at the table of my Aunt Frieda on the farm near Paynesville, Minnesota many years ago. We spent the night in Hong Kong and then began our flight back to the States on the 18th. We were delayed on the runway three hours because of a raging storm. The people were all seatbelted in their places and were not allowed to move around. Finally they unloaded some of the freight and we took off for our fourteen hour flight. That meant we were sitting in those narrow seats for seventeen hours before arriving in Los Angeles. With that long delay, I had missed my connecting flight from Los Angeles to Minneapolis. I was taken to a hotel and slept the sleep of exhaustion. The next day I was able to resume my flight back to Minnesota. It was wonderful to get home and be in my own bed.

Though one of the shortest visits ever made to another country, it was a challenge new to me. Three and a half years later at the Academy meeting, I ran into two of the lead doctors who were present during the time of our visit to Ho Chi Minh City in April of 1993. We were excited to see each other and had an extensive visit. They recalled the lectures and the demonstrations given. They were eager to report that over 25,000 extracapsular cataract extractions with intraocular lens implantations were done in 1996-1997 – half of them being done by the technique that had been observed and learned during Dr. Biernbaum's and my visit. The ophthalmologists had been very intent on the lectures and made full use of the assistant scope. With their native intelligence they surged ahead with the new procedure and shared it with other eye doctors.

It boggles my mind to realize how such a small group of twenty-three could ultimately be instrumental in making available 25,000 operations with the technique that was demonstrated in only a week's time in Ho Chi Minh City, Vietnam.

I will always remember Dr. Van, one of the chief surgeons who spoke English well. We spent a great deal of time together. In recalling his friendship, I was struck with the question, "What was a Minnesota farm boy doing so far away in Vietnam that became so significant to the surgical outreach of eye doctors in that part of the world?"

On to Cape Haitien, Haiti – 1993

On July 18, 1993, I set out for a flight to Cape Haitien, Haiti. The flight was delayed two hours because of a flat tire. I landed in Cape Haitien after only one stop for refueling in the Bahamas. It was a delight to be met by Dr. Hollis Clark and his wife Wanda. After touring their eye clinic, it was obvious to me that no help or suggestions were needed from an outsider. Dr. Clark and his associate Dr. Carmella had an efficient surgical theater with all the needed up-to-date equipment. Mrs. Clark ran a tight ship in the clinic and the storerooms. They had a new generator, automatic lensometer, autorefractor, and an alert staff who obviously were enjoying the work that they were doing.

My demonstration surgery was not particularly helpful in the presence of their skilled techniques. It was the old story of not being in your own familiar surroundings with your own instrumentation. My only contribution may have been sharing the ketamine regime that worked so well in Sierra Leone over a period of several decades. Volunteer ophthalmologists often face the problem of anesthesia for children as appropriate equipment and trained personnel are not always available in underserved countries.

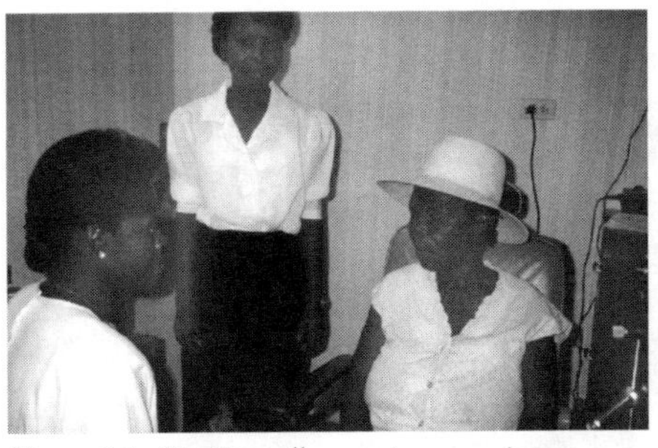

Figure 6.7. Dr. Carmella examines a patient.

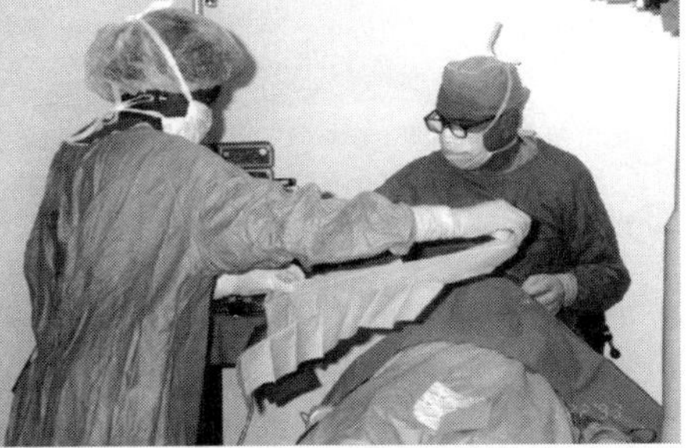

Figure 6.8. Dr. Hollis Clark prepares for surgery.

Over the years I learned that safe anesthesia can be obtained by using ketamine in conjunction with peribulbar, retrobulbar, VanLint, O'Brian, or Nadbath blocks. Ketamine comes in different strengths. If 100 mg/ml is used, the following calculations are made: The weight of the child in kilograms (kg) is multiplied by five. For example a 20 kg child needs 100 mg or 1 ml of ketamine. Fifty mg (0.5 ml) is placed beneath the facia lata on the anterior aspect of each thigh. The child will be ready for the local block within a three minute period. If the procedure lasts beyond twenty minutes, care must be taken not to stimulate the patient with loud talking or the touching of unanesthetized areas. The patient will continue to be somnolent even though the ketamine anesthetic has worn off. With the local block in effect, the patient is not stimulated to move or react. As a general rule for the local blocks, 2 ml of 1 percent Lidocaine can be used per year of age not to exceed 10 ml.

I enjoyed my stay in Cape Haitien very much. On one occasion Hollis took me to overlook the bay of Acol where Christopher Columbus spent Christmas while grounded on a reef.

All in all, many of their challenges at the Cape Haitien Eye Clinic were the same that we faced in Sierra Leone. It was good to see other missionaries and their work in underserved countries that were offering health, healing, and sight in the name of Jesus Christ, our Savior.

On to Zimbabwe, 1993 – The Stroke

On Thanksgiving Day, November 25, 1993, son Tim and wife Joanne with their family, picked Ruth and me up in their car to travel to daughter Mary's home in Minneapolis for Thanksgiving dinner. It had

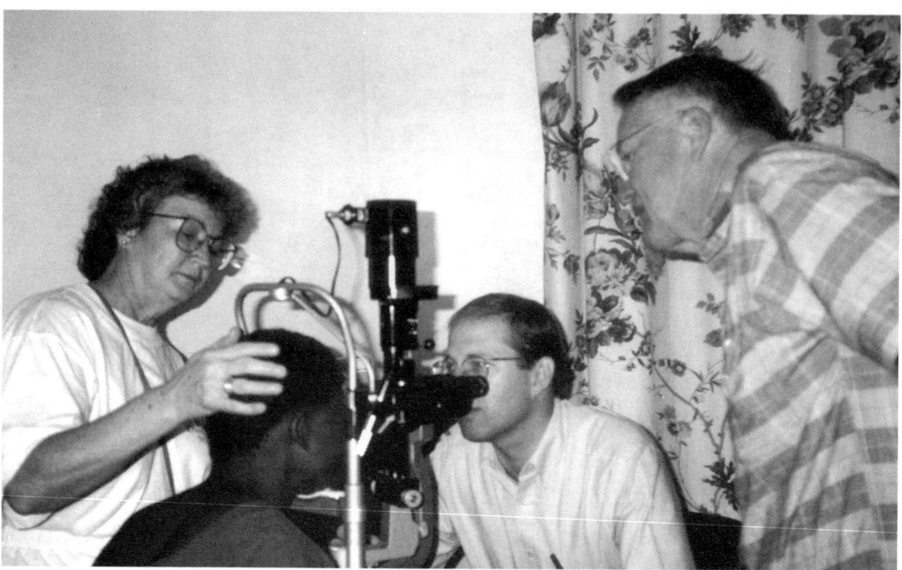

Figure 6.9. Dr. Dan Stephens at Slit Lamp.

been snowing and already four or five inches of snow had fallen. We passed three cars in the ditch. We were happy to arrive at Mary's by 10 a.m. The turkey dinner was lovely. Soon afterwards, Chris Boehlke, Mary's son, took us to the airport. The first leg of our journey was to Chicago. After a transfer, we went on to the London Heathrow airport. The following day we were in Harare, Zimbabwe, and got in on another Thanksgiving occasion. On the 28th Marybelle, who was the leader of our little group, took us to Dr. Dan Stephen's hospital in Karande. During the next week we were to do eye surgery, and it was my privilege to be able to teach Dan how to do extracapsular cataract extractions as well as the implantation of intraocular lenses. It is interesting to know that in the succeeding year when Dan's father (who is an ophthalmologist), came out to help in the program, Dan was able to show his father how to do the extracapsular cataract extractions with intraocular lens implantation. The father, although he was an expert eye surgeon, had not taken up doing intraocular lenses, and so the son (who was a general surgeon), taught his father, who was an ophthalmologist.

After we had been at Karanda, we did some teaching at a United Methodist Hospital in Old Mutare. Rather than returning home by way of England, we decided to go by way of Australia, the Fiji Islands, Hawaii, Los Angeles, and then Alexandria, Minnesota. It would be only

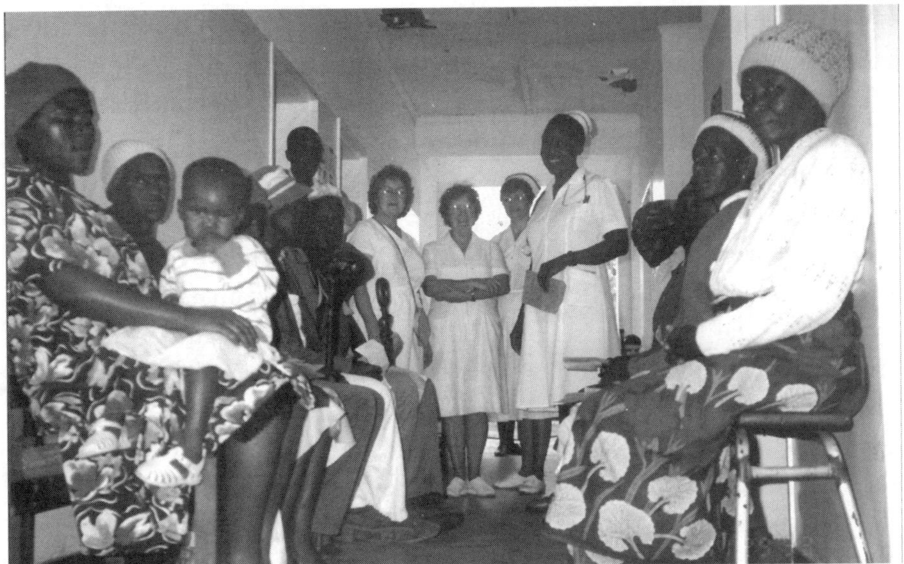

Figure 6.10. Patients of all ages at the Karanda Eye Department.

a little farther.

After an enjoyable time in Australia and Fiji, we arrived in Hawaii. It was strange that Ruth was not interested in touring Pearl Harbor where all the United States ships had been sunk December 7, 1941. She just wanted to sit. That night she became restless. She complained of a severe headache and on checking, it was apparent that she was ill. I was able to make a quick call, and we changed our date of departure. In a few hours we boarded a plane for Los Angeles. Our walk to the plane was long. When we got on board, Ruth settled back in the seat. She was not conversant. She was breathing all right, and her pulse was good. I was about to ask the stewardess if we could be let off the plane. However, the plane was already taxiing down the runway. It was apparent within the next few minutes that Ruth was suffering from a stroke of some kind. She maintained vital signs, but it was a very long 4 1/2 hours before we landed in Los Angeles. I asked the stewardess to have the pilot radio ahead for an ambulance to take Ruth to the nearest hospital. At the time that the people were to unload from the plane, there was an announcement asking that the passengers remain in their seats until someone left the plane who needed to have medical help. Expeditiously Ruth and I alighted to a waiting ambulance.

After the radio message had been sent, the politics of Los Angeles began working. The paramedics were sent to meet the plane rather than a hospital ambulance. The emergency crew felt that they had to examine the patient before anything could be done. I tried to reason with them that I, her husband, was a doctor and that by now I was aware of the fact that Ruth had lost peripheral vision to the right. I said, "My wife has had a stroke, and it involves an area affecting vision to the right." They still were reluctant to make any arrangements. In desperation I said, "Well, if you don't feel an ambulance should come, I will take her to the hospital in a taxi." They declared that we were under their control and care, and they would make the decisions as legally I had no status because I was her husband and not an objective or disinterested doctor in the situation. There were some heated exchanges. Finally, they decided to honor or humor me, and prepared to take Ruth and me to their emergency vehicle.

We needed to go up a series of fourteen tall steps. Ruth had been on a gurney, a stretcher with wheels. There was no elevator. I gathered up our suitcases, and on looking up, I saw that Ruth was off the stretcher and was walking up the steps with the two emergency men carrying only the stretcher. I could hardly believe that anything like that could be happening in the USA. At the top of the stairs, they replaced her on the emergency cart and put her into their vehicle. It was then that they wanted to apply their skill and their training by starting an intravenous drip. I knew that with all the shaking, swerving, and bumping, it would be very difficult to get a needle into the vein. I suggested, "We're only five minutes from the hospital. Wait until we get to the hospital and then an IV can be started." Again, there was a confrontation, but they gave in to a licensed doctor.

When we got to the emergency room of the Marina Hospital, Ruth was taken into the emergency room. As soon as I got to the emergency room, a lady directed me to another room for registration. I explained that I was a physician, that I knew what the problem was, and would like to share information with the doctor in charge. However, they isolated me. Finally I got up and walked through the doors and into the emergency room. I greeted the doctor who was examining Ruth. I explained that I was her husband and that I was a doctor and that Ruth had had a stroke and that it involved the visual tract on her left side. He said, "Why don't you come along with me," and so the two of us positioned Ruth for a CAT scan. A few minutes later, the findings revealed what had been predicted. On arrival, the attending physician could not believe the scenario involved in getting Ruth to definitive care. He immediately began treatment so that from the time we landed, even with all that confusion, there was only about a twenty minute delay before Ruth was getting heparin and other supportive treatment.

The next morning, because of that prompt treatment, Ruth was already talking. She had some anomia (nominal aphasia), which caused difficulty in recalling the names of people and objects. Over the next four or five days she improved to the point where we were able to get on an airplane and come the rest of the way home. We were met by our daughter Mary and her husband, Steve Boehlke, who whisked us up to Alexandria. Rather than being admitted, we simply stopped at the emergency room of Douglas County Hospital. While in the car, Ruth had bleeding and coagulation time specimens drawn by Dr. Richard Stewart, the doctor on call. We then took her home and put her to bed. We thank God for her speedy recovery under the care of Dr. Jerry McCrery. Now, years later, Ruth is reading again and has accommodated to her right peripheral vision loss. Together, we continue our volunteer eye surgery trips.

On to Mongolia, 1994

In August, 1994, I was part of a S.E.E. team of five that conducted an expedition to Outer Mongolia. On the last leg of our journey, we took off from Beijing, China, with its teeming millions. Our plane threaded between mountain ranges and eventually settled down in a long, green valley. Here was nestled Ulaanbaatar, the capitol city, with a population of 500,000 people. The additional 1,500,000 people of Mongolia are scattered throughout the country ranging from the lake country in the north to the Gobi Desert in the south.

We found the people to be poised and friendly. The streets were wide and motorized vehicles were sparse. There was no press of motorcycles as in Vietnam. The bicycles which fill the streets of Beijing were few in Ulaanbaatar. Herds of sheep, goats, cows, yaks, and horses roamed the countryside. My greatest surprise was never seeing a fence. Herdsman were everywhere riding the ubiquitous Mongolian pony.

The First Clinical Hospital in Ulaanbaatar has an impressive Eye

Figure 6.11. Dr. J. Baasanhuu, the eye doctor in charge with S.E.E. team.

Department headed by Dr. J. Baasanhuu, a well trained and accomplished ophthalmologist. Under her guidance extracapsular cataract extractions have been developed to perfection. Intracapsular cataract extractions are rarely performed.

The Mongolian eye doctors are respectful and self-assured. Our S.E.E. team dealt with 15 during our stay of nine days. Lectures on glaucoma were given by Dr. James Standefer, and I lectured on cataract surgery with IOL implantation. Dr. Harry S. Brown conducted a busy laser program with his portable Nidex laser. Mr. Wilfred Klein and Mr. Kelly Brown kept instruments in top performance.

The hands-on surgery was done on a one-to-one basis with the Welsh missionary scope set up. It is unlikely that Dr. Robert Welsh realizes the impact of his contributions to international volunteer eye surgery. He has been especially successful in encouraging service clubs to reach out and support eye projects. The booties on the new and improved stand made X-Y maneuvering easy. Here in Mongolia, a Jena (Zeiss) operating microscope with video monitoring, provided by Christoffel Blindenmission, made possible group instruction.

I have some indelible impressions about the patients on whom I performed surgery. Unknown to me, my first patient was a prominent professor from the University. Several years ago, a cataract extraction with

Figure 6.12. Herds of horses and sheep roam the countryside in Mongolia.

IOL implantation had successfully been done in Russia by Dr. S. Fyordorav, whom I got to know and visit with during the Academy of Ophthalmology meetings. An American ophthalmologist was to be tried this time – happily with success.

Among the medical doctors treated, one was strikingly beautiful and expressive. In spite of her diabetes and asthma, things went smoothly for her. No chances were taken with an anesthesiologist in attendance armed with steroids and asthmatic medications.

A second M.D. had to be led into the room with bilateral hypermature lenses. She was withdrawn and docile. We were hardly prepared for the extrovert the day following surgery. Her new interest in people and the surroundings gave her face a special beauty.

One my final day of surgery, I had the privilege of "assisting" three surgeons place their first posterior chamber intraocular lenses. These were deftly done with the help of a Dusek-McIntyre insertion forceps. Mr. Dusek graciously sent this helpful instrument to Mongolia for the eye program.

The Mongolian ophthalmologists were anxious for second opinions. Difficult eye problems were presented. They were encouraged to hear their diagnoses and methods of treatment confirmed by "American ophthalmologists," for whom they held an unusual respect. They were especially interested in techniques. Some instruments were left that were especially interesting or attractive to them.

The expedition was well received and plans were made for Dr. James Standefer to return to Mongolia in June, 1995 for a month's session of teaching, including newly developed glaucoma techniques.

What are the rewards of volunteer eye surgery? Dr. Harry S. Brown is fulfilling a dream that he had when he first began as an ophthalmologist that the best eye care be extended around the world.

Dr. James Standefer relates that he has never been happier than since he has been doing volunteer eye surgery in Latin America, Vietnam, the Solomons, and now Mongolia and China, with future plans to include Russia and the Far East.

There is something about being available to people in their need (their blindness). Were it not for ophthalmologists' life training and their willingness to share it, some people would not have the joy of seeing again...of having a new life opened to them. Once having participated in a program like this, the ophthalmologist is never the same again.

On to China, 1994

Beijing, the capital of China, is overwhelming in the mass movement of people. The 10,800,000 population needed expanded health facilities, as was the case for the Beijing Eye Hospital.

Professor Le Me-Yu, chairperson of the Department of Ophthalmology at the Beijing Medical University, had extended an invitation to the Mongolian S.E.E. team to lecture, do demonstrative IOL surgery, as well as participate in clinical pathologic conferences. Dr. Me-Yu was chief editor of the *Chinese Journal of Ophthalmology* and Vice President of the Chinese Society of Ophthalmology.

In a preparatory visit to the surgical facilities with Dr. Harry Brown and Mr. Wilfred Klein, we found a Zeiss OPMI-6 operating microscope in a side storeroom. Willie serviced it for the planned surgical procedures. I checked the preop patients.

The next morning I returned to the surgical suite alone. What I hadn't anticipated was a throng of gowned, capped, and masked doctors. After positioning myself at the head of the table following the local anes-

Figure 6.13. The Great Wall of China.

thetic which I had asked to do personally, I was unaware of the identity of the first assistant. Everything went well with efficiency and dispatch except that my elbows were of necessity kept close to my body because of the press of observers.

After the IOL placement and wound closure, I commended the first assistant on her expertise. When she removed her mask, I found I was visiting with Dr. Me-Yu herself.

On a subsequent case I was impressed again with the knowledge and dexterity of the first assistant. She was reserved and not quite as fluent with her English as Dr. Me-Yu. At lunch she happened to be sitting next to me. It was then that I learned that she headed up Beijing Eye Hospital, one of the largest and most prestigious eye hospitals in China.

During the lunch, I also commented that I had known about the Great Wall of China since my boyhood school days and that it was one of the world's great wonders. A tight patient and flight schedule the next day would make it impossible to visit the wall.

The next morning I received a call in my hotel room just after an early breakfast. I went down to the lobby and was met by one of the eye doctors who had observed the surgery the day before. With excellent English she informed me that she would take me to the wall in a limousine waiting outside. It was chauffeured by a professional driver. Arrangements had been made to delay the postop examinations and consultations long enough to make the trip possible.

The wall was impressive. It was a wonderful experience to fellowship and share methods of expertise with notable far Eastern scientists. I shall never forget my visit to China with all the kindnesses shown to me as a visiting volunteer eye doctor.

On to Zimbabwe, 1995

We were all packed and ready to leave for Sierra Leone the second week of January, 1995, when word came from the General Board of Global Ministries of the United Methodist Church that travel was not being advised to Sierra Leone. In consultation with Dr. Zebediah Marewangepo, it was decided to use our medicines and supplies in a volunteer eye surgery trip to Dr. Marewangepo's native Zimbabwe. His office would attend to notifying the country's church leadership. At the last moment I sent a fax myself to Bishop Jokomo's representative, Mr. Sam Mungure.

On arrival we were to learn from Mrs. Rose Mungure that the only notification to get through had been my last minute fax. She was successful in having the custom officials release our medicines and supplies.

Figure 6.14. Africa University underwritten by the United Methodist Church, Old Mutare, Kenya.

Figure 6.15. Postop ward.

It was another story receiving permission from the medical authorities to do volunteer eye surgery in Zimbabwe where so many expatriate M.D.'s were seeking admission to practice.

Following a temporary permit issued by the government, Mr. Mungure took us to old Mutare. Dr. and Mrs. Tendai Munyeza graciously welcomed us into their home.

Refracting and surgical instrumentation were set up in the hospital. We ministered to a sizable number of patients over the next two weeks.

By looking out of the windows of the old Mutare Hospital, with its outstanding special ward for the care of babies and small children, I could see the African University which was being built and underwritten by the United Methodist Church in the United States. Twenty million dollars are being invested for this needed educational center. Impressive on our tour of the University was a room filled with more than twenty computers. E-mails were not yet a common medium for communication or our unknown coming would have been more "known."

It was a joy to visit with Dr. Don and Ruth Rudy and nurse Delphine Jewel at Mutambara. While there we examined thirty eye patients. Theirs is a tremendous work. I wondered how they could handle such a demanding schedule and still retain their health. Less than

Figure 6.16. Dr. Solomon Guramatunhu and staff. Zimbabwe.

five years later I learned that Mrs. Rudy did yield up her life following this sacrificial service.

The United Methodist Church is strong in Zimbabwe. They have three well-equiped and efficient hospitals. We ministered in two of them. The dental facility in Harare is fulfilling a real need. The church also supports centers for orphans and the blind. The work of the United Methodist Church is a model to behold in Zimbabwe.

At Mutare, twelve miles from Old Mutare, we examined patients along with Dr. Chana, an Indian doctor supported by the Norwegian Association of the Blind. It is an excellent facility, even manufacturing their own eye medications. We brought out the Zeiss operating microscope from behind a door and set about doing extracapsular cataract extractions with intraocular lens implantations. Dr. Chana has made a tremendous contribution to that part of Zimbabwe extending also into Mozambique.

The last of our three weeks in Zimbabwe was spent at the Perirenwatwa Hospital in Harare. It was a special privilege to be able to lecture ten residents in eye training representing five different countries of Africa. In the group were Dr. Beata Tumushim and Dr. Ruth Welbeck who did excellent surgery as was the case with Dr. Fred Chikwanda and Dr. Mani, who also excelled in his presentation on the subject of retinal detachment. I was to appreciate three years later the skills of Dr. D.J. Kwendakwema during his time of surgery in Lilongwe, Malawi while participating in the S.E.E. supported Lilongwe eye camp.

Dr. Solomon Guramatunhu, with the help from outstanding surgeon Dr. John S. Jarstad, developed into a skilled phacoemulsification and intraocular lens implant surgeon. He was the only African to be doing that procedure in central and eastern Africa for a number of years. Dr. Jack Aaron, who had volunteered at Kissy UMC Eye Hospital as far back as 1986, took up the challenge along with S.E.E.'s help to annually do volunteer eye surgery in Zimbabwe.

Ruth and I enjoyed the people and the climate of Zimbabwe. Her days at the Bronte Hotel were spiritually invigorating. Our only regret was dropping in "out of the sky" without adequate notification. Church leaders and Dr. and Mrs. Tendai and Natalia Munyeza rose to the occasion and made us welcome.

On to Abak, Nigeria, 1995

We arrived in Lagos, Nigeria on September 17, 1995. Those who met us at the airport took us to a convent for the night. The single bed and sparse breakfast reminded us that we were far from home. The following day we flew on to Calabar. We were distressed that the driver who took us to the airport was fined for illegal parking when he left us off. In Calabar we were picked up by Sisters Theresa and Patricia.

When we arrived at the Mercy Hospital in Abak, we were not prepared for the hundreds of people waiting for us. A total of fifty-two bilaterally blind people were scheduled for surgery. Keratometric readings were done by Dr. James, an optometrist, whom we learned later was also a United Methodist minister.

The staff provided excellent help. Dr. Rosalen Duke was doing eye training in Calabar. She visited Mercy Hospital each day that we did surgery, and participated in some of the procedures. Because of her plans to go into full time eye care, we presented her at the end of the two weeks with a working set of eye instruments.

On the Sundays that we were in Abak we enjoyed the church services at the United Methodist Church. On one occasion we visited the Aluminum Smelting Company of Nigeria. We came to know the

Figure 6.17. Nurses and staff, Mercy Hospital, Abak, Nigeria.

Reverend Robert and Joan Dickinson who head up the Christian Bible College in Abak. At the time of our leaving we agreed to take a total of four pounds of mail to be mailed when we arrived back in Alexandria, Minnesota.

On the occasions when Joseph Innocent, (who gave us hanging drapes with Bible verses), or other staff people were unable to be present during the surgery, Sister Veronica filled in not only as an excellent assistant in surgery but also by doing the anesthetic blocks. She headed up the program and was a delightful person to know.

Our living conditions were enhanced by the excellent cooking of Friday, whose full name was Nyong Udoh. A broken window screen was discovered too late one morning. Ruth's practice of sleeping with her feet sticking out from under the sheet led to dozens of bites on her feet. The itching was annoying, but it was not until three weeks later in Alexandria that Ruth began to experience paroxysms of chills, fever, and sweating. It was frightening to witness her deterioration in spite of adequate chloroquine treatment. Visits to the doctor ultimately resulted in a blood smear which revealed plasmodium falciparum infection. We knew that she needed to have prompt treatment with an anti-malarial drug to which there was no resistance. Phone calls were made to the pharmacies and fortunately Mr. Jack Trumm replied, "Oh, we just happen to have a fresh supply of Lariam (Mefloquine). Our daughter recently made a trip to Africa, and we supplied her with Lariam."

Within several days of the treatment with Lariam, Ruth regained her strength and health. We tried not to think about the episode of a British pathologist and his wife who stopped in Kano, Nigeria on a return trip to the United Kingdom. When the pathologist's wife became ill three or four weeks later a blood smear was not done and she died for lack of treatment of malaria.

The work of Mercy Hospital is underwritten by Focus. This began decades ago because of the interest of Dr. James E. McDonald. They have built and equipped facilities for eye care in this area of southern Nigeria. The work has been carried on by Dr. Marilyn Miller, Dr. Ronald Fishman, Dr. James Standefer, and as many as fifty or sixty other volunteer ophthamalogists over the years.

On our last full day at Abak, we were aware that Friday's gas stove was being removed from the kitchen after he had served breakfast. We were to learn later that the Sisters spent much of the day cooking a sumptuous farewell dinner for us. Father Matthew along with other church leaders shared in this wonderful event.

It was a privilege for Ruth and me to participate in this extensive outreach and to know that fifty-two people who previously had been blind were now walking without being led, enjoying life, and being productive.

On to Chicuque, Mozambique, 1995

Fourteen hours after a non-stop flight from JFK Airport in New York, the South African Airways 747 touched down in Johannesburg, South Africa. A short hour connecting flight brought me to Maputo, Mozambique. United Methodist staff met me and put me up in the rest house next to the large and beautiful Malanga United Methodist Church. The following morning a formal visit was made to the Government Health Department for clearance to do surgery. Also a visit was made to the Government Eye Hospital in Maputo with a conducted tour of the facilities by Dr. Yolanda Zambujo. She was fluent in English which made our "shop talk" delightful. By 1 p.m. my pounding toothache that had begun a day earlier had to be treated. Mr. Schlomo

Figure 6.18. Beth Ferrell, administrator, Hospital Rural De Chicuque, Mozambique.

took me to a dentist who removed a filling and replaced it with a "temporary" one. Within a week I was able to chew on the tooth again.

Saturday morning, November 11, a hired bus containing six eye patients and me made the 300 mile trip north to the Hospital Rural de Chicuque in Inhambane Province. The patients were evaluated with the slit lamp and three were kept for subsequent surgery.

The following morning in the Chicuque United Methodist Church I received a warm welcome and a brotherly embrace from Bishop Joao Somane Machado, who happened to be in attendance. During the next two weeks 541 patients were examined and 51 surgeries performed.

The first patient during the first full day of surgery developed a raging endophthalmitis (infection). We were never able to trace the source. Desperate measures were taken with a new wonder drug and mercifully the eye was saved.

A large percentage of the patients were bilaterally blind before their intraocular lens implantations. It was thrilling to see the postoperative patients walking without being led on their way to the United Methodist Church where four long pews had been reserved for them. I was greatly moved when the pastor in front of the congregation presented me with a model Mozambiquean sailing ship.

The hospital staff is composed of co-administrators Mr. Armando Chitata and Mrs. Beth Ferrell along with five medical doctors – Emmanuel Mefor, Annette Gonsalves, Paul Wolff, Roberto Cordeiro and Beatriz Birchal. The last two from Brazil are Persons in Mission appointed by the General Board of Global Ministries. Dr. Stone, a general surgeon, would be returning from the USA in January, 1996. The remaining Mozambiquean staff are well trained and dedicated in their work. Mr. Adriano is the ophthalmic assistant. Mr. Alberto served as translator. Mrs. Ferrell in late 2001 was assigned by the GBGM to a ministry in Bo, Sierra Leone, West Africa.

The eye needs in Mozambique are staggering. Medicines and supplies are meager in Maputo. Bishop Machado is addressing this need by urgently requesting Christoffel Blindenmission to help develop facilities at the Chicuque Hospital which is centrally located in the country.

The Christian ministry of compassionate caring is a wonder to behold at Chicuque. The United Methodist Church is deeply committed to this outreach of the Gospel. There is a reason why 1500 overflow the church on the hospital compound. "Inasmuch as you have done it unto one of the least of these my brethren, you have done it unto me." (Matthew 25:40.)

Endophthalmitis, The Worst That Can Happen in Eye Surgery

On November 14, 1995, MCM was the first patient of the first full day of surgery. Reportedly instruments had been autoclaved and the operating team was gowned and gloved. Preop preparation included povidone application to the skin with some deliberately being allowed into the cul-de-sac. Peribulbar anesthesia then followed using 5 ml of 2 percent xylocaine mixed with a 5 ml .75 percent marcaine. A super pinky with light pressure was applied for 15 minutes. The povidone prep was repeated. A cloth drape was used with a hole twice the size of the orbital area. The upper and lower lids were separated and a Tegaderm drape applied. A slit was made, and it was observed that there were no lashes exposed in the operating field.

A fornix-based flap was prepared. After preparing a groove with a

Figure 6.19. This patient is smiling after learning that her endophthalmitis has successfully responded to treatment.

diamond knife, a 30 gauge 1/2 inch needle with a 45 degree bend on the distal 2mm was thrust through the groove into the anterior chamber and used as a cystitome. The can-opener capsulotomy was done with no egress of aqueous during the maneuver. The incision was opened with a 30 degree superblade. The capsular disc was removed with a Kelman McPherson forceps while the anterior chamber was maintained by irrigation from a 3 ml syringe with a 25 gauge Gills cannula. An irrigating vectis floated out the nucleus. Simcoe irrgation and aspiration was carried out without trauma to the endothelium or posterior capsule. 10-0 figure of eight sutures were placed at the sides of the incision and the IOL inserted under an air bubble. The IOL had been grasped by the surgeon and placed directly into the eye; there was no accidental dropping of the IOL on the operative field. Further 10-0 figure of eight sutures closed the wound. Three mg celestone and 20mg of gentamyscin were injected subconjunctivally inferiorally. Neodecadron ointment was placed and a sterile pad applied. The patient was given 250 mg tetracycline orally q.i.d. for an intended 4 day period.

The bandage was removed at 6:30 a.m. the following day and the eye was unremarkable. The patient was instructed to apply the neodecadron ointment six times a day by only pulling down the lower lid and not touching the upper. It was learned later that she administered the medicine herself, not having any relative with her. No eye pad was reapplied.

At about 10 a.m. the following day (less than 30 hours after the first examination) the patient complained of severe pain. A hypopyon level was nearly halfway up in the anterior chamber. Murkiness prevented seeing the pupil and hand motion was questionable.

Within minutes 25 mg of vancomycin, 20 mg of Ggentamycin, and 3 mg of Ccelestone were given subconjunctivally. Gentamycin drops were used every fifteen minutes and maxidex drops every hour. The subjunctival injections were repeated later in the afternoon.

Surprisingly the patient reported the third postop day feeling comfortable. A slit lamp examination explained the sudden relief. There was disruption of the temporal aspect of the wound, relieving the pressure.

In surgery 80 mg of gentamycin was mixed with a combination of 4ml of .75 marcaine and 4 m. of 2 percent xylocaine. Two ml of this mixture were slowly and periorbitally placed in the four quadrants of the orbit. Sufficient time was allowed for complete anesthesia and akinesia. A speculum with adjustable blades was used to ensure no pressure in the globe.

On the previous day the one gm of lyphilized vancomycin had been diluted with 20 ml of BSS to give 25 mg per 0.5 ml. At that time 25 mg was administered subconjunctivally. Now one ml (50 mg) was diluted with 4 mg BSS for a total of 50 mg vancomycin in 5 ml dilution. One ml of that dilution then contained 10 mg. The recommended one mg intrvitreal dose in the recommended 0.1 ml solution was then available for intra vitreal administration.

Since the state of the eye appeared hopeless and removal might be necessary later on, a decision was made to try to sterilize the anterior chamber and possibly save the eye even though the sight might be sacrificed by the toxicity of vancomycin on endothelial cells. It was known that 1 mg in the vitreous could be tolerated; and so 0.5 mg was injected through the disrupted wound into the anterior chamber prior to the resuturing (the quantity being 0.05 ml or the equivalent of 1 drop).

Following the wound repair, 0.1 ml (1 mg vancomycin) was injected through the pars plana into the vitreous cavity with a 30 gauge 1/2 inch needle. Also 25 mg vancomycin and 3 mg celestone were individually injected subjunctivally.

The patient responded dramatically. She became comfortable and the hypopyon disappeared in nine days, at which time she was able to count fingers. There was a good red reflex. Supportive medications included atropine and tobrex drops. Choloramphenical ointment was used at night. Within several weeks vision improved to allow for reading.

A goverment opthalmologist monitored the patient after I returned to the United States. It was wonderful to have the help of this eye specialist. All thanks are to God for overcoming in such a perilous experience!

On to Zing, Nigeria, 1996

Palm Sunday, March 31, 1996, was observed by worshipping at the Schiphol airport in Amsterdam. That afternoon I arrived at Kano, Nigeria, with six seventy-pound boxes of eye medicines, supplies, and equipment. No one was there to meet me as arrangements had been made to meet me on March 26th, five days earlier. Customs officers were appalled by the quantity of luggage. A military officer personally made arrangements for its clearance with not a single box being opened. He then arranged for two taxis to carry the boxes and accompanied them and me to a car park with the intent of securing transport to Jos, Nigeria, a six hour journey. On the way, however, my taxi driver suggested that it was dangerous to travel at night and suggested that we go to the ECWA Eye Hospital. (On a return trip from Jos to Kano we were stopped at eighteen road blocks by police and soldiers. At a similar road block near Zing the night before we passed, a man was accosted by armed robbers who took his car after killing him with a shot to the head.)

At ECWA, Terry Hammock, a SIM missionary, secured the boxes in a locked store and I was given a room for the night. The next day Terry arranged for a van to take the boxes to Jos. There was not enough room for me in the van but Steve Worley, a missionary evangelist had a place for me in his car. We arrived at the UMC rest house in Jos before evening. Frank and Delores Carter provided a meal and room. Beside their duties at the rest house they teach at Hillcrest School.

The next morning at 7 a.m., Frank and the driver, Daniel, took me to Bauchi. There Michael and Doris Vitzhum squeezed the boxes into their Toyota, and we took off for Zing. They have two lovely children, Yana and Analena. It was hot and the roads were poor. A flat tire occurred thirty miles before the end of our journey. Michael and Doris were an experienced team in changing the flat tire with a spare. Thankfully we arrived at Zing before dark.

During the next eleven days I was the Vitzhum's table guest while sleeping in a room in Bishop Done Peter Dabale's compound where the Chinese ophthalmologist Dr. Zhu and the Chinese general surgeon Dr. Zhang also had a house. Wednesday morning found us in the Zing UMC Eye Clinic seeing and treating patients and arranging for subsequent surgery. The boxes were unpacked and the Haag Streit slit lamp assembled as well as an American Optical keratometer and lensometer. A complete set of donated eye instruments was readied for surgery. Edward, the Nigerian registered nurse trained in eye care, was not available as his leg was in a full length cast following a fracture suffered in a recent car accident. Also, Dr. Zhu was unable to work in the clinic or participate in surgery due to a severe case of herpes zoster (shingles) of her upper body. Dena, an energetic assistant, did the sterilizing while Dr. Zhang, the general surgeon, and I did cataract extractions and intraocular lens implantations. We usually were able to do three a day except for one day when five patients were operated on. During the last three days, Markus, a registered nurse trained in eye care from Bambur, assisted in surgery.

While at Zing I participated in a Good Friday service and a beautiful Easter sunrise service on an expansive rocky plateau overlooking the city of Zing.

Ultimately it was time to leave. Postop patients cheerfully waved good-bye, thrilled with being given renewed sight. Some had been without vision for years. It is always our prayer that along with physically renewed sight there is a spiritual insight into the redeeming love of God as revealed in Jesus Christ.

During my stay at Zing I was invited to meet with Bishop Dabale on two occasions. We enjoyed a discussion about the eye program and the rural health program. He also shared his dreams for the future outreach of the United Methodist Church in Nigeria. When I visited Zing in 1953 during our 1952-1955 appointment at the Guinter Memorial Hospital at Bambur, the congregation was small. Now there are two churches in Zing, one of which is very large. Other churches are in Lankoviri, Jalingo, and surrounding villages.

I was not able to cross the ferry at Lau on the Benue River and proceed to Bambur on the return trip because of a very serious clash between Fulani and Hausa people in which hundreds of people were killed in the Karim Lamido area and our UMC dispensary burned down.

The trip back to Jos via Numan was a bit easier in a stronger vehicle with four-wheel drive. On arriving in Jos I was able to visit the ECWA Evangel Hospital where 43 years before I had participated in a gall bladder operation on one of our Bambur missionaries. I also visited Hillcrest School and walked around the campus where four of our six children had been in attendance.

Then on to Kano. On Monday, April 15, 1996, I spent the day in surgery helping Dr. Gazella Baghy do her first intraocular lens implantations as well as demonstrating the procedure with actual surgery of my own. After a busy clinic Tuesday, the operating microscope was packed and a flight taken from Kano to Amsterdam and then on to Minneapolis, Minnesota, and ultimately to Alexandria and a happy reunion with my wife, Ruth, and two of our children's families.

I came away from the experience with a sense of awe. There had been a tremendous growth and outreach of the United Methodist Church in the years following our initial ministry there forty-four years ago. We thank God that so many people are being reached for Christ and the new life in Him. Believers are being baptized in the Holy Spirit. Truly this is part of the witness to the uttermost part of the world referred to in Acts 1:5.

On to Maua, 1996

At Sunday noon October 6, 1996, I boarded Ghana Airlines in Freetown, Sierra Leone. It took some maneuvering, but I was not going to be separated from my carry-on travelpro bag. Stewardesses reported no room for it in the cabin but a friendly Sierra Leonean whisked it up the steps and promptly found a space near the door as well as a seat for me. Without assigned seats there is a free-for-all.

The flight to Abijan was without incident. However, the eight hour wait to board the Ethiopian airplane for Nairobi took some patience. The principal of the Theological College in Freetown, Rev. Nabieu, was most helpful in carrying my bag to the plane and up the steps. At the foot of the steps all luggage was meticulously examined. I thought I would be an hour showing all my medicines and instruments. The lady in front of me had to empty her hand bags. I explained that I was an eye doctor on my way to Kenya to do eye surgery and that the handbag and travel pro contained medicines, supplies, and instruments. He did not even open the luggage but waved me on with, "Have a pleasant flight." Apparently I looked too old and too harmless to be a security risk.

Again clearance was remarkably simple in Nairobi. I hired a Venture taxi, got clearance papers at the Medical Practitioners and Dental Board, stopped at a super market for sugar puffs, peanuts, cookies, honey, sandals, soap, tissue paper and bananas, and then set out the 300 kilometers to Meru. At the equator we stopped to rest. I bought an ebony turtle for Ruth to mark the occasion. We hurried on as it was getting dusk and travel is extremely dangerous at night. Before it got dark we had to give way to five bull elephants crossing the road just before arriving in Meru. The remainder of the trip was frightening with sharp curving roads and blinding car lights.

There was a warm welcome at the medical superintendent's home at Maua United Methodist Hospital. Drs. Lynn and Sharon Fogelman are both physicians appointed by the General Board of Global Ministries. They have three children, ages six to ten. A bed could not have felt better that night. Even the mosquitoes could not keep me awake. Thereafter I was comfortably housed in the boy's dormitory and had the privilege of having my meals with the Fogleman family.

English prayer services were held each morning at 7:30 with more than fifty in attendance. English Sunday services were at 5:15 p.m.

The day after arrival was spent lining up patients for surgery and preparing instruments. The Zeiss operating microscope was excellent. It also had a teaching apparatus on which I placed my 10 x 22 B binocular. Medical students and doctors could see the surgery as well as the operator.

Sylvester Intinyai did an excellent job assisting in surgery. Joyce Kimaru continued to see and screen patients. Ruth Charles was an experienced circulating nurse, and efficiently kept the surgery and clinic tidy.

Thirty one IOL surgeries were done with the inclusion of one trabeculectomy. Eight were bilaterally blind with mature cataracts. With surgery they had the joy of renewed sight. Two congenital cataracts were done, and one twelve year old patient easily accepted an IOL.

The surgeries presented some unusual happenings, but the most challenging occurred on the final scheduled surgery. In the middle of the operation the lights went out. We used an ophthalmoscope to provide illumination for the completion of the cataract removal and intraocular lens implantation. Mercifully, the eye did well.

Maua Hospital is the only hope for eye care in the northeastern sector of Kenya. Even at the provincial headquarters at Meru, which is thirty kilometers to the south, there is no eye surgeon at the present time. The people just sit and pray that someone with compassion will come to open their eyes again. In our prayers prior to the actual surgery we also pray that they would receive insight into the love of God as revealed in Jesus Christ. Working with "born again" staff was a thrilling experience. Two women patients came back later after successful implants to share with me that they knew they would be all right when they heard the prayer offered prior to surgery.

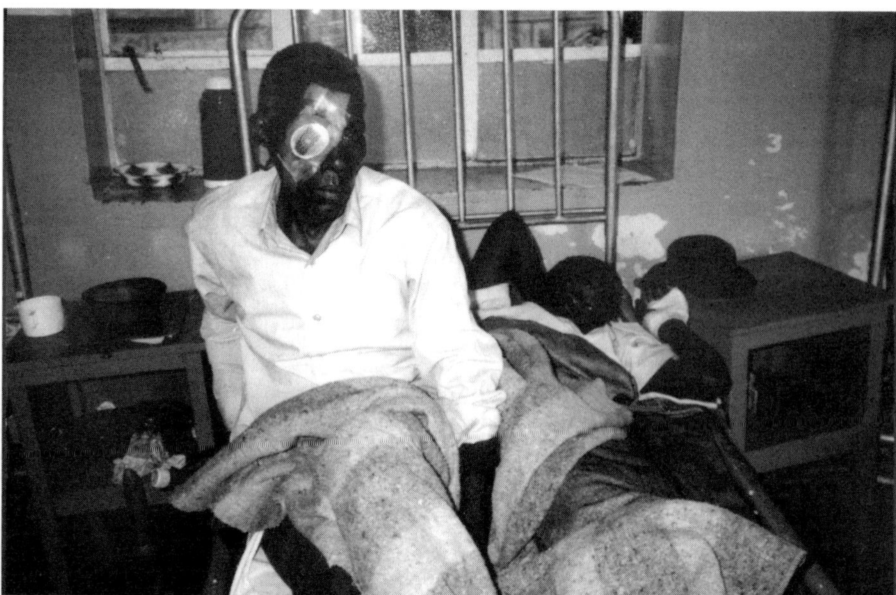

Figure 6.20. Two patients – one bed. Maua, Kenya.

We continue to pray for Maua United Methodist Hospital with its dedicated staff as they bring health and healing in the name of Jesus Christ.

On October 24, 1996, our KLM flight lifted off. I wondered if I ever would see Kenya again.

On to Maua Again, 1997

As the KLM plane lifted off from the Nairobi, Kenya, runway Monday, April 14, 1997, I thought back over the last two weeks when I had landed Easter Monday. It was nice to have been met at the airport by a van and two drivers from the Maua United Methodist Hospital, and to have 210 lbs. of medicines and supplies taken off my hands for direct transport to the hospital. Bishop Charles Makande also was there to discuss the fate of a container of ophthalmology and dental equipment and supplies that had been diverted to Nairobi from the besieged town of Bukavu in Zaire. Even though the deputy commissioner of customs would have allowed the removal of some items to be used in Kenya and then resealed, the finding of the appropriate crate, its opening and search for the right items, and the final repacking and closing of the crate and container loomed as too large a project even though fork lifts were available. Hopefully the war in Zaire would soon be over and the intact container directed on its way to Bukavu, Zaire.

Before dark on Tuesday, the Maua van and I arrived at the hospital. The next morning I faced a crowd of patients. Before noon four blind people had been selected and that afternoon their cataracts were extracted and IOLs placed. Four or five patients were done each succeeding day.

I never get over sharing the joy that blind people experience when their bandages are removed postoperatively. It is hard to realize that there are people sitting in darkness just waiting for someone in Christian compassion to help them into the light and a new life. Docile, unproductive people suddenly come alive and are independent and productive again. A 2 1/2 year old child with congenital cataracts was able to have an intraocular lens implantation. She found everything so interesting when sight was realized in the following days.

Two weeks of volunteer eye surgery may not seem a major event, but to the thirty people who regained sight it was very significant. I am constantly amazed that such ventures into areas where there is no help are still so appealing to me. I should be in a robe and slippers in front of a fire rather than junketing around the world. For the time being, however, the slippers will have to wait.

Never is your country and your home so meaningful or so dear as when you have been away for a time. After a transfer of planes in Amsterdam, the arrival in Minneapolis was followed by an uneventful bus trip up to Alexandria, where I was met by my dear wife, Ruth.

A word of commendation is due to the staff and missionaries in Maua United Methodist Hospital. Sylvester (Intinyai) Kaberia did all the sterilizing and assisting in surgery. He learned my routine so that instruments were deftly "there" at the appropriate time. Joyce Kimaru single handedly directed patient flow with work-ups and treatments and on occasion filled in as a circulating nurse. Drs. Lynn and Sharon Fogleman included me at their supper table along with their three children. After ten years at Maua, they are returning to practices at the Red Bird Mission in Kentucky.

Arrangements have been made for a visiting clinical officer from Meru to regularly visit Maua and perform eye surgery. Christoffel Blindenmission has been the driving force in seeing that eye care is available for this remote place in northeast Kenya which borders Somalia and Ethiopia.

Ophthalmologists who are willing to go to far off places, perform eye surgery, and want to see animals in the wild, might well consider a tour that includes Maua United Methodist Hospital, Maua, Kenya.

On to Bolivia, 1997

Doing eye surgery at 8000 feet above sea level at Cochabamba and Anzaldo, Bolivia, South America was a new experience as compared with the sea level at Kissy UMC Eye Hospital in Freetown, Sierra Leone, West Africa, where Ruth and I usually go two or three times a year. Our September trip to Sierra Leone had to be canceled because of the political instability that persisted following the May 25, 1997, military coup. Now in September of 1997, since medicines and supplies were already in place, it seemed appropriate to respond to the invitation of the Volunteer in Mission team from the Oklahoma Conference under the leadership of Larry Acton. He outlined the Christian purpose of the mission and took care of the many details without a hitch. He briefed the twenty-nine members who had flown into Miami from five different states just prior to take off for Cochabamba, Bolivia.

Ten minutes into the air the pilot announced: "We have some technical difficulties. We are returning to Miami." It was midnight. By 7 a.m. after a night of "rest" on the floor of the airport, a new plane was available which successfully carried us to Santa Cruz and then to Cochabamba, Bolivia, arriving at our hotel in time to go to bed – this time in nice surroundings and comfortable beds.

The next day, Sunday, the team was divided into four groups that visited four different churches. The group I was in ascended a mountain side and had a wonderful spiritual experience with a United Methodist congregation.

In the afternoon, unpacking and sorting was done for the start of the work week on Monday. On the trip to Anzaldo Hospital the eye team had an unforgettable experience. The road was narrow and steep without guard rails. Hairpin curves needed to be maneuvered and the inclines were steep. On occasion the side of the road dropped off for hundreds of feet. Some years ago a missionary couple had slipped off to their deaths from such a road.

The van in which we were riding seemed to be a rather recent model. Our driver was slow and careful. On completing a climb up a long incline, we leveled off for nearly 100 yards. A basketball size bolder lay in the middle of the road. Attempting to turn to the side of it, the driver realized that the steering wheel was completely disengaged and that he had no control. Frantic braking bought us to a stop. Without any comments we each climbed out and stepped over to the side of the road to peer down into the valley. Suddenly two words spoke for all ten of the passengers when someone said, "Thank God!"

With the help of local drivers with four-wheel drive vehicles, we were taken to Anzaldo Hospital. Our first sight of it was from an elevated point. It resembled Shangri-La with its beautifully tiled roofs on the twin-spired church and the cluster of hospital annexes. The hospital was entirely modern with excellent equipment. The floors were of white tile.

Figure 6.21. Oklahoma Conference Mission team to Bolivia.

One of the three surgeries was given over to the eye team and surgeries were begun. In spite of the delay on the road and late arrival, four surgeries were completed the first day.

Each day we faced fifty to seventy patients wanting help. We did as many as we could which was twenty-one, giving preference to the totally blind. The intraocular lens implantation technique was viewed by two residents in ophthalmology who came out from Cochabamba on our final day.

I can't say enough for the skill of the eye team in handling the patients as well as the eye instruments. Oklahoma State Senator Ben Brown fitted hundreds of patients with eye glasses. The line of patients waiting to see him exceeded the line waiting to see the eye surgeon.

The spiritual fellowship with the twenty-nine volunteers was a high point. They ranged from housewives to doctors (four), from construction workers to corporate managers, from a McDonald's owner to ordained pastors ranging in age from the mid-twenties to the sixties.

As Larry Acton expressed it: "Our purpose, our role as God's special servant – was to share Christ's love in ways that made a Christian difference." We endeavored to do this through the roof construction of Emmanuel United Methodist Church as well as the general medical clinics and the eye surgery program.

On to Chicuque UMC Rural Hospital, Mozambique, 1998

Our oldest son Tim and I flew out of the Minneapolis-St. Paul Lindbergh International Airport January 6, 1998, on board a KLM non-stop flight to Schipohl Airport, Amsterdam. We continued on to Johannesburg, South Africa, where we stayed at the transit hotel in the airport. The next morning we took the one hour flight to Maputo, Mozambique. Much of the following description is taken from Tim's impressions of his first return to Africa after nearly twenty years which he termed a "great adventure."

Walking on the tarmac at Maputo convinced us that we were in tropical Africa. While waiting to receive our luggage and initiate the difficult customs procedures, we were drenched with perspiration. New custom and immigration laws were in place overseen by a British firm called Crown Agency. It was intended to generate more income to meet the foreign debt Mozambique had incurred during its fifteen years of civil war. We had not obtained an official evaluation for our six boxes of medicines and supplies prior to our arrival making us subject to a 33.3 percent tax. Officials refused to release our luggage without full payment even with the intervention of Bishop Joao Somane Machado.

El Nino had struck. The streets of Maputo, Mozambique, were awash. Water stood everywhere. Cholera had reared its ugly head. Tim and I wondered what was ahead. Under the circumstances Tim and I checked air line schedules and the cost to take us back to Johannesburg for a possible flight to Nairobi, Kenya, to serve at the Maua United Methodist Hospital. We were preparing to call Dr. Mwenda at Maua. When it became known that we were making plans to leave Mozambique, the Bishop in desperation contacted the Government Department of Health to inform them of what was happening. Within two hours a directive in writing was delivered to the custom officials, and we walked out of customs without a single box being opened.

We then proceeded to the United Methodist guest house next to the United Methodist church with a membership of three thousand. The pastor, young and energetic, gave us a warm welcome. We enjoyed a good meal and headed for our beds. We hardly had gotten to sleep when it happened. A disco next door started blaring and did not let up until five o'clock in the morning. With only a couple of hours sleep we got

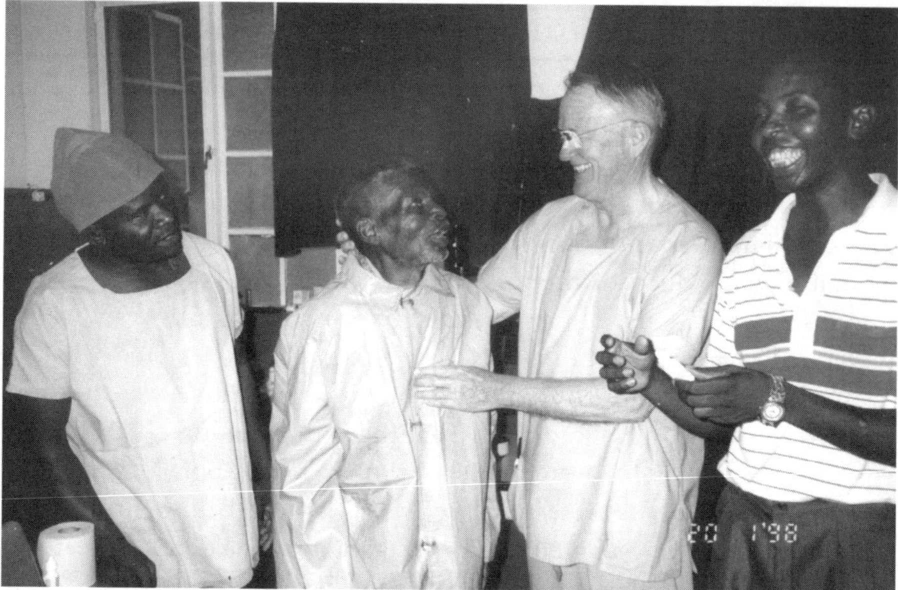

Figure 6.22. Surprised that his surgeon was a white man. Chicuque, Mozambique.

up at four a.m. Our six boxes were rushed to the bus depot from the church office to get ahead of the lineup for the trip to Chicuque. We were also helped by Dr. Emmanuel Mefore, a doctor at the Chicuque Rural Hospital to which we were going. He was from Nigeria and had just renewed his contract to serve another two years, during which his family would join him.

The six and a half hour trip with the Bluebird Express was quite comfortable, although accompanied by loud music the entire distance. The trip showed the evidence of the war with half standing cement walls of buildings. Mozambique still has the problem of buried land mines which cause injury and death. Moments of panic were experienced at one time when a sharp swerve upset some passengers as the bus avoided a slow moving tractor around a blind curve. Assured of the prayers of our loved ones we arrived safely in Maxixe. Dr. Beatriz Birchal, a thirty year old doctor from Brazil, escorted us the final three miles to Chicuque Rural Hospital. After a delicious meal at her house, she helped unpack the boxes in the eye clinic. Our housing accommodations were comfortable with an imposing view of the Indian Ocean with its beautiful beaches. Mr. Andreas Brose, effective Chicuque hospital administrator, arranged for the logistic management of our time of volunteer service.

Figure 6.23. Patients gathered at 5 a.m. We could not operate on all. Mozambique.

At the United Methodist church service the next morning, we were introduced to the congregation and participated in a three hour worship service that concluded with a farewell to the present pastor.

We had the privilege of meeting people like Nick and Gigi Vic. He is a retired urologist from the USA who was practicing several months at the Chicuque Hospital. Appointed by the General Board of Global Ministries, Bryan and Ann Stone were just completing a tour of general surgery. Yohan Zimmerman and his wife Sue Claussen from Combine brought their son, Jonas, for an eye check up for his accommodative esotropia. Yohan is a civil engineer reconstructing the hydroelectric dam that will provide continuous electric power for the mission. We had the opportunity of visiting Combine thirty miles distant from Chicuque. The dam had been destroyed during the war. Sue handles the hospital and clinic. The only other trip we took was to Inhambane with its Portuguese-style buildings. At the nearby Tofu beach Tim and Beatriz turned in dramatic swimming feats against huge waves.

For some reason sleep was denied us the first three nights. Consequently we got up at 3 or 4 a.m. and were at the clinic before 6 a.m. where we were always met by patients waiting for us. We began surgery on Monday and during out stay did thirty-six eye procedures –

mostly cataract extractions with intraocular lens implantaions. Pterygia and trabeculectomy procedures were also done.

Early on there were moments of apprehension with regard to instrument preparation and the maintenance of sterility. The assistants needed to get used to our manner of procedure in surgery. We found the keratometer without a bulb and placed a trans-Atlantic call to Allen Anderberg of Walmans for a replacement. However, we then found the bulb. It was being tried unsuccessfully in the lensometer. Happily it worked when properly placed in the keratometer. Fortunately we had also brought a proper bulb for the lensometer; so everything was shipshape and working.

The bad news was to follow the good news that the container was cleared the day of our arrival. It contained the Zeiss OPMI-6 operating microscope donated by Precision Lens and the Cilco DBR 310 A-scan ultrasound. Custom officials opened every box for examination, but they were not careful in closing them again. The probe to the A-scan was missing making the ultrasound nonfunctional. We were happy to have a small biopen ultrasound to determine IOL powers. The foot switch to the operating microscope was missing, but by using a manual Zeiss OPMI-1 to the stand, we were able to proceed. Improvisation was a constant challenge. Adriano, the ophthalmic assistant, was a great help in the clinic and surgical theater.

We thank God that always a way was found to provide quality surgery for the many blind. We felt badly that we could not do surgery for all who wanted operations. At least fifty were turned away – several of them with hardly any sight –they had come too late. One lady came to the clinic nearly every day. She had had a cataract operation with an IOL during my visit in 1995 and now wanted her second eye done. It was heart rending to put her off so that another with no sight might be done.

Perhaps the most dramatic moment came when Tim was successfully able to implant the first foldable introcular lens in this part of the world. The patient was a pretty sixteen year old young lady who will be grateful all her life for the visit of the Gesses.

We were well received by patients and staff. Albert was an excellent Portuguese and local language interpreter. Bishop Joao Somane Machado and United Methodist Conference personnel took care of all arrangements. Adolf, especially, was kind in transporting us from place to place and managing the heavy boxes. We could not have had a more gracious hostess than Dr. Beatriz Birchal. The meals were fit for kings.

Before leaving Mozambique a courtesy call was paid to Dr. Yolanda at the Maputo Eye Clinic. She is a gracious Portuguese lady who does a tremendous work in ophthalmology. We had the opportunity of leaving some posterior chamber intraocular lenses and viscoelastics with her.

We counted it a privilege to serve needy blind people in the name of Jesus Christ. Our prayer for them is also new insight into God's love. We will not soon forget Chicuque, Mozambique.

Figure 6.24. Carolina Health Foundation facilities. Honduras (Limon).

On to Honduras, 1998

Following correspondence with Dr. Henry W. Gibson and physician's assistant, Mrs. Vickie Glover, it was with great anticipation that plans were made to do volunteer eye surgery at Limon, Honduras. The Carolina-Honduras Health Foundation has underwritten an extensive health care program. Even in the fall of 2000 further improvements were still being made to enhance the facilities of the clinic as well as providing

Figure 6.25. Our chauffuer keeps our transportation running in Honduras.

two additional bedrooms and a bath for the volunteers. A satellite clinic is also in the making.

On April 2, 1998, members of the volunteer team traveling to Limon met in the Miami Airport for the flight to Honduras. Ruth and I had packed four large boxes, each weighing seventy pounds, which contained medicines and supplies, along with sophisticated instruments such as a Haag Streit slit lamp, Zeiss OPMI-1 operating microscope, keratometer, A-scan, and representative intraocular lenses.

The trip was a great success for the dental team. Debbie Johnson and Kaye Walker also were effective in miming the crucifixion in a dramatic and convincing way. Mrs. Vickie Glover had the help of her two big and strong sons, Slayton and Rhett, in the general clinic. Eye patients were seen but only several surgical procedures were done. A post trabeculectomy glaucoma patient treated at a previous eye camp told people that his surgery had not helped him. If anything, he let other people know that he perhaps saw less well since his surgery. We tried to explain that the successful lowering of his intraocular pressure by the surgery was to help protect him from deteriorating sight in the future. Nonetheless, the rumor grew that anyone submitting to surgery would be irrevocably blinded. Our deeply spiritual team counselor, Mrs.

Eleanore Cooper, ultimately advised us to understand and accept the situation.

It was with heavy hearts that we left Limon for our return to the USA. As Jesus said, *"How often I have longed to gather your children together – but you are not willing"* Matthew 23:37 NIV.

On to Lilongwe, Malawi, 1998 ❧ "An International Effort"

It was delightful to be welcomed to Lilongwe, Malawi, by Dr. Moses C. Chirambo, senior ophthalmologist par excellence. This South African country of eleven million was where Dr. David Livingstone had worked and explored for decades prior to his death in 1873. He had been feared dead but was found in 1871 by Henry Stanley of "Dr. Livingstone, I presume?" fame.

For Dr. Richard Yukins, his trip to Malawi started in Boston, Massachusetts, while I started from Minneapolis, Minnesota. From Amsterdam, Holland, it was an $8^1/_2$ hour overnight flight to Nairobi, Kenya, and then another $2^1/_2$ hours to Lilongwe. We had some concerns about going through customs with the huge supplies of medicines and equipment provided by S.E.E. International. However, in the baggage carousel area we were met by Dr. Chirambo. Taking our manifest papers he made a brief stop at the desk of the senior customs officer and with smiles all around, we were escorted out of the airport into waiting transportation without a single box being opened.

The hospital facilities were provided by Sight Savers and Lions International and the capitol city of Lilongwe. The equipment was state of the art. The wards were clean and orderly in spite of the great mass of patients. The surgical theater accommodated four operating tables with an operating microscope at each table. The surgical assisting was of the highest caliber consisting of doctors in training and nurses. The cordon of nurses involved in sterilizing the instruments kept the surgeons supplied with sterile instruments without a hitch and without the destruction or loss of a single instrument – the first time this had been achieved in my experience in overseas accommodations.

Especially appreciated were the viscoelastics and high quality IOLs provided by Surgical Eye Expeditions. The S.E.E. packet gave clear

Figure 6.26. Lilongwe, Malawi, 1998 – 102 eye operations.

instructions how to maximize this brief but intensive eye camp. Everyone wanted a S.E.E. certificate and badge.

The impact of this surgical eye camp was great in that it brought in patients from rural areas where eye care is not available. Already Dr. Chirambo was planning for another S.E.E. sponsored camp in Lilongwe for July, 1999.

Dr. Yukins capably handled the large surgical load presented to him. He became a familiar figure at the Wild operating microscope made available to the program by Sight Savers. A total of 102 cataract extractions were done. More than twenty were bilaterally blind. A patient's second eye was to be operated on by the staff doctors from the Lions Sight First Eye Hospital which is part of the Lilongwe Central Hospital the week after the initial eye camp ended. Patients are kept as inpatients for a minimum of five days as some come from distances as far away as 100 to 300 kilometers.

The ophthalmologists participating in the Lilongwe eye camp besides Dr. Yukins and myself were Dr. Moses C. Chirambo, Malawi; Dr. Nkume Baatumba, Congo (then practicing at Blantyre, Malawi); Dr. Joseph Msosa, Malawi (then finishing his residency in Nairobi, Kenya); Dr. D. J. Kwendakwema, Zambia; and Dr. Peter Mihale, Tanzania (in a support role).

Figure 6.27. The crowded wards, Lilongwe, Malawi.

Dr. Kwendakwema declared that the first thing he would do on his return to Zambia would be to write to Dr. Harry and Baillie Brown seeking a S.E.E. International eye camp in Zambia in 1999. He was impressed with the results of so many blind people seeing again because of the support of S.E.E. to make it happen with the availability of medicines and supplies.

The S.E.E.-supported Lilongwe eye camp achieved what had been hoped for by the Honorable Minister of Health and Populations who officially opened the eye camp September 7. The blind were made to see in this cooperative effort of the African countries of Malawi, Congo, Zambia, and Tanzania and as well as representatives from the U.S.A.

Return to Zing, Nigeria, 1999

I landed at the Kano, Nigeria, airport March 21, 1999, the day that General Olusegun Obasanjo was declared president-elect. Following years of strident military rule, the people were celebrating a democratically elected leadership.

The following morning I was in the air-conditioned surgery at the ECWA Eye Hospital. Dr. Gizella Baghy was the surgeon of the day per-

Figure 6.28. Zing. Most of the 82 postop patients slept under the trees.

forming intraocular lens implantations following cataract extractions and trabeculectomy cases. At another table a Diplomat of Ophthalmology was doing lid procedures and intracapsular cataract extractions (ICCE). It was a long day without a noon break.

The next day Dr. Abuh Sunday Omogahi expertly did the IOL cases. He is presently in his first year of ophthalmic residency at Kaduna but has been doing introcular surgery for more than ten years.

At noon I was picked up by Marcus, the Zing ophthalmic nurse, and Francis, the driver of the program's Hilux four-wheel drive. By evening we were in Jos for an overnight stay with Missionary Aviation Fellowship missionaries, Jim and Bernice Keech, who along with sixteen year old Michael and thirteen year old Sarah, gave us a hearty welcome which included a refreshing meal. I learned that they are presently the senior UMC missionaries in Nigeria, having come in 1989. Their first six years were at Bambur. They were continuing with their flying ministry as well as the supervision of the guest house facilities in Jos. Around the table after the meal Jim Keech expressed appreciation for the United Methodist Church. He felt it had a great program and base. To increase its strengths from the inside, he has given some thought to achieving a

Figure 6.29. Reunion with Bambur staff after 47 years.

seminary background.

Tomorrow I would arrive in Zing. Weeks of preparation were spent determining what medicines and supplies would be needed. I was determined to be of as much help as possible in the eye program. I was happy that I had equipment that could provide for the best care for the patients.

With this anticipation, I spent a near sleepless night during which a resume of my life's convictions were recorded and which are included in the *Appendix*. In the morning preparations were made for the last leg of the journey to Zing. The eight hour trip was hot and sometimes frightening (a herdsman stepped back from the path of our vehicle at the last moment), but we reached Zing safely before dark.

The size of the crowd of blind patients we faced the next day was overwhelming. Dr. Iorav James of Mkar Hospital, which was more than a hundred miles away, responded to the call for help. Several years earlier he had come to the Kissy UMC Eye Hospital in Freetown, Sierra Leone, for training. We each did forty cases; his were intracapsular cataract extractions (ICCE), and mine were extracapsular cataract extractions (ECCE) with intraocular lens implantations.

Two additional cases were done before Dr. James left, in which he

Figure 6.30. My hunting guide of 47 years ago.

participated in the intraocular lens implantation. The second one he did from start to finish with an expression of relief and joy. Postoperatively they looked so good that I would liked to have claimed them as my own.

The Zing UMC Eye Clinic is staffed by Ina Schoenfeld, a nurse from Germany, Edward Bawuro, Marcus Kank'n, and Alice Ibrahim . Shortly after my visit to Zing, Ms. Schoenfeld was united in marriage with Mr. Dearsely Dabale, son of Bishop and Mrs. Doan Peter Dabale. Her expert handling of the eye program prompted Christoffel Blindenmission to continue their support. An additional eye ministry is being extended to Bali.

This small staff prepared the drapes and instruments, did the preop preparations, and assisted in the surgery. Thanks to Carl Zeiss' world wide concern for the best of eye care, an OPMI-SH was available. The medicines, supplies, and IOLs were donated by Alcon, Allergan, and other surgical and pharmaceutical houses.

Surgery was begun early in the morning to try to beat the extreme heat which built up each day by 11 am. However, on several occasions, surgery was still being done into the evening hours. Facilities were not available to house these eighty-two people and their relatives. Some slept on mats underneath trees while others were in a carport. Only one patient had the luxury of a bed.

In spite of the austere environment, the results were stunning. The joy of newly restored sight nearly matched that of an evangelical camp meeting.

At Zing I had the opportunity to provide intraocular lenses following cataract extractions for two pastors and one pastor's wife from Bambur, where we served in the Guinter Memorial Hospital from 1952 until 1955. Most surprising of all was being able to restore the vision of my hunting companion and guide of forty-seven years ago. On the operating table he reminded me that he was the one who helped me capture a more than two-ton hippopotamus. I told him I still have the skull. Again he reminded me that he had prepared the skull by burying it and letting ants and termites remove the tags of meat from the bones.

After the two week stay, the journey back to Kano was begun by way of Bambur. It was thrilling to meet former staff members of the Guinter Memorial UMC Hospital. Some were still engaged in medical work, while others had become teachers, pastors, and one, whom we knew as Baba, was now chief of the Kulung people in that part of Taraba state. Our reliable and respected cook, Mai Doki, was also there to greet me.

Up at 3:30 a.m. on our final lap to Kano, I had breakfast with Wolfgang and Gerlinde Bay, principal and nurse at Banyam Theological Seminary. It was then twelve hard and hot hours of pounding the road to Kano where Ishvan Patkai and his wife, Dr. Gizella Baghy, made us comfortable for the night. On Friday and Saturday more eye surgery was done at ECWA Eye Hospital which included the remarkably expert participation of Dr. S. Kirupananthan, the ECWA Eye Hospital Chief Surgeon and director, who with his wife have been in ministry in Kano for over a decade. Since responding to the call of Jesus Christ to world service, they have only rarely returned to Sri Lanka, the place of their birth.

On Monday, March 22, at 12:55 a.m. I was on board a KLM flight from Kano to Amsterdam and then Northwest to Minneapolis and ultimately to Alexandria, Minnesota, all in one day's span.

It was wonderful to get home to Ruth's cooking. I had lost fourteen lbs. in weight but never had experienced more satisfaction knowing that eighty-two people were seeing again, more than half of them having been totally blind before this volunteer eye surgery expedition.

Many people, including missionaries, had a hand in this outreach, not the least of whom were representatives of pharmaceutical and optical houses. My thanks to all of them in making this exhilarating experience possible.

An Injury at Maua, Kenya, 1999

Never before had I experienced such convenient travel arrangements. I left Alexandria, Minnesota for Minneapolis on a Twin City passenger shuttle at 7 a.m. on Saturday, April 24, 1999. Five seventy pound boxes of medicines and supplies were graciously transported free of charge. Mr. Fred Bursch has assisted in this way for nearly twenty years, literally carrying what amounts to tons of sight-giving medicines and supplies. On one occasion when there were nineteen boxes, he arranged for a separate driver and bus to manage the load.

I boarded a Northwest plane shortly after noon for an eight-hour trip to Amsterdam. After a layover of several hours, a KLM plane transported me the rest of the way to Nairobi, Kenya.

After identifying myself as a volunteer eye surgeon in transit to Maua United Methodist Hospital, none of my five pieces of luggage was opened or examined. Representatives from the hospital escorted me to the Methodist Guest House for a sound sleep.

The following morning, I was picked up by Mr. Ikotha, the hospital administrator and his driver. Several stops were made for additional hospital supplies before setting out on the 300km drive to Maua Methodist Hospital. A stop was made at the Kikuyu Eye Hospital for flourescein strips, which I had forgotten to pack; Goldmann tonometry would be a must for postoperative patients.

It is always a thrill to cross the equator from one hemisphere to the other. On this trip, we did not have to wait for five bull elephants to cross the road, as I had experienced several years back on a previous visit. Not even giraffes showed up as on two of my previous trips, but we did have to veer away from cows, sheep, goats, chickens, ducks and two pigs.

I stayed at the Maua Basin Hotel. My room had a shower and a mosquito net. The hospital driver picked me up on call each morning and returned me each evening.

Mr. Silvester, the optical nurse, had everything ready for surgery. Pre-packed and pre-sterilized surgical packs, which were prepared by the

Surgical Eye Expeditions (S.E.E.) International staff in Santa Barbara, made the surgical procedures convenient. Sutures, viscoelastics and IOLs made for successful surgery. Mrs. Joyce Kima oversaw the screening of patients and took care of the many common eye problems. She had just had a baby girl and was happy to be back at work. Mrs. Grace was our excellent circulator, and was expecting her first baby.

During my first week, some dramatic surgeries had taken place involving children. A nine year old girl and a ten year old boy were delighted with their newfound sight following IOL implantations. A sixteen year old girl was able to see faces clearly for the first time. She was looking forward to finally being able to attend school. I also was moved by the intensity in which a three year old viewed a doll after IOL implantation.

The mother-in-law of the hospital administrator had been led about for several years because of her mature cataracts. Previously, she had been too fearful to have surgery. This time she decided to go through with it. She was so pleased with the result that she immediately wanted the second eye done. It was scheduled for the coming Monday.

However, because of an injury to my leg in the operating theatre, of all places, I was unable to move about to work-up patients, let alone do their surgery.

Figure 6.31. Mother-in-Law of Maua Methodist Hopital administrator.

After being confined for two days and realizing that it would be extended for several more, the medical superintendent, at my request, arranged for my return trip to the airport. It was nearly Sunday noon. Packing took only a few minutes. Dr. Claire Smithson, acting medical superintendent, and Nurse Barbara planned to personally accompany me to the airplane. Hurriedly we set off down the road as the plane was scheduled to leave by 8 p.m. It was then that I realized that my passport and ticket were safely residing in the hospital safe. We retraced our five or six miles back to the hospital. The staff member with the keys to the safe lived several miles from the hospital. The road was so bumpy that we needed to crawl at times. Arriving at his home, we were greeted by his wife. He was away on a visit to a friend several more miles away. She could not locate the keys in the house. Our dash to the friend's house was another "crawl." After picking him up, it was back to the hospital, securing the visa and ticket, and then setting out again, speeding down the road. The estimated travel time would give us a leeway of about thirty minutes. In spite of a severe rain storm, the expert driving of Dr. Smithson enabled us to arrive just before the plane was to take off. In the frantic scramble (while I was able to move at only a snail's pace), my coat was left in the back of the van. I would not miss the coat but in the pocket was a favorite pair of gloves that had in the past accompanied me to a number of countries in the world.

The ticket counters were empty, save for one at the far end being manned by the person in charge. He informed us that the plane was fully booked and then disappeared. Stunned, we did not move. Moments later he reappeared saying, "I'll get you on." After a quick wave to my Maua friends, he escorted me right to the seat I was to occupy.

My leg did not swell any further. In fact, by keeping it bandaged and quiet during the two eight-hour return flights, the swelling was subsiding by the time I arrived home. This was a welcome surprise, as some people actually develop leg edema on long flights. It took another five days until I could walk without experiencing discomfort. I was sad to have missed the last week of surgery. Several weeks later, my gloves arrived in the mail.

On to Ghana, 1999

My trip to Ghana September 6-21, 1999, was a most enjoyable one. Being met at the airport by Mr. George Wood, Regional Director for International Aid and its Christian Eye Ministry branch, as well as by Mr. Badu of Emmanuel Eye Center, made my entry into Accra effortless. They were known and respected by the officials, and so they were receptive of me.

After a night of rest, Mr. Wood and his brother, Kojo, drove me to Cape Coast. Medicines and supplies were made ready for the following day's clinic and surgery. The staff was well organized and surgery was done for fifteen patients in three days.

On Saturday, Mr. Wood drove me to Sunyani. I attended Father Jackson's Anglican Church Sunday morning. It was a dignified service at its beginning. However, a couple had been married in it on Saturday and now on Sunday were receiving communion. The bride was a member of the Anglican Church but the groom was from a charismatic church. Later in the service, his friends contributed to a very lively worship.

Sunday afternoon the operating microscope was put in place and readiness made for the week's clinic work and eye surgery. It was a joy to minister to twenty patients in need. Several were totally blind and needed to be led. Successful surgery brought great joy.

One such patient was a young man in his twenties. Several times he had been skipped over for surgery as there was little hope for a successful outcome. However, with the intervention of Evelyn, who headed the clinic team, it was agreed to put him on at the end of the schedule. If time permitted, we would at least try to help him. There was time – and the next day he walked out of the clinic with no guidance. We all accepted this as the Lord's doing and rejoiced with him.

Only one full day was spent at the Emmanuel Eye Center in Accra where Dr. Herbert Billman purchased property and established a premier eye facility. The staff is exceptional and is serving an international clientele effectively. While I consulted with a few patients in the morning, most of the day was spent in surgery with Dr. James Clark who deftly operated on ten patients, one of them being an important leader from the Central District.

I have been privileged to do volunteer eye surgery in fourteen different countries, but never have I been more impressed with the leadership and efficiency of the personnel than in the Christian Eye Ministry in Ghana. The Lord is using this ministry in a wonderful way – not only for the restoration of physical sight but also for the sharing of spiritual insight into the love of God as revealed in Jesus Christ. I am grateful for being able to be a part of it.

Color Print 3.1. On the Road to Bo. Reduce Your Speed. (see page 196)

Color Print 3.2. On the Road to Bo. You Have Been Warned. (see page 196)

Color Print 3.3. On the Road to Bo. The outcome of those who do not heed signs. (see page 196)

Color Print 3.4. Missionary Retreat at Leicester. (see page 196)

Color Print 3.5. School survey revealed no glasses being worn in this school of 1100 students. (see page 196)

Color Print 3.6. Our four sons visit us in Bo. (see page 196)

Color Print 3.7. Bo, 1975, Missionary Fellowship. (see page 200)

Color Print 3.8. Ms. Doreen Tilghman with Conference Treasurer, Mr. H.R.N. Jusu. (see page 207)

Color Print 3.9. The Five Original Volunteers: Roger Reiners, builder; Arvid Liebe, pharmacist; Loren Ebsen, builder; James Mundwiler, mortician; Floyd Bohn, accountant. (see page 207)

Color Print 3.10. Volunteer builders of Kissy UMC Eye Hospital. (see page 208)

Color Print 3.11. Kissy UMC Eye Hospital under construction. (see page 208)

Color Print 3.12. Staff at Kissy UMC Hospital. (see page 211)

Color Print 3.13. Hannah Koroma, Assistant Administrator, and three daughters. (see page 212)

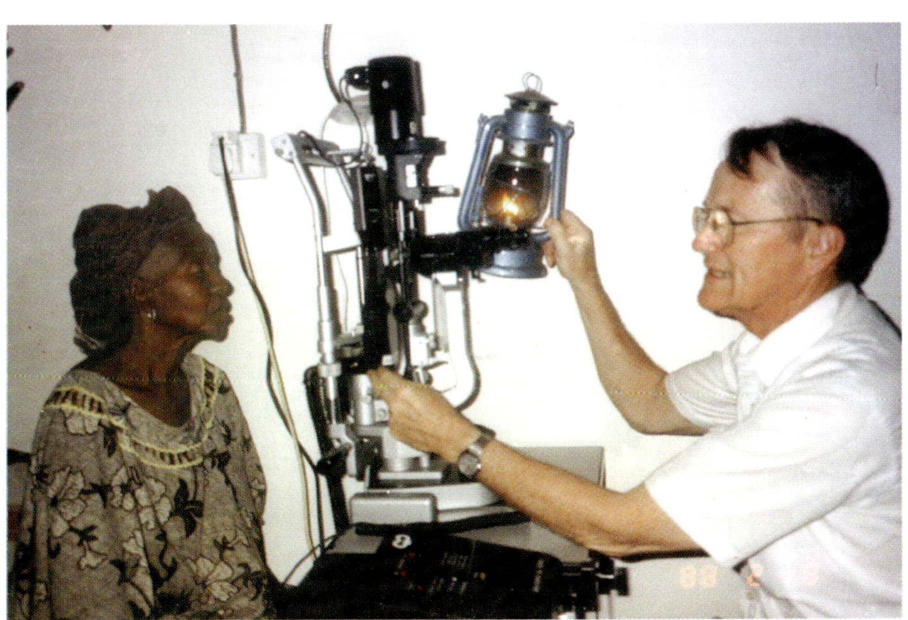

Color Print 3.14. When city electricity fails. Kissy UMC Eye Hospital, Freetown, Sierra Leone, Africa. (see page 213)

Color Print 3.15. In the white suit: Dr. S.N. Fyodorov, internationally known ophthalmologist, in attendance at the International Eye Foundation, Society of Eye Surgeons V World Congress, meeting in Cairo, Egypt, 1984. (see page 313)

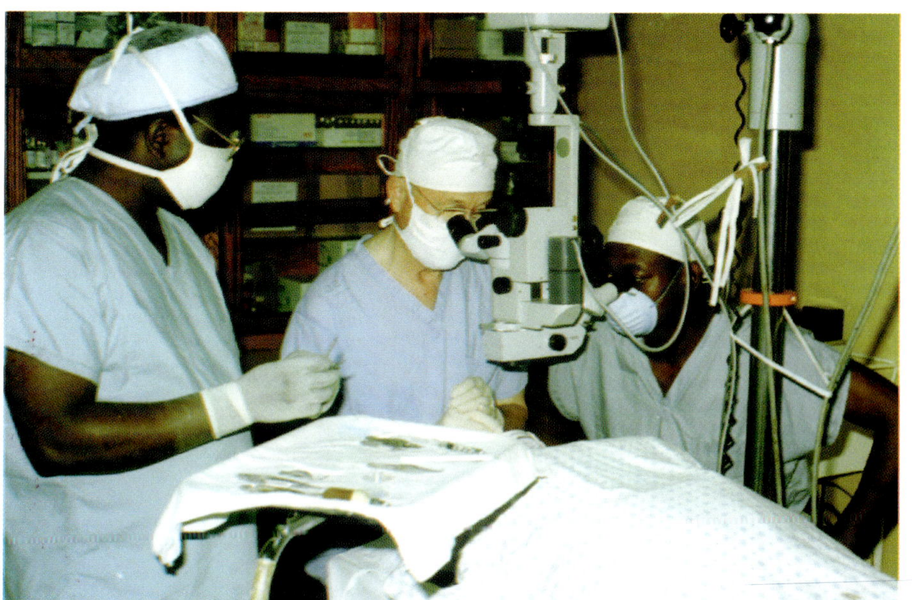

Color Print 3.16. Visiting doctor observes. African physicians learn to do eye surgery at the Kissy UMC Eye Hospital first by observing. (see page 215)

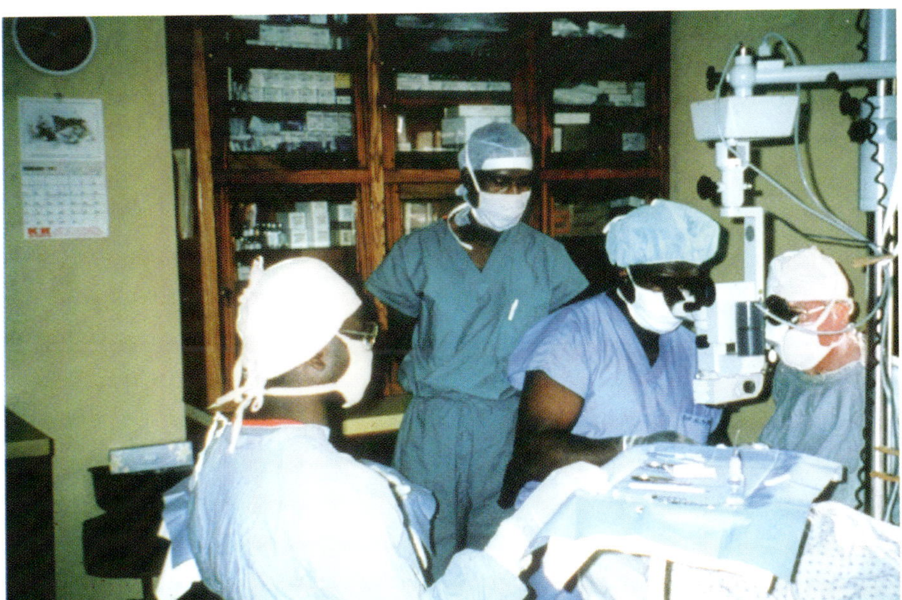

Color Print 3.17. Trainee now doing the surgery. (see page 215)

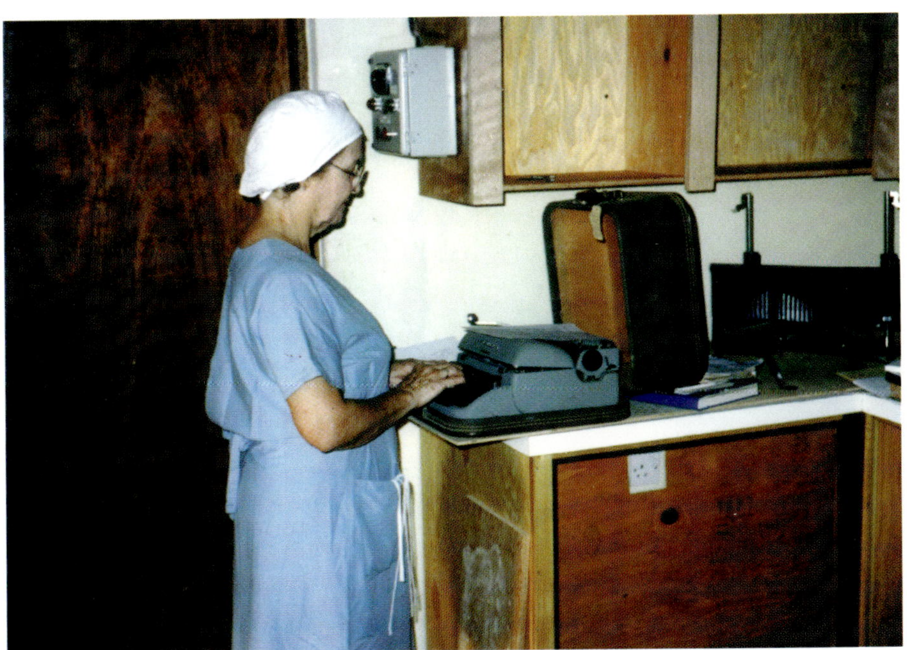

Color Print 3.18. Ruth assisting in surgery and in typing thousands of letters. (see page 217)

Color Print 3.19. Not all of Ruth's time was spent in the Eye Hospital. She taught in many Sunday Schools. (see page 217)

Color Print 3.20. Metra Heisler and others lived through this. (see page 217)

Color Print 3.21. Boughman Memorial United Methodist Church with the senior Pastor, Dr. Frank B. Davies, in the right foreground. Rev. Francis Tommy is standing second from the left. (see page 220)

Color Print 3.22. Watchmaker who had IOL brings his mother for cataract surgery. (see page 254)

Color Print 3.23. Pete Shearer and Dick Reeves repairing water supply to eye hospital. (see page 224)

Color Print 3.24. Dr. Ainor Fergusson and his wife Cassandra return home to Sierra Leone. (see page 228)

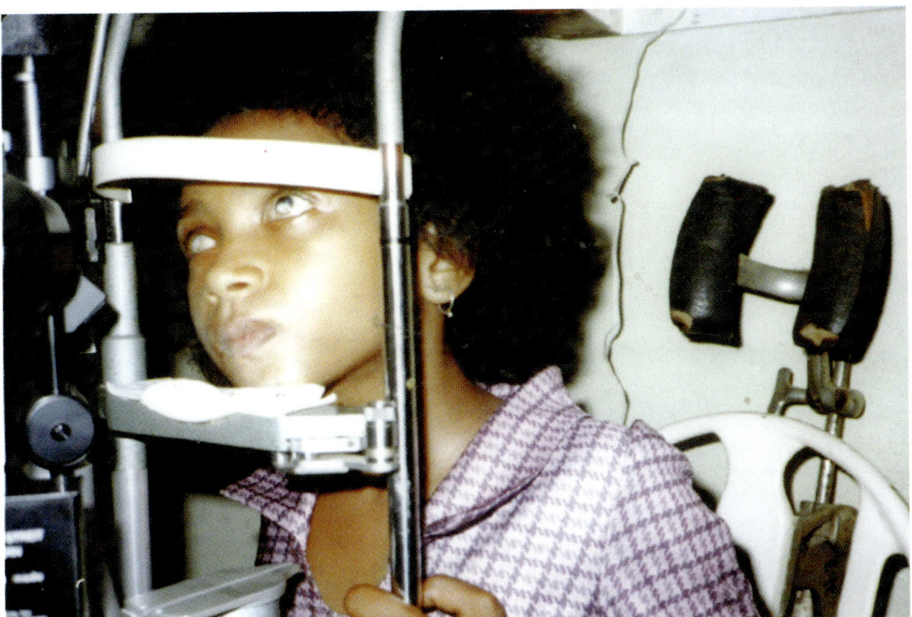

Color Print 3.25. Measles complications. (see page 234)

Color Print 3.26. The Rev. Joseph Christian Humper elected Bishop of the Sierra Leone Conference of the United Methodist Church. (see page 237)

Color Print 3.27. Repeat surgery after 37 years. Fatu after her cataract operation and IOL. (see page 241)

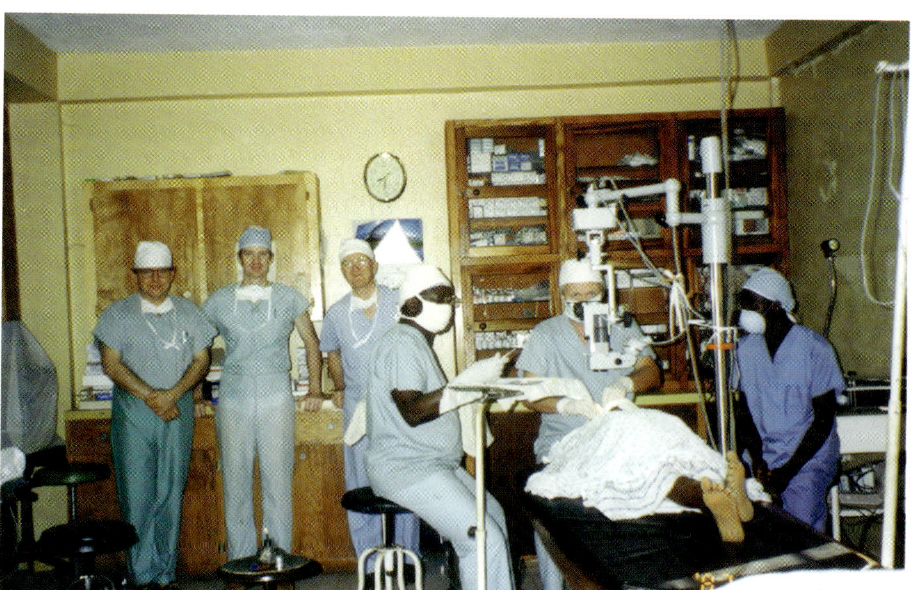

Color Print 3.28. Dr. Donald Doughman, corneal specialist; Dr. Richard Lockwood; Dr. William McElroy (at microscope). (see page 246)

Color Print 3.29. The family of Crispin and Theresa Renner with Dr. and Mrs. Willie Fitzjohn (second and third adults from the right). (see page 247)

Color Print 3.30. Christopher Boehlke with Pastor W.B. Clay at Rotifunk. (see page 248)

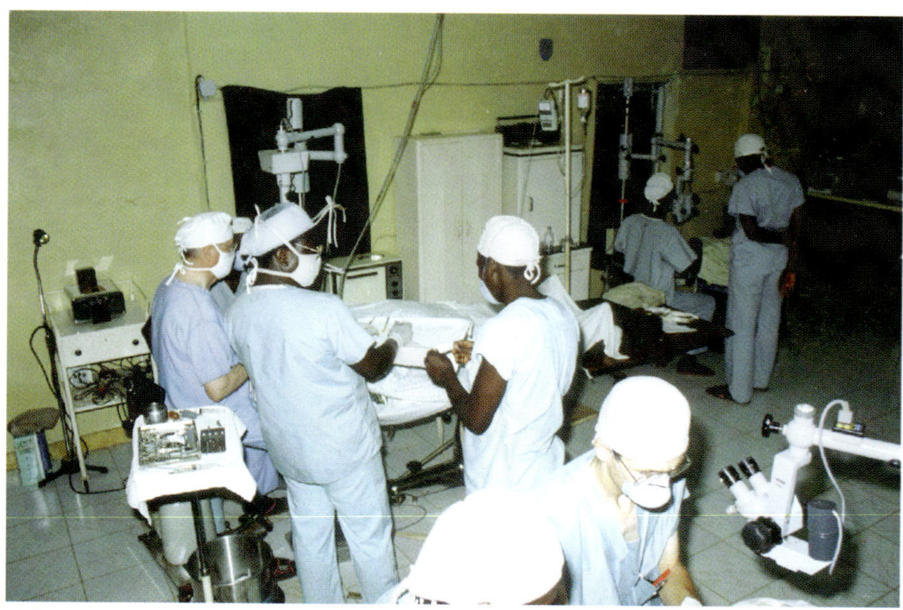

Color Print 3.31. Three Zeiss operating microscopes are utilized at Kissy. (see page 253)

Color Print 3.32. Missionary Retreat at Mission House, Leicester, 1973.

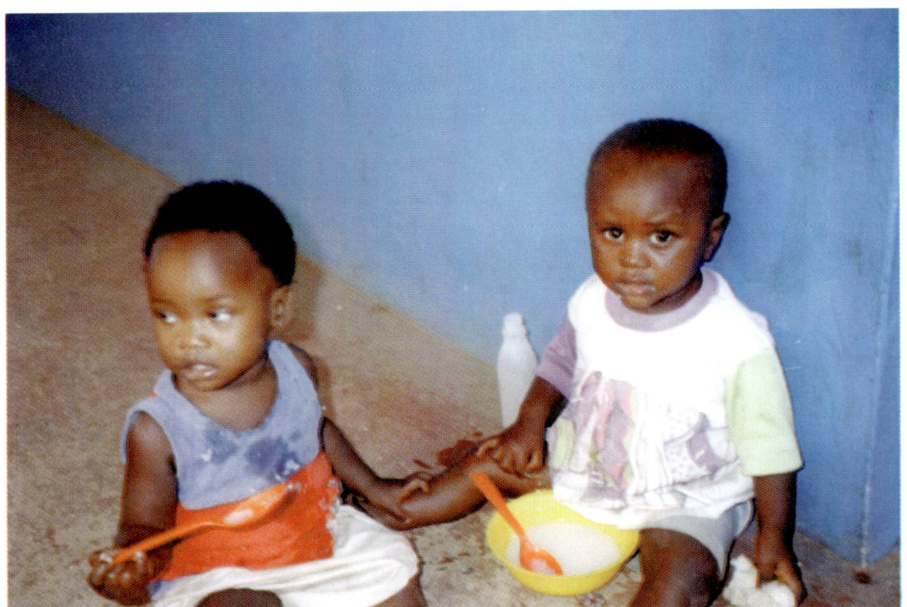

Color Print 4.1. Sharing one bowl of rice, two spoons. (see page 254)

Color Print 4.2. Spared Life. Following a congenital cataract extraction the child aspirated. (see page 261)

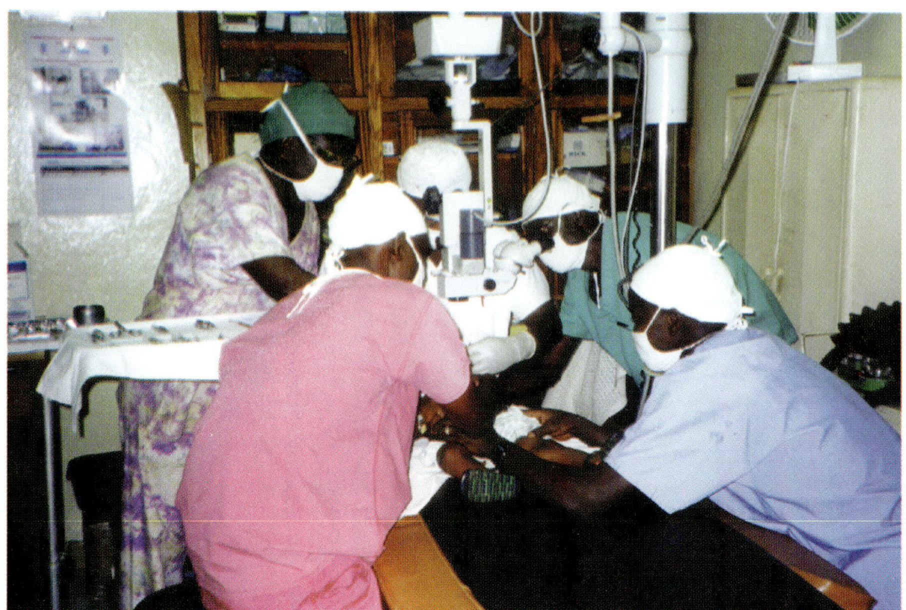

Color Print 4.3. "Half" the staff participated in this congenital cataract extraction of 10 months old child. (see page 262)

Color Print 4.4. Our driver, Paul Tarawally, is flanked by amputees of the Rebel Conflict. (see page 285)

Color Print 4.5. Mr. Kamara being rehabilitated following his tragic amputations, 2001. (see page 286)

Color Print 4.6. Watching the sun set over the ocean to the west where our family members are located. (see page 288)

Color Print 4.7. Children in front row: Becky Hopkins, Christie Hopkins, David Hopkins, Peter Gess, Britta Gess, Aaron Gess, Sarah Gess. Second row: Beth Hopkins, Ruth E. Gess, Adam Gess, Ruth A. Gess, Becky Gess, Elly Gess, Joanne Gess, Debbie Gess, Jennifer Boehlke. Third row: John Gess, Lowell Gess, Tim Gess, Mary Boehlke, Chris Boehlke. Fourth row: John Robert Hopkins, Bob Hopkins, Andrew Gess, Steve Boehlke, Paul Gess. (see page 288)

Color Print 4.8. Missionaries meeting at the Lighthouse for Christ, Mombassa, Kenya. (see page 299)

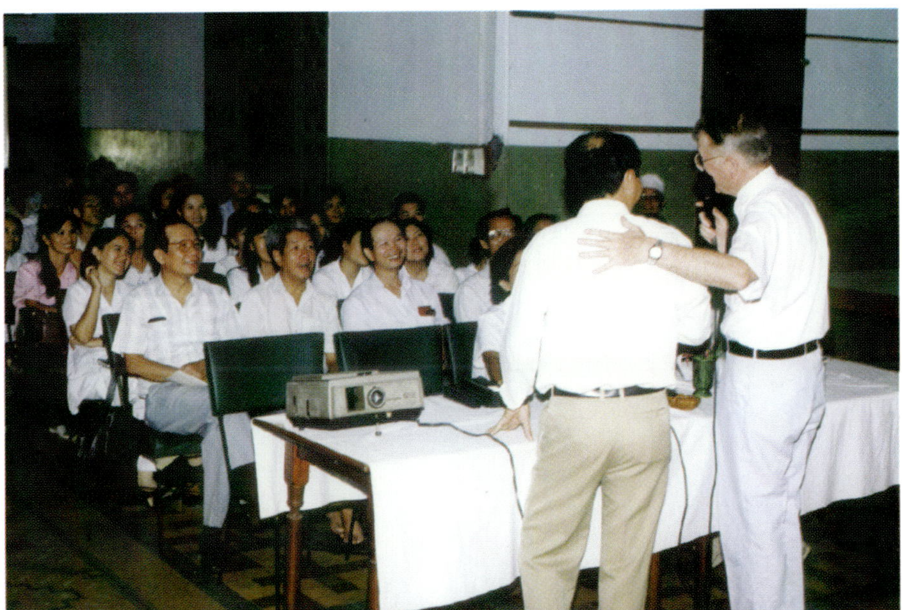

Color Print 4.9. Sharing ophthalmological expertise in Ho Chi Minh City. (see page 304)

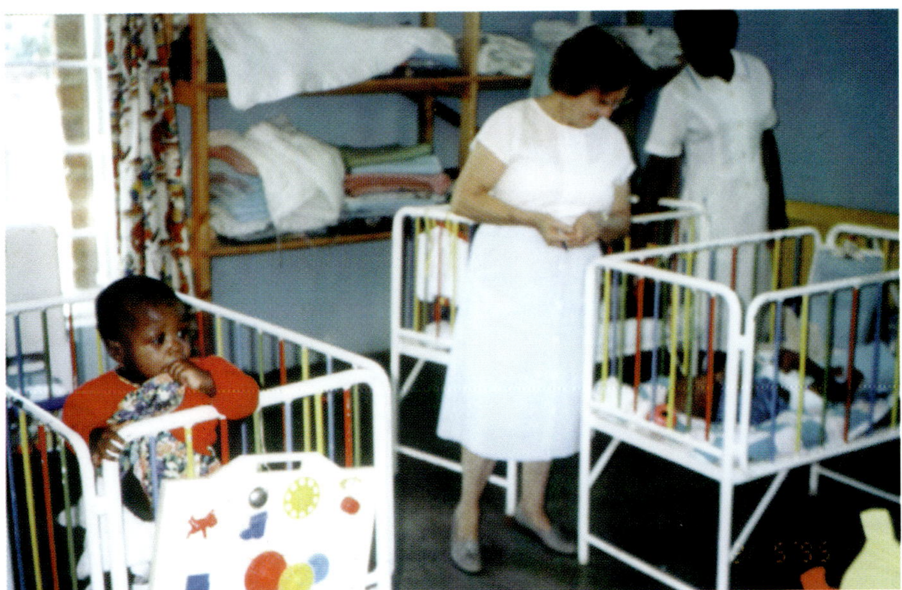

Color Print 4.10. Pediatric care at Old Mutare, Zimbabwe. (see page 308)

Color Print 4.11. Mongolian children visiting the Ulaanbaatar Eye Clinic, Mongolia. (see page 313)

Color Print 4.12. Flanked by six ophthalmologists from Beijing, China, in front of the large eye hospital. (see page 314)

Color Print 4.13. Dr. and Mrs. Tendai Munyeza, Old Mutare Hospital, Zimbabwe. (see page 317)

Color Print 4.14. Mother and child waiting while a relative is being examined at Maua, Kenya. (see page 329)

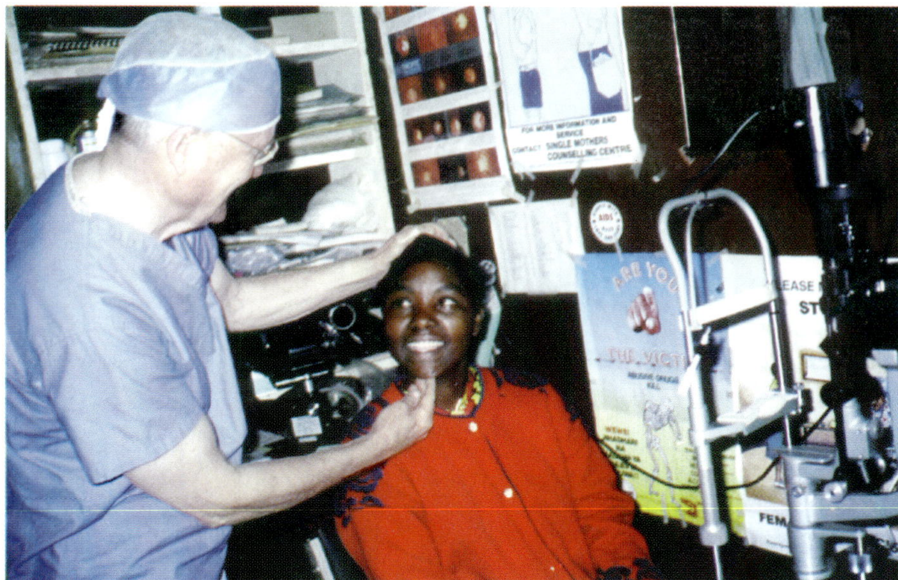

Color Print 4.15. Sixteen year old girl planning to "go to school" after cataract extraction and intraocular lens implantation. (see page 329)

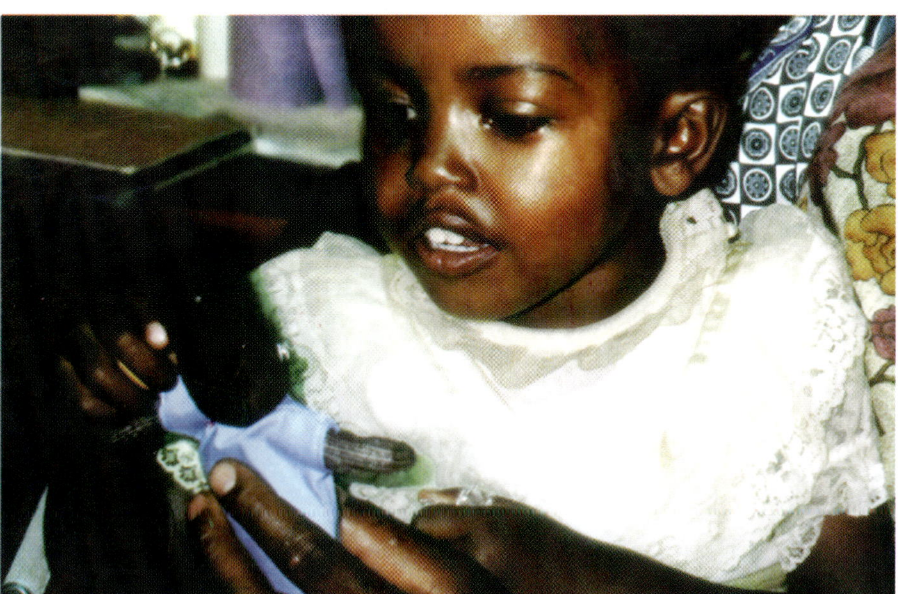

Color Print 4.16. Three and one-half year old after congenital cataract extraction. (see page 330)

Color Print 4.17. A typical intraocular lens implant patient in Bolivia, 1997. (see page 333)

Color Print 4.18. The surgical team, Lilongwe, Malawi. The three in the middle: Dr. Moses Chirambo, Dr. Richard Yukins, Dr. D.J. Kwendakwema. (see page 341)

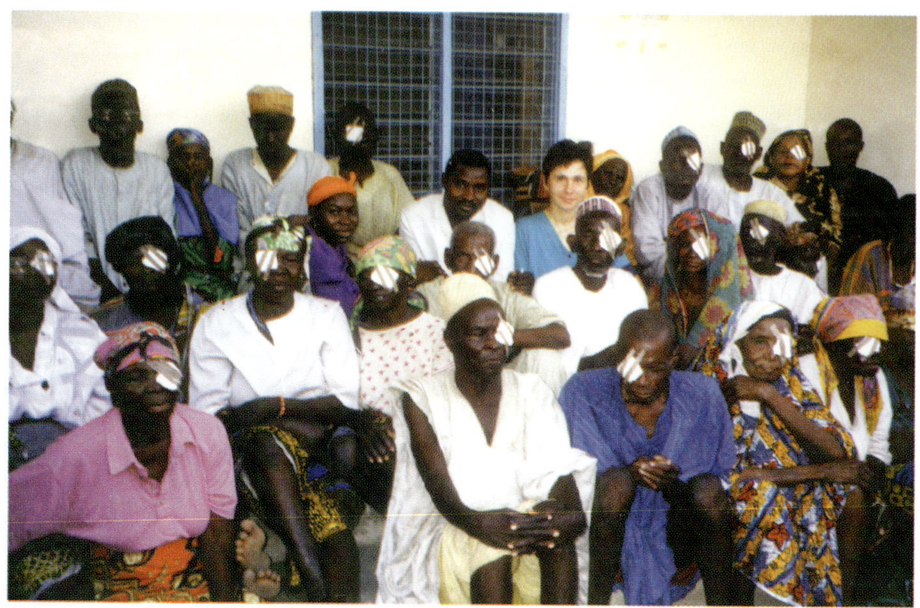

Color Print 4.19. Zing Eye Clinic under direction of Ina Schoenfeld Dabale. (see page 347)

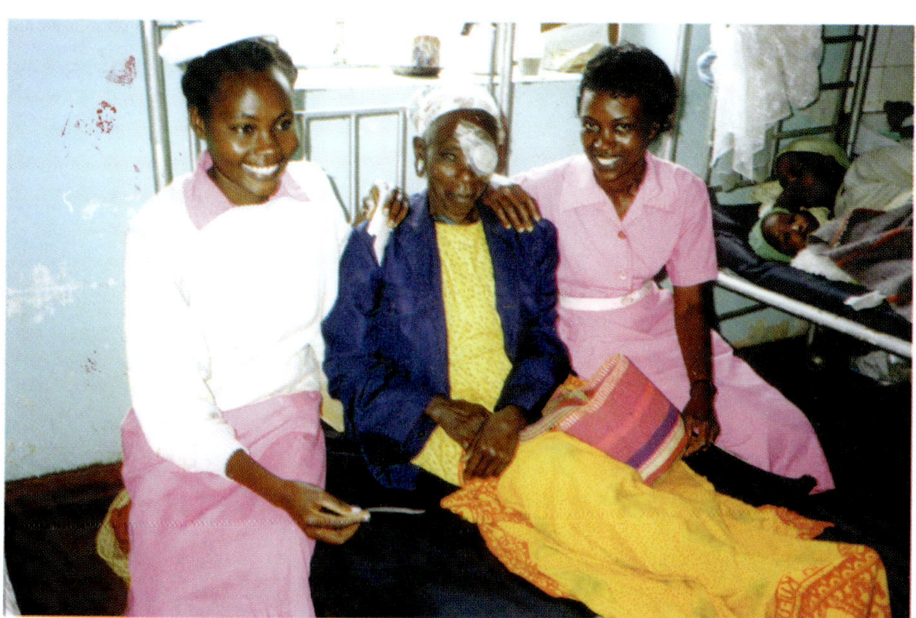

Color Print 4.20. Expert nursing care, Maua Methodist Hospital. (see page 350)

Color Print 4.21. There is only one reason for this broad smile ... being able to see again. (see page 351)

Color Print 4.22. Inside the Koronis Assembly Grounds Tabernacle. Here in 1935 I publically accepted the call to a life of Christian service. (see page 387)

Color Print 4.23. Karl Kuglin with captured baboon. (see page 403)

Color Print 4.24. Land Rover without brakes. (see page 404)

Color Print 4.25. Akron General Hopital, 1958, general surgical residents and spouses in, or in preparation for, missionary service. Top row: Maynard Seaman, Donald Duckles, Donald Goering, Howard Wadstrom, John Bennett, Rev. William Troup, Robert Schenck, and Lowell Gess. Front row: Sue Duckles, Dorothy Seaman, Betty Bennett, Ann Wadstrom, Louise Goering, Pearl Troup, Ruth Gess, Ruth Schenck. (see page 405)

Color Print 4.26. Gate to Kissy UMC Eye Hospital. Will it always offer an entrance? (see page 409)

Color Print 4.27. Dr. Zebidiah Marewangepo of the General Board of Global Ministries (center) with Mr. David Kinyon on his left. (see page 415)

Color Print 4.28. Carolyn and Joe Wagner of Operation classroom, Ruth Gess, and the Rev. Doris Langham Koroma, Paramount Chief candidate Kagboro Chiefdom. (see page 416)

Color Print 4.29. Christian Ophthalmology Society friends, Dr. Arthur and Marilyn Pellicane. (see page 416)

Color Print 4.30. Lake Koronis Assembly Grounds chapel. The scene of Andrew and Carrie's wedding. (see page 418)

Color Print 4.31. Dedication to Ruth: Our love still growing after 56 years. This picture taken after our third baby. (see page 424)

Color Print 4.32. Cottonwood tree, Freetown, Sierra Leone under which slaves were sold ... many of them being sent to America. (see page 444)

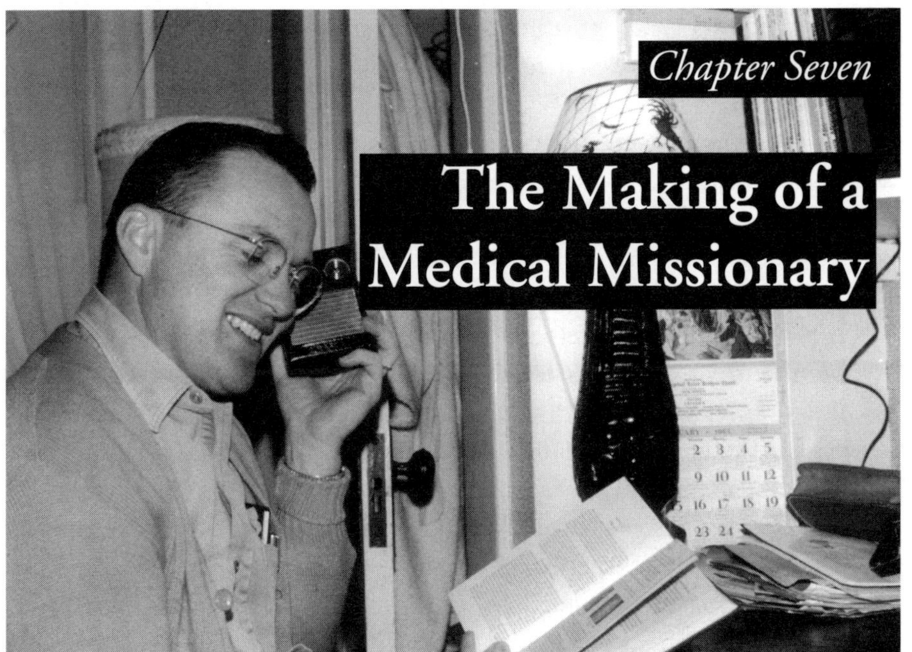

Hitting the books in Medical School

The Prologue

Ruth and I were kneeling at the altar rail of Calvary Evangelical Church. On our heads were the hands of Bishop E.W. Praetorius, the Rev. Frank Spong, and the Rev. Floyd Bosshardt, the latter who is still alive at the time of this writing. We were being commissioned as medical missionaries of the Evangelical United Brethren Church, formerly the Evangelical Church and then later as the United Methodist Church. I had just graduated from the Washington University School of Medicine and had completed a rotating internship at the St. Paul Ancker Hospital. Earlier, Ruth had obtained her registered nurse's degree from Winnipeg General Hospital, Winnipeg, Manitoba, Canada.

How had we come to this momentous moment? We were of simple stock. Ruth was born in Brookdale, Manitoba, Canada. Her life was greatly changed at age fifteen when her banker father died of a heart attack at the young age of forty-five. She needed to work as a secretary to help support her mother and two younger sisters, even though she continued to dream of training as a nurse to fulfill a call to medical missions. Ultimately she was able to complete her nurses training. At this point Ruth and I were married, having found each other out of all the world.

My beginnings were at Paynesville, Minnesota. I was baptized at the Salem Evangelical Church. It would continue to be at the center of my life – Sunday School, Daily Vacation Bible School, Youth Fellowship, and all the social events germane to a German community surrounded by Scandinavian Lutherans and German Roman Catholics. The church was our social center as well as our place of worship.

Members cared about each other. Mr. William Sack prayed for me, his daughter, Lily, was my first Sunday school teacher, and later on Mr. Rudolf Heitke had a major impact on my life. In spite of our squirming and rowdiness and the appearance of no one listening, Mr. Heitke and his prepared lessons got through to me, influencing my "conversion" at age nine. It was two years later, at the age of eleven, that I received my "call" to medical missions. Before he died, I was happy to be able to thank him for his marvelous help in presenting to me the Christian message and the claims of Jesus Christ on my life.

The Call

Incredible! Is it possible for an eleven year old Minnesota farm boy half a world away from Africa to receive a "call" to medical missions in that vast continent? Except for grade school information, I knew nothing about Africa. However, I knew about missions. As Dean S. Gilliland states in *My Pilgrimage in Mission* (International Bulletin of Missionary Research, Vol. 24, No. 3 July 2000):

> *My denomination, the Evangelical Church, had a program for mission education at all levels. In 1948 this group became the Evangelical United Brethren Church (E.U.B.) and later in 1968 merged with the Methodist Church to become the United Methodist Church. As a child, it was impossible not to know about missions.*

I, too, was fully aware of Livingstone, Carey, Borden of Yale, Judson, Paul White, and others. I had never seen or talked to a live African missionary, but the "cause of missions" was ever before me. Would anyone believe that God would speak to a boy whose only activities were cultivating corn and playing softball? I confided with no one about that call.

Unlike the Old Testament Samuel, I did not make further inquiry. I would not have said, "Speak, for your servant is listening," (I Samuel 3:10). Most assuredly I would not have said, "Here am I, send me," (Isaiah 6:8). Africa was far away. To my boyish mind it was dark and dangerous. I had no intention of leaving home and friends.

At the age of nine I stepped forward during an evangelistic service and knelt at the altar of Salem Evangelical Church (Evangelische Gemeinschaft), a church similar to Lorraine Esterly Pierce's description of Evangelical churches in her excellent book *Marching Through Immanuel's Ground.* At the altar I sought and received forgiveness of sins and the assurance of a new life in Christ Jesus.

Two years later the clarion call to medical missions was laid upon my heart. It was to be another ten years before I would share with parents, Sunday School teachers, pastors, counselors, or friends that I had received an unmistakable call to medical missions.

As a lad of fifteen at the Lake Koronis Assembly Grounds, I walked down the aisle in Billy Graham style to dedicate my life to Christian service. It was assumed that I was heading for the ministry. It would be another eight years before I actually had a meeting with Billy Graham.

With design, I avoided any subjects in college that related to medicine. One science course was required for graduation. I chose geology, the study of rocks, the farthest subject away from information relating to the human body and the pursuit of medicine. However, the moment came while on my way to begin seminary training, that I came to realize that if I did not honor the Lord in His calling, He might not be able to use me effectively in the pastoral ministry.

With this new commitment to prepare for medical missions, I was required to pick up physics, comparative anatomy, chemistry, calculus, genetics, biochemistry and the other premedical requirements for medicine, during my years at the Evangelical Theological Seminary in Naperville, Illinois, and two summer courses at Garrett Biblical Institute in Evanston, Illinois.

Upon completion of seminary and premedical work, I was accepted to the University of Illinois Medical School. World War II, however, drew so many pastors into the service that I agreed to fill a pastorate for two years in Minnesota. These were wonderful years. Ruth and I were married and served at the St. Cloud-Graham Evangelical Churches as well as at the Mayer Evangelical Church during which time our oldest son, Tim, was born. Unknown to me, this period drew me out of the succession to the medical school in Illinois which was being overwhelmed with medical applications from Illinois war veterans.

After all these years of preparation I was finally ready to be trained as a medical missionary, and there was no place to go. It seemed that all returning veterans had decided to study medicine. My application to be one of eighty admissions to the Washington University School of Medicine in St. Louis, Missouri, was but one of over 5000!

Had I really been called to medical missions? Obviously, there was no place to begin. Some forty years later Merlin Schendel, son of Pastor E.M. Schendel, told me how he remembered his father praying that Lowell Gess might be accepted into medical school to fulfill his calling. Applications were made to five medical schools but rejections were forthcoming from all except the Washington University School of Medicine in St. Louis, Missouri. I felt led to write to the dean of admissions to inquire of my status. It already was past mid-August 1947, and the new class was to begin in September. Within several days a letter of acceptance was received and medical training became a reality.

It was not until I was halfway through medical school that I learned the details of my acceptance. The mail that brought my letter of inquiry to the dean's desk also brought a letter from a previously accepted student who had decided not to attend Washington University School of Medicine. The dean simply handed my letter to his secretary saying: "Let this applicant have the opening." Providential? Perhaps the 4,800 remaining applicants didn't have prayer warriors interceding on their behalf.

In 1996, I was honored by the Washington University School of Medicine with the "Alumni Achievement Award." During the honors banquet Ruth and I were visiting with Dr. and Mrs. William H. Danforth. He was to receive the "Distinguished Service Award." Dr. Danforth had been the chancellor of Washington University for a period of 24 years of exceptionally dedicated and capable service. During our conversation it was learned that while Dr. Danforth accepted Harvard Medical School's opening in 1947, graduating in 1951, he had also been accepted to the Washington University School of Medicine in 1947, the same year that I was accepted. Out of interest, I asked him if he could remember about what date he sent his letter declining the

Washington acceptance. He said that it was late, just several weeks before classes were to begin, about mid-August. Apparently it was our letters that reached the dean's desk at the same time. It was a thrill beyond words to finally be able to thank the person who relinquished his acceptance that allowed me to begin medical training.

The need for further training was recognized after the three year appointment to Nigeria. I was given the opportunity of taking a surgical residency to equip me for a new surgical program at the Hatfield-Archer Hospital at Rotifunk, Sierra Leone, West Africa, where we met a multitude of people needing surgery – many of whom were blind. Ultimately a three year ophthalmology residency equipped me for a bonafide eye outreach in Sierra Leone. Ruth and I have conducted an eye program in Sierra Leone for over a forty-six year period. To date we have crossed the ocean 132 times.

The foreseeable future is filled with plans for the continuation of an evangelical outreach through medicine and surgery at the Kissy UMC Eye Hospital, Freetown, Sierra Leone. We thank God for His wonderful kindness and compassion. With joy we seek to minister to the blind that they might receive physical sight and spiritual insight through Jesus Christ, our Lord.

The Boy

The phrase "when I was a boy," would bring groans from our teenage children, for it usually signaled a lecture about their excesses as compared to the Spartan life style of my youth. "But, Dad, things are different now!" When they were small, however, they loved to hear stories of my youth while on a farm in the Salem community north of Paynesville, Minnesota. As a small boy, it was my responsibility to close the chicken house door at night. Sometimes it would get dark before accomplishing this chore. Every sound along the way was threatening. At such times I would call my dog, Sport, and together we would make the trip to the chicken house.

There came a time when I could no longer call him and enjoy his company. A neighbor's sheep were being molested. He determined that is was Sport. I found Sport lying along the fence, shot through the heart.

My world stopped. There were tears. Little comfort was found in the half-hearted reasoning of my parents that a rogue dog could not be permitted. I insisted that Sport couldn't have done such a thing. In the nights that followed, the molestation of the sheep continued. Sport had been mistaken for another errant dog.

While the above story didn't bring copious tears to my eyes, another one did. I was given a purebred Guernsey heifer by my parents. From the day of her birth I spent time with her. I fed and trained her. She was a thing of beauty. I called her Donna. When I showed her at the Stearns County 4-H fair, she was awarded a grand championship which rewarded me with a free trip to the Minnesota State Fair. Spending a week with all the other 4-H'ers was a thrill.

On approaching the gate to the judging area, I was asked to present papers verifying the heifer to be of purebred stock. I had been unaware of this technicality. I thought all of my father's herd of thirty-three Guernsey cows were purebred and that this was one of the heifers, so there should be no problem. They were adamant. "You have to present your credential papers to qualify for the main showing."

Donna and I returned to the cow barn. An official encouraged me to show her as a grade rather than a purebred and so after a delay of several hours, we again approached the judging area. Somehow my calf sensed the confusion and disarray and became so nervous that I couldn't present her in proper stances. We ended up twelfth out of a field of 87.

While disappointed, I bravely led my charge back toward the barn. On the way, someone commiserated with me about the registration mix up. For what was to come next I was not prepared. This person told me the news. Danny's purebred heifer had won the Minnesota Grand Champion purebred Guernsey award. Danny's heifer was the runner up to Donna at the Stearns County Fair! Again my world stopped – more like a crash! Silently Donna and I went back to the stall. She lay down in the straw. I buried myself in it and sobbed.

Thirteen year olds bounce back quickly. Within a few days I was to start high school. The freshmen boys were to play the seventh and eighth graders in football. In the tryouts I won the race. Consequently I was to be the ball carrier. Our uniforms were so awkward and heavy that I felt like David being weighed down by Saul's armor. In fact, on the field I could hardly get started with all the excess baggage. We suffered a humiliating defeat to a younger team.

The following year in St. Paul, Minnesota, softball became my passion. Next to my parent's grocery store I ran an icehouse – chipping chunks of ice and loading them onto the bumpers of cars or delivering them to iceboxes in people's homes. In between customers I pretended that I was Johnny Volmer, the famous softball pitching great of that time. I would throw a mushy ball against the back of the icehouse. One day it happened. All the right moves came into place and the ball shot to the icehouse like a bullet. I tried it again, with the same phenomenal result. Within a few days, neighborhood boys were refusing to catch my pitch. It took someone of the stature of Russ Praetorius to pound the glove and say "Put 'er there." (In seminary it was Lynn Schendel.) This was a phase of my life that was to open many doors, in community events, church softball leagues, pitching at Koronis against the ministers and one day pitching for the ministers. The career extended even through medical school and internship before the glove was finally hung up. Someone will ask how I kept in condition during medical school. Ruth has some tender fingers to remind us even though she used a big baseball catcher's mitt. She had been a very good catcher in a girl's league and was the gamest person in the world.

Bumps Along the Way

Some people are unwilling to own up to near and actual failures. Mine were only too real and sometimes potentially devastating.

After my freshman year in high school at Paynesville, Minnesota, my parents sold the farm and moved to St. Paul, Minnesota. The drought of the early 1930s had taken its toll. We had had no crop for three years running. The herd of thirty-three purebred Guernsey cows could not be fed for lack of grass and fodder. At the time of the auction, my mother was unable to face the ordeal of seeing the herd auctioned off and split up. We knew each animal by name. The 5000 dollars from the sale of the farm and livestock was used to buy a grocery store in St. Paul, Minnesota. It was two blocks from Central High School, with its outstanding English department. My junior high preparation was not adequate for coping with the Central High School English department's requirements. It was soon apparent that I would not be able to proceed with the class. The teachers decided that I was not of college caliber, so preparations were made for me to be channeled into a course for manual skills.

When my mother and father learned that I was being directed to this commercial stream, they realized that I would not have college preparation. While Dad manned the grocery store, Mother accompanied me to visit Miss Cora Timme, my homeroom teacher and consultant, and ultimately to Principal Marshall's office. The consensus was repeated that I would not be able to handle college training. However, they did offer an intelligence quotient test and an aptitude test, in later years to be called the SAT. The results were acceptable (surprising), and everyone agreed to allow me six weeks to prepare for readmission to the college preparation group. Mother was a trained teacher, having taught school before her marriage. She literally went back to teaching when she tutored me. Along with the English teacher in Central High School, Mother put me through the paces. Finally the time came for me to join my peers.

From the first minimum requirement test until the last, which was taken three years later, the results were in the 95 to 100 percent range. On the basis of these scores, I was employed while a freshman in Macalester College to correct English papers for Professor McLean. My job would be to especially note sentence structure, grammar, and spelling. I was required to give a mark on each paper, but I was never in a position to cause a failing grade.

It was not until the 50th reunion of my class at Macalester College that I admitted to my classmates that I had been employed to correct their papers. I reminded them that I never presumed to give a failing grade to any of my peers. That decision was left to the professor. After this confession, one of my classmates collared me later on during the reunion activities, and with a twinkle in his eye said, "Thanks for the 'A'."

Another High School (speed) Bump

After receiving my driver's license, I was eager to drive any one, any time, any where they wanted to go – even my sister, June, to a meeting at church. Calvary Evangelical Church (before it was E.U.B. or United

Methodist) had a large and active youth program. Some years as many as thirty would go to the summer Koronis Assembly at Paynesville. Calvary was well known to other Evangelical Churches in Minnesota. It was not unheard of for the youth to arrange first-class drama productions with a Christian message because of the skills of Fred Kobler, one of my life's closest friends.

June was a member of a sewing circle. I was happy to take her to church with our 1933 Plymouth. St. Anthony Avenue had no stop signs from Lexington to Snelling. It was not brightly lit and my right foot became heavy on the accelerator. A squad car's flashing lights brought us to a halt. I turned down the driver's window which moments later seemed to be filled by the uniformed officer. A detached and monotone voice asked, "And where are you going in such a hurry?" June and I looked at each other. Suddenly I blurted out, "To church." "And what is happening at church to require such speeding?" Again, a pause before I answered, "A sewing class." The body at the window shifted. "Watch it – take it easy," he said as he retreated to his car and pulled out ahead of us.

We followed slowly and cautiously. At Snelling he turned right; we turned left and began breathing again. At church nobody believed our story.

"Bump" from Medical School Threatened

Another dramatic bump occurred when I was beginning medical training at the Washington University School of Medicine. The spectre of failure is ever present in the minds of beginning students. So much had been involved in being accepted into medical school training. While other students frolicked, the premedical student continued to be buried in the books. Once accepted, the pursuit of a life goal was not going to be allowed to flounder.

At the Washington University School of Medicine, St. Louis, Missouri, we were about eight weeks into Dr. Mildred Trotter's dissection anatomy course. Our first examination was to be a turning point for a number of students who would decide to opt out of medicine as not being for them. Others who did poorly would also reevaluate their plans and possibly pursue a career other than medicine. There was no doubt in my mind that I was in medicine for a purpose. I was looking forward to a medical missionary career.

When the test papers were returned I was not prepared for the shock of receiving a failing grade. I had studied hard and diligently during the weeks of dissection. Instead of proceeding to the assembly hall, I went to Dr. Trotter's office. She was at her desk. With permission I approached her and presented her my test paper. With a voice choked with emotion I said, "If this is a failure, I don't belong here." She perused the paper, got up, and strode into the assembly hall. She went up to the podium and announced that all of the test papers were to be passed to the center aisle where she gathered them.

That afternoon some students were devastated with the new grades while others of us were reprieved. An incorrect marking key had been used in the grading. Until I die, I will never forget Dr. Trotter's understanding smile as she handed me the final result. I was still in medicine.

Finances

A serious bump at the time of acceptance to medical school was the fact that we had no money, except a $385, 1937 Chevrolet. I needed $600 for the first year's tuition at the Washington University School of Medicine. A can of gun-metal gray paint renewed the car's appearance. A "For Sale" sign with my address was placed on the windshield with the car parked on University Avenue. A rain shower left droplets on the car causing it to sparkle. Within an hour, two prospective buyers were vying for it. When asked about the price, without blinking an eye, I said, "six hundred dollars." That afternoon a letter with an all-important check was in the mail to the medical school.

It was no different years later at the time of retirement. Apart from a $12,500 plot of real estate from my parents and grandparents, we had only $1700. $1500 was immediately spent qualifying for intraocular lens implantation following cataract extraction. A home was purchased with no down payment due to the gracious action of the president of a Home Loan and Savings Association who apparently felt sorry for us as returning medical missionaries. Perhaps he felt that he could take a chance on our future earning power. We did not disappoint him.

Within three years, the mortgage was retired.

In medical school finances were a constant plague. Expenses far exceeded the income of summer painting with my father and the scholarship from First Evangelical Church, Naperville, Illinois. During the first year of medical school, we initially rented a third floor one room apartment. Water was secured from the second floor. There was no wallpaper on the walls.

After a period of time, we found another third floor one room apartment with running water. We shared a refrigerator in the hall with a neighbor. The bathroom was on the second floor.

We attended a Presbyterian Church around the corner. Pastor McIntyre visited us one day in our cramped quarters. Within a week, he was back with an offer too good to refuse.

A Presbyterian-Congregational Community Church in East St. Louis had no pastor. The lovely and spacious parsonage was offered to us. Since I was an ordained pastor, would I preach once each Sunday?

We invited Ted and Jane Feierabend to live with us – they on the second floor, we on the first. They were also in preparation for medical missions. Ruth and Jane shared an evening nursing shift at a local hospital. It was a wonderful arrangement. We shared their excitement and joy when in 2001 he received the Alumni Achievement Award during the fiftieth anniversary of our class graduation at the Washington University School of Medicine, St. Louis, Missouri.

What we had not anticipated was the effect of that little church having a regular pastor. The Sunday school became active. There were weddings and funerals. It became a growing church that involved more and more time of the "preacher in the parsonage."

The second year of medical school is a demanding one. Pathology and other subjects give no quarter. I was burning the candle at both ends. My grades began to slip. I was not getting adequate sleep, which led to an illness (infectious mononucleosis) that required ten days of hospitalization. My classmates had moved on without me. Could I catch up? Would I flunk out? I was perilously near the bottom of the ranking of the second crucial year.

It was at this stage that I was called in to see the Dean. When he learned of the schedule of church and school activities, he was speechless. Then, recovering, he told me the story of my acceptance with the exchange of two letters. He went on to say that he didn't want to be proven wrong in accepting me. If I would give up the pastoral duties in East St. Louis, he would take one more chance on me. He offered a Jackson-Johnson scholarship, usually reserved for the most accomplished scholars, not the needy ones.

Along with that scholarship and the intervention of Mrs. H.S. Frank, a prominent member of the Board of Missions, financial help became available. The Franks had been missionaries to China. Fifty years later, financial help was still coming from the Frank family. Their son, Joel, arranged a brilliant piano and organ benefit concert at the Hennipen Avenue United Methodist Church with the proceeds going to the Kissy UMC Eye Hospital.

We moved back to within several blocks of the medical school. I was able to utilize the library facilities at night and our apartment had all the amenities of a home. During the third year, I was not crowding the lower one third of the class. I had the thrill of reaching the upper fifteenth percentile in some of the subjects. I missed preaching and pastoring, but I needed to be reminded that my call was to "medical missions."

Please, No Bumps On This Trip

Following a periodic trip to Jos, Nigeria, for supplies, we were half way home to Guinter Memorial Hopital in Bambur when Para, a school boy who helped us in our home, asked if he could ride on the bonnet (hood). He had purchased some fish for family and friends. In the confines of the back of the Land Rover the smell was overpowering. I assumed that he wanted to cradle himself with the spare tire which rested on the hood. Instead, he positioned himself on the fender hanging onto the spare tire with his hand while supporting his feet on the front bumper. With a smile of confidence he shouted, "Let's go."

It was a common sight in Africa to see passengers as well as driver assistants hanging on to various places on the sides and backs of lorries (trucks). What I didn't know was the position the police took on people being on the front part of the vehicle. After another ten miles as we were approaching Gombe, a Nigerian policeman who was leaning on his bicycle waved to us. A bit surprised by his friendliness, I waved back to him and continued into the town. This was our last chance to fill up with petro (gasoline). Just as we were preparing to load up, this same policeman came pedaling up so out of breath that he could not speak for a few moments. He wrote out a ticket with a court summons date. I reasoned with him that with the start of the rains I would not be able to get out of Bambur to attend the court session. Also, being away from Guinter Memorial Hospital would make it difficult for the staff attending the patients.

Several weeks later a letter arrived explaining that the court hearing had been moved back by several months when travel would be more convenient, but that I need not be in attendance since the arresting officer had failed to "submit his charges." After getting his breath back, he apparently reverted to the same "friendly policeman." Never again were we prompted to allow someone to "ride up front."

Guilty, Your Honor

While serving at the Rotifunk Hospital, it was necessary from time to time to make a trip into Freetown to obtain supplies at the New England Medical Stores. After January 1 all vehicles were required to display on their wind screens (windshields) the current year's license. Mail deliveries were sometimes slow. Our new license sticker put in the mail by Hank Baldwin in early December had not reached Rotifunk by the second week in January. Undaunted, we made the trip to Freetown and at the first round-about were hailed down by the police. No explanations were acceptable.

With a policeman occupying the passenger's front seat, I was directed to the police station. A court session was already in progress with a gowned judge handing out sentences. I spied an usher from the King Memorial United Methodist Church. He obligingly agreed to take my hurriedly scribbled note to Pastor S. M. Renner which read, "Help! I am being sentenced and fined because the vehicle license sticker was held up in the mail."

Even though the number of people being brought to justice was great, my turn was imminent. Suddenly from a side door behind the judge's desk, Dr. Renner slipped in and without so much as a glance around approached the judge. Without expressions, the two men exchanged several words and Dr. Renner disappeared as ethereally as had appeared. Moments later the usher from King Memorial slipped a note into my hand containing two words: "Plead Guilty."

This was not what I had expected. I thought that Dr. Renner would have explained that I was a medical missionary securing supplies for the hospital and that the license sticker had been purchased but was delayed in the mail. They had exchanged only several words and now I was being instructed to plead "Guilty."

Dr. S. M. Renner was one of the most repected clergymen in Sierra Leone. Two of the first four presidents of the country sat under his ministry. Judges and lawyers were part of his congregation. In the succeeding moments when I was called before the judge and he inquired how I intended to plead, I dutifully said, "Guilty, your Honor." His reply – "Case dismissed."

I walked out into the hot noonday sun, brushing past my captor. He broke into an all-knowing friendly smile.

Harrowing and Life Threatening Experiences

My reference to close calls pales in comparison to those experienced by my peers during their military service as related in *Front Line*, Allan Taylor's biographical story of Delbert Kuehl, WWII chaplain.

In my making of a medical missionary, there were some close calls, even harrowing and life threatening experiences along the way. As a small boy I was not immune. While in my preschool years, my father needed to go to a neighbor for equipment to repair some farm machinery. I had wanted to go along with him, but he was in a hurry and did not want to wait for me to get ready. I secretly positioned myself on the running board, squeezing between the fender and battery that in those days was positioned on the side of the car. It was a wild two-mile trip. When we arrived at the neighbor's place, I got off and came around the car. My father almost fainted. He had sped around curves in race-driving fashion. All the time, I had been hanging on to the battery box for dear life.

Experience 2: Crash Into Grain Binder. A second incident was the day that our small truck was left unattended on our farm. I was crowding age six by this time. I knew by watching my father how he started it and how he shifted the gears. I decided that since nobody was around and the truck was in a wide-open field, I would take it for a spin. It turned out to be much more difficult to handle than I had realized. I was small and the turning of the steering wheel was more than I could manage. I ran into a grain binder that was stationed near by. After the incident, I was not so much afraid of what my father would say. My fear was of my uncle who jointly owned the grain binder. I had been a truant and had to face the music.

Experience 3: Runaway Horse, Age 11. I came in from the field with three horses that had been pulling the two-row corn cultivator. I could not unhitch the horses because I wasn't old enough, tall enough, or strong enough to lift the tongue of the cultivator. Usually I waited for adult help. However, on making the last round in the cornfield, I saw a car coming down the road with a red bicycle tied to the side of it. I recognized the car as one belonging to my aunt and uncle from St. Paul. I had the feeling that the red bicycle must be for me. With this added incentive, I was able to unhitch the horses all by myself.

Usually the horses were quite willing to go by themselves to the barn after a days work. This time, I decided I would ride one of them. Unfortunately, I selected Nelly, the most unruly of the three. Nelly spooked and took off at a gallop with me on her back. That wasn't so unusual except that she had a harness on and when we approached the barn, I noticed that the barn door was open. I had to make a decision whether to jump off the horse, or to stay with the horse and try to go through the barn door on top of the horse. At the last moment, I spread myself out on the back of the horse and we hurtled through the door without my being brushed off by the doorframe.

Experience 4. That same horse caused me other troubles. One day I was putting corn stalks in her bin. Fortunately, I had on a heavy coat. Suddenly, she nipped me on the shoulder. A heavy coat prevented any serious injury. However, there was a hurt to my "feelings." There were not only vocal recriminations, but one of the corn stalks was used to persuade her not to do it again.

Experience 5: Overturned Car. While attending the first year of high school, a number of students from the Salem community drove together in a Model A automobile. The senior student who was driving was licensed. The old Model A Fords had a high center of gravity. On the way to school we hit a patch of sand, and he lost control. We turned over, and when the dust settled, my head was sticking through the canvas top of the car, which was lying on its side.

Experience 6: Koronis Tabernacle – Fourteen year-old Bravado. At considerable expense curtains had been prepared and delivered for the Lake Koronis Assembly Grounds tabernacle's stage. Belatedly, the problem of hanging them was realized before a scheduled program that evening. Professional help could not be secured on such short notice.

I was attending the boy's camp. Someone suggested that I could hang them as my father was a painter. With long extension ladders, I worked with him on high buildings, including the steeples of our Nerstrand and Faribault churches. I was too young when my father and Harvey Miller painted the Salem steeple.

The height of the tabernacle's ceiling was daunting. No long extension ladders were available. A sudden thought prompted me to ask for a large step ladder, three 12 foot 2X10 inch planks, ten large nails, and a hammer. The roof was low at the rear of the tabernacle which allowed me to get up on it and shove the planks through the front windows laying them on the rafters on each side directly above the front part of the stage. The plank on each side was nailed in place and then the third one mounted on the two side ones. It was a dizzying height, but the curtains were hung. Moses came down from Mount Sinai with the Ten Commandments on stone. I left ten nails in wooden planks in the rafters of the "sacred" Koronis tabernacle. Sixty six years later the planks are still in place.

Experience 7: Tire Blowout. My first car was a 1937 Chevrolet two-door. It was apparent that it had been rolled over because there were dents in the top, and we could not be sure of its alignment. It was during World War II, and good tires were not always available. On one trip as I was coming down an incline rolling along within the speed limit, which was fifty miles per hour, the rear tire blew out with a large bang.

I'll never forget the panic of trying to hold the car from going from one ditch to the other as it rocked and reeled, before finally coming to a stop. This was the car whose sale financed the first year of tuition to medical school.

Experience 8: Get Back! It's Going To Explode! As a college freshman with my green beanie cap, I was busily engrossed in a chemistry class experiment. Total silence with no visiting or tinkling of chemistry glassware, prompted me to look up. The class in front of me was missing. Turning to my right I spotted the lab assistant near the door way through which most of the students had been directed. He hoarsely shouted, "Get back! It's going to explode!"

Reflexively I turned to my left and on a shelf just above the level of my head, a glass jar was burning. I turned to leave when a violent explosion occurred shattering the windows of the laboratory. Joining the others who had exited the door I saw green beanies scattered around with a number of students bleeding from cuts on their arms and faces. I had been less than six feet from the explosion and was without a scratch.

By accident water had been poured into a jar that housed a chunk of solid sodium. In spite of the kerosene covering, the water reacted with the sodium producing sodium oxide and hydrogen. After a brief period of burning, the hydrogen exploded!

Besides the loving care of my Lord, it was felt that the shattered glass passed over my head and on its downward projection struck students at a distance. I was willing to accept my explanation. What I could not understand was – since I was so near to the explosion – why was I the only student who still had a green beanie on his head.

Experience 9: Heatstroke, Nigeria 1953. After we had been in Nigeria for about a year, I was able to take some time off to do some hunting. The two guides and I anticipated capturing an antelope, wild boar, or buffalo. In our trek, we walked far afield. It was very hot and we ran out of water. The guides noticed that I was beginning to stray from the path. Shade or shelter was not available except for a small thorn tree, under which they laid me. After a period of fanning, I came around but was so weak that they literally had to assist me in walking, even carrying me part of the time on the long journey home. It was more serious than we had realized. Heat strokes, when no water, shelter, shade, or ways of cooling are available, can be fatal.

Experience 10: Angry Crowd, Sierra Leone. While returning to our Kissy UMC Eye Hospital on one occasion, we came upon a throng of thousands of people blocking the road. The pandemonium was threatening. A bus ahead of us had been turned over and the windows broken. It frightened us to think what might have happened to the passengers. Now the menacing mass turned its attention to our car and began to rock it. Oblivious to the danger, Ruth opened the door to remonstrate. Each time they pried open the door, Ruth would say, "lef it" and then shut the door again. One of our patients, a passenger in the back seat, encouraged Ruth to lock the door, but she just faced off each would be intruder. One person in the crowd, a man of about twenty years of age, recognized us. He sprang to the top of our hood (bonnet) and hollered to the crowd saying that this was a doctor who was returning to the Eye Hospital. He explained that we had nothing to do with the cause of the civil unrest that was at the base of this fury. He waved to part the crowd, and we went through as the Israelites went through the Red Sea. A Land Rover behind us, seeing that we were allowed to go through, tried to follow in our path. The crowd's fury then was directed to it, overturning it and again breaking the windows. We never learned what happened to the driver.

Experience 11: Hunting. Hunting occasionally involves danger. One would think that a missionary would be a little sensible about the excitement of hunting, but strange things do happen. On one occasion we were going after a hippopotamus. He had slipped into the water. We took off after him in a canoe. Later, I learned that one does not go after hippopotami in canoes. The hippotamus surfaced exposing his nose and eyes. A well placed shot caused him to disappear under the water. He did not reappear. The next morning, we found that there was a place where some weeds were higher than other places. The men cut through the weeds and up floated the hippopotamus. The hippopotamus was harvested. It is customary to give a quarter of the kill to the chief of the area. We were in an area where there were five chiefs. There were only four quarters; so we asked the fifth chief, the one farthest down on the totem pole of authority, to make his selection of the part he would like. He chose the neck and all were happy. However, not all the hunters continued to be happy. Some were Ibo and some were Hausa. An altercation arose during the butchering.

I was sitting some distance away with my gun leaning against my chair. Suddenly, there was a terrible commotion, and one of my assistants came running and excitedly called me to come quickly. There had been a dispute about the division of the meat. The men were poised with their menacing machetes. When I got to the place where the butchering was being done, the hunters had lined up according to their tribes and were glaring at each other. Without hesitation, I lowered the gun and fired a shot over their heads. This got their attention. Then, shoving another shell into the chamber, I used my best Hausa to shout, "The next person who raises a machete gets this gun." It was successful in cooling the situation.

Other potentially dangerous hunting incidents did occur. One involved stalking a buffalo. It had led us into a bushy place in which we could hardly move. Suddenly, there was a commotion, but instead of coming at us, the buffalo went out the other side. This also happened with an elephant. After the elephant experience, I decided there should be no more of this. I wouldn't mind dying in the line of duty as a missionary, but by no means was I going to be found in extremis because of some hunting incident.

One incident was entirely unforeseen. In Nigeria baboons are real problems, and at times, dangerous. Some are large and fierce. A male baboon can weigh more than a hundred pounds, with most of the muscle in the shoulder areas. The hindquarters are small.

On one occasion, as we were passing through Senge Pass, we were stopped by some excited people who explained that a troop of baboons was ruining their peanut field and were aggressive to anyone trying to scare them off. They pleaded with us to come with a gun if we happened to possess one. I did have a rifle in the car and obligingly walked with them to the area where the baboons were feeding. I could not believe the size of these animals and the fact that they seemed to have no fear of people. I leveled my rifle and fired to strike the big male. Following the shot, there was pandemonium. The baboons ran but only for a distance of seventy-five yards and then stopped and assumed challenging stances.

I felt that it was necessary to make sure that the baboon, which had been struck, was not just wounded. I prepared to find him and make sure that he would not be a danger. I had walked only a very slight distance when suddenly, no more than twenty feet ahead, a huge baboon arose. There was a wound in his shoulder and one arm was not functioning. The other arm was very much intact. Without my knowledge, the passenger in my car had followed me up the high hill. He was on the other side of the baboon that was glaring at me. There was no way that I could fire again. By slowly moving to the side, I was eventually able to get the baboon in my sight without anyone else being in the line of fire. The animal was dispatched. This was an incident that I determined never to let happen again.

Experience 12: Land Rover Without Brakes. On a return trip from a medical clinic to Zing, during which I had been able to take my family, we were coming down a long incline. As the speed increased, I attempted to brake. It was a terrifying moment when I realized there were no brakes. We were gaining momentum and were approaching the foot of the long incline where a stream usually flowed. During the dry season, the road crews had decided to replace the bridge and had cars going through the dry stream bed to the side. All the time I had been trying to put the car into a lower gear. I turned off the ignition, trying to slow the momentum. When we came to the bottom we were still going much too fast. We hurtled through the streambed with a bump that sent us sailing through the air. Thankfully we remained upright and limped the rest of the way home. I never again drove that vehicle as I immediately placed an order for a new Land Rover that would be safe for my family.

Experience 13: Armed Robbery, Rotifunk. After Ruth and I returned to the Kissy UMC Eye Hospital following a short furlough, we decided to check the hospital at Rotifunk before seriously unpacking the more than fifteen boxes of medicines and supplies that had accompanied us. Larry and Marge Chambers had volunteered to spend a year at Rotifunk repairing and renewing the buildings. We had much to visit about and decided to stay overnight. The following day, arriving back in Freetown at the Kissy UMC Eye Hospital, some somber-faced conference officials, including the Reverend David Caulker, met us. He explained to us that in our absence, a group of fifteen armed robbers had besieged the Kissy UMC Eye Hospital and broken into it by going through our bedroom door. They had carried off medicine and supplies, but in the confusion, one of the robbers was shot and killed. No one ever knew how this took place. Indeed it was providential that we were not sleeping in our bed that night in the direct line of intrusion.

Some of these harrowing experiences were life threatening. I thank God for His presence and protection when, because of human frailty and poor decisions, serious personal harm could have resulted.

General Surgery Residency

With the blessing of the Board of Missions a leave of absence was granted for training in general surgery. The residency was begun at Akron General Hospital, Akron, Ohio, in the fall of 1955. The successful acceptance to this program had been engineered by Dr. Roger Troup, a missionary colleague in Nigeria, with whom I had the privilege of doing surgery from time to time.

The program and surgical staff at the Akron General Hospital was of high caliber and attracted surgical residents nationally, as well as internationally. Nine of the staff were either missionaries seeking greater skills or were doctors planning to go into missionary service. Even at this writing in 2001, Dr. Maynard Seamens and his wife, Dorothy, continue to serve in far off places such as Tibet and Nepal, Dr. Jim and Martha Foulkes are presently in the Sudan after having served nearly four decades in Zambia, and Dr. Tom and Elaine Coleman, minister in the Cameroons for months at a time after having spent many years in Ethiopia.

Dr. Daryl Angus, the chief resident at Akron General Hospital, enjoyed challenging his fellow residents with responsible patient care. The visiting staff also allowed us to actively participate in the actual surgical procedures.

One urologist, who had had a successful career, was now aging and appreciated the help of eager youthful residents to perform a large part of his surgery. I had scrubbed with him a number of times and knew his procedures. He simply stood back until the critical moment of removing the prostate suprapubically, which he always performed himself, and then stepped back again and watched as the resident closed.

One day on the way to the hospital, I was flagged down for traveling 40 miles an hour in a 30 mile zone. I was issued a ticket as well as a summons to appear in court several weeks later. After this delay I rushed into surgery for the first case. The patient already was under general anesthesia. The surgical procedure was that of a suprapubic prostatectomy. I participated in the way described above.

Filling out the chart at the end of the surgery I was made aware that the patient was a traffic court judge. While he was at the hospital, I visited him each day, taking care of his needs, along with the oversight of the urologist in charge. As I remembered later, my visits were usually following other surgical procedures while I still was capped and gowned, with a mask dangling down that obscured part of my features. Several weeks later I stood before my patient, the judge, and was not recognized in my street clothes.

I received his sentence of $35.00. I was proud to see that he was fit. He never knew that he had just sentenced the doctor who several weeks earlier had done ninety percent of his surgery.

I look forward to someday appearing before the judgment seat of Christ and hearing the final verdict, "Forgiven, enter into the joy of your Lord."

Sword Swallowing

As a boy I could never accept the truth about sword swallowing. Like so many other magical tricks, I assumed that the sword collapsed upon itself and never truly was thrust for any significant distance into the body of the performer.

While I was doing a surgical residency at the Akron General Hospital, Akron, Ohio, in 1955 through 1957, the world had yet to learn of Brad Beyers, who eventually set a Guinness Book record for swallowing ten swords at one time. He claimed that no harm was done to his body even though he used real 28 inch blades. X-rays taken with the swords in place showed their going all the way to his stomach.

During my time on the Chest Service at Akron General Hospital, bronchoscopies needed to be done for the diagnosis of certain disorders. Washings were used for microscopic examination.

After anesthetizing the mouth, throat, and air passages of a middle-aged man, I was preparing to insert the bronchoscope. The patient spoke up and what he said was the unthinkable – the impossible. He confided that he was a circus performer and did sword swallowing. Now that I had anesthetized his air passages, it would be possible for him to position the bronchoscope without violent coughing or choking. I believed him and transferred the scope from my hands to his. Deftly he placed it into the trachea rather than having it course to the stomach through the esophagus. While in place he allowed me to manipulate the bronchoscope to view selected areas in the right and left lung fields. Since he had placed it, in all fairness I asked him if he would like to remove it at the conclusion of the examination period. This he did, ending with a look that suggested he could do what we thought never could be done.

What was an exciting incident for me turned into a future embarrassment. A senior resident was present. During all that was happening he said not a word. However, in the days to come, he bandied about a more interesting story that got larger with each telling. Ultimately the story was that I could not accurately place the bronchoscope so that the patient came to my rescue.

As an adult I came to believe what a child could not believe, that sword swallowing is a bona fide procedure, and with a little local anesthesia, the performer could actually direct the sword, or in this case the bronchoscope, into the passageway leading to the lungs.

"Is Jesus Going to Let Me Die?"

During a time of surgical residency at the Childrens Hospital in Akron, Ohio, I performed a number of tonsillectomy and adenoidectomy procedures. Always at the close of the day these patients would be checked, and again around midnight. On one such occasion all the postoperative children were sleeping, but I passed one bed where there was a little four year old girl. She was not a postop. I stopped and noticed that her eyes were wide open. I said to her softly, "Hi, sweetie, aren't you going to go to sleep like all the others?" At first she did not answer – but realizing that she had my attention, she asked, "Is Jesus going to let me die?"

I was aware of her case. Everything possible had been done for her. Her parents and professional staff were committed to provide quality care in her final days. Her intense gaze into my eyes demanded an answer. Moving very close I bent over and clasped her hand. "My dear," I said in a low but clear voice, with all the assurance I could muster, "Jesus isn't going to let you die. He promised that whoever lives and believes in Him will never die." Then I added, "I promise you with all my heart that this is true." I felt her hand tighten. I sat down and stayed with her for a few moments. When she closed her eyes, I resumed my rounds. In the morning as I checked my patients, I passed her bed. It was empty. During the night she had gone to be with Jesus.

I have often thought about that incident, as I was apparently the last person to whom she spoke. What and how much should be told to a patient in moments like this? Or if the condition is hopeless, and the patient may never be able to see again, how much does one say? Ambrose Pere once stated, "I bind up the wounds, God heals them." Is it not true that by faith and intercessory prayer relatively "hopeless" conditions have improved? To me it would seem wrong to leave a patient without "hope." God is great and can do wonderful things. How can we limit His healing grace?

It is not intended ever to deliberately falsify the situation. In lay terms, the physician must confront and comfort the patient as well as the family members. This is one time that the personal relationship cannot be filled by another staff member. The patient wants to hear from the doctor's lips what happened, what the condition is, and what might be expected. Again it is not kind to paint a completely dark or hopeless picture with no ray of hope for improvement as the days and weeks progress.

The patient doctor relationship is a two-way experience. While healing may not come to the patient, I can affirm that healing has come to me because of the stalwart faith of some of my patients. My life has been enriched, not merely because of my wanting to help in the healing process but because of those who have been healed and who in turn have been a blessing to me.

Projections for the Kissy UMC Eye Hospital

Will there be a Kissy UMC Eye Hospital in the future? It is true that it is located in a vulnerable part of Freetown. When rebel forces moved into the city January 6, 1999, the hospital was in the direct path of the invaders. It was broken into and savagely looted. An itemized listing of the damage in dollars amounted to $119,862.00. The United Methodist Church, Christoffel Blindenmission, and interested doctors and friends were quick to underwrite a portion of that which had been destroyed. At the present time the program is moving on in full force.

We look forward to the hospital again ministering to the people upcountry as well as those in Freetown. Mobile clinics were done in the past and are planned again to extend to Wellington, Rotifunk, Taiama, as well as occasional visits to Yonibana, Monjama, Bo, and Jaiama. This is possible as CBM has donated a sturdy, four-wheel drive Toyota Hilux.

It is anticipated that as political stability comes to Sierra Leone, volunteer eye surgeons will again come to help at the Kissy UMC Eye Hospital. With their coming, they bring medicines, supplies, and new expertise. Housing facilities are available in the apartment over surgery.

Ultimately we are hoping for the eye care to be done by indigenous ophthalmologists assisting Dr. Ainor Fergusson in his wonderful work. Training of ancillary staff is always foremost in our minds and we are especially grateful for the part CBM has played in this emphasis in the past. We continue to pray that the United Methodist Church will continue its support through the Advance Special program of the General Board of Global Ministries.

It is always thrilling to be present when patients experience new sight. They can hardly contain their joy and often their expression is, "Thank God, I can see!" This is a joy that is vicariously shared by each member of the staff. There is similar appreciation for the fitting of eye glasses that allow patients to read and see the world. Also there is the prevention and treatment of glaucoma and other sight endangering diseases such as trachoma and onchocerciasis (river blindness). In this compassionate Christian ministry we always rejoice when because of the care given at the Kissy UMC Eye Hospital there has been a new realization of God's love and care.

We do not know the future, but we know who holds the future.

"I know the plans I have for you," declares the Lord, "plans to give you hope and a future."

Jeremiah 29:11

What is the Future for Medical Missions?

This book has been written with a hidden purpose. It was meant to be informative, interesting, and perhaps even entertaining. Above all it was meant to bring to the realization of people the need that there is for medical missions today and surely for the future. It is my prayer that there may be a stimulus with this writing of anecdotes that will prompt some to respond to the call of medical missions.

The situation of the medical missions outreach today is quite different from that which presented when Ruth and I responded a half century ago. One wonders what the fields will be like in the 21st century. In the *Today's Christian Doctor* magazine there are some statistics that are almost unbelievable. Dr. Harold Adolph, M.D., notes that there are thirty mission organizations at the present time reporting thirty-three hospitals worldwide without a single doctor or nurse on their staff. Of the doctors who felt the call of God to go as missionary doctors, only twenty percent still have that interest when their training is completed and their debts paid off. To pay off debts nearly a decade is involved. By this time the family and medical practice are well established. It is difficult beyond words to uproot after that length of time.

We are seeing at the present time a phenomenon known as short term missions. Some feel that they can fulfill God's requirements for world evangelism by simply making a two week commitment once a year or so. They reason that it is not necessary to give a lifetime commitment. I hurry on to say that tremendous blessings have come from the multitude of short term mission projects that have been sent around the world in recent days. My only thought is, "Where are those who are willing to respond to the call of Christ to serve in his name through medical evangelism, not just for a short term but as a career response?" One survey found that of a hundred feeling the call of God to missions, only twelve completed training for such a calling, only two actually went, and only one stayed.

Dr. Adolph's survey also revealed that medical missions were used by God in a way that was striking. Eighty percent of the Christians in India relate their conversion to a mission hospital experience. In Sierra Leone and Nigeria we found that a large percentage of the Christians were impacted by the medical evangelistic outreach of hospitals and clinics. Sometimes, years later we would learn of patients who had come to believe in Jesus Christ as their savior. Relatives thought we would wish to know. To be sure, we were thrilled with the news that fulfilled our calling.

Besides the spiritual impact, sobering statistics relating to the simple medical conditions are frightening. For example, in Africa only one in twenty women needing a C-section for obstructed labor can get that operation. Only fifteen percent of patients with hernias in Africa can get the operation they need during their lifetime, even if their hernia is strangulated. Of the twenty million people worldwide who are blind, remedially blind, hardly one half will have the joy of seeing again.

Just prior to the writing of this I had the privilege to visit with an eye resident who confirmed that he was looking forward to a lifetime career in ophthalmology in underserved countries of the world. This thrills my heart to know that of the best trained and most promising young people there are those who are responding to a lifetime commitment of, "I'll go where you want me to go, dear Lord."

"Helping Hands" Acknowledged

I cannot imagine a more thrilling, and fulfilling life, than what Ruth and I have enjoyed over the many years that the Lord has given us life and breath. We were allowed, even encouraged, to speak on behalf of Jesus Christ, the Son of God. It was our privilege to minister to others for renewed life and sight. We vicariously experienced the joy of our patients when they were freed from the shackles of sin and had the privilege of sight restoration, allowing them to be productive and independent.

Yet this supreme joy would not have been possible except for the help and sacrifices of others. In later years I learned that my parents did as

Figure 7.1. Salem Evangelical Church.

Hannah in the Bible, who offered Samuel to the Lord's service. My parents gave spiritual guidance. They were careful in seeing that their children were in Sunday school and church. Bible school was important no matter how it may have conflicted with the chores that needed to be done on the farm or with the harvesting of the crops. Members of Salem Evangelical Church cared about each other. Mr. William Sack prayed for me and his daughter, Lilly, was my first Sunday School teacher. In spite of our squirming and rowdiness and the appearance that no one was listening, Mr. Rudolf Heitke and his prepared lessons got through to me. Before he died, I was happy to be able to thank him for his marvelous presentation of the claims of Jesus Christ on my life.

In wintertime I can still remember how we were bundled beneath bear rugs in Reuben Arndt's box sled. Being at the end of the line, he and his wife with their children Floyd and Jeanette, would pick up other families on the way to church. The joy of the Christmas celebration at the Salem church was especially meaningful. It is wonderful that to this very day the church, though officially closed, has been restored and again is open for special occasions such as the August Salemfest and the Christmas program in December. Curtis and Carol Wegner, along with Mr. and Mrs. Rick Miller, have given of their time, talents and tithe to continue the presence of Salem Evangelical Church. Enthusiastic sup-

WASHINGTON UNIVERSITY

SAINT LOUIS (10), MO.

SCHOOL OF MEDICINE
OFFICE OF THE REGISTRAR

August 15, 1947

Mr. Lowell A. Gess
219 B 8th Avenue S. E.
Minneapolis 14, Minnesota

Dear Mr. Gess:

I am pleased to inform you that your application for admission to our first year class has been approved by the Committee on Admissions. Please indicate your acceptance or non-acceptance of the place on the enclosed blank and return it together with the required fifty dollar deposit within the next five days.

I am sending you a sheet of information concerning registration etc.

Very truly yours,

W B Parker

Registrar, School
of Medicine.

Figure 7.2. Letter of Acceptance to Medical School.

port is offered by such people as Carol and Bob Heitke, Lon and Robin Moon, and many others.

In remembering those who impacted my life specific individuals come to mind. My sister, June, two years older than me, was able to let my wishes be known even before the time that I could speak. It became a concern to my parents when, at the age of three, I still was not conversing. In the years that followed there was no loss for words and my intelligence was felt to be strong enough to skip a grade in school.

In those early days relatives played a strong role in my life. We were always welcomed at my Aunt Freda's where we could sit down and enjoy her prepared fricassee chicken. The only other time in my life that a comparison could be made to hers was on a Vietnamese flight from Ho Chi Minh City to Hong Kong seven decades later.

Christmases were bleak and sparse in my childhood. The Great Depression following the stock market crash of 1929 left farmers with no currency. It is true that we had milk from the cows, eggs from the chickens, corn from the fields, and meat from the cows and pigs. Nonetheless, there still was no money to buy Christmas gifts. My earliest remembrance of Christmas consisted of an orange and peanuts as gifts. The exception was a wonderfully anticipated box from my Aunt Alma in St. Paul, Minnesota. Each day we would wait for the postman to deliver that Christmas box with wrapped gifts from her.

The Bradley Kellogs took me into their home as a Macalester freshman where I shared their son Frank's room as well as his bed. District Superintendent J.G.Heidinger risked appointing me to pastor the New Trier Evangelical Church while still a college student.

Wonderful help also came from teachers such as Theresa Bries, Emiline Miller, Cora Timm, Professor Maclean, Glen Clark, Dr. Harold Heininger, later to become bishop of the Evangelical United Brethren Church, Dr. Paul Eller, President of Evangelical Theological Seminary, Dr. Wilbur Harr, chair of missions at seminary, New Testament Professor, Dr. Keen, (with his thoughtful interest in students exemplified by his mentoring promising and future church leader Dwight Busacca), the Rev. Dewey Eder, who arranged for a scholarship during our medical days, and the Rev. Wilmert Wolf who guided me as his assistant pastor during my days of training at the seminary. There were also important persons such as Pastor McIntyre in St. Louis, Missouri, who shepherded us, making sure that we had a roof over our heads.

Physicians who guided my thinking and medical training were Drs. Graham, Woods, Moore, and Dean Watson of the Washington University School of Medicine who was responsible for my acceptance letter signed by Registrar Parker.

Certainly helping hands include the Advance Special, with its hallowed number 009229.3RA, a program within the General Board of Global Ministries of the United Methodist Church, to which churches and individuals may donate money for the program of the Kissy UMC Eye Hospital. In the late 1980s the gifts were small in numbers and amounts. Ruth personally acknowledged each gift. When questioned if the gifts were really directed to the program without any administrative amount being taken away, assurances produced a dramatic increase both in numbers and amounts. Dr. Randolph Nugent and Dr. Zebediah Marewangepo were especially supportive, as were Ms. Sue Robinson and Ms. Pat Rothrock. The interview of Ms. Doreen Tilghman with Dr. Ainor Fergusson which resulted in Dr. Fergusson's being added to the hospital staff as a Person in Mission was an important high point in the support of the eye ministry. Individual churches such as our own Alexandria United Methodist Church have continued to give donations for the support of the Kissy UMC Eye Hospital through the Advance Special.

Christian Blind Mission, known as Christoffel Blindenmission, in Germany has been supportive of the eye program in Freetown as noted in the 1992 report. Besides supplying medicines, supplies, and equipment, they have been solicitous and thoughtful. When Mrs. Ainor Fergusson suffered a serious laceration of her scalp during an armed robbery and Dr. Fergusson had to flee for his life, CBM transferred them to Guinea Bissau to be out of harms way for a period of recuperation. Unbelievably they had to be rescued in less than a year when a coup erupted in Guinea Bissau. CBM's emphasis on training made it possible for Mr. John Fornah and Mr. James Koroma to take training in Ghana. Dr. Fergusson was given three months training in India. CBM arrranged for doctors from Nigeria, Liberia, and Togoland to receive training in intraocular lens implantation at the Kissy UMC Eye Hospital. They provided a thirty KVA generator, central to the working of the program because of unreliable city power, as well as two motor vehicles which unfortunately were destroyed in the coup. The only transportation for the outreach of Kissy in 2001 is the Toyota Hilux, again a donation to the hospital. Dr. Richard Lockwood, Dr. Nick Cook, and Dr. Ainor Fergusson have all been sponsored by CBM as part of their marvelous outreach to more than fifty-two countries of the world.

The Central Global Vision Fund, (501 (c) (3) status with a tax number of 46-0381749), was established by the original volunteers from Central United Methodist Church, Milbank, South Dakota to support the work of the Kissy UMC Hospital. Individuals and organizations make contributions though this vehicle to make the continuation of the Kissy Hospital possible. Volunteer eye surgeons have been able to secure tax credits with regard to their travel and supplies expenses. Donations are honored by the Internal Revenue Service. The counsel of the Board of Directors has been invaluable spiritually and financially. We thank God for the concerned and compassionate people who respond to the eye needs of people in Sierra Leone and other countries that allows for the mandate of our Lord Jesus Christ, "the blind receive their sight, the lame walk, the lepers are cleansed, the deaf hear, the dead are raised up, and the poor have the gospel preached to them." (Matthew 11:5).

Crucial help has come from Operation Classroom, the inspiration of Bishop John L. Hopkins on his 1985 survey of Sierra Leone and Liberia, accompanied by Indiana laymen John Shettle and Bob Bowman. Rev. Joe and Carolyn Wagner, who were brought in to head up Operation Classroom and participate in its explosive growth since 1987, have included the Kissy UMC Eye Hospital in their important consultations with church leaders. In a very practical way they have made space available for eye medicines, supplies, and equipment for the hospital when they ship containers to West Africa.

Further personalities who have been so effective and have meant so much include no less than forty volunteer eye surgeons like Dr. Justin Sleight and his wife, Marg, as well as some eye doctors who had never visited the Kissy UMC Eye Hospital but still heartily supported the program such as Jon Tierney. In addition to Enid Young's painting of Africa on the cover of this book, she and her husband, Loman, did creations and murals at the Kissy UMC Eye Hospital. The Rev. Bill and Mae Zahl along with Lynn and Doris Schendel, Earl and Eileen Werner, and our faithful children gave prayer and financial support. Daughter Mary had

Figure 7.3. Prayer warriors and supporters: Bill and Mae Zahl on each side; next to Mae is her brother Lynn Schendel and his wife Doris.

long discussions with me in the evaluation of the thrust of the book. Though separated by three time zones in Alaska, Beth and Bob offered encouragement in their telephone calls and then shortly before the completion of this book, Beth helped me firm up some theological points. Ruth, John's wife, made no complaints about the many hours it took John to keep the computers running. Paul and Arlet showed me tricks in the computer use. Andrew and Carrie spent precious time during their Christmas vacation setting up the framework for my anecdotes and doing some typing. Steve Boehlke expertly set up a web site, www.medicalmissionchallenges.org. With all our comings and goings to Africa, cousins Mae and George Farnum always made us welcome for overnight stays. However, there was never any doubt about their entertaining angels unaware. They, and Kevin, knew what they were doing, and the members of our family were no angels.

Especially encouraging and challenging to me were college friendships with Russell Sargent and my roommate, Roscoe Hoiosen. In Kirk Hall's Section Nine at Macalester College we participated in a meaningful Bible study in the plush visitor's suite given us by the authorities for this weekly meeting. Both men were outstanding athletes. I had the thrill of winning the 1942 college handball championship meeting my hockey player-coach in the finals. In a friendly handball match just before graduation, Roskie defeated me. I had to live with that and Roskie's chuckling for the rest of our lives. From that upper room, our callings took Roskie and Char to Alaska as teachers, Russ and Nancy to Latin America as preachers, and Ruth and me to Africa as healers.

With all this support Ruth and I have been able to enjoy the ministry of reaching out to blind people in the world. Even in the present day there are couples such as Howard and Lorraine Pierce who not only support financially but with their skills help make known the Kissy UMC Eye Hospital's ministry in West Africa.

It must be emphasized that no matter how clear the call to serve as a medical missionary was, it would have been impossible without the nurture of the church. Daily Vacation Bible Schools, evangelistic services, and especially Lake Koronis Assembly Grounds had great impacts on my Christian nurturing. I was able to attend the Lake Koronis Assembly meetings every year of my life for the first twenty-one years, having been carried to the first meeting as a babe in arms. My father, along with Pastor P. A. Lang, and Mr. Wm. C. Miller, had the privilege of stepping out the boundaries of the original assembly grounds.

The youth assemblies at Koronis were determinative in my life. The pastors of the Evangelical and later the Evangelical United Brethren Church, met together with the young people for a week's fellowship and Christian education. There were spiritual challenges for life commitment. It was during one of the evangelistic services at age fifteen that I stepped out and made public my call to Christian ministry. Little did pastors such as F.A.Spong, Floyd Bosshardt, and D.C.Trapp realize how much they influenced my spiritual life in those days at Koronis.

As time passed I realized that I was just a helping hand, a cog in a very large and wonderful wheel. The friendship and subsequent marriage to Ruth (Bradley), a registered nurse, enabled us to serve as a team. She was a devoted wife and mother during the years of my medical training. In Africa she was involved in the schooling of our children, assisting in surgery, participating in Sunday School and women's work, and entertaining visitors. At Taiama she conducted the general clinic and at Bo she coordinated the eye program, which she did again at Kissy UMC Eye Hospital along with the selection of the staff. She has participated in the program of reaching out to underserved countries of the world as evidenced by the voluminous correspondence involved.

Our medical missionary service would not have been possible except for the help of others. Medicines and supplies were and continue to be made available from charitable pharmaceutical and optical houses, Douglas County Hospital, and individual doctors. Other medicines are secured through Trumm Drug and Thrifty White's Pharmacy at cost. Helen Paulson, and more recently Karen Olson, sterilize supplies with the blessing of Bill Flaig and Jim Bergsrud. It all started innocently enough in the 1970s and 80s when we would spend three months each year in West Africa. After retirement at midnight, December 31, 1989, Bill Flaig suggested a hospital party recognizing our retirement. I respectfully declined such an event but mentioned that if the hospital would be willing to continue sterilizing donated items, I would be most grateful. This has been continued now for over ten years. I am sure they never dreamed that I would live this long, let alone still be doing eye surgery in Africa.

Many times I have been picked up by the Minneapolis-St.Paul Airport Shuttle, a service of the Bursch Travel Agency in Alexandria, Minnesota. Their help in carrying boxes of medicines and supplies was that of going the second mile. In spite of the number of boxes carried over these almost twenty years, no charges ever were made for their handling. On one occasion when the boxes numbered nineteen, they dis-

Figure 7.4. MSP Airport Shuttle with driver Reg Johnson.

patched a special van to handle the load. The remaining room accommodated only the driver, Ruth, and me.

Such acts of helpfulness have continued over the years. Ruth and I are quick to recognize that our ministry has been a cooperative venture, and it is only fair to acknowledge some of those who have made our calling possible. The length, breadth, and scope of this encouragement and assistance covers our entire lives from our parents onward.

Individual donations have been remarkable. Bob and Bea Swenson donated a beautiful computer with all the components to the Kissy UMC Eye Hospital only to have it completely destroyed in one of the coups. With no fanfare they made available a replacement. Their daughter, Nancy, has supplied valuable sutures and other needed supplies. Mark Schendel has made available a number of computer supplies. Roger and Linda Cole, Bruce and Kathleen Pohlig, and the doctors in the congregation of the Alexandria United Methodist Church made sure that there was support for Dr. Ainor Fergusson at the eye hospital. Other people have given portable typewriters that are manual because of the uncertain supply of electricity. Steve and Linda Lovrien have given support to pastors. Allan Schoening's metal working expertise has kept our machines in repair. Frames and lenses to provide glasses for indigent patients were made available by Gary and Marilyn Threlkeld.

The Lions, through Al Nelson, have supplied thousands of glasses and cases. One doctor, an ophthalmologist who heads the international volunteer surgery program, Dr. Yale Solomon, upon learning of the $100,000.00 damage to the eye hospital in the recent civil war, pulled out his American Express card and conducted me to exhibit booths for a shopping tour of ophthalmoscopes, surgical and refractive instruments amounting to over $9,000.00. Zeiss optics have made available sophisticated operating microscopes. Alcan has annually donated medicines and supplies worth $20,000 or more. Allergan, Helen Keller Worldwide, Brothers Brother, and Interchurch Medical Assistance have been supportive. Northwest Medical Teams International through the interest shown by Carrie Gess have shared valuable eye medicines and supplies. Furnishings were supplied by the Carrie Park May Fund of Steelton, Pennsylvania. Ms. Kate Tiedemann and Michael Vedral at Katena have donated instruments which can be found in many of the countries in which I have done volunteer eye surgery. Storz and Dr. Luther Fry have made available instruments. Mr. Bruce Perkins also donated beautiful stainless steel instruments as far back as 1957 with the encouragement of his pastor, the Rev. John Paul Jones, serving at that time in Toledo, Ohio.

"Twice in recent years the Christmas reunion of the Wolf clan in Nerstrand, Minnesota, with the encouragement of Opal and Elizabeth Wolf, has made generous individual contributions to the Kissy UMC Eye Hospital instead of giving gifts to each other. For many years the Nerstrand, Paynesville, and Alexandria Sunday Schools and congregations have faithfully remembered the Kissy eye program with donations. Persistent prayer support was always assured by life long friends, Orlando and Lenora Tesch, and by my Aunt Sadie Fisher, who sweetened our furlough returns by treating us to banana splits."

In the wake of the $119,000 war damage suffered by the Kissy UMC Eye Hospital, Bishop John L. Hopkins was led to challenge pastors and churches to underwrite the cost of restoration. One thousand five dollar bills were distributed at the Minnesota Annual Conference in May, 2001, as seed money for fund raising projects that might be blessed twenty fold.

It is serious to have so many people trust us to see that their prayers are answered in their concern for needy eye patients, especially those blind who can be sprung into a new life of independence and productivity by a half hour's surgery involving a cataract extraction with intraocular lens implantation. Kiwanis, Rotary, as well as the Lions have been involved in these ministries. We are proud to represent them and do the actual laying on of hands in helping needy people. While eyes may focus on us, we are quick to acknowledge that we have been, and are, supported by others. There was no such intention of "going it alone." It is with all the sincerity that we can summon that we thank these helping hands in the thrilling life of ministry that has been given to us.

Being able to experience the exploits described in this book does not make Ruth and me any more important than the many prayer warriors who support us. In fact without their silent, solid support, spiritually and financially, we would not have been able to even venture forth to fulfill the Lord's mandate to assist the sick and the blind or to hear statements like the blind man in John 9:25, "Now I see," or to have known people like the two blind men in Matthew 20:34 who after "their eyes received sight, followed him."

Epilogue

Dedication to Ruth

My dearest, please hear me while there is yet life and breath.

I thank God that out of all the world we found each other and that we had the privilege of growing in our love, which has gotten better and sweeter with the passing years. I love you more today than ever before.

Besides being the love of my heart, in all your winsome ways, you have been an ideal mother as well as wife.

You were willing to leave the country of your birth to share your and my calling to a healing ministry in the name of Jesus Christ. It has been such a joy to bring people new sight and insight into the love of God through our work from day to day.

Our children could have had no more wonderful a mother than you. You were there for them from their earliest years when they reached out their hands and hearts. They knew security and understanding.

It may have taken a little longer to the do the baking with all those little "helping" hands, but you were not only fashioning a cake, you were helping to mold precious lives.

As the Lord continued to open new doors to us, you simply bundled the family together and we took off for Africa where we were to spend the best part of our lives. You always made do whether it was as teacher to our children or whether it was the making of clothes or the sifting of little visitors out of our flour.

You were a nurse administrator par excellence, with an uncanny intuition in understanding the character of staff applicants.

Above all, you made things happen ... a true helpmate!!!

Never once did I hear you complain that I wasn't doing my best to make provision for you...even when our annual income was less than $3000 for a family of six. We were immensely rich spiritually.

For all these blessings I am deeply grateful. You have blessed me in a way I never thought possible.

We look to the Lord for His continued leadership and grace in the days that He yet allows us together, for we hold to the promise that we are *"heirs together of the grace of life"* ***1 Peter 3:7***

I am happy that it was possible to give this tribute while you were still able to appreciate and comprehend it. You need to know of my deep love for you as well as our children. You have exemplified the commendation of Jesus...You have done *"what you could."* ***Mark 14:8***

God uniquely created you.
Your husband, children, grandchildren,
and all your friends and patients thank God for your wonderful and long life.

Ruth, you and I have enjoyed recalling past memories and experiences, but encouraged by the apostle Paul,

"We are forgetting those things which are behind, and reaching forth unto those things which are before, {We} press toward the mark for the prize of the high calling of God in Christ Jesus" ***Phil 3:13-14***

It is still our firm conviction that:

We face a humanity too precious to neglect
We know a remedy for the ills of the world too wonderful to withhold
We have a Christ who is too glorious to hide
We have an adventure that is too thrilling to miss.

Fifty Year Tribute To Lowell

To Lowell, My Dear Husband:

I was really touched as I read your tribute to me on our 50thWedding Anniversary. I feel that my reading of your Curriculum Vitae and list of professional awards was not sufficient to pay tribute to you as an outstanding example of a Christian husband, lover and companion.

In the early years of our marriage when you were so involved with your medical training, I was happy to devote myself to you and our children, and because I came from a frugal background, I cheerfully accepted our limited resources. (You know that I still find it difficult to spend money.)

I must admit that leaving my country and my people was not easy, but the sense of God's calling was very real. It was a joy to become your partner in many ways, as wife, mother of our children, nurse, teacher, administrator, secretary, and partner in sharing the Good News of the Gospel. I was never concerned about our meager income during years of training and serving in West Africa. We often had more than those around us.

I really admire you for your careful, conscientious, yet brave ventures in ophthalmology, which have proven beneficial to so many in Africa, the Orient and here in the United States.

The Lord knew us better than we knew ourselves, and our being together happily for 50 years is His great gift to us!

I LOVE YOU and I'm grateful for every day He allows us together.

"Heirs together of the grace of life." ***1 Peter 3: 7***

Your Loving Wife,

Ruth

Statement of Belief, Ruth

I believe in God as the creator and sustainer of the universe. I believe in Him as a personal, loving Father, forgiving, healing and reconciling. I believe His plan is for full and abundant life for all of His creatures, and I believe that people are continually being brought into a new relationship with Him through Jesus Christ. I believe Christ showed us by His life and teachings what God was really like, and taught us how God wanted us to live. I believe that His life and His death on the cross reconciles us to God. My response to Christ has been, and is constantly, an inviting of Him into my heart and life, that He may live in and through me.

Prayer is an exciting and living experience to me. I am always anxious to be a part of small prayer groups, which are a blessing to me. I treasure the Bible, because in it I learn of God's ways and of his promises and demands upon us. Only through this book do I have contact with the earthly life of Jesus, His followers, and the early church. I believe God speaks to us through the Bible.

I believe that the community of believers, the church, is Christ at work in the world today. We are "ambassadors for Christ" in seeking to bring people back into friendship with God. However, I do feel that as times and cultures and customs change we must adapt our methods and ways of expressing the unchanging love of God.

In person-to-person relationships I feel called to love and to care, and to have honesty and integrity in all my living. I feel we are called as Christians to fight intolerance, injustice, racism, indifference, and violence itself, by being actively involved in the political and public structures of our society, that all may have equal opportunity to enjoy and benefit from the plenty that is available.

I respect others of non-Christian faiths. However, I believe that Christ was unique, and the most complete expression of God that man can know. I would seek to understand their faith and way of life, that I might confirm them in the truth they understand and help them to enlarge their understanding of God.

I believe that God's intention for humanity is that a full, creative, meaningful, and abundant life may be experienced, and I feel that this life is possible for every person, especially as they come to know God's forgiveness and love, which he revealed to us in Jesus Christ.

I believe that "word" and "deed" are inseparable in God's intention. I believe we are called as Christians to good works, but then to be ready always to tell of the *"hope that is within you"* (1Peter 3:15), that the thanks and glory may be God's.

I believe, however, that we are justified before God by faith, and that our deeds are the outcome of a love relationship that exists between God and us, which can only find expression in our love and concern for others, as so beautifully expressed in Matthew 25:40 NEB *"anything you did for one of my brothers here, however humble, you did for me."*

I am a Registered Nurse, and hope to continue to use these skills in our Kissy UMC Eye Hospital. I also hope to help build bridges of understanding between the people from different backgrounds. I hope to be a link between the church in the U.S. and the church in Africa. During our married life we have lived in rural areas, in urban ghettos, in suburbia and on the mission field in Africa. I believe I can continue to work in each area, but in view of our years in West Africa feel drawn to continue our involvement there.

Statement of Belief, Lowell

To try to match Ruth's "statement of belief" would reveal a stark inadequacy.

The Apostle's Creed serves as an all encompassing statement of my belief:

I believe in God the Father Almighty,
Maker of heaven and earth. And in Jesus Christ, his only Son,
our Lord; who was conceived by the Holy Spirit, born of the virgin Mary;
suffered under Pontius Pilate; was crucified, dead and buried. The third
day he rose from the dead; he ascended into heaven;
and sitteth at the right hand of God, the Father Almighty;
from thence he shall come to judge the quick and the dead.
I believe in the Holy Spirit; the holy catholic Church;
the communion of saints; the forgiveness of sins;
the resurrection of the body and the life everlasting.
Amen.

God's will for my life, as with Ruth, was to make known the Gospel of God's love as revealed in Jesus Christ and to bring people to God through Him, whom to know is life eternal. I wanted to share the Lord Jesus Christ as Savior rather than truth or healing that is not redemptive. I entered my field as a medical missionary because I felt a "call" to that specific mission. Important to me is, Mark 16:15 ...

"Go into all the world and preach the good news to all creation" **NIV**

Ruth was trained as a nurse before our marriage. I had seminary training, but I still felt called to include medicine as a method for sharing the Gospel.

For me, being a missionary is being obedient to Christ's command *"You will be witnesses for me . . . to the ends of the earth."* **Acts 1:8. KJV**

It was my desire to share Christ as a solution to the world's need.

The immediate appeal of suffering tugged at my heart. Christ had compassion on those in need, and healed all manner of diseases of mind and body.

I am constrained to follow Him as best I can.

I believe we build schools, churches, hospitals not only to make Christians out of non-Christians, but because we cannot be Christian without sharing them.

I am persuaded that one does not throw away one's life by losing it in service, but rather finds it in the natural expression of the will of God.

We preach not only to bring people to the Lord Jesus Christ, but because we cannot help but share with others the overflow of our own abundant faith for victorious living.

We go to needy places in response to Christ's command, *"Heal the sick....say, the Kingdom of God is come near you."* **Luke 10:9 KJV**

We go to foreign fields, not to be Christian by making Christians... but to make Christians by being Christian.

I am convinced that merely the maintenance of life is not important. It is important to remain faithful. As a missionary, I seek to identify myself with the needs of people.

Our hearts are moved by the great need of the neglected poor. We believe we have the solution in Jesus. We cannot deny them the chance for newness of life. II Corinthians 5:17, *"If anyone is in Christ, he is a new creation; old things have passed away; behold, all things have become new."* NKJV.

It is thrilling to be present when blind patients experience new sight. They can hardly contain their joy ... "Thank God I can see"... a joy that is vicariously experienced by each member of the staff.

There is similar appreciation for the proper fitting of glasses that enables patients to read and see the world.

Also there is the prevention and treatment of glaucoma and other sight endangering diseases, such as trachoma and onchocerciasis, known as river blindness.

As Christian missionaries, we are especially thrilled when because of the eye ministry, patients gain insight into the love of God as revealed in Jesus Christ.

We cannot miss such a wonderful opportunity for the fulfillment of their lives as well as our own.

To such a service of love I am willing to sacrifice friends, comforts, and if need be, life itself.

Midnight Convictions

On the way to Zing in 1999 I was cordially entertained at the Jos Rest House by Jim and Bernice Keech. After an evening meal, I slipped away for an intended night's sleep.

I dropped into a deep sleep at 9 p.m. but was wide awake at midnight. Even after enjoying "Twenty Hymn Classics, Volume 1" on my stereo headset, it was evident that sleep was not forthcoming. The messages of the hymns flooded my mind. I replayed some. Suddenly I realized that my hands were raised and audibly I was giving praise to God. The words that came out were Psalm 8:

"Oh Lord, our Lord, how excellent is thy name in all the earth! Who hast set Thy glory above the heavens. Out of the mouth of babes and sucklings hast Thou ordained strength because of thine enemies, that Thou mightest still the enemy and the attacker. When I consider Thy heavens, the work of Thy fingers, the moon and the stars, which Thou hast ordained; what is man that Thou art mindful of him? And the son of man, that Thou visitest him? For Thou has made him a little lower than the angels and hast crowned him with glory and honor. Thou madest him to have dominion

over the works of Thy hands; Thou has put all things under his feet; all sheep and oxen, yea, and the beasts of the field; the fowl of the air, and the fish of the sea, and whatsoever passeth through the paths of the seas. Oh Lord, our Lord, how excellent is Thy name in all the earth!"

What a joy to be able to serve Jesus Christ by serving others. The restoration of physical sight was important, but so much more the sharing of insight into God's love as revealed in Jesus Christ.

In the night hours, I determined to be of as much help as possible to the eye program in Zing. I was happy that I had equipment that could provide for the best care of the patients. Also, I would have the opportunity of working with James Iorav, D.O. who was to be available to do some surgery at Zing during my stay there.

My thoughts then centered on Ruth. What a shame that she wasn't sharing this experience as we had done over the three decades of our missionary work and later on in our eye practice in Alexandria, Minnesota. I wondered how I could manage being away from her for three weeks. I looked forward to being with Ruth in Seattle at the ASCRS meeting during our visit with Paul and his family in the near future. Also there was to be the visit with Beth and her family in Anchorage, Alaska. Perhaps the trip to Maua, Kenya, should be postponed for awhile even though it might mean a loss of a large portion of the invested ticket.

My thoughts then swept to Garrett Evangelical Theological Seminary and the alumni award coming in June. It would be a nice event, but even more enticing would be an invitation from President Fisher for a chapel speaking engagement someday. I would like to address the students in training, as I remember the impact of a speaker during my seminary days who left an indelible impression on me with his simple testimony of being called "to preach Christ."

I have paid my dues:

1. The response to the call to medical missions.
2. The thirty years of academic training.
3. The overseas ministry spanning four decades which involved Ruth and our six children.

I would like to challenge the seminary students that it is first and foremost a commitment to Jesus Christ as Lord for the doors of service to open. In my youth we sang this meaningful hymn: "It may not be on the mountain height, or over the stormy sea, it may not be at the battle's front my Lord will have need of me; but if, by a still small voice he calls, to paths that I do not know, I'll answer, dear Lord, with my hand in thine, I'll go where you want me to go... I'll go where you want me to go, dear Lord, over mountain, or plain, or sea; I'll say what you want me to say, dear Lord, I'll be what you want me to be."

In the quiet of my room, in the middle of the night, in far off Jos, Nigeria,I determined that the quality of service that I would be privileged to render would always be of the best. Anything less would not do. It would not be fair to the Gospel. If we have the best Gospel, only the best and most skilled service will do.

There is good news and bad news in all of this. The bad news is that heaven cannot be attained with brownie points. The good news is that heaven is available to anyone, everyone, through faith. Faith in the Lord Jesus Christ. Believe on the Lord Jesus Christ...and there is salvation.

We are not thinking of our seminary as holding to a unitarian emphasis where one can only use "God" in prayers and challenges. We are in the Wesleyan tradition: God...Jesus Christ...Holy Spirit. Empowering is through the Holy Spirit. You plant... conversion and consecration is of the Holy Spirit.

I have had my ups and downs spiritually. In seeking the answers to my questionings and doubts I did what I could. I majored in psychology and philosophy at Macalester college. Socrates, Plato, Aristotle and the others left their marks. But it was a project in seminary that was life determining in my faith. I researched a paper on the factors that led to the conversion of Augustine. He had come out of a sensuous past. He realized the urgency of his mother's prayers for his salvation. A dear friend of his in his dying moments reached out to the Christian faith. A Scriptural passage to which he, by accident, opened as recorded in Romans 13: 13-14, *"Not in rioting and drunkenness, not in chambering and wantonness, not in strife and envying; but put ye on the Lord Jesus Christ and make not provision for the flesh to fulfill the lusts thereof,"* made a final impact. Augustine needed to read no more, for instantly as the sentence ended it were as a light or a security that came into his heart and all the gloom of doubt vanished away. It is well known in history what this saving experience in the life of Augustine meant to the early church. His was a new and redeemed life.

With this background it can safely be said that it is important not just to read the Word. It is important to preach it, rather than expound on one's own thoughts on the matter. There is to be reason, yes; experience, yes; tradition, yes; Scripture: by all means! Reason can be manipulated. It can be faulty. Experience can be doing the same thing incorrectly over and over again. Tradition can stifle new advances. The church was wrong...Galileo was right. As far as Scripture is concerned... this is the authority that is needed to preach the Word. It will inspire even those who are not great preachers by simply letting the words of Scripture be accountable in that hour. Preaching the word in season and out is the mandate of the clergyperson.

The place of prayer in all of this must not be minimized. Before doing any eye procedure over the last four decades I have prayed with the patient, for healing, for the ministry of those caring for the patient's needs. This I have done more than 15,000 times. With prayer in one's heart and the Bible in one's hand it is impossible not to succeed to help and bless. It was Jesus who said in Mark 16:15-18 *"Go into all the world and preach the good news to all creation. Whoever believes and is baptized will be saved, but whoever does not believe will be condemned. And these signs will accompany those who believe; in my name they will drive out demons; they will speak in new tongues; they will pick up snakes with their hands; and when they drink deadly poison it will not hurt them at all; they will place their hands on sick people, and they will get well."*

It is appropriate that I recount a sermon that was preached at the Evangelical Theological Seminary when I was a student back in 1942-1945. I have no idea who the preacher was. His central theme was "Jesus." Seminary students come from many different countries. Their backgrounds are very different. Certainly the cultures are different, but there is one common element and that is "our love and loyalty to Jesus Christ...Savior." This was not only for the Jews first but also for the Gentiles. It was for black, white, yellow, and brown.

Going to seminary involves different motives. Some attend seminary because a degree is needed for leadership in the church. All want to sharpen their skills in sharing the Gospel. There are those who want to reach a certain class of intellectuals in the congregation which calls for sophisticated techniques. There is no way that we can match the intellectual background and capacity of all of our parishioners. It behooves us that we are solidly planted in the important aspect of being a pastor... that is, a pastor in ministry. We can only credibly stand up to our parishioners and be intellectually respectable and rationally justifiable as we are being led by the Holy Spirit. As the disciples were assured... it will be given you in that hour what you are to say. The background, however, is paying the price for complete surrender to the Holy Spirit and careful preparation in the ordinary things. The Old and New Testaments need to be mastered as well as the other courses in seminary. Homiletics helps in learning the most persuasive way of imparting the Gospel. It is important that grammar be given its due importance. A pastor can lose his audience by incorrectly using such simple things as pronouns after prepositions...it is not "between him and I"..."it is between him and me!"

What is prayed for is a conversion experience, an enlightenment, a sudden awareness of the majesty of God. We can be impressed by the extent of the universe. But the only real clue we have to God is in the revelation of His love and person through Jesus Christ. "The Father and I are one," the Scriptures enjoin us. "No one has seen the Father but through me." A magnificent sunset, beautiful mountains, expanses of grain and corn, the vastness of the sea, ...these help inspire. However, they certainly did not prompt early Christians to face the wild beasts in the amphitheater. The apostles based everything on Jesus. Paul admitted he knew nothing in his preaching but Christ Jesus. People approach truth in different ways...Pilate uttered the famous question "What is truth?" Philosophers down through the ages have immersed their lives in that pursuit.

I thought it would be a good thing to be knowledgeable about what had been discerned by the best minds. I was anxious to learn from the great philosophers of the past as well as from those of recent times such as Kierkegaard. However, it was during the early morning dawn on Lake Geneva, Wisconsin, that all that is relevant finally came down to the Christ of the Scripture. Not Scripture per se. It was the Christ of the Scripture. This freed me from seeming inconsistencies so boldly brayed by the doubters and unbelievers. The Bible contains 39 Old Testament books and 27 New Testament books. We cannot be sure how many authors are involved. The theology of some is radical... hard to understand, seemingly inconsistent. Not so with the person and work of Jesus Christ. No one censures Jesus (apart from his contemporaneous scribes and Pharisees). You never hear someone decrying Jesus Christ as a bad person. The Christ of the Scriptures is inviolate.

In my thinking, it is important to stick to essentials. I want to be careful about expositions that are pet subjects. I want to avoid the politically acceptable harangues, the fine points of sensual orientations, the outlines of what will happen, and when it will end. We know how it is going as we see the moral degradation of our country and world. We are not to avoid really important questions such as the question the lawyer asked of Jesus, *"What must I do to inherit eternal life?"* Luke 10:25 It is important for people to know. They want to know about heaven and how to get there. Jesus threw the question back to the lawyer for the answer and received the correct one when the lawyer said, *"Thou shalt love the Lord thy God with all they heart, soul, mind and strength and thy neighbor as thyself."* And when the lawyer asked who his neighbor might be, Jesus took the occasion to give the parable of the Good Samaritan and the compassion that was evidenced. And so in the final analysis when Jesus asked, "Who now of these three thinkest thou was neighbor to him who fell among thieves?" The lawyer said, "He who showed mercy." The response of Jesus to him was, "Go and do thou likewise."

We don't send missionaries into the world to make Christians out of non-Christians. We send missionaries to make Christians by being Christian. We don't build hospitals, schools, churches, to make Christians out of non-Christians. We do this because we cannot be Christian without providing schools and churches and hospitals. Jesus preached as no one else ever has preached. He taught as no one else has ever taught. He healed in miraculous ways. He lived with people. He loved with a matchless love. He shared. That's the word... He shared all that he had with others. I suppose that if you and I preached, taught, healed, lived, loved, and shared, and if we did this long enough, heaven would come to earth. However, we have been trying this for 2000 years and the world still is unredeemed. This is because the way of love is the way of the cross. There is no other way. When we realize that in spite of all the wonderful preaching and teaching and healing and living and serving and sharing that Jesus did, it meant the way of the cross for him to really become the Savior of the world. Does that mean that we have to die? It does for some. A friend of mine in Sierra Leone, a pastor, was killed because he was preaching in an area that was violent and did not accept the challenges of the Christian message. It may not mean that we have to be killed in body. What it does mean is that we may have to be willing to be humble rather than great, to live in ordinary circumstances rather than in luxury, to be willing to let go being the president of a company, a famous person, a politician, or one wielding great power and still be willing to serve in the name of Christ in a way that is lowly. I don't mean to infer that all of us have to die the way of the cross as Jesus died, but we are being asked to die to our own needs, our own wants, our own wishes, and to consider God with all our strength, mind, and power, and our neighbors as ourselves. We face a humanity that is too precious to neglect. We know a remedy for the ills of the world that is too wonderful to withhold. We have a Savior who is too glorious to hide. I believe that this is an adventure that is too thrilling to miss.

The entire night was spent recording these thoughts.

With the dawn, preparations were made for the final eight hour trip to Zing on hot and occasionally dusty roads rather than an enjoyable and comfortable flight in Jim Keech's aiplane. There was an acute shortage of aviation fuel in Nigeria, the country which supplies one third of all the USA's fuel needs.

Before dark, we safely reached Zing.

I look forward to a safe arrival in the mansion prepared for "believers" as promised in John, Chapter 14. I am not troubled because I believe in God and the Lord Jesus Christ. Human and medical "challenges" will no longer be in my hands. To be with Him will complete my journey.

Appendices

History, Sierra Leone

Contentment is Great Gain, a gripping account written by talented missionary nurse-midwife, Lois Olsen, contains a chapter beautifully and briefly describing the history of Sierra Leone and the Church. She graciously agreed to allow her research to be used again for another audience.

She writes:

"Sierra Leone is a small country on the west coast of Africa. During the fifteenth century, the Portuguese, encouraged by Prince Henry the Navigator, sailed along the west coast of Africa; the first Europeans to make this adventuresome journey.

The first Portuguese ship anchored in the estuary of the Rokel River in 1447. This river forms the northern boundary of the peninsula on which the current city of Freetown is located. In 1462, Pedro da Centra named the peninsula Serra Lyoa, from which the current name of the country is derived, probably because the hills in the center of the peninsula resembled lions.

Although the early Portuguese carried slaves and gold to Europe, Sir John Hawkins was the first Englishman to conduct a slaving voyage to Sierra Leone in 1562. The English continued to dominate the slave trade, although other Europeans were also involved in the transportation of slaves from the area until the British outlawed the slave trade in 1807.

In a 1772 landmark decision, the English chief justice ruled that a slave could not be forcibly removed from England. This resulted in a measure of freedom for slaves in England. In 1787, the first group of about 400 "Black Poor" was sent to Sierra Leone. The group also included about 60 white women and a few white men. In 1792, the new settlement was named Free Town. This changed to Freetown in 1792 by the settlers from Nova Scotia. In 1791, a private company, the Sierra Leone Company with headquarters in London, took over the administration of the area and it became a British colony.

The next black settlers arrived from Nova Scotia in 1792. They had been slaves in the United States and had been set free at the time of the American War of Independence. Some of them had fought as members of the British Army and were no longer welcome in the United States and so settled in Nova Scotia. They had appealed to the Sierra Leone Company which offered them land in Free Town. They were Christians and brought their churches with them: Methodist and Baptist. Some of them also brought with them an obscure sect of Christianity called the Countess of Huntingdon Connection. The Countess of Huntingdon had been the leader of a group of Anglicans in England who had separated from the Church of England, much as had the Methodists. Her movement had quickly spread to the American colonies and was found among the Nova Scotia settlers.

A third group of settlers was the Maroons. Originally, they had been slaves in Jamaica. After a slave revolt, they were captured and shipped to Nova Scotia. They suffered from the bitter cold weather and asked to be sent to Africa. They arrived in Freetown in 1800.

In 1807 the British government passed the Abolition Act which made slave trading illegal for British citizens. In 1808 the British up-graded Freetown to a British Crown Colony. The British Navy began to capture ships carrying slaves. Instead of returning the captives to the country of their origin, they brought the slaves to Freetown. By 1815 over 6,000 were settled there.

In 1804, the Church Missionary Society, (CMS) a Church of England institution, sent out two missionaries. The strong Christian influence of the early settlers encouraged the captives to adopt Christianity. Although the captives came from numerous language backgrounds, English soon became the common language. Many people also adopted English names. The settlers blended into a single group called Creoles. Today, the term Krio is the commonly accepted spelling.

The Krios were, and still are, separate and distinct from the indigenous people of Sierra Leone. Although much of the Krio culture was European based: clothing, houses, and religion, there were certain distinguishing characteristics that separated them from their western origins. The Krios, from the beginning, wore European-style clothing: coats, trousers, and top hats for the men; dresses and feathered hats for the women. Although rice was the staple food for both Krios and indigenous people, certain dishes were a feature of Krio menus: Jollof rice (rice cooked in a tomato sauce); foofoo (boiled and fermented cassava root); and palaver sauce (a peppery stew of greens served over rice).

But the outstanding feature was their language. Although English provided the base, words and phrases from many languages were grafted in. For example, the verb "sabby," to know, is from the Portuguese "sabeir" while "borku," meaning much, is from the French "beaucoup." Some phrases were direct translations from indigenous languages. For example, an angry person is told "Cool your heart," which is a translation from a Mende phrase. A distinctive grammar and vocabulary evolved. For instance, the English sentence "This is the man," in Krio becomes "Nar de man dat." Krio is a common language in Sierra Leone and its use has spread along the coast and is used in Ghana and Nigeria.

In 1896, the British Governor, Frederic Cardew, declared the rest of the country to be a British Protectorate while the peninsula remained a British colony. The Protectorate was organized into five districts, each governed by a British District Commissioner. Districts were divided into chiefdoms, administered by elected indigenous chiefs.

The use of imported administrative officials meant that expenses increased. To meet the cost of the new administration, Governor Cardew imposed a hut tax in 1898. Each house owner was to pay a tax to the government. The tax was exceedingly unpopular. The resentment of the tax, plus the animosity against the government, when they lost their independence to the authority of British administrative officers, was a major impetus that led the people of the Protectorate to declare war on the British government.

During the first months of 1898, sporadic fighting broke out over the whole of the Protectorate. On April 27, a mass rebellion erupted. The uprising was carefully planned by the chiefs and covered the entire Protectorate. The plan was to destroy all Europeans, all Krios, and all government servants. This was extended to anyone who had learned to speak English or who had adopted a European life-style. One historian states that the common statement was "Every man in trousers, every woman in a dress."

The rebellion was soon overturned. The British army, along with a contingent of local troops, advanced through the country. The army soon captured those towns that were of strategic importance, where a powerful chief held authority. This included Rotifunk. In Tiama, a tall, thick wall with a moat in front of it, surrounded the town on three sides. Unable to scale the wall, the army attacked the town from the unprotected bank of the river and Tiama was captured.

The British government enacted swift retribution for the rebellion. Chiefs, in particular, were singled out for arrest and punishment. The historian Fyfe, reports that 96 people were hanged. After the rebellion, the British government consolidated its hold over the country and the number of Europeans in administrative authority was increased.

Following the rebellion, there was consistent development. From 1800 to 1961, the government and the Krios made education a high priority. Christian missionary organizations established a number of schools. The CMS started the Grammar School and the Annie Walsh Memorial School; the Wesleyan Methodist Society established the Methodist Boys High School in 1874 and a girls school in 1880. In 1827 the CMS founded the Christian Institute of Fourah Bay which in 1848 became Fourah Bay College.

A number of Krios went to study in Britain. The first barrister, John Thorpe, a Maroon, qualified in 1850, and James Africanus Horton became the first western-trained doctor in 1859. Samuel Adjai Crowther, the first registered student at Fourah Bay, qualified as the first Anglican Bishop in 1864. Samuel Lewis became the first Sierra Leone Knight in 1896 and was the first to be granted Cambridge and Oxford degrees.

Krio influence extended throughout all of West Africa. Krios were ubiquitous traders, but they were also missionaries, educators, and engineers and were involved in the legislatures of the British West African colonies. Fourah Bay College became the center of learning for the West Coast.

Although control of the country was firmly in the hands of the British authorities, there were some small efforts to involve local people in the governing process. In 1924 a new constitution provided for a Legislative and Executive Council. The Legislative Council of 22 members had eight Africans, three of them elected and five members appointed by the governor.

The Protectorate Assembly was organized in 1946. This was a central representative body which allowed the people a voice in Protectorate matters. It was still under the authority of the Legislative Council. Eventually, some of these elected members were given responsibilities for government ministries. In 1954, one of these men, Dr. M.A.S. Margai, became the Chief Minister and later Prime Minister.

After World War II, the British colonies throughout the world intensified their demands for independence. In most British colonies, Britain granted these demands with few objections. In West Africa, there was no armed struggle such as occurred in Kenya with the Mau Mau Opposition. In Africa, the Gold Coast was the first and became the country of Ghana in 1957. Sierra Leone celebrated its independence on April 27, 1961.

The United Brethren Church

The first missionaries of the United Brethren Church (UBC) came to Sierra Leone in 1855. Instead of settling in Freetown, they moved south along the Atlantic Coast and settled in Shenge. Prior to their arrival, work had been established by the American Missionary Association. Eventually, this association transferred all of its property to the UBC. The UBC extended their field of work beyond Shenge to Rotifunk in 1875 and later to Moyamba and Tiama. Although the UBC missionaries concentrated much of their work among the two largest ethnic groups in the Protectorate, the Mende and Temne people, they also established the King Memorial Church in Freetown. In 1904, they also opened a Boys' High School, the Albert Academy in Freetown. King Memorial had a Krio membership, but the Albert Academy was called the "Mende" school. The majority of the students came from outside the colony.

During the Hut Tax War, the UBC suffered much in the loss of missionary personnel, church members, hired workers, and property. The five missionaries living at Rotifunk were killed [see anecdote, "Martyrs"]. Rev. L.A. McGrew and his wife, Clara, who had been living in Tiama since January of 1898, were taken to a rock in the middle of the Teye River, were killed there and their bodies washed downstream.

After the rebellion was over, the UBC expanded all aspects of their work. New missionaries arrived and some who had been on furlough to the United States returned to continue their tasks. The UBC people, who placed a strong emphasis on education, developed numerous primary schools, usually staffed by local people. In addition to the Albert Academy, the Harford School for Girls was opened in Moyamba in 1898 and in 1937, became the first secondary school for girls in the Protectorate.

In 1904, evangelistic work was started in Jaiama in the Kono district near the border with French Guinea. In addition to the hospital at Rotifunk, the church started small clinics and maternity units at Jaiama, Tiama, and Manjama. Increasingly, local staff were in charge of all institutions. After independence, the Sierra Leone government ruled that all heads of schools had to be non-Europeans.

In 1946 the UBC and the Evangelical Church in the United States merged into one organization called the Evangelical United Brethren Church. This organization united with the Methodist Episcopal Church in 1968 and became the United Methodist Church (UMC). These changes, both in name and structure, were adopted by the church in Sierra Leone.

As the church expanded, the number and authority of the expatriate missionaries decreased and the church and its associated institutions were delegated to Sierra Leoneans. Much of this delegation was necessitated by the rapid growth of the church. Some of the delegation of authority came as both missionaries and Africans were aware of the need of the church to become autonomous and independent. The first African bishop was the Rev. B.A. Carew. Temne by birth, he lived in Mende country for many years and spoke a classical Mende. After Carew's retirement, the Rev. Thomas Bangura was elected bishop. In 1993, he was succeeded by the Rev. Joseph Humper.

Expatriots continued to perform the medical work except during the services of Dr. John Karefa-Smart and Dr. Moses Mahoi at Rotifunk. All of the medical institutions had Sierra Leone staff who worked under the supervision of the missionaries. For a short period of time, a school for midwives was established at Rotifunk. After graduation, these midwives were able to carry some of the responsibilities at the other clinics."[1]

The Amistad Saga

Although Shenge was the birthplace of the present United Methodist Church, emancipated Amistad captives were ministered to by committed Christians in 1842 in the Bonthe area as well. It was for the express purpose of serving the Amistad people that the Rev. and Mrs. William Raymond, two black American teachers and their wives, and the Rev. and Mrs. James Stick, sailed across the ocean in a ship named *Gentleman.*

The Rev. Walcott B. Williams' March 1, 1905, account (written nearly a century before Director Steven Spielberg's movie, Amistad) in *The Religious Telescope* is intensely interesting. He tells how in April, 1839, a vessel (*Tecorah*) with a cargo of Negroes who had been kidnapped in Africa, left that coast for the West Indies, and in the following July landed at a small village near Havana, Cuba. It is impossible to describe the hardships and sufferings of that weary, two-month's sea voyage. During the night and a large part of the day they were confined between decks scarcely four feet apart, without any beds but the bare planks of the deck, suffering from foul air, and excessive heat, from hunger and thirst, from seasickness and homesickness, ignorant as to their destination and their fate. Once or twice a day they were allowed upon the upper deck for a little fresh air, food and drink. Some days after their arrival near Havana, they were bought by two Spaniards, named Pedro Motez and Jose Ruis, and put on board the Spanish schooner *Amistad*, to be taken to plantations in the province of Puerto Principe, in Cuba. The cook on the vessel told them, jokingly, that when they reached their destination they were to be killed and eaten. This alarmed them greatly. Among the captives was an African chieftain named Singbe (Cinque),a man of giant frame and great physical courage. Among the goods on the vessel were a lot of large knives or machetes, used by the Cubans for cutting up cane. When they had been out four days, Singbe armed himself and some of his friends with these machetes, and killed the captain and some of the crew, and took possession of the vessel. Two of the crew escaped in a boat. The lives of the two Spaniards were spared. Singbe had noticed by the sun that the vessel had sailed westward from Africa, and compelled the surviving white men to work the vessel to the east, and he kept close watch to see that they did so; but he did not know how to use the compass, and in cloudy weather and in the night-time the vessel was turned northward, so that during August they had drifted to the east end of Long Island, and went ashore to get water. Their strange actions excited suspicion, and on the 25th of August, 1839, they were captured by Lieutenant Gedney, of the United States brig Washington, and taken into New London. When arrested the Negroes cried out, frantically, "Sierra Leone! Sierra Leone!" These were the only words they could use that were understood by their captors.

Judge Andrew T. Judson conducted an examination on board the Amistad. There were 43 Negroes in all, and among them were three little girls, a boy eight years old, and a cabin-boy named Antonio. The rest were young men who had been taken prisoners in war, though some had been kidnapped. They had belonged to different tribes in Africa, and had followed different occupations. Some were very bright and intelligent, others were stolid and brutish; but no one could understand their language so as to get their side of the story. A great number of legal questions arose at once in regard to the disposition of the vessel, the Negroes, and the cargo. Montez claimed four of the Negroes and part of the cargo as his property. Ruis claimed the rest of the Negroes with the exception of the cabin boy, Antonio, who belonged to the captain of the vessel. The Spaniards wanted the slaves delivered to them at once. Lieutenant Gedney wanted salvage on the vessel and cargo. It was finally decided that Singbe and 38 others should be tried for murder and piracy on the high seas, and they were sent to New Haven and put in jail.

The case attracted widespread interest in the country, and a few friends of the black men met in New York and appointed Lewis Tappan, S. S. Jocelyn, and Joshua Leavett a committee to secure funds and counsel for the prisoners. They employed Seth Staples and Theodore Sedgwick, of New York, and Roger S. Baldwin, of New Haven, to look after the legal questions involved.

It was of the utmost importance to find some one who understood the language of the prisoners, and who could act as interpreter. Professor Josiah Gibbs, of Yale College, visited them, and laying down his pennies, counted them as he laid them down, and so got them to count; thus he learned to count in Mende. Thus equipped he went to New York City, and going among the vessels, he found on a British war vessel a Negro named James Covey, whose countenance lighted up when he heard Professor Gibbs counting in the Mendi language. It seemed he had been stolen in Africa, and was sold to a Portuguese slave trader, which was captured by the British, and he had been sent to school in Sierra Leone, where he learned English, and found employment on this English war vessel. Captain Fitzgerald, learning the object of Professor Gibbs, kindly consented to let him go to New Haven as interpreter.

The courts finally decided that Lieutenant Gedney was entitled to salvage on the vessel and cargo, but not on the Negroes; that the cabin boy, Antonio, was born a slave, and must be returned to Cuba. The prisoners were acquitted of the charge of murder, and were free; but the Spaniards, assisted by the Spanish Minister at Washington, appealed from this decision to the Supreme Court of the United States. Between these two trials the Negroes were removed to a long building at Westville, about two miles from New Haven, where they were taught by Sherman Booth, a theological student, and others. It had been so confidently assumed by President Van Buren and the secretary of state that the decision of the District Court would give them up to the claimants, that a vessel was kept in readiness near at hand, on which they could be hurried at once, and returned to Cuba before their friends could appeal to the Supreme Court.

The case came before that court February 20, 1841, and was argued by Roger S. Baldwin and John Quincy Adams, and on the ninth day of March the court decided that they were unconditionally free. They were then taken to Farmington, Connecticut, until arrangements could be made to send them to Africa. Here they were domiciled in a large, new barn belonging to Mr. Austin F. Williams. The three little girls, Tay-Mi, Margru, and Kee-Ya, were taken into the families of three hospitable ladies. While they were in Farmington they were taught by Mr. Booth and by Rev. William Raymond and wife, and much interest was created in their behalf, and a conviction that some missionaries should go to Africa with them. Rev. James W. C. Pennington, pastor of the First Colored church in Hartford, called a meeting in his church, May 5, 1841, to consider a mission to Africa. A little later another meeting was called in Hartford to consider "a special mission to Africa." It appears that when the courts gave their final decision that the captives were free, there was still some money left in the hands of the committee, and it was determined to use this toward sending missionaries. Rev. William Raymond and wife volunteered to go with them as missionaries, and James Steele, a theological student at Oberlin, also the interpreter, James Covey, and Mr. and Mrs. Henry R. Wilson, colored members of Mr. Remington's church. Mr. Wilson was born a slave in the Barbadoes, and Mrs. Wilson was brought up in Brooklyn, Connecticut. We hear no more of them or of James Covey.

In order to interest people in the Negroes, and raise money for the mission, Mr. Booth took twelve of the brightest of them to New York, and held two great meetings in the Tabernacle; thence he went with them to Philadelphia, where they held three meetings, which were largely attended by the leading citizens. The chieftain, Singbe, spoke in his own language, and in describing the mutiny when the captain and cook were killed, he so excited the emotions of his hearers (though to the Americans it was only pantomime, as they could not understand a word he was saying) that the whole audience rose to their feet; and Mr. Booth adds, "It was the finest and most exciting exhibit of eloquence I have ever known." A farewell meeting was held in the Broadway Tabernacle, Sunday evening, November 21, 1841. The company had a tedious voyage, landing in Freetown January 15, 1842. Owing to wars among the petty tribes, it was found impracticable to reach the proper Mende country, and as some came from the Sherbro country, a site was selected on the little Boom River, about one hundred and fifty miles southeast of Freetown, Sierra Leone, and about forty miles from the coast, near a village named Kaw-Mendi.

On their arrival, they were received by King Henry Tucker. A great multitude of men, women, and children gathered around the new comers, for Mrs. Raymond was the first white woman they had ever seen.

The chieftain, Singbe, on his return to Africa, visited his people, and then came to the mission, and was married at the house of an old Mendian preacher, but turned out badly, and went to Jamaica. Why he went, and how long he remained is uncertain, but he did return to the vicinity of the mission. Rev. Albert Miller, who knew him, says: "He remained until death within the zone of the mission, but was never noted for his piety or fine ethical distinctions. He preferred his native dress and customs, yet was not prejudiced against Christianity, and sometimes acted as an interpreter for the missionaries. He lived in a rude, native hut, and there died in July, 1879, and was buried in the mission graveyard at Good Hope."

Margru (Sarah Kinson) returned to Africa with the other captives, in December, 1841 but in 1846 Mrs. Raymond found in necessary to come to this country on account of failing health, and brought Margru to Oberlin for further education; she remained there some three years, and in scholarship compared well with the white girls in her class. She rejoined the mission in February, 1850, and Mr. Thompson says "The meeting of Margru and Tay-Mi (the two Amistad girls) was a joyful one. They now met not only as former fellow-sufferers, but as sisters in the bonds of the gospel." From this we learn that Tay-Mi retained her connection with the mission as a Christian, but learn nothing more of her. We have not been able to discover any trace of the other little girl.

Margru proved to be a valuable teacher. After a time she married a trader named Green, but did not sever her relations with the mission. "One Sunday in March, 1854," Mr. Thompson says, "I called on Mrs. Green (Margru) to 'turn the Word'; she was diffident, and did not like to stand before the congregation, but yielded to my judgment and desire, and stood beside me on the platform, the best interpreter in the mission. She afterward interpreted for me when occasion required, and I was always glad to have her, as I could speak more freely." He also speaks of her very great kindness to his wife and children. She subsequently went up the river with her husband, and was taken sick and died.

In January, 1849, Mr. Thompson writes: "This evening my class was increased by four workmen, three of them Amistads. All Prayed, and most talked excellently; and in the following April all four of the Amistad captives were members of the church. Among these was probably the little girl, Tay-Mi, and also Kenna, who soon became his favorite interpreter, visitor, exhorter, counselor, and much beloved; and yet, later on, he wandered into sin, absented himself from meetings, traded on the Sabbath, and took other wives. Although he was most faithfully labored with, he had no satisfaction, but scoffed at divine things, and even whipped his wife for attending the meetings. As he proved to be incorrigible, he was finally excommunicated."

On one of Mr. Thompson's trips, he reached a town about nine o'clock at night, and the first man he met was Kale, one of the Amistads, who hastened to find him a place to sleep.

Some years later another kind-hearted, but impenitent former Amistad captive came to the missions, but none of the others were seen again. With this Rev. W. B. Williams ends his account.

Going back into the history of missionary endeavors in Sierra Leone it is reported that the English Church Missionary Society began sending out missionaries as early as 1802. Sierra Leone proved hazardous to their health and fifty three missionaries reportedly died within the first two or three decades. The Amistad Saga pointed up the intense mission activity and interest during the mid-nineteenth century. The author of the article on the Amistad included a listing of missionaries making the supreme sacrifice during and following the time of the Amistad story in the mid-nineteenth century.

About the year 1843, Miss Harnden went out, but was permitted to labor but a few months, when she died. Mr. Garnick reached the mission February 4, 1847, and died July 10, 1847; Rev. William Raymond reached the mission in February, 1842, and died November 26, 1847; Anson J. Carter reached it in July, 1848, and died eight days later. The first Mrs. Brooks died of African fever, in 1849, before reaching the station; Miss Joanna Alden died at the mission-house in Freetown, May 3, 1851, Mrs. Minerva Dayton Arnold died June 9, 1851, the same year that she arrived, and the next day Mrs. Elizabeth Tefft died. Rev. Mr. Condict reached the mission in 1854 and died April 24, of the same year; Rev. Matthew Mair went out in 1857, and died in Freetown before reaching the mission; Rev. Barnabus Root, a young colored minister of great promise, sailed in 1874, and died soon after; Rev. Franklin L. Arnold died in connection with the mission; James Cutler Tefft arrived in 1852, and died October 15, 1855. A second Mrs. Brooks also died in connection with the mission; also a Mrs. Miles, who died at Mo Tappan, and her husband, who died in England, on his way home. A Mrs. Whiton died at Good Hope in 1864; Mrs. Burton died on the way home, and was buried at sea. Mr. Winship died of African fever soon after reaching home, and Mrs. Jane Winters arrived at the mission in March, 1855, and died Mary 4, 1855, having been in Africa only two months.

With these sacrifices the Mende Mission was founded.

A More Recent History

Within a year of the earlier account by Ms. Olsen, the Hatfield-Archer Hospital at Rotifunk was destroyed in the present civil war conflict. It had had a proud history, at one time being one of the preeminent hospitals in the country. This was due largely to the skillful practice and presence of Dr. Mabel Silver. Other doctors following her who shared in this ministry were: Dr. Alvin French, Dr. Lowell Gess, Dr. George Harris, Dr. David Stephenson, and Dr. Donald Megill, brother of Ms. Esther Megill who served many years in the medical program while also doing educational projects. She also was to serve as the Board representative for West Africa for a period of time in the 1960s.

The nurses with whom I had the privilege of working in Sierra Leone were, without exception, deeply committed in their Christian calling to service in the name of Jesus Christ. All of their energies were poured into the care of desperate and needy people with whom, many times, they were not even able to speak to with a common language. Long periods of isolation severely tested them.

No doctor appointed by the General Board of Global Ministries has served in Sierra Leone since 1975. In 1983 the Kissy UMC Eye Hospital was built in Freetown and dedicated by the then President, Siaka Stevens, in 1984. The succeeding years have found 40 volunteer eye surgeons serving for periods of one to three months. Mrs. Lettie Williams has efficiently assumed the administrative role from the beginning. A Sierra Leonean ophthalmologist, Dr. Ainor Fergusson, joined the staff with a continuing presence since 1991. On the same Mango Brown Compound, the Kissy Health and Maternity Centre has made great strides in ministering to the sick and needy. Operation Classroom under the guidance of the Rev. Joe and Carolyn Wagner supplied a doctor in the person of Dr. Dennis Marke. While the initial vision of Bishop John Hopkins and others was to help in the classrooms, the challenges of clinics and the church eventually were included.

Sierra Leone, about the geographic size of South Carolina, with a 1999 estimated 5 million population, has white sandy beaches, mangrove swamps, jungles and bush areas extending into the expansive Savannah. It encompasses Mount Bintumani, which at 6390 feet, is the highest mountain in that part of West Africa. The country has rich stores of titanium ore, bauxite, iron ore, gold, chromite, and diamonds. At the present time only diamond mining continues.

The politico-historical events of recent years were aptly summarized in the Episopal Address to the One Hundred and Twenty-First Representative Session of the Sierra Leone Annual Conference of the United Methodist Church held on Tuesday, February 13, 2001, at Rogers Memorial United Methodist Church, Njagboima, Bo, by Rt. Rev. Dr. Joseph Christian Humper, Resident Bishop of the Sierra Leone area.

1970s: - President Siaka Stevens consolidates power through violence, corruption and intimidation, creating an Internal Security Unit with Cuban assistance, 1977 elections are rigged and marred by violence, after which Stevens declares a One-Party state.

1985: - The economy in ruins, Stevens hands over Government to former Army Chief, Joseph S. Momoh.

1990: - Momoh relaxes press restrictions; moves to re-introduce multiparty democracy; UNDP Human Development Report places Sierra Leone last out of 160 countries; Charles Taylor begins his war in Liberia; 30,000 Liberian refugees flee to Sierra Leone, ECOMOG is established with Freetown as the rear base.

1991: - Former army Corporal, Foday Saybana Sankoh on 23rd March leads the Revolutionary United Front (RUF) attack on Sierra Leone border towns (Bomaur) from Liberia; attack continues, marked by brutality against civilians; children are kidnapped and inducted into the RUF; Momoh doubles the army, recruiting hooligans, drug addicts and thieves and children.

1992: - ***April:*** A meeting by unpaid soldiers becomes a coup. Momoh flees; National Provisional Ruling Council (NPRC) assumes power under Captain Valentine Strasser (age 27); brutal war continues; RUF attacks target civilians. Their hallmark is crude amputations of feet, hands, lips, ears, noses—with special attention to women and children. When atrocities are committed by his followers, Sankoh does nothing to stop it. Two officers who object to torture and amputation are tried on trumped up charges and executed leaving Sankoh in undisputed leadership. 120,000 refugees flee to Guinea; widespread internal dislocation.

1993:- Kamajor (traditional hunters) militia begins fighting against RUF along with Republic of Sierra Leone Military forces (RSLMF) and ECOMOG: Rebel atrocities continue.

1994:- RUF overruns diamond areas, bauxite and titanium (Sierra

Rutile); economy essentially bankrupt; Freetown threatened. By now an estimated 50,000 have been killed and about half the country's 4.5 million people have been displaced.

1995:- ***February:*** NPRC employs Gurkha Guards for combat duty, but following setbacks they withdraw; ***May:*** Executive Outcomes (mercenaries from South Africa) contracted by NPRC; by June, the RUF is beaten back from Freetown and diamond areas liberated; rebel activities subside.

1996:- ***January:*** Palace Coup in which Julius Maada Bio replaces Strasser; Peace talks with RUF begins in Abidjan; Women take to the streets in support of elections;March: elections marred by RUF violence but reported to be otherwise free and fair by international observers; Ahmad Tejan Kabba becomes President; November 30th Foday Sankoh and Kabba sign a Peace Accord dubbed: ABIDJAN PEACE ACCORD.

1997:- ***May 25th:*** Dombolo-Day soldiers, (Junior army men) stage a coup, release 600 prison inmates (some die-hard criminals serving life imprisonment) and seize power, forming the Armed Forces Ruling Council (AFRC). Kabba flees. Major Johnny Paul Koroma, a former coup plotter, becomes Chairman and after forty-eight hours invites RUF to join the government. AFRC/RUF rule characterized by systematic murder, torture, looting, rape and shut-down of all formal banking and commerce throughout the country. ***October 23rd:*** an aborted Guinea Peace Accord crippled by AFRC.

1998: - ***February:*** ECOMOG under General Khobi, launches offensive on Freetown, driving the AFRC/RUF out of Freetown and power; President Kabbah returns from exile in Guinea. Sierra Leone armed forces disbanded. Towns and villages throughout the country experience continued attacks and extreme brutality from AFRC/RUF forces. July: Security Council creates UN Peacekeeping operation, UNAMSIL, and sends 40 military observers and later human rights observers. ***October:*** An estimated 10,000-12,000 ECOMOG troops continue to battle with AFRC/RUF. An estimated 800-1200 Nigerian soldiers killed and cost is estimated at $1 million per day. ***October:*** trials of soldiers and civilians result in death sentences for many, including Foday Sankoh. Attacks continue, RSLMF regroups.

1999: - ***January 6:*** Dombolo-Dooms Day: AFRC/RUF elements attack and enter Freetown resulting in two weeks of arson, terror, murder and dismemberment. Cabinet Ministers, journalists and civil servants are tortured and killed. Parts of the city razed; over 6,500 civilians are killed before ECOMOG pushes them back. 200 children are reported missing. ***February:*** Nigerian Presidential candidates agree that Nigeria should get out of Sierra Leone soon after Nigeria's return to civilian rule on May 29. The UN Security Council discusses Sierra Leone. July 7: Government of Sierra Leone (GOSL) concludes a negotiated peace agreement with the RUF, giving Foday Sankoh and several other RUF and AFRC leaders Cabinet positions. All RUF and AFRC leaders are given "blanket" amnesty. August: phased out Nigerian Troop withdrawal begins. ***October:*** UN Security Council approves a 6000 member peacekeeping force for Sierra Leone with authority to use force when required. ***December:*** Kenya and India contingents of the UNAMSIL peacekeeping force begin to arrive in Sierra Leone.

2000: – ***January-March:*** UN Security Council approves sending additional troops, Jordanian and Ghanaian troops join UNAMSIL. ***April:*** RUF atrocities intensify; brutal attacks continue. Westside Boys (Okra Hill) AFRC/RUF 'baranta." ***May 3:*** peaceful demonstration by women – Foday Sankoh refuses to see them. ***May 8:*** peaceful demonstration by population turns tragic, Foday Sankoh's boys open fire killing 26 demonstrators in all, Foday Sankoh in hiding; ***May 11:*** Foday Sankoh is spotted and arrested, he is then detained in solitary confinement; 121 other RUF high echelon and collaborators taken to Pademba Road maximum Prison. ***June:*** British paratroopers arrive in Sierra Leone to protect Lungi International Airport; helps to quell rebel atrocities; RUF seize UNAMSIL weapons and Armed vehicles; 500 UNAMSIL forces held hostage in Makeni and Kailahun; some 50 are released, ***July:*** UN Security Council sends 6000 more troops with mandate to use robust force. ***August:*** UNAMSIL on rescuer mission, rescues 241 UNAMSIL force held hostage in Kailahun; UN Security Council approves training 5 battalions – robust force; Endorses trial of Foday Sankoh and collaborators for crimes against humanity; a tribunal to be set up in one West African country; Obasanjo, Konare and Kabbah visit Sankoh; Sankoh no longer the leader of RUF: ***August:*** Issa Sesay appointed new leader of RUF. British army force abducted by Westside Boys; 5 are released; British paratroopers use force to rescue 5 British and 1 SLA solider when negotiations fail. ***September 3:*** RUF attack Guinea soldiers at Pamlap; President Conteh of Guinea orders removal of Sierra Leonean and Liberia refugees stranded in Guinea. President Kabah invites ECOWAS leaders to resolve border problem. They agree to send an observer group alone Guinea, Liberia and Sierra Leone borders. ***October-December:*** Struggle continues.

2001: – RUF involved with rebel forces in Guinea. Fighting continues to isolate Sierra Leonean and Liberian refugees especially in the "parrot beak" area creating the world's greatest humanitarian crisis; March: UNAMSIL troops arrive in RUF-held town of Lunsar with hope of consolidation of the cease-fire throughout the country; RUF makes political demands, especially calling for a new interim government.

During the closing months of 2001 the RUF became open to a political solution and the need for general elections. Disarmament was being carried out overseen by UNAMSIL forces. Prayers are for a peaceful Christmas 2001.

With the present socio-economic impact on the country, the church and other areas of ministries have been rendered non-functional. Congregations had to escape for their lives. Some found themselves in refugee and displaced camps, while others lost their lives. Pastors, evangelists, teachers, women's workers, nurses – all became part of the tragic consequences of war. Uprooted, they lost all of their little possessions – the Shepherd and the sheep were scattered with the exception of churches in cities like Bo, Kenema, Bonthe Sherbro, Moyamba (though Moyamba too went in the Diaspora for some time), and Freetown where the church doors remained open. And yet, in spite of this tragic picture, Bishop Humper's affirmation is that we cannot but raise our hearts and hands in praise to God for sustaining us and leading us and guiding us to continue in His service.

It is generally agreed that diamonds are at the root of much of Sierra Leone's troubles. Partnership Africa Canada reported early in 2000 that politics or ethnic conflict played a very small role in the decade long civil war which has caused more than 75,000 deaths, half a million refugees, and which has displaced half of Sierra Leone's 5 million people. The continuation of the war provides the opportunity for profitable crime under the cover of warfare. It has been important to certain interests that the rebels be supported and supplied in order to have access to the lucrative diamond mining and trading market.

It can be said that diamonds have fueled Sierra Leone's conflict, destabilizing the country for the better part of three decades, stealing its inheritance from past distinguished generations, and robbing an entirely new generation of children, putting the country last on the United Nations Development Program Human Development Index.

With respect to the diamond industry Bishop Humper suggests that no single recommendation alone will solve its multifarious and complex problems, but his 2001 Episcopal Address outlines comprehensive steps toward a solution.

In spite of the democratically elected government of President Ahmad Tejan Kabbah and the help of the United Nations, the neighboring West African countries in the ECOMOG alliance, and the western powers, a consensus emerges that peace and stability can only be realized when controls are imposed on the illegal selling of diamonds.

In the early months of 2001, the heavy presence of UNAMSIL troops especially in the Freetown area has allowed for some stability and safety. Non-government organizations are responding to the food and health crises. Worldwide interest and concern has centered on the plight of the thousands of amputees who lived through their ordeal. Non-government organizations including World Hope International have responded to the challenge of helping the victims regain a measure of independence and self sufficiency with the fitting of prostheses. An article by Orthopedist Craig D. Cameron as told to Susan Cameron appeared in the March/April, 2001, *Focus on the Family's Physician.*

Urgent prayers for peace continue. I believe the people of Sierra Leone have the moral fiber to achieve it.

[1] Lois Olsen, *Contentment is Great Gain*, (Milwaukee, 1996), pp. 16-21.

Curriculum Vitae of Lowell Arthur Gess, BD, MD

Lowell Arthur Gess was born July 13, 1921, in Paynesville, Minnesota. He attended a country school and the Salem Evangelical Church in rural Paynesville. Throughout his early years he participated in the camping program at Lake Koronis Assembly Grounds, becoming active in the Evangelical Youth Fellowship on a state and national level, and was also active in interdenominational Christian Youth Fellowship. His family moved to St. Paul, Minnesota, where he graduated from Central High School in 1938. He attended North Central College of Naperville, Illinois, for one year, but completed college at Macalester College, St. Paul, Minnesota. At the age of nineteen he was licensed to preach by the Minnesota Conference of the Evangelical Church, and served a rural church. He graduated from Macalester College in 1942 with a B.A. degree. He attended the Evangelical Theological Seminary at Naperville, Illinois, graduating with a B.D. degree in 1945. Shortly thereafter, he and Ruth Bradley, a R.N. from Winnipeg, Canada, were united in marriage.

Dr. and Mrs. Gess served the St. Cloud-Graham circuit and the Mayer Church, while completing his pre-medical studies. In 1947 he entered Washington University School of Medicine. He received a Jackson Johnson Scholarship, and a scholarship from First E.U.B. Church of Naperville, Illinois. Dr. and Mrs. Gess served a small Federated Church in East St. Louis, Illinois, for two years. For the last two years of medical training and internship at Ancker Hospital, St. Paul, they were placed under appointment by the Board of Missions of the Evangelical United Brethren Church.

In 1952 Dr. and Mrs. Gess and their family were appointed to the Bambur Hospital in Nigeria, where they served three years. On their return to this country he entered a surgical residency in Akron, Ohio, following which he was sent by the Board of Missions to Rotifunk, Sierra Leone, to establish a surgical program. During this period Dr. Gess became aware of the many people who were blind because of cataracts. In 1960 he was accepted into the ophthalmology residency programs at Washington University School of Medicine and the University of Minnesota Department of Ophthalmology. To be near his aging parents he trained at the University of Minnesota. In 1964 he returned to Sierra

Leone, and established an eye program at Taiama. In 1967 he went to Bismarck, North Dakota, working for the Quain and Ramstad Clinic as an ophthalmologist. Further postgraduate ophthalmological training was done in 1969 at Harvard. The General Board of Global Ministries of the United Methodist Church renewed Dr. and Mrs. Gess' missionary appointment in 1972. They were assigned to an eye ministry in Bo, Sierra Leone, for a three year period. He returned to private practice in Alexandria, Minnesota, and since that time has served the church in Sierra Leone as a volunteer medical missionary. During this period an eye program was established and the General Board of Global Ministries constructed a new hospital, the Kissy UMC Eye Hospital, to serve the eye needs in Sierra Leone.

Dr. Gess has been actively involved in the latest advances in the ophthalmological field, including intraocular lens implantation. He has designed and copyrighted his own intraocular lens. The program at the Kissy UMC Eye Hospital has made available this advanced surgical technology to the people in West Africa.

He has had the following Papers published:

1. Onchocerciasis in Sierra Leone, Africa, *The Sierra Leone Medical and Dental Bulletin*, Jan. 1974, Vol. 1 No. 2, pages 57-60

2. Granulomatous Dacyoadenitis caused by Schistosoma haematobium, *Archives of Ophthalmology*, Feb. 1977, Vol. 95, pages 278-280, Jakobiec, Gess, Zimmerman

3. Scleral Fixation for intraocular lenses. *American Intraocular Implant Society Journal*, Fall, 1983, Vol. 9 No. 4, Pages 453-456

4. Trabeculectomy with Iridencleisis, *British Journal of Ophthalmology*, Vol. 69, No. 12, pages 881-885, Dec. 1985

Dr. Gess delivered article #3 at the annual meeting of the American Intraocular Implant Society in New Orleans in 1983. He delivered article #4 at the annual meeting of the Welsh Cataract Surgical and Intraocular Lens Congress at Houston in 1980, and an updated rendition at the International Congress of Ophthalmologists in Cairo, Egypt, in February of 1984.

Dr. Gess is an honorary member of the Lions Club as well as Rotary.

He received the "Service to Mankind Award" from the Alexandria Sertoma Club in 1979, a Doctor of Humane Letters from Westmar College in 1985, the order of the Rokel for Distinguished Service from the Republic of Sierra Leone in 1991, a Distinguished Citizen Award from Macalester College in 1992, the Outstanding Achievement Award from the Vision Foundation of the University of Minnesota's Department of Ophthalmology in 1992, a Distinguished Humanitarian Service Award from the American Academy of Ophthalmology in 1993, the Alumni Achievement Award from Washington University School of Medicine in 1996, and the Distinguished Alumni Award in 1999 from Garrett Evangelical Theological Seminary, and the 2001 Christian Ophthalmology Society J. Lawton Smith Award.

Dr. Gess is an ordained minister and member of the Minnesota Conference of the United Methodist Church. He serves as an interpreter of the mission outreach of the church. He also serves the people of Sierra Leone as a volunteer ophthalmologist at the Kissy UMC Eye Hospital in Freetown. In recent years he has done teaching and demonstration surgery for extracapsular cataract extractions with intraocular lens implantation in Sierra Leone, Ghana, Nigeria, Kenya, Zambia, Zimbabwe, Mozambique, Malawi, Bolivia, Honduras, Haiti, Vietnam, China, and Mongolia.

Few joys match those which people experience when they are delivered from blindness.

"Inasmuch as you have done it unto one of the least of these my brethren, you have done it unto me." **Matt. 25:40**

Finally, Intraocular Lenses

We had been under appointment to the General Board of Global Ministries from 1952 to 1975. At the end of this period I was fifty-five years of age. We had no financial assets. Three of our six children were in graduate school. An annual missionary's salary of less than $10,000 was inadequate. It was necessary to establish a private ophthalmological practice and an opportunity was found in Alexandria, Minnesota.

With the beginning of this new practice, I was concerned that patients might be skeptical of an aging missionary, feeling that perhaps he was not adequate for modern medicine after having been in "deepest

Africa" for over twenty years.

I needed to prove that I was a bonafide eye surgeon. That opportunity came on my 1976 return visit to Africa. A friendship with Peter Choyce of England had developed over the years. He invited me into his home. In surgery I had hands-on experience with him as he deftly placed anterior chamber intraocular lenses following intracapsular cataract extractions. His doing it so well was the result of having developed a procedure over time that was safe and effective. He had chronicled the do's and don'ts of this new modality that he had worked out while assisting Harold Ridley as a resident during the history making first intraocular lens implantation in England in 1949. Ridley had noted that polymethylmethacrylate (PMM) was an inert material. Fragments from exploding canopies struck by anti-aircraft fire had been observed in the eyes of flight navigators of the Royal Air Force. The canopies had been fashioned with PMM. Consequently, he asked Rayner, an optical house, to fashion some artificial lenses of various powers and began inserting them into the eye following cataract extraction. The era of intraocular lens implantation had begun.

Mr. Choyce provided me with fifteen intraocular lenses which I took back to Alexandria, Minnesota. To qualify for intraocular lens implantation I attended a workshop in California directed by Dr. Dennis Shepherd. I hung up the framed certificate, and on February 16, 1977, I did my first Choyce anterior chamber intraocular lens implantation.

The drama surrounding this occasion was almost as stressful as my first general surgery in Nigeria, Africa in 1952, and my 1958 first eye surgery at Rotifunk, Sierra Leone. Annie Halvorson wanted to have vision restored in her right eye. She had been legally blind for several years. Now the blurred left eye was preventing her from reading the road signs. We mentioned to her the availability of a lens that could be put inside her eye following the removal of the cataract. The advantage was that it would still allow her to use her better left eye along with the operated eye. The standard operative technique required a thick lens in her glasses which did not allow for a balanced use of vision between the operated and unoperated eye.

The advantage of the IOL appealed to Mrs. Halvorson, and she elected to go with it even though I explained that I had never done it before on a human being. She only asked, "Do you think it will work?" I answered, "Yes."

Mrs. Halvorson was the first of over 16,000 patients that I have been able to help to date. The outcome? A delighted patient and a delighted surgeon!

News of patient satisfaction spread like wildfire. By word of mouth patients learned from other patients where the intraocular lens implantation was available. Patients came from Minneapolis and St. Paul as well as some from states surrounding Minnesota. The age of the intraocular lens definitely had begun.

I was not the only ophthalmologist befriended by Peter Choyce. Dr. Thomas Ellingson visited Mr. Choyce at South-End-On-The-Sea and in his subsequent busy practice alerted the opthalmological world about the UGH (uveitis glaucoma hemorrhage) syndrome. Dr. Richard Horns also visited Mr. Choyce. Dr. Malcolm McCannel utilized implants other than Choyce's Mark VIII and contributed the famous "McCannel suture" for IOL stability.

During a relatively short period of time over 150 anterior chamber lenses were placed in Alexandria where my son, Dr. Timothy Gess, and I were practicing. While a significant number of early lenses needed to be removed, we were spared that complication.

In those early days there was significant resistance and disapproval of the use of IOLs. Doctors who used them were referred to as "dangerous buccaneers." Hidden away in the boondocks, it was almost a year before it became known at the University of Minnesota's Ophthalmic Department that IOLs were being implanted in patients attending the Gess Eye Clinic in Alexandria. In 1978, I was invited by Dr. Richard Lindstrom, chief eye resident at the university's eye department, to describe my experiences with the first 150 lens implantations done in Alexandria. It was a humbling experience to address my peers who had been immersed in the best eye care for over twenty years while I was off in "deepest Africa," and for them to hear my description of the newest procedure on the horizon.

The preeminence of the anterior chamber IOL was not to last indefinitely, even though ophthalmologists appreciated them since they were able to continue with their intracapsular extraction technique.

Led by the late John Pearce of Bromegrove, Warwickshire, England, attention was redirected to the extracapsular cataract extraction as used by Harold Ridley in 1949. Dr. James Gills and Dr. Robert Welch were sensitive to this new emphasis and conducted training periods for the removal of lens and cortical material. I was fortunate to be one of their early pupils and later in 1979 have a one on one training experience with John Pearce himself. Pearce graciously invited me to stay in his home and to participate in his surgery. He described the benefits of having the IOL placed in the posterior chamber rather than the anterior chamber. He emphasized that this was intentioned by nature. Actually he was saying that the lens should be placed where God had originally placed the natural lens of the eye.

My first posterior lens implantation was on December 4, 1979. From that moment on, my choice was that of placing the IOL in the posterior chamber following an extracapsular cataract extraction. In the early 1980s I evolved four methods for the scleral fixation of the Pearce-style posterior chamber intraocular lenses. The results of a series of 303 lenses fixed by one of these methods during a three year period were presented at the U.S. Intraocular Lens Symposium, New Orleans, Louisiana, March 1983 and printed in the *American Intra-Ocular Implant Society Journal*, Volume 9, Fall 1983, pages 453-456. With improved styles of lenses it was not necessary to routinely utilize a fixation method. In subsequent years, I was invited to a number of countries to teach and demonstrate intraocular lens insertion techniques.

That this modality of dealing with cataract extractions and that this expertise would be made available in Sierra Leone was inevitable. Previously patients were fitted with +10 heavy aphakic glasses. In time they were lost, broken, or stolen. Placing a refractive lens inside the eye provided excellent vision without glasses. Acceptance of this new method was again slow in coming. Happily within ten years, Christoffel Blindenmission, a funding partner of the Kissy UMC Eye Hospital realized the merits of IOLs and offered financial help in providing them along with viscoelastics and instrumentation for the inserting of the intraocular lenses in over fifty countries of the world where they supported eye centers.

Intraocular lenses were finally accepted.

Get A Patent!

With the experience gained by my association with Mr. Peter Choyce for anterior chamber lenses and Mr. John Pearce, also of England, advocate for posterior chamber lenses, I was in a position that interested optical houses in the United States. Precision Cosmet of Minneapolis, Minnesota, was doing much of the pioneering in intraocular lens research with their sophisticated facilities. They worked with Dr. Jerald Tennant whose angled modification of Mr. Choyce's Mark VIII anterior chamber lens alleviated the pupilary block syndrome which plagued early designs. Mr. Noel Bissonette and Mr. Charles Gay were knowledgeable about design, testing, and manufacturing. Of my five models drawn up for fabrication, three were used in series of patients; i.e., two were anterior chamber lenses while the third, called the alpha omega lens, could be used either as an anterior or posterior chamber lens.[1] The use of these lenses was closely controlled by strict guidelines and local hospital surgical committee surveillance. Members of the committee included medical and surgical doctors, as well as a hospital administrator, a lawyer, and a clergyman from the community. Continued successful results eventually caused the dissolution of the committee, especially when my son, Timothy, a phacoemulsification specialist, also doing surgery at the Douglas County Hospital, brought successes to new highs with greater numbers of cases. He was to remain the only "phaco" surgeon in North Central and Western Minnesota for nearly a decade.

With the success of the new designs of IOLs, I was encouraged to apply for a patent.

A lawyer was engaged. As in many legal affairs, the process was slow. Ultimately the drawings and descriptions were sent in late spring to another lawyer in Washington D.C. who specialized in patents. The letter languished on his desk throughout the summer while he was on vacation.

Meanwhile, outstanding ophthalmologist Dr. Charles Kelman and his "bank" of lawyers presented a similar design in mid-summer. It was actively processed.

When my application was received at the patent office, a letter was written informing me that my patent application infringed on the recently accepted Kelman lens. It is of great satisfaction to note that Dr.

Kelman's lens had true character and is being used on occasion to this very day.

Another model of mine was accepted. It never was developed beyond the original series of patients in which it was successfully used, as Precision Cosmet was taken over by IOLab and only a handful of the many models produced by Precision Cosmet were continued.

Nevertheless, I am a patent holder. It is unlikely that this achievement has ever impressed anyone. Only my loyal wife, and the cleaning lady have ever viewed the license certificate hanging in my office.

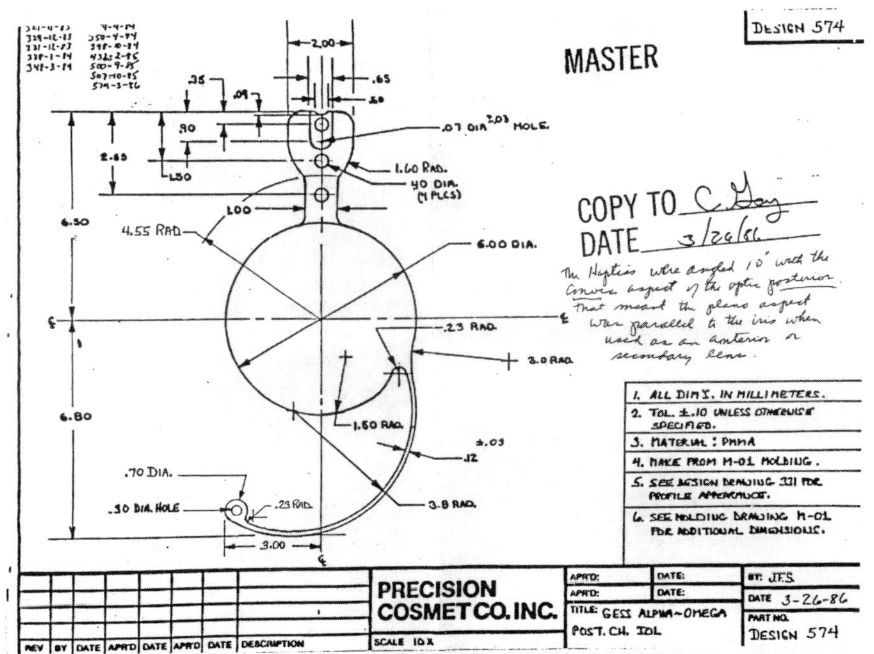

1. **The Alpha-Omega IOL.** The haptics are angled 10 degrees with the convex aspect of the optic posteriorly when used as a posterior chamber lens. When used as an anterior chamber IOL or as a secondary lens, it is flipped over with the plano surface of the optic parallel with the iris (the convex portion then being anterior).

Scleral fixation is secured by utilizing a small hole recessed in the solid haptic. The end of a 10-0 prolene suture is threaded through the hole. The heat of a cautery causes the end of the suture to shrivel up into a smooth, round ball which cannot be pulled back through the hole. The needle on the other end of the suture is passed through the ciliary body (several red cells on one occasion in 303 cases), and buried in the sclera under a flap or by passing the suture horizontally half the thickness of the sclera and then bringing cautery to the suture's end forming a smooth, round ball which prevents it from being pulled back into the eye.

The ALPHA-OMEGA lens was used successfully both anteriorly and posteriorly. The series which used no 10-0 prolene fixation for posterior IOLs also was without complications when placement was in the capsular bag.

Listing of Helping and Healing Hands in Underserved Countries

Visits by Lowell Gess, M.D. as of Retirement from Alexandria Practice in 1989:

l990: May 10–June 2, Lusaka, Zambia
Aug. 29–Oct. 3, Maua , Mombasa, Masai Mara, Kenya

l99l: Nov. 3–Nov.13, Cairo, Egypt, Jerusalem, Israel

l992: May 11–May 16, Cape Coast, Ghana

l993: April 10–April 18, Ho Chi Minh City, Vietnam
July 18–July 25, Cape Haitien, Haiti
Nov. 25–Dec. 20, Karanda, Zimbabwe

l994: Aug. 4–Aug.15, Ulaanbaatar, Dr. Baasanhuu, Mongolia
Aug. 15–Aug.20, Beijing, China

l995: Jan. 18–Feb. 19. Old Mutare, Zimbabwe
Sept. 17–Oct. 3, Abak, Nigeria
Nov. 9–Nov. 29, Chicuque, Mozambique

l996: Mar. 30–April 17, Zing, Nigeria
Oct. 7–Oct.24, Maua, Kenya

l997: March 30–April 15, Maua , Kenya
Sept. 19–Sept. 28, Cochabamba, Anzaldo, Bolivia

l998: Jan. 6–Jan. 23, Chicuque, Mozambique
Apr. 2–Apr. 12, Honduras
Sept. 3–Sept. 20, Lilongwe, Malawi

l999: Feb. 27–Mar. 22, Zing, Nigeria
Apr. 24–May 3, Maua, Kenya
Sept. 3–Sept. 22, Cape Coast, Sunyani, Ghana

Visits to Kissy 1990 – 2001 Since Retirement

1990: Jan. 9 - March 16

1991: Jan. 1 - March 1
April 23 -May 28
Sept. 27 - Nov. 3

1992: Dec. 29, 1991 - Mar. 1, 1992
April 16 to May 11 (coup)
Sept. 10 - Oct. 19
Dec. 31 Minneapolis to Amsterdam

1993: Jan. 1 - Mar. 14
Sept. 2 - Oct. 3

1994: Jan. 1 - Feb. 4
April 15 - May 15
Sept. 15 - Oct. 24

1995: Feb. 24 - Mar. 17
Sept. 1 to Sept. 17

1996: Jan. 26 - Feb. 23
Sept. 13 - Oct. 6

1997: Jan. 24 - Feb. 25

1998: June 24 - July 12
Oct. 19-Oct. 31

1999: RUF Invasion Freetown Jan. 6

2000: Feb. 11 - Feb. 28

2001: Feb. 16 - Mar. 5
Oct. 12 - Nov. 5

Volunteer Work Teams: Sierra Leone, Africa:

Team #1

Departing Minneapolis, Wednesday
January 19, 1983, 7:30 A.M.
US Air 172 & 86 & KLM 585
Returning Minneapolis, Sunday,
Februay 13, 1983 2:55 P.M.
US Air 94 & 89

Jim Mundwiler – 1982, 83, 87
402 E. 34d Avenue
PO Box 511
Milbank, SD 57252
432-4545

Laron Krause – 1983
Route 1 Box 21
Clear Lake, SD 57237
874-2442

John Luecke – 1983
Gary, SD 57237
272-5669

Loren Ebsen and
Marsha Ebsen – 1982, 83
305 Gause Avenue
Milbank, SD 57252
4320-4830

Martha Gerrard – 1983
140 N. Beverly Circle
Oak Ridge, TN 37830
615-483-0162

Kurt Knutson – 1983
RR1
Page, ND 58054
701-668-2303

E. Walter Erdmann – 1983
202 South 5th Street
Milbank, SD 57252
432-4766

Daryl Stengel – 1987
Milbank, SD 57252

Alfred Pay – 1987
Milbank, SD 57252

Team 2

Departing Minneapolis Wednesday
Februay 9, 1983 7:35 A.M.
US Air 172 & 86 & KLM 585
Return Minneapolis Sunday,
March 6, 1983 2:44 P.M.
US Air 94 & 89

Arvid Liebe – 1982
104 West 8th Avenue
Milbank, SD 57252
432-5272

Floyd Bohn – 1982, 83, 87
104 Randall Drive
Milbank, SD 57252
432-6790

Rev. John and Fran Rebstock – 1983, 84
9333 East University
#38 Silver Springs Village
Mesa, AZ 85207
JFRebstock@webtv.net

Roger Reiners – 1982, 83, 84
RR1 Box 147
Milbank, SD 57252
432-4239

Berniece Ankeney – 1983, 84
202 East 19th Street South
Newton, IA 50208
515-792-2629

Wilmar H. Nelson – 1983
Box 11
Newton, KS 57114
316-283-3295

Rev. Ralph Dunn – 1984
Clear Lake, SD

Edwin Reiners – 1987
RRI Box 147
Milbank, SD 57252

The Kissy UMC Eye Hospital, Freetown, Sierra Leone, West Africa

Dedicated in February 18, 1984, by His Majesty, President Siaka Stevens

Volunteer ophthalmologists serving since 1984:

1984

January - March	Dr. Lowell A. Gess
March - April	Dr. Russel R. Boehlke
April - May	Dr. Albert H. Bryan
June - July	
August	Dr. John S. Dunn
	Dr. Winston T. Cope
September - October	Dr. Ricky Russell
November	Dr. Frank J. Cerny

1985

January-March	Dr. Lowell A. Gess
March -April	Dr. Justin L. Sleight
April-May	Dr. Russell R. Boehlke
June	Dr. Knute M. Guldjord
July	Dr. Larry J. Gerbens
August	
September	Dr. John C. Roberts
October	Dr. Frank Moran

1986

January-March	Dr. Lowell A. Gess
March- April	Dr. Albert H. Bryan
April-May	Dr. Robert Searle
June	Dr. Jack A. Aaron
July	Dr. Richard A. Yook
September	Dr. Hillmer A. Fonken
September-October	Dr. Russell R. Boehlke
November	Dr. Norman F. Woodlief

1987

December '86 - March '87	Dr. Lowell A. Gess
March- April	Dr. Edward P. Hurst
May-June	Dr. Allen K. Larson
June-July	Dr. Wesley D. Sonddreal

1987 – *(continued)*

July-August	Dr. L. Ray. Cain
September	Dr. Bill G. Prater
October-November	Dr. Russell R. Boehlke
November-December	Dr. Arland K. Faust

1988

January-March	Dr. Lowell A. Gess
April	
May	
June 2-30	Dr. Branson Call
June 30-July 28	Dr. Royce O. Hall
August	Dr. Robert E. Jardinico
September	
September-October	Dr. Russell R. Boehlke
	Dr. Hillmer A. Fonken
November 3-30	Dr. John P. Ritchey

1989

January-February	Dr. Lowell A. Gess
February	Dr. Justin L. Sleight
March	Dr. Marc Sirota
April	Dr. Michael Gottner
May 9-25	Dr. Richard H. Yook
June	
July 5-27	Dr. Michael H. Cunningham
July 29-August 26	Dr. Royce O. Hall
September	Dr. Charles B. Carter
October-November	Dr. Michael H. Cunningham

1990

January-February	Dr. Lowell A. Gess
March	Dr. Edward P. Hurst
April	Staff
May	Staff
June	Dr. Richard H. Yook
July	Dr. Thomas Walker
August	Dr. Drew Logan
September	Dr. Royce O. Hall
October	Dr. Russell R. Boehlke
November	Dr. John P. Ritchey
December	Staff leave

1991

January-February	Dr. Lowell A. Gess
March	Dr. Michael H. Cunningham
April-May	Dr. Lowell A. Gess
June	Dr. Michael J. Gottner
July-August	Dr. Richard A. Bowers
September	Dr. Jerry D. Harrel
October	Dr. Lowell A. Gess
November	Dr. Charles B. Carter
	Dr. Robert Letson
Continuing	Dr. Richard Lockwood

1992

January-February	Dr. Lowell A. Gess
March	Dr. Albert H. Bryan
April-May	Dr. Lowell A. Gess
April 29	Coup
September-October	Dr. Lowell A. Gess
Continuing staff:	Dr. Ainor Fergusson
	Dr. Richard L. Lockwood

1993

January-March	Dr. Lowell A. Gess
February	Dr. Charles B. Carter
March	Dr. Donald J. Doughman
April	Dr. Anne-Lise Lauffenburger
May	Dr. Russel R. Boehlke
August	Dr. Nick Cook (began 2 year appt)
September	Dr. Lowell A. Gess
October-November	Dr. Russell R. Boehlke
Continuing staff:	Dr. Ainor Fergusson
	Dr. Richard Lockwood

1994

Continuing staff:	Dr. Ainor Fergusson
	Dr. Nick Cook
January-February	Dr. Lowell A. Gess
April - May	Dr. Lowell A. Gess
September 15-October 23	Dr. Lowell A. Gess

1995

Feb.19-March 17	Dr. Lowell A. Gess
September 2-17	Dr. Lowell A. Gess

1996

January 26-February 22	Dr. Lowell A. Gess
September 13-October 6	Dr. Lowell A. Gess

1997

January 25-February 25	Dr. Lowell A. Gess
June 24-July 12	Dr. Lowell A. Gess

1998

October 19-October 31	Dr. Lowell A. Gess

1999

No visitors...active fighting

2000

February 11-February 28	Dr. and Mrs.Lowell A. Gess

2001

February 16-March 5	Dr. and Mrs.Lowell A. Gess
October 12-November 5	Dr. and Mrs.Lowell A. Gess
December 4-December 17	Dr. Cathy Schanzer

Ophthalmologists Who Have Served at Kissy UMC Eye Hospital, Freetown, Sierra Leone, West Africa:

1. **Jack A. Aaron**
6565 E. Carondelet Dr.
Tucson, AZ 85701
(602) 721-5440
or home: 350 S. Treston Lane
Tucson, AZ 85711

2. **John S. Barker**
Arvada Family Health Center
9950 W 80th Ave.
Arvada, CO 8005
(303) 422-2305

3. **Russell R. Boehlke**
1017 Robertson St.
Fort Collins, CO 80524
(303) 484-5322
or home: 1924 Navejo Dr.
Fort Collins, CO 80525
(303) 484-0194

4. **Albert H. Bryan**
401 S. 12th Ave.
Yakima, WA 98902
(509) 837-3845

5. **Ray L. Cain**
2828 Highway 31 S.
Decatur, AL 35601
(205) 233-2914 or 355-1726

6. **Bronson Call**
324 10th Avenue, Suite 185
Salt Lake City, UT 84103
(801)534-6400
or home: (801) 359-8566

7. **Charles B. Carter**
3200 Main Street
Vancouver, WA 98663
(206) 696-4691

8. **Frank J. Cerny**
80 Sheboygan St.
Fond Du Lac, WI 54935

9. **Beverly A. Clark**
75 N. Federal Hwy (US #1) Suite 108
Delray Beach, FL 33483

10. **Nick Cook**
Kissy UMC Eye Hospital
P.O. Box 115
Freetown, Sierra Leone 251120

11. **Winston T. Cope**
415 Seventh St. S.
St. Petersburg, FL 33701
(813) 894-3138

12. **Michael A. Cunningham**
Inland Eye Center
S. 842 Cowley
Spokane, WA 99202

13. **Donald J Doughman**
5228 W. Highwood Dr.
Edina, MN 55436
(612) 938-2020

14. **John S. Dunn**
1200 Michigan Avenue.
East Lansing, MI 48823
(517) 337-2225

15. **Arland K. Faust**
Suite 117, 1801 S. 5th
McAllen, TX 78503
(512) 682-2463

16. **Ainor Fergusson**
Kissy UMC Eye Hospital
PO Box 115
Freetown, Sierra Leone 220583

17. **Hillmer A. Fonken**
1029 Luke St.
Fort Collins, CO 80524
(303) 221-2222
or home: 1904 Navajo Dr.
Fort Collins, CO 80525
(303) 484-1545

18. Larry J. Gerbens
2855 Michigan N.E.
Grand Rapids, MI 49506
(616) 949-2600

19. Lowell A. Gess
111-15th Avenue East
Alexandria, MN 56308
(320) 762-1888

20. Michael J. Gottner
1608 2nd Street NE
Auburn, WA 98002

21. Knute M. Guldjord
2655 Wheaton Way
Bremerton, WA 98310
(206) 377-3703
or home: (206) 377-0302

22. Royce O. Hall
5632 26th St W.
Bradenton, FL 34207
(813) 756-0669
or home: (813) 383-2653

23. Col. Jerry D. Harrell
411 Whitefield Ave.
St. Simon Islands, GA 31522
(912) 638-7629

24. Edward P. Hurst
PO Box 1277
Greenville, TX 75401
(214) 455-4824
or 771-4068

25. Robert E. Jardinico
5800 Gratiot
Saginaw, MI 48603
(517) 793-9230
or 791-3616

26. A. Richard Johnson
202 Lawrence Lane
Yreka, CA 96097
(916) 842-6181

27. Kai-Lewis
Liberian address unknown

28. Anne-Lise Lauffenburger
4147 AESCH
Hauptstr 69
Switzerland 061-784888
FAX: 41 5061 784346

29. Robert D. Letson
Dept of Opththalmology
Box 493
University of Minnesota Hospital
Minneapolis, MN 55455
(612) 625-5435 or (612) 823-7432

30. Richard Lockwood
79 West Fifth St
Chillicothe, OH 45601
(614) 773-6347
or home: (614) 772-4295

31. Bill G. Prater
Suite 2000, 1965 S. Fremond
Springfield, MO 65804
(414) 887-1965

32. John P. Richey
6816 Uppingham Rd.
Fayetteville, NC 28306
(919) 484-6141
or home: (919) 424-3862

33. John Roberts
4366 Manauwea St.
Honolulu, HI 96821

34. Cathy Schanzer
5350 Poplar, Suite 950
Memphis, TN 38119
(901) 683-4600

35. Robert F. Searle
408 N. Walnut St.
Pittsburg, KS 66762
(316) 231-7164

36. Marc A. Sirota
31-27 41st St.
Astoria, NY 11103
(718) 728-3400

37. Justin L. Sleight
3001 Westchester Road
Lansing, MI 48910
(517) 482-6476

38. Wesley D. Sondreal
Edina Eye Clinic
#200, 3939 W. 50th St.
Edina, MN 55424
(612) 920-2020

39. Tom M. Walker
2880 Dauphin St.
Mobile, AL 36606
(205) 473-1900
or home: 3359 Venicia Rd.
Mobile, AL 36605

40. Norman F. Woodlief
2421 Willow Lane
Cedar Falls, IA 50613

41. Richard H. Yook
8940 Reseda Boulevard
Northridge, CA 91324
(818) 993-5575
or home: 6168 Jared Court
Woodland Hills, CA 91367
(818) 340-7005

Missionaries of the United Brethren in Christ Church, The Evangelical United Brethren Church, and the United Methodist Church Sierra Leone, Africa 1855-2001

A

Name	Years served
AKIN, Angie E.	1904-1941
AKIN, Rilla (see Southard)	1902-1920
ALBERT, Ira E.	1899-1902
ALBERT, Mrs. Mary Richards	1899-1902
ANGMAN, Arne	1986-1994
ANGMAN, Ulla-Gua	1986-1994
APPLEMAN, Rev. Donald	1958-1969
APPLEMAN, Mrs. Joyce	1958-1969
ARCHER, Mary M.D.	1895-1898
AVERY, Dr. Leslie	1969-1974
AVERY, Mrs. Leslie	1969-1974
AYRES, Rev. (Dr.) Carl	1947-1954
AYRES, Mrs. Helen	1947-1954

B

Name	Years served
BABBITT, Wavelene	1941-48, 1956-58, 1964-65
BACHMAN, Susan	1923-1929
BALDWIN, Eugene	1962-1966
BALDWIN, Mrs. Jean	1962-1966
BARAKAT, S.J.	1900-1901
BARAKAT, Mrs. S.J.	1900-1901
BARNHART, Florence	1947-1959
BAUMGARTNER, Hannelore	1979-1980
BECKLEY, Mabel	1930-1951
BEEKEN, Emily	1876-1878
BEVERIDGE, Betty	1953-1965
BILLHEIMER, J.K.	1856-1864
BILLHEIMER, Mrs. J.K.	1861-1864
BISCHOFF, Marilyn	1962-1964
BITTLE, Elma	1891-1892
BLOEDE, Gertrude	1949-1958
BONEBRAKE, P.O.	1892-1893
BOWERS, Patricia	1989-1992
BOWMAN, Lissie	1876-1877
BOWMAN, Lloyd	1929-1936

Name	Years served
BOWMAN, Lela	1922-1936
BRADFORD, Dr. Lester	1952-1966
BRADFORD, Dr. Winifred	1948-1966
BRENNEMAN, Ida Elizabeth	1926-1937
BROOKS, Ethel Lindell	1948-1954
BROWN, Dorethra.	1992-1999
BURTNER, L.O.	1892-1898
BURTNER, Mrs. L.O.	1892-1898
BUTZEK, Miss Margarita	1965-1968

C

Name	*Years served*
CABBAGE, Dr. Richard	1971-74,76-79,80-84
CABBAGE, Mrs. Richard	1971-74,76-79,80-84
CAIN, Isaac Newton	1892-1898
CAIN, Mrs. Mary Mutch	1892-1898
CARLSON, Friederike	1990-1993
CHAMBERS, Larry and Marg	1990-1991
CHAPMAN, Mrs. Allan	
CLARK	1930
CLIPPINGER, Lula	1914-1919
CLOSSON, Rev. Frank	1959-1963
CLOSSON, Mrs. Natalie	1959-1963
COLBERT, Donna M.	1958-1966
COLE, Helen (see YOUNG)	1932-1934, 1937-1947
CONNER, E.I., M.D.	1927-1932
CONNER, Mrs. E.I.	1927-1932
CRIM, Harry	1920-1922
CRONISE, Florence	1894-1898

D

Name	*Years served*
DARBYSHIRE, Gwyneth	1957-1967
DEL ROSARIO, Romeo.	1985-1988
DOUGHERTY, ALICE (see Musselman)	1907-1947
DOUGHERTY, R.P.	1904-1913
DOUGHERTY, Mrs. R.P.	1911-1913
DUDLEY, Tom and Berma	

E

Name	*Years served*
EATON, Minnie	1894-1938
EBERLE, Jane	1959-1971
EBERT, Walter	2000-2001
EBERT, Patricia	2000-2001
EMBREE, R.L.	1918-1923
EMBREE, Mrs. R.L.	1920-1923
EMERY, E.W.	1915-1918

Name	Years served
EMERY, Mrs. E.W.	1915-1918
ENYART, Arabelle	1944-1947
EPPEL, Dale E.	1984-1989
EPPEL, Mrs. Evelin A. Bryant	1984-1989
ESAU, Betty L. (Wight)	1955-1967
ESBENSHADE, Rev. Lucille	1952-1960
EVANS, D.M.	1915-1924
EVANS, Mrs. D.M.	1915-1921
EVANS, J.A.	1871-1899
EVANS, Mrs. J.A.	1875-1899
FAUST, Miriam (Matthews)	1951-1956

F

Name	*Years served*
FICHTNER, Anne C.	1952-1961
FLICKINGER, D.K.	1855-1862
FORREST, David	1985-1988
FORREST, Mrs. David	1985-1988
FRASETTE, Margit	1965-1968
Married: Bendu	
FRENCH, Alvin E., M.D.	1954-1957
FRENCH, Mrs. Barbara	1954-1957
FRIDY, Edith	1920-1925
FRITZ, Doris	1978-1983
FRITZ, Ursula	1982

G

Name	*Years served*
GALOW, Rev. Clyde	1954-1974
GALOW, Mrs. Gladys	1954-1974
GASSER, Miss Elaine	1953-1964
GASTON, Rev. Fred and Margaret	1949-50,54-57, 64-78
GASTON, Mrs. Margaret	1987
GESS, Lowell, M.D.	1957-67, 72-75
GESS, Mrs. Ruth	1957-67, 72-75
GILBERT, Dorothy	1982-89
GIPSON, Lela (see Bowman)	1922-1936
GOEBEL, Brunhilde	1966-1976
GOODMAN, Chester	1935-1937
GOODRICH, Morris	1912-1914
GOMER, Joseph	1870-1892
GOMER, Mrs. Mary	1870-1894
GRIGGS, Zenora, M.D.	1900-1919
GROENENDYKE, Ellen	1889-1902
GROVE, Carlyle	1972-1974
GROVE, Mrs. Esther	1972-1974

GROVE, Dwight, M.D.	1939-1941
GROVE, Mrs. D.D.Kathryn	1939-1941

H

Name	*Years served*
HACHE, Lennie	1988-1991
HADLEY, O.	1866-1869
HADLEY, Mrs. A. Mahaha	1866-1869
HAGER, Mrs. Marjorie	1955-1963
HANSONS	1980's
HARDING, Miss Ruth	1946-1954
HARRIS, Alice M.D.	1891-1892
HARRIS, George A., M.D.	1956-1965
HARRIS, Mrs. Norma	1956-1965
HARTRANFT, June	1945-1964
HATFIELD, Marietta M.D.	1891-1898
HAUST, Cora	
HEIN, Kurt	1963-1970
HEIN, Mrs. Hilde	1963-1970
HEISLER, Metra	1955-1974
HERON, Bud	1970-1971
HERON, Jane	1970-1971
HERBOLD, Ernst August	1976-1977
HERBOLD, Edelgard	1976-1977
HEYER, Ed	1968-1971
HEYER, Jane	1968-1971
HIGH, Estelle	1922-1948
HOERNER, Jessie	1915-1918
HOERNER, Mae	1913-1920
HOLMGREN, Ingrid	1989-2001
HORN, Renate	1970-1976
HORST, Cora (Mrs. Moyer)	1946-1952
HORTON, Frank	1997-1999
HORTON, Carolyn	1997-1999
HOUGH, Albert	
HOUGH, Mrs. Albert	
HOWARD, A.T.	1894-1898
HOWARD, Mrs. Mae	1894-1898
HOYLE, Maud	1921-1930
HUMPHREY, Dan	1971-1975
HUMPHREY, Mrs. Dan	1971-1975
HUNT, Rev. Robert G.	1946-1948
HUNT, Lorena	1946-1948
HUNTER, William	1969-1972
HUNTER, Kathleen	1969-1972

Name	Years served
HURSH, E.M.	1905-1921
HURSH, Mrs. E.M.	1907-1921
HUSCHER, Gladys M.D.	1934-1949
JAMES, Stanton	1954-1959
JAMES, Nellie	1957-1959

J

Name	*Years served*
JOHNSON, Marcia	1966-1973
JOHNSON, William Mott	1969-1972
JOHNSON, Meryl Marie Tally	1969-1972
JUDY, C.	1903-1906
JUDY, Mrs. C.	1903-1906

K

Name	*Years served*
KECK, Waldo and Mary	1973
KENNEY, Rev. D.E.	1947-1953
KENNEY, Mrs. Nellie	1947-1953
KING, E.A.	1894-1912
KING, Mrs. E.A.	1894-1912
KING, J.R.	1894-1912
KING, Mrs. J.R.	1894-1912
KINGMAN, E.	1907-1918
KINYON, David	1991-1993
KINYON, Kelly (K. McFeeley)	1991-1993
KLINE, Edna	1962-1963
KOPP, Marilyn	1967-1976
KUMLER, Daniel	1855-1855
LANDIS, Sarah E.	1912-1914

L

Name	*Years served*
LANDIS, Ralph	1980-1982
LAW, Les	1965-1968
LAW, Mrs. Hope	1965-1968
LEACH, Lester	1929-1932
LEACH, Susannah	1929-1932
LEADER, Rev. Charles	1925-1964
LEADER, Mrs. Bertha	1923-1964
LEAMING, Rev. Vaughn	1938-1940
LEFFORGE, E. Everett M.D.	1946-1949
LEFFORGE, Mrs. Virginia	1946-1949
LEHMAN, Miss Lois	1958-1965
LESHER, J.M.	1883-1887

LESHER, Mrs. J.M.	1883-1885
LIND, Ruth	1980's
LIPPERT, Miss Mary Alice	1955-1964
LOMAX, Susan	1976-1980

M

Name	*Years served*
MAIR, Mrs. Mary	1879-1883
MALCOLM, James	1969-1974
MALCOLM, Mrs. James	1969-1974
MALLORY, Mr. John	1972-1974
MALLORY, Mrs. Luella	1972-1974
MESSENGER, Frank	1983-1986
MESSENGER, Mrs. Sue, Rev.	1983-1986
MARTIN, W. N.	1920-1926
MARTIN, Mrs. Grace	1920-1926
MATTHEWS, Mrs. Miriam E. Faust	1951-1956
McGREW, L.A.	1896-1898
McGREW, Mrs. L.A.	1896-1898
McKENZIE, Mary	1929-1949
McQUILLEN, Kyle	1969
McQUILLEN, Mary Louise	1969
McQUISTON, Rev. James	1949-1959
McQUISTON, Mrs. Nancy H.	1949-1959
MEGILL, Donald M.D.	1965-1969
MEGILL, Mary Alic	1965-1969
MEGILL, Esther	1950-1962
MIGNEREY, L.B.	1921-1924
MIGNEREY, Mrs. L.B.	1921-1924
MILLER, H.T.	1906-1913
MILLER, Mrs. H.T.	1906-1913
MILLER, Jacob	1890-1892
MILLER, Mrs. Jacob	1890-1892
MINSHALL, F.	1896-1898
MINSHALL, Mrs. F.	1896-1898
MONNINGER, Dieter	1986-1991
MONNINGER, Andrea	1986-1991
MORFORD, Anne	1965-71, 1979-83
MORRIS, Sally	2001-2002
MUELLER, Rev. Howard	1965-1968
MUELLER, Mrs. Mary Alice	1965-1968
MUKENGE, Ida Rousseau	1962-1964
MURELL, Mary E.	1902-1906
(MUSSELMAN) DOUGHERTY, Alice	1907-1947
MUSSELMAN, J.F.	1908-1947

N

Name	*Years served*
NEUSCHWANDER, Irmgard	1978-1983
NEY, Emma	1916-1922
NICHOLS, A.S.	1923-1925
NICHOLS, Mrs. A.S.	1923-1925

O

Name	*Years served*
ODLE, Etta	1910-1925
OGREN, Ronny	1989-1992
OGREN, Eva	1989-1992
OLFERMANN, Sabina	1983-1986
OLSEN, Lois	1947-1964
OLSON, Rev. Gilbert	1962-1973
OLSON, Mrs. Beverly	1962-1973
OLSON, Vivian	1947-1980, 1986

P

Name	*Years served*
PARSONS, Dr. Robert	1929-1939
PARSONS, Mrs. Hope	1929-1939
PERRIN, Eileen	1937-1948
PHELPS, Rev. Vernon (Dr.)	1955-1961
PHELPS, Mrs. Mary J	1955-1961
PICKARTS, Virginia	1949-1989
PICKENS-JONES, Alan	1982-1985
PICKENS-JONES, Linda	1982-1985
PLETSCH, Rev. Donald	1962-1973
PLETSCH, Mrs. Helen	1962-1973

R

Name	*Years served*
RENN, Grace	1920-1923
RICHARDS, W.S.	1901-1902
RICHARDS, Mrs. W.S.	1901-1902
RICHTER, G.M.	1912-1925
RICHTER, Mrs. Fanny	1911-1925
RIEBEL, W.E.	1903-1905
RIEBEL, Mrs. W.E.	1903-1903
RIFE, Erna	1928-1939
RISLEY, F.A.	1909-1924
RISLEY, Mrs. F.A.	1913-1921
ROSSELOT, Glen	1920-1939
ROSSELOT, Mrs. Grace	1928-1939

	Name	Years served
	RUDOLPH, Neil	1971-1974
	RUDOLPH, Mrs. Elise	1971-1974

	Name	*Years served*
S	SAGE, W.S.	1883-1890
	SAGE, Mrs. W.S.	1883-1890
	SAINT, Allis (Riblet)	1963-1967
	SCHAFER, Anna	1939-1941
	SCHENCK, Ella	1891-1898
	SCHENDEL, Jeannette	1953-1958
	SCHILLING, Dagmar	1987-1989
	SCHILLING, Heike	1988-1990
	SCHULZ, Mechthild	1986-1989
	SCHUTZ, Walter	1923-1952
	SCHUTZ, Mrs. Edna	1923-1952
	SHANKLIN, ELLA	1908-1914
	SHEPP, Phyllis	1944-1947
	SHIRLEY, Rev. L.O.	1943-1968
	SHIRLEY, Mrs. Grace	1943-1968
	SHUEY, W. J.	1855-1855
	SHUNK (see RICHTER), Fanny	1911-1925
	SILVER, MABEL	1930-1962
	SIMPSON, Mr. James	1960-1968
	SIMPSON, Mrs. Cleo	1960-1968
	SKARTVED, Amy (R.N.)	1953-1955
	SLEIGHT, Dr. Justin	1973-1974, 1985, 1989
	SLEIGHT, Mrs. Marg	1973-1974
	SMITH, J. Hal	1909-1915
	SMITH, Mrs. J. Hal	1909-1915
	SNYDER, C.W.	1903-1906
	SNYDER, Mrs. C.W.	1903-1906
	SOUTHARD, H.D.	1906-1908
	(SOUTHARD) AKIN, Rilla	1902-1908
	SPENCER, J. Dean	1957-1968
	SPENCER, Mrs. Ramona	1957-1968
	STAUFFER, Mary E.	1906-1912
	STAUFFER, Mildred	1906-1912
	STEPHENSON, David V., M.D.	1960-64, 1968
	STEPHENSON, Mrs. Alberta	1960-64, 1968
	STORZ, Renate	1982-1988
	STUCK, Elizabeth	1950-1953

	Name	*Years served*
T	TEMPLE, Rev. Paul R.	1948-1953
	TEMPLE, Mrs. Mariana	1948-1953
	THEDE, Mrs. Joy (Mrs. Gayle C. Beanland)	1953-1958
	THEUER, Mr. Donald	1956-1962, 1989
	THEUER, Mrs. Lilburne	1956-1962, 1989
	THOMAS, H.H.	1916-1937
	THOMAS, Mrs. H.H.	1920-1937
	THOMAS, Rev. Jack	1955-1966
	THOMAS, Mrs. Dolores	1955-1966
	THOMAS, Lydia	1892-1894
	TODD, E.E.	1899-1904
	TODD, Mrs. E.E.	1899-1919
	TOWNSEND, Ted	1989-1995
	TOWNSEND, Mrs. Rosemary	1989-1995
	TOZER, Earle	1926-1942
	TOZER, Mrs. Earle	1926-1942
	TREBES, Stan	1961-62, 1970-75
	TREBES, Helen	1961-62, 1970-75
	TREDER, Rita	1985-1989

	Name	*Years served*
V	VESPER, Nora	1915-1948
	VAN JOLLE, H.	1988-1991

	Name	*Years served*
W	WAGNER, Joseph, Rev.	1985-2002
	WAGNER, Carolyn	1985-2002
	WALKER, Rev. Fred	1945-1957
	WALKER, Mrs. Elizabeth	1945-1957
	WALTER, Bernhard	1989-1992
	WALTER, Petra	1989-1992
	WARD, Arthur	1897-1898
	WARNER, Peter	1873-1875
	WARNER, Mrs. Peter	1873-1875
	WEAVER, Lee	1996-2000
	WEIDLER, D.E.	1912-1921
	WEIDLER, Mrs. D.E.	1915-1921
	WEST, Richard N.	1882-1894
	WEST, Mrs. Lida M.	1882-1894
	WHITFIELD, Jimmy	1998-1999
	WHITFIELD, William	1998-1999

WIESS, Darrell	1974-1977
WIESS, Mrs. Darrell	1974-1977
WILBERFORCE, Daniel F.	1878
WILBERFORCE, Mrs. Lizzie	1878
WILLIAMS, Frances	1889-1892
WILSON, C.O.	1860-1861
WILSON, Naomi	1918-1946
WIMMER, W.N.	1910-1928
WIMMER, Mrs. W.N.	1910-1928
WINARSKE, Friedbert	1985-1986
WINARSKE, Donate	1985-1986
WITT, W.B.	1856-1858
WOLF, Joseph	1874-1878
WREN	
WRIGHT, Hilary	1977-1982

Y

Name	*Years served*
YOUNG, Rev. Parker	1937-1947
YOUNG, Mrs. Helen	1932-1934,37-47

"Missionaries of Hope": John Yambassu, Allan Leary, Marcus Quee, Alice Kumba Matturi, Eugene Omesombo Muembo, Suizzane Porter, Patricia and Walter Ebert.

Registered Nurses: Ida Elizabeth Brenneman; Mrs. E.I. Conner; Margit Frasette Bendu; Gladys Galow, Ruth Gess, Dorothy Gilbert; Brunhilde Goebel; Ruth Harding; Metra Heisler; estelle High; Lois Olsen; Helen Pletsch; Delores Thomas; Nora Vesper.

Sent out by the Women's Missionary Association: Dr. Archer, Emily Beeken, Elma Bittle, Mr. and Mrs. Cain, Florence Cronise; Minnie Eaton; Ellen Broenendyke; Dr. Hatfield; Mrs. Mary Mair; Mr. and Mrs. McGrew; Mr. and Mrs. Jocob Miller; Rev. and Mrs. Sage; Ella Schenck; Lydia Thomas; Mr. and Mrs. West; Frances Williams.

Some of the early missionaries who died in Africa: I.E. Albert (drowned); Mary Archer, M.D. (1898); Elma Bittle; Mr. and Mrs. Cain (1898); Joseph Gomer; O. Hadley (died soon after returning home); Dr. Hatfield (1898); Lester Leach (killed by lightning as he stood at the entrane of the church at Rotifunk); Mr. and Mrs. McGrew (1898); Mrs. R.E. Riebel; Ella Schenck (1898); J. Hal Smith; Richard West (1894); Frances Williams.

Special thanks are given to Ms. Esther Megill who rallied to help complete this listing.

This great host of "called" people have had, and continue to have, the joy of Christian service in Sierra Leone, West Aftrica.

Missionaries of the Evangelical Church, The Evangelical United Brethren Church, and The United Methodist Church: Nigeria, Africa Sudan United Mission – United Methodist Church Branch: 1923 - 2001

*GMH = Guinter Memorial Hospital

Name (and Years on Field)	Location	Assignment	Nationality
Addicott, Ernie (1971-72) & Addicott, Ruby	Bambur	Pilot	USA
Anders, Christine (1982-84)	Jos	Hillcrest Teac.	USA
Armold, Rev. John (1927-52) & Armold, DíAlta (1927-52)	Pero, Kirim, Bambur, Banyam Bible School	Evangelist	USA
Armold, DíAlta (1957-61)	Jos	Hillcrest, Dietician	USA
Armold, Rev. & Mrs. Shirley			
Arnett, Dr. Charles (1963-64)	GMH	Student	USA
Dr. Charles, Pearl (1968-74)	GMH	Doctor, Nurse	
1977-80	GMH	Doctor, Nurse	
Baker, Miss Marion L.			
Baldwin, Eugene (1952-55)	Gwatan	Maintenance	USA
Baldwin, Jean (1952-55)	GMH	Engineer, Nurse	
Bay, Wolfgang and Gerlinde	Banyam	Theological School	Germany
Benfer, Dr. Kenneth, Mrs. (1953)	GMH	Volunteer Doctor,	USA
Benfer, Mrs. (1953)	GMH	Nurse	USA
Bensch, Mrs. Christa (1973-76)	GMH	Nurse	
Benson, Rev. Charles (1978-84)	Bambur	Agriculture Christian Ed.	USA
Bernhardt, Mrs. Otto (Thekla Kuglin)			
Bertsch, Miss Ilse (1972-98)	Gwatan Waram	Midwife Rural Health	W German
Bocher, Dr. John, Clara (1969-70) & Bocher, Clara	GMH	Doctor	Danish
Bohr, Rev. Alfred, (1966-80) & Bohr, Marianne	Zing, Banyam, Bible School, Jalingo, Jos	Evangelist, CRK	USA
Bollinger, Mrs. Alfred (1953-56) ("Ruth")	GMH Pero	Nurse	USA
Brass, Miss Mattie (1966)	GMH	Nurse	USA
Brewer, Mrs. James (Edna Kline)			
Brewer, Dr. R. John (1977-79) & Brewer, Carol	GMH	Doctor, Nurse	USA
Bringlaw, John			
Brodbeck, Miss Ulrike (1985-87)	Banyam	Teacher	W Germany
Buckwitz, Uwe, Beate (1991-97)	Zing-TTP		Germany
Budding, Mrs. Jean (1986-89)	Jos, Hillcrest	Teacher	USA

Name (and Years on Field)	Location	Assignment	Nationality
Burtner, Rev. Roger (1962-69) & Burtner, Sylvia	Bambur, Lankaviri	Evangelist	USA
Carter, Franklin, & Carter, Delores	Jos	Educator	USA
Cassen, Ian (1974)	GMH	Student	
Chivers, Alan, Jean			
Churchill, Mrs. Robert (Mary Martin)			
Cook, Mr. and Mrs.			
Current, John, (1983-86) & Current, Minerva	Jos	Field Treasurer	USA
David, Cletus	Jalingo		
Dennis, (nee Schneider) Heidy ('51-52)	Waram,Jalingo	Education	Swiss
Dennis, Rev. Duane, (1953-69) & Dennis, Heidy	Zinna, Djen	Evangelism	USA
Draeger, Miss Virginia (1954-60)	GMH, Zinna	Nurse	USA
Eberle, Miss Jane (1971-78)	Jos	Teacher, Treas.	USA
Eckerd, Dr. Everett			
Elliot, Dr. Harold, Bernita (1946-53)	Kirim, GMH	Doctor, Nurse	USA
Ellis, Miss Roberta (1988)	Jos, Hillcrest	Teacher Education	USA
Enyart, Miss Arabell (5 years)			USA
Erbele, Rev. Walter, (1945-73) & Erbele, Ruth	Bambur, Pero, Lankaviri, Kassa, Banyam, Zing	Evangelism, Education	USA
Erbele, Terence (1954-73)	Kassa, Jos	Student	USA
Terence, Evelyn (1989-)	Jos	Treas. Business Manager	
	Hillcrest	Nurse	
Faust, Dr. Arthur, Aletha (1930-70)	Pero, Zinna Bambur, Waram Bukuru	Evangelism Education Theological Ed. Special Village Christian	USA
Finch,			
Fitzgerald, (1978-87) Rev. William, Barbara	Zing	Agriculture	USA
Flachsmeier,Horst (1964)	Kano	Eyework	Germany
Frey, Friedlinde (see Wernli) (1969-74)	GMH,Gongola	Nurse	W German
Friedrich, Christa (1964-67)	GMH	Nurse	W German
Garris, William, Virginia (1978-79)	Bambur	Pilot	USA
Gehm, Rev. Philip (1960-64)	Lankaviri, Bambur	Evangelism Education	USA
Geissbuhler, Mrs. Hildi (1961-)	GMH	Nurse	Swiss
George, Rev. Larry, Mickey (1978-80)	Jos Hillcrest	Field Treas Teacher	USA
Gess, Dr. Lowell & Ruth (1952-55)	GMH	Doctor, Nurse	USA
Gilliland, Dr. Dean, Lois (1956-66)	Banyam Bukuru	Evangelism Theological Ed.	USA
Gripentrop, Gertraud (1982-91)	Waram, Zing	Nurse	W German

Name (and Years on Field)	Location	Assignment	Nationality
Guinter, Rev C.W., (1906-23)	SUM	Evangelism	USA
Guinter, Laura (1909-23)	SUM	Translation	USA
Guinter, Rev. C.W., Laura (1923-29)	Kirim, Bambur	Evanglism	USA
Gulley, Rev. James, Nancy (1972-78)	Bambur	Agriculture	USA
Addicott, Hanke, Sabina (1996-2000)	Zing-RHP	Nurse	Germany
Harr, Dr. Wilber, Juanita (1936-39)	Bambur	Evangelism	USA
Hart, Miss Susan (1986-87)	Bukuru	Education, TCNN	USA
Hartenstine, Marion (1962-65) (see Lugo)	GMH, Pero	Nurse	USA
Hein, Mrs. Becky			
Heimgardner, Mr. William			
Hernand, G.W.			
Heydenberk, Rev. W. Jerry, (1972-74) & Heydenberk, Valerie	Jos, Hillcrest Zing	Evangelism	USA
Hilgenfeld, Joan (see Zoeller) (1956-58)	GMH	Lab Technician	USA
Hilton, Dr. David, Laveta (1959-68)	GMH	Doctor	USA
Hinegardner (now Turner) Elizabeth (1961)		Volunteer, Lit-Lit	
William, Elizabeth (1968-69)	GMH	Maintenance	USA
Hoesch, Rev. Armin (1946-52)	Bambur	Education	USA
& Hoesch, Margaret (1956-59) Djen			
Hoffman, Dr. Rudolph (1950-52) & Hoffman, Annelies	GMH	Doctor	W German
Horn, Miss Doris (1977-80) (1982-91)	GMH, Waram Zing	Nurse	W German
Hostetter, Mrs. Gwendolyn (1982-85)	Jos	Hillcrest Nurse	USA
Hundrieser, Rev. Richard (1966-70) & Hundrieser, Erika (1975-80)	Jos, GMH	Hillcrest Field Treas.	USA
Jam, Mr. and Mrs.			
Janke, Ardis (see Wamsley) (1955-60)	Bambur,	WakaTeacher	USA
Jewell, Miss Delphine (1957-59)	GMH	Nurse	USA
(1968)	Jos	Hillcrest Nurse	
Johnson, Miss Ethel (1985,87,88)		Volunteer	USA
(1989-91)		Leadership Development	
Johnson, Miss Junann (1986-87)	Jos	Administrative	USA
Kaelberger, Dorothea, (1970-73) (see Moller)	GMH	Nurse	W German
Keech, James, Bernice (1990-99)	Bambur, Jos	Pilot, Education	USA
Kemper, Miss Ann (1978-84)	Zing, Jos	CRK Teacher	USA
(1988-91)	Bambur, Banyam Theological Sem		
Kline, Edna (1963-69) (see James Brewer)	Lankaviri Jos	Teacher Hillcrest Teacher	USA
Kohler, Lois (1980-84)	Jos	Field Treasurer	USA
Krebs, Vreni (1967-70)	GMH	Nurse	Swiss
Kuglin, Rev. Karl, Thekla (1938-60) (see Bernhardt)	Bambur, Bambuka, Zinna	Evangelism	USA
LaBumbard, Mrs. Lon (1971-74) (Billie Jean Rydberg)	GMH	Nurse, Rural Health	

Name (and Years on Field)	Location	Assignment	Nationality
Lear, Mrs. Dorothy (Dorothy McBride)			
Leidenroth, Miss Edith (1987)-	Waram	Nurse Midwife	W German
Lotze, Donald, Joan (1973-75)	Jalingo	Education	USA
Ludwig, Miss Phyllis Jean (1956-59)	Djen, Zinna	Education	USA
Lugo, Mrs. Marion (5 yrs in Nigeria) (Marion Hartenstine)			
Lumbert, Dr. Clifford, (1981,85) & Lumbert, Nola (Short Term Volunteer)	Hillcrest	Dentist	USA
MacDonald, Alastair, (1973-77) & MacDonald, Margaret	Jos	Air Engineer	British
Macke, Wilma (nee Vandersall) (1946-64)	Pero, Gwatan,	Educ. Field Treas	USA
Mr. Woodrow (1950-64)	Gwatan	Construction	Canadian
Mader, John, Shirley (1972-73)	Jalingo	Education	USA
	Gwatan	Maintenance	USA
Mallery, Harold, Mrs. (1969)	Gwatan	Maintenance	USA
Mallery, John, Luella (1972-74)	Jalingo	Education	USA
Maneval, Miss Onnolee (1963-65)	Bambur	Education	USA
Martin, Mary (see Churchill) (1961-63)		Nurse	USA
Mason, Walter, Mona (1976-78)	Gwatan, Bambur	Pilot, Nurse	USA
Mathison, Drs. Jerrell, Joyce (1971-86)	GMH	Doctors	USA
	Yola	Epidemiology	
McBride, Dorothy (see Lear) (1949-51)	Banyam, Bambur	Christian Ed.	USA
McBride, Ira (1923-62)	Bambur	Evangelism	USA
Mrs. Ruth (1923-33)	Bambur		USA
Mrs. Betty (1937-41)	Bambur		Irish
Mrs. Kathleen (1946-62)	Bambur		Irish
McGuinnis, Thad, Jeannie	Jos, Jalingo	Rural Agriculture	
McQuillen, Rev. Kyl, (1970-71) & McQuillen, Mary Louise	Jalingo	Education	USA
Megill, Miss Esther (1968-72)	N.Y.	Area Secretary	USA
(1990)	DWM	VIM	
Mercer, Crystal (1950-61)	Zinna, GMH	Nurse	USA
Mercer, Mrs. Favirner			
Miner, Miss Dorothy (1947-58)	GMH, Gindiri	Nurse, Teacher	USA
Mittwollen, Mailies (1990-95)	Jos	Nurse	Germany
Mohr, Natalie (1968-78)	GMH	Nurse Dispenser Trainer	W German
Moller, Erling, Dorothea (Dorothea Kaelberger)			
Morgan, Miss Ulrike (1970-73)	GMH	Lab Tech	W German
Nease, Mrs. Richard			
Olewiler, Dr. Dean, Jane (1953-67)	GMH	Doctor	USA
Peterson, Dr. Robert (1991) & Peterson, Mary	Hillcrest	Dentist	USA
Piburn, Dr. Marvin, (1974-75) & Piburn, Carolyn	GMH	Doctor, Nurse	USA
Quigg, Steve (1979-88) & Quigg, Gail	Bambur	Pilot	USA

Name (and Years on Field)	Location	Assignment	Nationality
Rauch, Helmut (1971)	Gwatan	Maintenance	W German
Ray, Dr. Ronald, Diane (1978-)	Bukuru	Theological Ed	USA
Rees, Betty (see Roby) (1962-65)	GMH	Nurse	USA
Richart, Rev. Frederick, Carol (`81-84)	Jalingo, Jos, Lank	Christian Ed.	USA
Rickard, Rev. David, Marian (`63-65)	Pero	Evangelism	USA
Roby, Mrs. Alvin (Betty Rees)			
Rott, Dr. Ludwig, Helmina (1970-74)	Bukuru	Theological Ed.	W German
Rowe, Lucy (1946-53)	Pero, GMH	Nurse	USA
(1957-60)	Kano	Bible Translator	
(1961-64)	Bambur	Secretary	
Rydberg, Billie Jean (see LaBumbard)			USA
Savuto, William, Jerri (1985-89)	Jos	Field Treasurer	USA
Schaefer, John			
Schmidt, Lois (1952-86)	Zinna, Bambur, Pero, Waka, Jos	Education	USA
Schoenfeld, Dabale, Ina (1997-2001)	Zing/Bali	RHP Eyework	Germany
Seaman, Alan, (1986-90) & Seaman, Norma	Zing	Agriculture, Nurse	USA
Skartved, Amy (196-62)	Kirim, GMH, Djen	Nurse	USA
Spores, Darrel, Anna (1969-73)	Jalingo	Construction, Education	USA
Springborn, Crystal (see Mercer)			
Stanley, Mr. and Mrs.			
Stettler, Rev. Martin, Ruth (1953-61)	Pero, Lankaviri, Djen	Evangelism	Swiss
Strachan			
Tanner, Miss Elizabeth (see Heingardner)			
Tett			
Thompson, Dr. Arnold, (1966-72) & Thompson, Marj	Garkida, Gwatan	Doctor	USA
Titus, Donald, Martha (1981-82)	Jos	Hostel Parents	USA
Trautwein, Hildi (see Geissbuhl)			
Trebes, Stanley, Helen (19 8-70)	Hillcrest Bambur, GMH	Field Treasurer	USA
Tryon, Vernon (1974-76)	Bambur	Pilot	USA
& Mrs. Ruth (1975-76)	Hillcrest	Grandparent	
Tschannen, Miss Emmy (1952-66)	GMH, Pero, Djen	Nurse	Swiss
Vernon, Tom (1985-88)	Bambur	Pilot	USA
Vitzthum, Michael, Doris (1991-96)	Zing	Medical	Germany
Vossler, Otto, Irene (1982-83)	Lankaviri	Church/Youth	W German
Wahl, Ingeborg (1970-75)	GMH	Nurse	W German
Walter, Miss Florence (1952-82)	Zinna, GMH, Jos	Nurse	USA
Walter, Victor, Mabel (1927-35)	Pero	Evangelism	USA
Wamsley, Mrs. Roger (Ardis Janke)			

Name (and Years on Field)	Location	Assignment	Nationality
Warner, Miss Mary Lue			
Weekley, Miss Colleen (1952-65)	Bambur, Waka	Education	USA
Weibel, Rev. Roscoe, Ruth (1963-66)	Jos,	Field Treasurer	USA
	Hillcrest	Dietician	
Wernli, Mrs. Hans (Friedlinde Frey)			
Westley, Rev. Eugene, Helen (1955-69)	Waram, Lankaviri	Evangelism,	USA
	Bambur, Zinna	Nurse, Field Rep.	
		Treasurer	
Westley, Helen (1978)	Jos	Hillcrest Nurse	
Westley, Rev. John, Pearl (1960-67)	Jos	Field Treasurer	USA
		Dietician-Hillcrest	
	Gwatan	Maintenance	
Whitfield, William, Jimmye (1979-83)	Bambur	Agriculture,	USA
		Education	
Willey, Dr. Ronald, Lu Ann (1979-83)	GMH	Doctor	USA
Williams, Miss Esther (1974-79)	Jos	Hillcrest Teach	USA
Wittmer, Ruth (see Bolliger)			
Woodyard, Vivian (1992)-		Education	USA
Zuren, Miss Ulrike (1991-)		Medicine	Germany
Zlotkin, Dr. Stanley (1973-)	GMH	Doctor	
Zoeller, Mrs. Kenneth (Joan) (4 years)			

BIBLIOGRAPHY

Adolph, Harold. *Todays Christian Doctor.* Summer 1999.

Alldridge, T.J. *A Transformed Colony Sierra Leone.* London: Seeley and Co. Ltd., 1910.

Behney, J. and Paul H. Eller. *The History of the Evangelical United Brethren Church.* Nashville: Abingdon, 1979.

Candale, G.S. *West African Snakes.* London: Longmans, Green and Co. Ltd, 1961.

Cox, Emmett D. *The Church of the United Brethren in Christ in Sierra Leone.* William Cary Library, South Pasadena, California.

Dong, Peter, *et al. The History of the United Methodist Church in Nigeria.* Nashville: Abingdon Press, 2000.

Eller, Paul H. *History of Evangelical Missions.* Harrisburg, PA, The Evangelical Press, 1942.

Faust, Arthur and Aletha. *From Pero Station.*

Fyfe, Christopher. *A Short History of Sierra Leone.* London: Longmans, Green and Co. Ltd, 1962.

Matchette, Katharine E. "When the Dog Bites," *Good News*, March-April 1983.

Mills, J.S. *Mission Work in Sierra Leone, West Africa.* Dayton: Memorial Edition, 1998.

Olewiler, Dean and Lowell Gess. "Uterine Rupture," *West African Medical Journal*, 1954.

13. Olsen, Lois. *Contentment is Great Gain.* Milwaukee: Leone Press, 1996.

Olson, Gilbert W. *Church Growth in Sierra Leone.* Grand Rapids: Wm B. Erdmans Pub. Co., 1969.

Qualls, Alyssa. Internet Report, 2000.

Sibthorpe, A.B.C. *The History of Sierra Leone.* London: Elliot Stock, 1968.

Williams, Henry. *The Gospel and Medicine,* notes.

INDEX

AA

BB

CC

DD

EE

FF

GG

HH

II

JJ

MM

SS

YY

ZZ

In March 1993 I had a lifetime inspirational experience, ophthalmologically and spiritually, while spending two weeks working and living with Dr. Lowell Gess and his wife Ruth at the Kissy UMC Eye Hospital, Freetown, Sierra Leone. I had responded to Dr. Gess' invitation to bring donor corneas and then perform eight corneal transplants as well as fifty cataract operations with intraocular lens implantations.

At the eye hopital I found a modern, up-to-date clinic and operating room as modern as those in my own University of Minnesota facility.

With outstanding ophthalmological qualifications, Dr. Gess has performed thousands of eye operations with exceptional success. With his kind, gentle, and humble approach to the patients in the operating room and clinic, he evidenced the hands, heart, and soul of a missionary healer. In a wonderful way some patients found Christ as well as new sight.

Donald J. Doughman, M.D.
Professor, Ophthalmology (past Chair)
Department of Ophthalmology
University of Minnesota
Minneapolis, Minnesota